Rush
to
Destiny

By

L. J. Martin

Dedicated to a
quintessential western man,
who I'm proud to say,
is my good friend…

Rock Creek Ron
Ron Clausen

Rush to Destiny – L. J. Martin

PROLOGUE

Summer 1828

The nation's capital bustled with activity.

A tall, whipcord-lean man with a shock of gray hair flaring from under his black high hat dodged a gig pulled by a red-roan horse. He waited for a beer wagon clattering and bouncing behind a team of matched grays, then strode across Pennsylvania Avenue near the White House. His gold-handled cane tapped the brick street in a jaunty manner as he enjoyed the warmth and pleasant breeze of the summer's day. Then he stiffened and rose to his full height, his prominent chin thrusting forward in a determined set when he noticed two boys in a rough-and-tumble scrap in the gutter.

In four quick steps he was within reach and rapped the nearest boy a stiff one across the shoulders. Both boys, scuffed and puffing, stopped, their fists balled at their sides, to glare at the intruder.

"Here, here, you boys save that energy for the school-room, where it'll bring you more than a useless black eye."

The boys glared at each other for a moment more, each thinking a black eye on his opponent would not be so useless; then the taller of the two, who had received the stout rap of the cane, broke and ran down the street.

"What caused such a ruckus, young man?" the gentleman asked reproachfully, then crouched to kneel eye to eye with the smaller boy, who couldn't have been over six years old.

"He called Andy-by-God Jackson a name, sir." The gray-haired man bristled; then his blue eyes glinted in mischief under bushy gray brows, and looked down his long nose—but he didn't smile. "And what name was that?"

"A . . . a jackass, sir."

This brought a half smile that softened his angular features. He cut his eyes after the escaping youth and winced as he unfolded back to his full height—both his back and partially mobile left arm pained him from lead balls taken in duels, and the ball in his back so near his spine remained a continual reminder of his encounter with Senator Thomas Hart Benton's brother. His attention came back to the boy, and he smiled for the second time.

"Well, son, ol' Andy Jackson does have sort of a long face, an' a by-God donkey-long nose that some say pokes into where it's not wanted, an' his attitude can sometimes be downright stubborn. Still an' all, his ears aren't long as any decent jack's, or he'd listen to what folks are advising him. An' some lady-folks would say he's not near as good-looking as Adam's off ox, or ass, in this case."

The boy's expression soured; Andy seemed to be getting the same disrespect from this gentleman as he had been getting from his former playmate turned combatant.

"Andy-by-God Jackson is going to be our next president, sir," the boy said, looking the man square in the eye but keeping his respectful manner. The boy's hard stare—one that belied his young age—betrayed that he would as soon kick the tall man in the shin. "And my father says he's the man for the job."

"And your father is?"

"George Beale, sir."

"The son-in-law of Thomas Truxtun?"

The boy's chest puffed a tad and his chin raised. "Commodore Thomas Truxtun, sir."

"Well, son, I'm proud to meet the grandson of so fine a man and so brave an American hero."

The man again stooped and, shifting the cane from right to left, extended his bony hand. The boy shook, but remained hesitant.

"You give your father and mother my respects, and all of you call on me once I'm rightfully ensconced in the White House."

"Sir?"

The man chuckled. "Why, I'm the jackass, son. Andrew Jackson is my name. And yours?"

The boy grew wide-eyed. "Edward Fitzgerald Beale, sir."

"Well, Andy-by-God Jackson is proud to meet you. Any man who'll fight for my good name, no matter what his age, is a friend of mine."

Jackson tipped his hat and grinned broadly, then continued down the walkway. The boy stared after him until the man hesitated and thoughtfully turned back.

"Young Master Beale, you come call on me if I can ever be of service."

"My friends call me Ned, sir."

"Ned then." Jackson tipped his hat again and took up his jaunty stride.

The boy watched him disappear around a corner, then scampered for home, wondering how he would tell his mother that he had met Andrew Jackson—without telling her about the scrap.

CHAPTER ONE

February 4, 1837

The late afternoon wind whistled mournfully, whipping wet-frigid air off the bay, rattling the many lines of the barren tri-masted vessel against wood and furled canvas. Her thick-based masts rose out of a dark hull, tapering and fading up into the mist, standing with wide cross arms like three gaunt, denuded elms above a bleak winter forest. Ice clung to her rails, decks, and lines, taunting and challenging those who would have to chip it away.

As the slender, dapperly uniformed youth stood on Philadelphia's dock, staring up at the masts, spars, and rigging of the seventy-four-gun *U.S.S. Independence*, he wondered how wise it had been to take President Andy Jackson up on his invitation—eight years had passed before Ned felt the desire, and family necessity, to take advantage of the offer.

But when his father had unexpectedly died, he and his older brother, Truxtun, had been called home.

Ned and Truxtun Beale would normally have walked the few miles to Bloomingdale, the family farm just outside of Washington, but this time his mother had asked that they take a hack and hurry. With some trepidation, they paid the driver, who quickly reined the gig away. The lane from the road to the farm's small cluster of buildings lay lined with coaches, and drivers lounged about, smoking and talking quietly, not meeting the boys' eyes.

Ned and Trux walked across the wide lawn between two stately elms and entered their mother's two-story white farmhouse. A number of men in trousers and frock coats sat in their mother's parlor, sipping coffee or tea. They greeted the boys with tight but encouraging smiles and extended hands. Even though Truxtun was his older brother, Ned knew he was the stronger of the two in many ways.

As soon as he arrived home, Trux seemed to wilt and sank slope-shouldered to a love seat. With wet eyes, he accepted the condolences of the gathered mourners. Ned maintained his upright demeanor, kept his shoulders back, shook hands all around—but under that facade, wanted his mother's company.

Emily Beale entered from the kitchen, even in this situation remaining the stern head of the household and directing the servants in serving her guests. Dressed in black, except for the better of her several white lace dust caps, she seemed all business, greeting her sons with a small buss on the cheek as if they were home on any Saturday night to spend Sunday with the family before returning to school.

It took two days after the funeral before the house quieted, and she called her two sons to join her in that same parlor. Ned sat quietly across the table while Truxtun paced the floor, hands folded behind his back, trying desperately to appear older than his seventeen years. Trux cleared his throat. "If it is all right with you, Mother, we should be returning to Georgetown and our classes. I'll be behind in chemistry if—"

"That's why I've asked you two to come and talk with me, Trux."

His mother seemed genuinely saddened, Ned thought as he watched her. Then she steeled her resolve and went on.

"I'm sorry, but it seems your father has left us in a somewhat dire financial condition. He owes . . . now we owe . . . a great deal of money on some lots he purchased in town,

11

among other debts. And without him here to—" Truxtun Beale's eyes widened. "No school?"

She sighed deeply. "At least not for some time."

"That's fine with me, Mother," Ned said with an encouraging smile. "A break would do us good. I can get on as an apprentice—"

"You'll both have to make up your minds to work somewhere," she said quietly, and her shoulders slumped, but not nearly so much as Truxtun Beale's did. He looked as if he had been slapped in the face.

"No school," he mumbled.

Ned rose with a smile and laid his hand on his brother's shoulder. "No school, Trux. No tests, no professors, no walking five miles home on Saturday nights and back on Sunday." He stepped around the table, put a reassuring arm around his mother's shoulder; and gave her a much wider smile than he really felt. "Everything will be fine, Mother. "

"You two should spend the evening thinking about what you want to do with the next year, at least one year...maybe more."

"I could work here at the farm," Trux said hopefully.

"I may have to sell Bloomingdale," Emily Beale said, and for the first time her lip quivered, ever so slightly. Truxtun's face fell.

"I think you would enjoy city living, Mother," Ned said quietly. "Things are more convenient, and now that Father's not here to watch over things . . . . " His attempts to console her seemed only to make her quiet grief worse. He bit his lip and wished he could say something, and even more so, wished he had the money to solve her problems.

"Think about what you want to do with yourselves," she repeated, and rose, a hanky clasped in a thin hand. "I think I'm going to lie down a while."

Emily Beale took a deep breath, looking from son to son. "We arc going to be fine," she said, her voice gaining strength. Then her shoulders squared and she headed for the stairs leading up from the entry, across the highly polished parlor floor.

Truxtun looked at Ned as if the whole thing was his fault, but Ned knew he did not truly believe that. It was just Truxtun's way. His brother seemed not to know which direction to go to leave the room, just turned this way and that. Finally, without speaking, he walked through the dining room, down the long hall, and Ned heard the back door bang, its counter-weight closing it.

Ned Beale walked to his father's study and quietly moved from bookcase to bookcase. He paused and studied the frame resting on a shelf, and his eyes misted. His father had once scolded him for picking the framed medal up. Now, feeling some of that childhood guilt, he again lifted it and ran his hand gently across it. The Congressional Medal of Honor— the highest award in the land. Returning it carefully, he turned and ran his hand across the finely polished cheery wood desk his father had spent so much time at; then his eyes drifted up to the ceiling. With determination in his step, Ned left his father's room and took the stairs two at a time. He passed his mother's bedchamber. The paneled door was closed, and he hoped she was resting. He had noticed the sinking and darkening of her eyes over the past several days, and she looked years older than she ever had before. Quietly, he went to the end of the hall, opened a narrow door, and ascended the stairway into the attic.

Even the servants seldom dusted the attic, and lined with trunks and crates, it would not be easy to do so. Dim with only high small windows at each end. it smelled of dust and mildew—but it was a familiar smell Ned liked. He moved across to a scarred leather trunk with wide brass buckles on leather straps, worked them, and opened it. He carefully brushed off his hands before he began to rummage through his grandfather's things. Picking up a blue wool jacket

13

trimmed in gold braid, he admired its big silver buttons for the hundredth time since he had been old enough to find his own way to the attic. By the time he had finished sifting through the things in the trunk and had carefully refolded and replaced the jacket and reworked the brass buckles, he knew exactly what he wanted to do.

He turned to leave, and saw his mother standing quietly near the stairway door, watching him. She smiled softly and leaned back on a trunk, seemingly unmindful of the dust.

"He was a great man," she said, a hint of pride in her voice.

"Do you think I could—" Ned tenuously started to ask, but his mother interrupted.

"You can do anything you set your mind to, Ned Beale." She glanced over her shoulder at the stairway, as if to assure herself of their privacy, then centered her strong gaze on him. "Many times, I thought you should have been the one named Truxtun, after your grandfather. You even carry yourself the same sure way he did. And your laugh . . . sometimes I think he's in the room again when you laugh."

His mother's tone strengthened, and her deep-set eyes seemed to darken. "Some men are cut out to do great things, Ned. I have always felt that about you." For a moment, her eyes seemed far away. "Don't let lack of money be a setback . . . . There is destiny about you, Ned. If you want to follow in your grandfather's footsteps, and your father's, I will do everything in my power to help you."

Within the week, Ned found himself and his mother in President Andrew Jackson's office, and before the year was out, in a uniform on his way to Philadelphia.

Now he took a deep steadying breath and stared at the great ship in front of him; suddenly he felt very small.

Today was his fifteenth birthday, the first day he could legally report to the Navy. His warrant as a midshipman had been approved during the prior year, at the recommendation of Andy-by-God Jackson and Senator James Buchanan, a family friend. And Ned knew, no matter how small he felt at the moment, he met the warrant's basic specifications: He was fifteen as of today; well over the required five feet, one inch in his bare feet; more than thirty inches around the chest; could read and write; was of robust frame; was intelligent— or so his mother continually told him, though his marks testified only to average; was of perfectly sound and healthy constitution, free from physical defects or malformation; and was not subject to fits. Truxtun, who had taken an office apprenticeship in Washington, had teased him continually about this last requirement, claiming he had fits of temper on many occasions.

But now his backbone shuddered slightly, and he wished he could ascribe it to anger. Luckily, under the uniform and the heavy greatcoat he wore, no man could detect the tremor. Ned thought of the strength his mother had shown over this past year, and steeled his resolve. Emily Beale had managed to sell the town lots and save the family farm, but it had been very difficult for her, and the future looked little better.

Still, as the activity of the restocking of the *Independence* bustled about him, and butterflies teased his stomach, Ned wished he was back at Bloomingdale milking Heather, the Beale family cow. Here it was only hard men working among the lines, crates, barrels, and accouterments of the sea, and the birds of a dozen varieties that oversaw it all. But even the gulls that lined the top of the warehouse crouched with heads recessed into puffed feathers, respecting the damp cold, and only an occasional raucous complaint from them chided the workers below.

"You hunting a berth aboard *Freedom*, son?"

Ned turned his head toward the gravely voice and noted the ruddy-faced sailor among those working.

"You goin' aboard the *Independence*, young middy?" the man repeated.

"Yes, sir, the *Independence*, not the *Freedom*," Ned answered, a little louder than necessary.

"She's called that by those of us who love her. Hoist that locker and I'll be showin' ye to the middies' berth . . an' save yer sirs for the officers. God knows ye'll be needin' them." The man's wind-and-sun-creviced face broke into a warm smile. "Normally First Lieutenant Conners shows the new men to their places, but he's ashore on the captain's business. I'm Chief Gunner's Mate Rosco Handley," he offered, extending a callused hand as rough as the barnacled hull of the ship looming above them.

Ned shook, then swung his locker up to his back, having to stoop to bear its leaden weight.

"Take 'er in yer left, boy," the gunny gently prodded.

Without questioning the older man's advice, Ned set the locker back on the rough-planked wharf, then picked it up so it hung from his left hand. As the gunny led the way to the gangplank, Ned allowed himself a sigh. The trip up the planks meant more than the excitement of boarding a fighting ship of the line, for when he moved up that ramp, it meant a commitment from which there was no turning back.

When they reached the gunwales the gunny paused and, even though he needn't, since he was part of a working shore party, he smartly saluted the quarterdeck. Ned paused at the same spot and did the same, realizing Handley was only making sure he did what was appropriate—and why he had advised him to keep his right hand free. He felt a spot of warmth for the old gunny, and hurried along behind him as the broad-shouldered sailor worked his way across the holystoned pine, threading his way through myriad lines and deck gear to the forecastle.

Having to back down the fo'c'sle ladder, Ned carefully picked his way, following into the first hatch on the larboard side of the passageway, and found himself in the midshipmen's berth, a long, narrow cabin lined with bunks on

16

either side. He dropped the locker and his heavy greatcoat to the deck.

"Stow yer gear against the bulkhead at either end and any berth without a blanket can be yer'n." Rosco eyed the youth as he again picked up the heavy locker. He had seen many a lad come aboard a ship of the line, and this one did not seem special. The boy did have a look of determination about him, though he was slender in stature, but Rosco knew he would fill out with hours high in the rigging and more hours drilling with cutlass and pike—if he could cut the rigors of shipboard life. He seemed a receptive enough lad and carried, at least so far, none of the smart-mouth that so many of them seemed cursed with.

Yes, this one would do, Rosco decided. He would bet his next ration of grog on it.

As Ned found a spot into which to slip his heavily packed leather trunk, the gunny moved on out and back to the ladder. "Good sailin', young middy," the man's gravely voice echoed.

"Thank you, sir," Ned called after him, then bit his tongue, remembering "sir" was for officers only.

He took a moment to look around. Thirty cramped berths, three high and five long on each side of the narrow cabin. Nets packed full of personal gear hung from the bunks above and further intruded into the tiny twenty-four inch personal space each man claimed. There was a cold, damp chill about the place. This tiny cubicle would be his home for how long? Maybe years, maybe all his working life, if he didn't pass his midshipman's exams—but that, at the earliest, loomed two years in the future. And seldom had any midshipman passed them in less than four. For now it was learn and survive, and more importantly, as his mother had admonished him before he left Bloomingdale, keep the honor of the Beale and Truxtun names alive and well.

With his blue wool coat sleeve, he polished the deep sculptures of the damp-misted silver buttons on his coat—

17

lovingly sewed there by his mother after being removed from the long-unused coat of his departed maternal grandfather, Commodore Thomas Truxtun, the hero of the Revolution and later of the undeclared war against the French in 1798. Ned's father, George, was also a naval hero, and had received the Congressional Medal of Honor for his courageous acts in the War of 1812.

With silent determination, Ned un-strapped the trunk lid and removed his blanket, carefully folding it to fit the bunk he selected—one of seven remaining and all in the top rows. Though he had to climb to get there, and it was more difficult to make up, it did seem to have a couple more inches of vertical space.

"Well, well—new meat, lads."

Ned turned from his precarious stance on the bunk-side to see four other young middies enter the cabin. He carefully climbed down and extended his hand to the first of the men.

"I'm Ned Beale."

The large boy in the lead who had spoken shook quickly, then reached a finger out and poked one of the silver remembrances of his grandfather.

"By the saint's, that's as fancy a button as ever graced a middy's blouse . . . are those Rhode Island Reds I see there?"

Ned dropped his eyes to the sculptured spread-winged eagles on each button, and the man brought his finger up and flicked it under Ned's nose. The four joined in a chuckle. Ned could feel the heat at the back of his neck. His shoulders bunched and his fists balled at his sides, but another boy quickly stepped between them and extended his hand.

"William Anderson, Master Beale, pleased to meet you."

While they shook, the first boy moved away, plopping his large, thick-chested frame into a lower bunk.

Anderson dropped his voice. "Don't mind Johanson, Mr. Beale. He's the senior rniddy on board and thinks it's his duty to haze the rest of us." Anderson's voice lifted again, and he

18

motioned with his head at the other boys. "This is Thomas Tucker, and your bunkmate, Horace Abemathy. "

"My grandfather's name was Thomas," Ned said with a glint of pride in his eyes as he shook their hands.

"Oh? It's a proud name. How did your old grand-pappy make his mark on the world?" Thomas asked. His abrasive tone seemed to echo that of Johanson's.

"He sired a fine line of sailing men, among other things," Ned said through a tight jaw, refusing to bring up his grandfather's or father's rank and illustrious record. Sometimes, his father had instructed him, things were better left unsaid.

"Stow your gear, Mr. Buttons, and get that rag of a coat off our common deck." Johanson's voice rang from his berth, where he spoke without looking up. He lay with a book open, one Ned recognized, for he also had a copy in his locker, Blunt's *Theory and Practice of Seamanship*.

"The bosun will pipe the supper call in ten," Johanson said, "and we wouldn't want our fresh meat to miss his grub and lose his strength . . . he'll be needing it."

Ned felt his anger surge, but the others just chuckled. He would bide his time. His father had also taught him as he had been taught by his father before him—dogs bark when a bull walks by.

He would bide his time.

Twenty-four young men assembled at a single long table in the midshipmen's wardroom, which doubled as a classroom where the middies would be tutored by a civilian teacher who would be with them for the duration of the voyage. Two black wardroom boys served hardtack and a stew of heads, trotters, and fresh vegetables—a succulent delicacy Ned knew would soon be only a memory after the vessel put to sea. The stew of pig heads and feet could be flavored with bottles of vinegar or olive oil that flanked a wheel of cheese in the center of the long table.

Norvell Johanson had the head of the table, and had been responsible for offering the grace. He also seemed to carry the conversation, which finally got around to Ned who sat as far from Norvell Johanson as he could get, and across from the only vacant seat at the table.

"I see that young Mr. Buttons managed to find his way to the wardroom," Norvell said. "You are the youngest man here, are you not, Mr. Buttons?"

Ned refused to grace Johanson's name calling with an answer, and continued to eat as if he had not been spoken to.

"Mr. Buttons!" Johanson goaded. "Your senior midshipman is speaking to you." The boy next to Ned, Horace Abernathy, elbowed him in the ribs to gain his attention.

"Ah, Mr. Buttons is conscious . . . ." Johanson pressed as Ned raised his face from his plate. But Ned looked Abernathy, not Johanson, directly in the eye.

"Did you want something, Horace? My name, as you will recall is Beale, Ned Beale, and though I do wear buttons that have seen more naval engagements than all the officers of the *Independence* combined, I still don't answer to any name other than my own. Beale, Ed-ward Fitz-ger-ald Beale." He mouthed every syllable.

The slight confrontation had garnered the attention of every boy in the room, and when Ned finished, all faces turned back to Johanson.

"Ah, the chickens on Master Beale's uniform have been 'round the barnyard, have they, and they have learned to crow? Well, Mr. Buttons, buttons don't make the man."

"Nor does mouth," Ned snapped, cutting the guffaws of the other boys short, his voice ringing with a confidence he didn't truly feel.

Johanson dabbed at his mouth as he studied the much smaller boy at the end of the table. Setting his cotton napkin aside, he rose and stalked toward Ned.

Ned continued eating. The senior midshipman, slightly red-faced, stopped directly behind him.

"As the latest and youngest here, Mr. Buttons, you should learn to mind your manners."

"Ned Beale's manners have been well taught," Ned said without turning.

"I think not. A jaw stiffened by a few stout slaps would seem inclined to flap less. You and I have an appointment, Mr. Beale, atop a deck box."

The clatter of wooden spoons stopped, mugs hung suspended between tabletop and mouths—some of which hung open in surprise.

Johanson had challenged the smaller midshipman to a slapping match on the deck atop a box where the first boy to be knocked off would be the loser. Sometimes a shipboard means of passing the time, more often a way to settle grudges, the game had come to be known as a boxing match.

"I would be more than pleased, Mr. Johanson," Ned managed, but with little enthusiasm.

"Eat hardy then, sogger, for I will knock the most of it out of you." Johanson spun on his heel and returned to his seat.

The conversation picked back up, though not until many of the boys had cast admiring, if somewhat doleful, looks at Ned Beale. Though they knew he would be bested, he had stood up for himself.

Even half full of stew and hardtack, Ned's stomach churned with the flittering wings of butterflies, and suddenly the food had lost its flavor. He forced the rest of his meal down in silence while Horace Abernathy mumbled beside him.

"He's not one to mess about with, Beale. He beat poor Thomas into submission on the first night here. How could you get yourself—"

"Thanks for the encouragement, Horace," Ned muttered without looking at the boy next to him.

The wardroom door swung wide and a tall, redheaded lieutenant, Sean Conners, stepped inside. As one, the midshipmen rose and snapped to attention.

"Gentlemen, you're to report topside to witness the flogging of Midshipman John Specter. Be there in fifteen minutes, properly buttoned and slicked down."

As the door slammed, they sat as one.

"My God," Horace said, breaking the silence and nodding toward the empty seat, "I wondered where he was . . . . What has Specter done to get himself punished so soon?"

No one answered, and the meal was finished in silence. A pall had been cast over the room by the coming exhibition.

Over six hundred men lined decks wet with the evening mist. A four-by-eight-foot wooden grate pulled from one of the hold accesses leaned against the raised poop deck, where a spread-eagled boy lay tied face down to it, his bared back exposed to the bosun's mate, who held a deceptively limp cat-o'-nine-tails in hand.

Flanking the grate on each side, lining the bulwarks and the quarterdeck rail, stood forty Marines with bayoneted muskets at ready arms. Each wore his leather shako hat with a brass plate with eagle and anchor, blue coat trimmed in red, white pantaloons, and black gaiters that reached to the knee. The sailors wore customary striped shirts and duck cloth pants. Few wore their flat-brimmed ribboned hats, even with the sullen fog, for they complained about them getting in the way of their work—and they complained that the Marines did no work, other than guard against a mutiny, an act they particularly worried about now, when the unpopular act of flogging was to be carried out.

Every man on deck wore one thing in common—a somber expression.

The captain of the *Independence*, John B. Nicholson, stood atop the poop deck amid the Marines and almost directly above the boy the lieutenant had called Specter.

"Gentlemen!" the captain's voice rang out over the deck. "You have been assembled to witness the flogging of Midshipman John Specter, who was absent without leave this afternoon. Mr. Specter will receive five rashes, which he has earned by casting a cloud of doubt as to the honor of each and every crew member of this fine vessel. Mr. Baxter, apply the punishment."

With painful slowness, Bosun's Mate Baxter completed the whipping, and the crew remained so silent that each blow echoed across the deck of the frigate. When he had finished, two black loblolly boys, surgeon's helpers, hurried forward and applied a balm of lard and calomel to Specter's back while two other sailors unbound him. The boy had not cried out nor collapsed under the heavy blows, but when turned, his face was streaked with tears—tracks of pain and anger, not submission, across a mask of stone. With the punishment complete, the captain dismissed the crew.

Ned completely forgot about his confrontation with Johanson, as it appeared Johanson and the others had. All of the boys returned to either the wardroom or the middies' berth. Ned went straight to his upper berth, folded and stowed his uniform, donned his nightshirt, and climbed in. He hoped he would never have to witness another man being whipped—it was a sobering, revolting, and demeaning sight, one that seemed to diminish each and every man there. And one that made Ned think listlessly about home—the serenity of Bloomingdale.

The berth door slammed open and Ned jumped, expecting the senior middy to be there taunting him, but it was the subject of the punishment, Specter. One sorrowful loblolly boy followed him into the berth, and watched as he slipped into the bottom bunk directly below Ned.

"Now ya'll come down to the surgeon, Mr. Specter, if'n that back starts to fester," the boy offered sympathetically. He stood a moment as if wishing there was more he could do, then turned and left.

Ned wanted to say something to ease the tension in the room, but did not, nor did Specter, whose heavy breathing Ned could hear.

With every man in his bunk, whale oil lanterns were doused at ten o'clock, and the quiet lapping of the sea against the hull, the occasional creak of a timber, a cough or two, and the sleep-muffled moan of John Specter in the bunk below were the only good nights Ned received.

He lay awake for a long while and wondered at the miles and years ahead, between his carefree boyhood at Bloomingdale—which suddenly seemed a fading memory through the fog enveloping the ship—and the command of his own ship of the line.

And how to react there without sullying the name Beale.

Mornings were spent learning various skills. The bending and splicing of line with fid, horn, heavers, and marlin spikes. Bowlines, cask hitches, harness hitches, timber hitches, fisherman's bends, and on and on until all the knots began to look like the same tangle but still were patiently taught by the old bosun's mates. When the mind became boggled, the muscles were tested with heavy cutlass and pike, taught by the senior Marine officer on board, Captain Phinias Walton, or his second-in-command, Lieu-tenant Matthew Halleran.

Then the mind was tested again.

Ned spent afternoons in the wardroom-classroom, where a prudish, watery-eyed civilian instructor, Thadius Tallywort— quickly nicknamed Tallywacker by the boys—drilled the middies in math, grammar, ethics, geography, classics, and history. Evenings were spent with the bosun's mates or minor ship's officers touring the *Independence* and studying the practical application of new skills. When they left port, the boys would be expected to demonstrate what they were only beginning to learn.

Ned was enthralled with the ship, built in Charlestown, Massachusetts, by Hartt and Barker, and displacing two thousand, two hundred fifty seven tons. At one hundred ninety feet, carrying the better part of six hundred fifty men, the *Independence* spread fifty feet in beam and stood four levels deep, with a working-hold depth of twenty feet above the bilge. She required twenty-three feet of draft. Her seventy four guns rode on two gun decks—twenty long thirty-two-pounders, thirty-two medium thirty-two-poun-ders, twenty thirty-two-pound carronades, and a swivel two-pounder fore and aft. The *Independence* required an armory and powder storage of fearsome size in both the powder room forward and the magazine aft. The armory, or gunroom, also maintained and stored the small arms—muskets, pistols, pikes, and cutlasses—and cast bullets, grapeshot, and balls from bulk lead.

As Chief Gunner's Mate Rosco Handley led the inspection of the armory, Ned wondered how many pieces the ship— along with her men—would be blown into if an enemy charge ever penetrated deep into her bowel to find the tightly packed powder room.

The bosuns had given the boys a full tour of the spacious floating fort. And Ned had learned her well. The *Independence* boasted a full-blown carpentry shop. A cooper. A blacksmith shop—forge and bellows and tools kept her ironwork shipshape, and a tinker worked on her lighter metal. A paint shop and crew of painters were continually busy.

Separate messes and wardrooms fed the captain and senior officers. The officers' wardroom included the senior lieutenant, six junior lieutenants, the sailing master, purser, chaplain, surgeon, Marine officers, and Professor Tallywort. The officers' private cabins opened off their wardroom. The middies enjoyed a separate wardroom. The mid-ranking boatswain, gunner, carpenter, and sailmaker ate together, neither qualifying to eat with the senior officers nor deigning to eat with the common sailors. Also apart from the sailors, the lower-ranking master-at-arms, purser's steward, ship's corporals, Marine sergeants, and ship's yeomen found a private spot that was respected by the sailors; but they and the sailors and Marines were fed from a common mess cooked in a great five-foot-square pot called the copper, eating wherever they could find room—usually, legs crossed in front of them, on the floor of the gun decks among their hammocks. The captain ate in his own spacious cabin, or with the officers—or anywhere he damn well pleased.

A cordage and canvas room repaired block, tackle, line, tarps, and sails that could not easily be tended by the common sailor. The ship boasted her own organized band with fife, drum, brass, and cymbal, not to speak of the instruments played by half the sailors aboard. A surgeon and two loblolly boys manned the hospital, located in the orlop, or the issuing room, deep in the hull and as far from action as possible.

The purser maintained a storeroom: tallow for grease; tar; whale oil for lamps; a dopchest to replace uniforms; tools; sailcloth; and shelves and bins holding every other imaginable item that might be of need for both ship and personal use in the middle of the wide Atlantic; kegs of rum, dried vegetables, pickles, salt pork and beef, salt cod, flour, beans, suet, raisins, butter, bread, wine, brandy, condiments; vinegar, olive oil, mustard seed; and livestock. Prunes, pickled sorrel, onions, and sugar were kept, but only for the captain's table or the sick.

To both the joy and bane of the middies, the *Independence* kept a complement of live chickens, sheep, and hogs aboard, the only way to provide fresh meat when at sea. Hog, sheep, and chicken pens—for meat only, as the hens promptly stopped laying when on board—huddled first gun deck forward, where they provided some of the least desirable duty, slopping and sloshing, for those who needed dressing down.

And under it all, the holders. A group of gnomes who handled the thousands of barrels of water—a gallon a day for each man—rum, oil, and other liquids on the lowest deck nearest the bilge. These men spent their daily lives without sun, and a deck or topsail man could be aboard a vessel for a three-year tour and never meet one.

Rising above it all towered three masts: the middle, or mainmast rose over eighty feet in three stepped sections; the foremast rose seventy feet, also in three sections; and the mizzenmast, aft, rose fifty in two sections. The bowsprit and jib boom stretched almost fifty feet in front of her bow, and her dolphin striker hung ten feet below. Fourteen yardarms spread sail and other canvas flew from mizzen aft to jib forward. Over thirty sails captured wind—full-spread for the slightest whisper or reefed for the stiffest gale—enough canvas to cover thousands of square feet. And the topsail men were the most respected of the sailors.

Her numbers of halyards, sheets, and ratlines, clews, gaskets, and stays would have stretched for miles if laid end to end, but rather wove a spider's web of line from deck to mast, deck to yard, and mast to mast—and each with its purpose. Knowing the ropes was a term common to even the landlubber. Those lines fixed in position, her stays, were tarred for weather and wear protection. But running lines wear and continually needed replacement.

The capstan, with ten spokes, had an axle from the main deck, to where it was stepped into the hull far below and could be manned on both gun decks. Twenty men could put their backs to it and raise twenty thousand pounds of iron anchor, chain, and heavy hemp rode, or forty men could if her hook was fouled in reef or mud deep below her hull.

Her blocks and tackles, belaying pins, capstans, pumps, and other paraphernalia seemed too abundant to count—though the boys would be expected to name each and every

27

piece of equipment aboard ship and know its operation and maintenance as second nature.

With all he needed to learn. Ned knew he would have little time for outside interests or distractions. He believed that Norvell Johanson had forgotten about the boxing match, and he was just as pleased that the incident had passed over. They were scheduled to make way on Saturday, a week from tomorrow, for a ten day trial run at sea, and Ned wanted nothing to distract him from his performance.

But when Ned retired to his bunk after supper to begin memorizing Blunt's thick *Theory and Practice of Seamanship*, Johanson paused on his way to his own bunk.

"Well, Mr. Buttons, Sunday is just around the corner and we have an appointment atop a deck box—a short appointment for you, I fear. Unless, of course, you'd prefer to admit to these fellows that you've got a mouth the size of a hogshead barrel and that it's overloaded your slimy sardine brain."

Before Ned could answer, John Specter, in the bunk below, countered, "If any among us has a driveling mouth, it's you, Johanson."

"Mind your manners, Mr. Specter, or I'll have to take you down and pick the cat-a-nine-tail scabs from your sogger back."

"My back will heal, Johanson, but your mouth will always be oversized and full of your own overgrown clumsy foot." The boys all laughed, drawing a hateful, silencing look from the senior middy, but he retreated to his own bunk.

So Ned's appointment atop the box had not been forgotten. On Sunday, when the boys would have a few hours of free time to engage in whatever sport they wished, Johanson's sport would be Ned.

He felt the fluttering of his stomach, only this time it was sharp-edged wings the size of flying fish, not fluttering butterflies.

CHAPTER TWO

Sunday morning, the first clear day since Ned had boarded the ship, the boys reported to the main deck after a breakfast of cooked wheat—gruel covered with a dab of molasses—coffee, and hardtack. A group of diving birds worked the frigate's bow in the quiet bay, their slick backs flashing the reflection of the bright sun as they ducked and dove. Even the gulls—two dozen black-legged kittiwakes—sang the cries that gave them their names in loud exultation of the relatively pleasant weather. For two hours, from a spot that served as pulpit on the poop deck a half dozen feet above the men, the ship's chaplain, Walter Colton, entreated the crew to emulate the Lord Jesus and study the Good Book, after which the band played and the crew sung "Rock of Ages." Then most of the crew was given free time.

Ned leaned on a long thirty-two-pound cannon near John Specter, who had been staring out into the bay during the sermon. A dark-complected, dark-haired boy with striking iron-gray eyes, Specter had not said two words to anyone, other than his exchange with Johanson, since he had been flogged.

"How's your back?" Ned asked.

Specter turned and eyed Ned with a piercing look. "Fine," he snapped, then gazed back out to sea.

"Not festering?" Ned pressed.

"Do you need data for your journal, Mr. Beale?"

29

"Hardly, Mr. Specter. You stepped up when Johanson was flapping his jaw, and I appreciate it. If it bothers you to talk about it, I'll close mine."

The corner of Specter's mouth betrayed a hint of a smile. "I don't much like Johanson, Mr. Beale. It really had little to do with you. My back is better, thank you. But I would advise not making friends with the cat and his many tails, if you can avoid it."

"And you couldn't?"

"I got word that my mother was ill, and they would give me no leave . . . not that it's any of your business."

"I'm sorry."

"'Not your concern."

"Couldn't you have waited until your next day ashore?''

"Mr. Specter!" Baxter, a thick-faced man with the red cheek and forehead blotches of too much rum, stood nearby. "It's my understandin' that you'll be mindin' the holystone for the next four Sundays."

John Specter returned the hard look of the man whose duty it had been to whip him, but said nothing.

"Turn to on the foredeck. Ye'll find a crew of soggers like yer'sef already at work, and an extra stone. Bend to it, you'll be none the poorer fer it."

Specter stepped away, then hesitated and turned back to Ned. "She was dead when I got there, Mr. Beale. Neither waiting, nor going, did any good."

Ned remained silent, watching the boy walk away. He wondered what he would have done in the same situation. The Navy would have had to lay the whip to him, too, he decided as Specter disappeared.

Several groups of men had formed on the deck of the *Independence*. Some played whisk, some played cribbage using crib boards of exotic hardwood from the South Seas or carved from the tusks of walruses and scrimshawed with intricate scenes. Many men had their mending on deck, and worked on shoes or uniforms. Others played mouth organs to the accompaniment of guitars and mandolins or the cranking of a hurdy-gurdy. Groups of men, one on each end of the waist deck, competed in volume and vigor with rousing sea chanties, drowning out the cries of the seabirds and the bleating and snorting and cackling of the stock on the decks below. The main deck was divided into four sections—forecastle, or most forward; waist, second quarter back; quarterdeck, third quarter back; and poop, the raised portion aft.   The groups of men stopped abruptly at an invisible line at the main hatch where the quarterdeck began. No common sailor was allowed on the aft half of the ship unless part of a work crew or to-and-from mizzenmast topsail crew. Only officers and midshipmen were allowed there during leisure. The junior officers, midshipmen, and crew working aft also avoided the windward, or uphill side of the quarterdeck, where the captain and senior officers strolled. Shipboard etiquette was learned well and strictly observed.

"Mr. Beale!" a voice interrupted Ned's perusal of the chaotic scene. He turned to see three midshipmen. Thomas Tucker led the boys and gave Ned a smirk-smile. "Mr. Johanson wonders why you're not aft on the quarterdeck."

"Am I expected aft?" Ned asked nonchalantly.

"All the middies await the entertainment you offered. I believe you stated you would 'slap Johanson's jaw sore and shut,' an' there's a nice size tackle box just aft of the mainmast. . . generally out of sight of the poopdeck watch."

"That's not exactly the quote or the source, Mr. Tucker, but nonetheless I will be happy to provide the afternoon's entertainment by doing so." Ned rose and followed the boys, who spun on their heels, laughing and bantering among themselves as they hurried aft.

Ned's stomach did flip-flops, but he steeled himself with a memory of his father's advice: There's no shame in losing, particularly to a bigger man; the shame is in not standing up

31

to him. I'll give a good account of myself, he promised, as if his father listened.

Horace Abernathy stepped out of the group of boys as Ned approached. "There's no need for this—"

"What do you mean, no need?" Johanson asked. "This match has been scheduled for days." The senior middy already had his blouse removed. Ned eyed the boy's well developed arms and shoulders, and the rippling stomach muscles. Already a line of masculine blond hair split his chest and disappeared into his duck pants.

No shame, Ned repeated to himself, hoping to steady his nerves.

Nearby, John Specter rose from working the stone amid sudsy water on the pine deck, and caught Ned's eye. "Slap the bejesus out of the muck raker!" he shouted, before the sailor who oversaw the crew admonished him to get back to work.

Ned removed his own blouse and handed it to Horace, who gave him a pleading look but said nothing.

Johanson mounted the three-by-five-foot deck box with a jaunty leap. "Care to join me, Mr. Beale . . . for a second or two?"

Ned said nothing, but stepped forward, and with his back half turned to Johanson climbed up on the box. "Now, the rules—" Johanson began.

Ned's stinging slap left Johanson teetering on the edge of the box, his arms failing for balance. Twice more Ned connected with both hands, and Johanson fell on his rump to the deck three feet below.

The boys laughed nervously as the senior middy stared up, eyes bulging and red faced.

"Is that all there is to this?" Ned said, climbing down from the box, a sly smile on his face.

Thomas Tucker stepped out of the crowd of boys. "You cheated, Beale. Norvell wasn't ready."

"I didn't come to talk, Tucker. You and Johanson seem more suited to that. I came for a boxing match. Now that it's over, I believe—"

"It's not over, Beale," Johanson roared and regained his feet. His face blotched in anger, reddened from Ned's quick, stinging slaps, he clinched his fists at his sides so hard the veins bulged in his arms.

"I thought the rule was that it was over when one man was knocked off the box?" Ned asked, feigning innocence.

Johanson calmed himself, but his eyes still flashed fire. "How would you know the rules, Beale? I didn't get a chance—"

"You had all the chances you get today, Mr. Johanson." Ned spun on his heel and started to stride away, but the other boys raised a groan of ridicule. Ned took a deep breath and stopped in his tracks. He obviously wasn't going to get off so easily.

He turned back. Johanson was already atop the box, chiding. "You shouldn't turn your back on your fellows, Beale. They can see your yellow stripe."

In two strides, Ned reached the box and leaped up, only to be met by two stinging slaps. He ducked the next and landed his own glancing blow, but was stung in turn by two more. He dodged from side to side, but on the narrow box there was no room to avoid the bigger boy. Another stinging blow racked his head to the side, then he felt his wind escape as a fist buried itself deep in his stomach. Another slap and he found himself sprawled on the deck, tasting blood and bile in his mouth, his ears ringing, and gasping for wind.

"You cheated, Norvell," Horace screamed over the laughs of the other boys. ''You used a fist.'' Ned raised his head and saw his small bunkmate, his own head raised like a bantam rooster, nose to nose with Johanson.

"I guess maybe you would like to mount the box, sogger?" Johanson growled down at Horace.

"No," he answered sheepishly, "but you did cheat."

"Say it again an' I'll slap you over the rail into the briny."
Horace backed away.

Ned struggled to his feet, gasping for breath. When Horace dropped his eyes from Johanson's, the senior middy moved to face Ned.

"Now, Mr. Buttons, you know your betters."

"Two out of three, Johanson?" Ned managed, and received a surprised look from Johanson and a gasp of admiration from the others.

''Not today," an authoritative voice rang out over the murmur of the middies.

Ned and Johanson looked over to see redheaded Lieutenant Sean Conners atop the poop deck, looking down in smug knowledge of what was taking place.

"Not today, gentlemen," he repeated when he had their attention. "Since you have so much energy to spare, Bosun's Mate and Chief Gunner's Mate Rosco Handley is going to take you gentlemen on a tour of the gun decks and demonstrate the use of our weaponry."

Almost immediately the boxing match was forgotten, for every midshipman was most interested in the sharp teeth of the *Independence*. So interested, there was no complaint of giving up free time. Her cannons were the very essence of her being as a warship, and the boys had yet to be exposed to their intricacies.

Ned cut his eyes to Johanson and got a contemptuous and vindictive look that signaled the incident was anything but over for him. Then the senior middy turned his attention to the ruddy-faced bosun's mate, Rosco Handley, who led the way below via the aft ladder. The boys followed to the first gun deck. They wove their way among suspended hammocks, for the common sailors bunked where they could find room on both the upper and lower gun decks. Men sat in groups passing the time with cards, mending, and musical instruments, much as those on the upper deck. Handley took a position beside a long thirty-two-pounder. Next to the gun stood a dozen able seamen.

"Young gentlemen," Rosco began, "each thirty-two-pounder ideally has a gun crew o' twelve, including the gun captain," he pointed to a serious looking sailor, "a second captain," he pointed to another, "a loader, a powder boy, and eight gunners."

As did many of the other boys, Ned calculated twelve times the ship's seventy four guns and realized the ship didn't carry that many men. Before he could question the bosun, Handley added, "Of course, we are most often shorthanded, and while one gun is being swabbed, or loaded, or aimed, the gunners may be turning-to on the neighbor and running another out, and unless we are in the heat of battle and in a very bad position, only the larboard or starboard cannon are in use at one time."

Handley methodically went through the firing orders and explained them. "Gunners to yer stations. Cast loose yer guns. Take out yer tampions. Stop yer vents. Sponge out. Cartridge." And they actually loaded a five-pound cotton-sacked powder charge, taking care to keep the seam down.
"Ram home an' seat 'er well so she puts 'er ball deep in their gut." They drove a wad of hemp down on the sacked powder.

"Shot your guns . . . course, we're not doin' so in the harbor." The men went through the actions of loading a massive ball, but did not.

"Ram home ... again she would normally get a wad." They also did not load the wad that would have followed the shell.

"Run out." They fell to the blocks and tackles and heaved the cannon into position.

"Prime." The gun captain pierced the cartridge through the vent with a long venting wire, explaining that it had been necessary to keep the seam down so the wire would easily pierce the cotton sack. Then he filled the vent with powder, using the same wire to pack and make sure he got a true full vent.

"Aim your gun." The gun captain supervised the aiming and explained the method of leading a moving target, also taking into consideration the heaving of the moving ship.

"Stand by to fire." The crew moved out of harm's way, except for the gun captain.

"Fire!" He touched a lighted match made of twisted hemp to the touchhole, and the cannon responded with a roar louder than Ned could ever have imagined, shooting a tongue of flame a dozen yards out over the water and recoiling a half dozen feet back against its restraining block and tackle. The smell of powder hung in the air as the boys regained their hearing. Then the middies applauded, bringing a wide smile from Handley. "I love the smell, don't ye, boys?"

"In a battle, gentlemen," Lieutenant Conners brought them quickly back to the seriousness of the matter at hand, "these men might have been performing this rather complicated task while their comrades fell bloodied around them; while burning canvas, line, and even yards and masts fell across them, crushing the life from some . . . while they looked into the very face of death's ugly self. 'Tis a procedure that must be mastered by each and every one of you, for the lack of a shot, or a shot gone awry that could have been made properly, might mean the decisive failure of an encounter . . . yes, a battle . . . yes, even a war. You recall your literature . . . for lack of a nail a shoe was lost, and so on. Well, this is the same principle."

Conners walked over and leaned against the bulwark, eyeing each of the twenty-four midshipmen individually before he continued.

"I personally have seen a crew forget one seemingly small step in this process. They forgot to swab, sponge out with the wet sponge. When the cartridge was rammed home, it ignited from a bit of flaming wad left in the barrel. The ram took a man with it, and it was just as well, for he was blown nearly in half. Two others died from the explosion and two more were retired with limbs gone, blown away with ram splinters. Learn. . . it. . . well."

Conners paused for effect and, when he got no comments from the boys, knew he had their undivided attention.

"Now, gentlemen, we'll go through it again, then each of you will have a go at a position on the gunnery crew."

And so went their afternoon's recreation for the first Sunday aboard the *Independence*.

The following week, they cast off for their first ten day sea trial.

As of yet, none of the boys had met the true test of a common sailor: working in the rigging.

Ned had made it a point to avoid Norvell Johanson as best he could, but when ordered up the ratlines found himself directly above the senior middy.

"Move it, barnyard, move it," Johanson prodded as Ned made his way up the precarious ratlines. He kept up with the boy ahead, but still Johanson prodded. A cold wind, in addition to the swaying of the masts as the *Independence* heaved in the heavy seas, buffeted them about in the rigging. The bosun in charge of the unfurling of the foretopsail had already instructed them in adjusting the starboard and larboard braces, thus adjusting the angle of the yard, and now came the setting of the sail itself.

Ned, as he had been advised, tried to keep from looking down, but Johanson continued his badgering. Finally, feeling the heat in his neck, Ned glanced down just as Johanson slapped at his heel. A sinking feeling flooded Ned as he thought he was going to lose his balance. He stared down at the deck far below—and clung to the tarred ratlines desperately.

"Bastard," Ned managed, resuming his foothold.

"Watch your lip, sogger, or you'll find it slapped silly."

Ned hesitated, timing it just right. When Johanson reached up and grabbed the tarred rope rung directly below, Ned stepped back down and ground his heel into Johanson's half-frozen fingers.

"Yeeow!" Johanson yelled, clinging with one arm wrapped in the rigging while he sucked at the fingers of his offended hand. "That was on purpose!" he yelled after Ned, who had gained a few precious feet up the tarred rope ladder.

"Move it, move it," the boy beneath Johanson prodded.

"The rule is silence," a sailor below chided them all. On the deck below stood the bosun, singing out orders through a mouth trumpet, and every man was expected to maintain absolute silence in the rigging so the orders could be heard. Carefully, Ned worked his way out on the starboard side of the yard, his feet feeling their way along the lines, called Flemish horses, suspended below. He reached a position next to a boy who had stopped in front of a line bound around the furled sail. He waited in front of his own tightly tied restraint. He had hoped Johanson would move to the larboard side, but glanced back to see the senior middy take up a position beside him.

"All right, young gentlemen," the bosun below called out to the twenty boys fifty feet above him, "loose the outer gaskets!"

The outer ends of the massive sail began to fall free.

"All gaskets away!" Ned fought with the tightly tied line until he loosened it. The sail, two thousand square feet of canvas, dropped away and caught the wind. He felt a curious surge of accomplishment as the huge sail filled with wind and snapped taut. He could sense the power of it.

"Lay down from aloft!" the bosun called out. It was a welcome order as the boys retraced their steps and began moving back to the relative safety of the ratlines.

Just as Ned began to slide his feet along the Flemish horse, Johanson kicked backward and caught him squarely in the ankle.

Both Ned's feet left the safety of the line, flailed madly for footing in the air, and he felt himself falling.

The Flemish horse bit into his hands as he grasped it and clung for life itself, feeling as if his arms would be jerked from their sockets beneath his full weight. He felt the rush of both anger and fear as he swung. Johanson glowered down at him, with no look of remorse—in fact, he looked pompously pleased.

"Heave that man back to the yard!" the bosun below bellowed, and all eyes over the ship turned to Ned.

"Clumsy fool," Johanson said, loud enough so every man on the yard could hear, but along with the man behind, reached down and grabbed Ned by the back of his shirt and hoisted him back to where he could get his feet on the Flemish horses.

Ned clung to the yard for a moment, waiting for the fear and anger to subside.

"Lay down from aloft!" the bosun repeated his order, and Ned moved along the line to the mainmast. It was all he could do not to kick Johanson's legs out from under him, but he contained himself. He would bide his time.

As soon as their feet touched the deck, Lieutenant Conners worked his way among the excitedly jabbering middies. "Mr. Beale, Mr. Johanson, follow me."

Ned cut his eyes to the senior middy, who gave him another vindictive yet cautioning look. Conners led the way aft to the poop deck, and they climbed the ladder. Captain John Nicholson stood at the windward rail, his hands folded behind him.

"Here, sir," Conners said as they approached.

The tall captain turned and eyed each boy up and down. "Gentlemen, shipboard is no place for shenanigans. Your childish ways—"

"I have no childish ways. . .sir," Johanson stammered.

"Don't interrupt me, midshipman." Nicholson's eyes looked cold as the wind that whistled across his command deck. "I repeat, shipboard is no place for childish ways. Johanson, you've been given a position of responsibility as senior midshipman. If I even suspected that you purposefully—"

"My clumsiness, sir," Ned said quietly.

"No horseplay involved?" Nicholson's gray brows lowered over his eyes.

"Missed my step, sir."

Nicholson looked doubtful, but he gave the senior middy a nod. "In that case, Mr. Johanson, you're to be commended for your fast action in assisting your shipmate." The captain turned to Conners. "Mr. Beale will not work the upper rigging until you're convinced he's mastered his clumsy ways." Nicholson turned back to the rail, and continued speaking as if to himself. "And if you don't, Mr. Beale, there'll be no need for you to study for your exams. No man becomes a passed midshipman, no matter how proficient in his studies, until he masters all aspects of shipboard life."

"Yes, sir," Conners snapped smartly, but Ned thought he caught a glimmer of disappointment in his eyes, then a glint of anger as he glanced at Johanson. Ned had a sour taste in his mouth.

"You're excused, gentlemen," Conners said. "Report back to Bosun McCracken."

"Yes, sir," both boys said simultaneously, but Ned almost whispered his response.

Ned and Johanson hurried back to the poopdeck ladder.

"I knew you didn't have the backbone to come against me, Beale. You're a damned fool," Johanson murmured.

Ned glanced over to see a triumphant look in the senior middy's eye, and he again felt the rush of anger. "We'll   see who's the fool, Johanson. The cream always rises to the top."

"And sours," Johanson said with a laugh while he sauntered away.

For three days, Ned was confined to learning the workings of the jibs and spankers, and never allowed more than twenty feet above the deck.

On the eighth day out, the *Independence* turned back toward Philadelphia. Ned and four other boys who had been deemed clumsy, or too frightened in the rigging, were learning the intricacies of letting go the sheet anchor, when the other middies passed them on their way to the mainmast.

As Johanson strode by, he couldn't resist a jibe. "Beale must have stepped in the tar pot. He seems stuck to the deck." A few of the boys laughed, but Horace Abernathy, Ned's bunkmate, got red in the face.

"Only because he spoke up, and you were too cowardly to!" Almost as soon as he spoke, Horace regretted it.

"You and I have a date atop the box, Mr. Abernathy," Johanson demanded.

"I think not," Horace said sheepishly.

"Then who be the coward?" Johanson's tone cut to the bone as he stressed the last hateful word.

"I'll not gain the attention of the officers in any negative way." Horace tried to mask his reluctance to face the bigger boy.

"I'd be happy to give you another lesson!" Ned yelled out after the retreating middies.

But Johanson ignored him. Instead, he glowered at Horace. "There are other ways, sogger."

They continued forward to the mainmast ratlines and began to ascend. Ned stared after them; then his attention returned to the anchor captain, who continued with his lecture.

41

The rest of the middies had graduated past the foresail and were ascending all the way up to the topgallant. Ned continued to glance up as his classmates took up a position where he should have rightfully been.

"Are you with us, Mr. Beale?" the anchor captain snapped, bringing Ned's attention back to the matter at hand.

"The rode must be clewed tightly—" the anchor captain continued, but was interrupted by the loud screams of the men working on the quarterback.

All eyes raised to the topgallant, where Horace Abernathy hung much as Ned had from the Flemish horse, and just as Ned looked up, Johanson reached down to grab him by the shirt. In a panic, Horace grabbed for Johanson's wrist but lost his grip with the other hand.

Johanson followed Horace off out of the rigging. End over end, they cartwheeled through the air. Horace hit the holystoned pine deck with a crunch that resounded across the silent ship, but Johanson barely cleared the rail, disappearing over the side.

With a sickening look at the growing pool of red under Horace's splayed and broken body, Ned moved to the rail to see if he could spot Johanson. He sputtered to the surface just under the aft anchor where Ned stood. Ned could see the way Johanson was slapping at the water that he was obviously unable to swim.

"Throw the corks!" Ned yelled at his other failed middies, then mounted the rail and dove overboard.

The thirty feet of freeboard was farther than Ned had ever attempted to dive before, he realized, sailing down and down before crashing into the churning wake of the *Independence*. The cold numbed him almost immediately, and saltwater stung his eyes when he kicked to the surface. He wiped the water away and spotted Johanson, kicking and screaming as he frantically beat the surface of the water.

Ned stroked toward him, then worried that he would be dragged down with him if he got in reach.

Wild-eyed, Johanson yelled. "Help! Help me!" Then his mouth filled with brine and he disappeared beneath the churning surface.

Ned spun in the frigid foam, searching for the cork floats used for a man overboard, and spotted one twenty yards away, bobbing on the surface. Thank God someone had heard his cry.

He quickly contemplated the distance and knew he could never reach it and return before Johanson disappeared forever beneath the waves—or both of them succumbed to the numbing cold.

Johanson was no longer yelling, and his mad beating of the water had almost stopped. He slipped beneath the surface, then managed to gain it again, gasping for air but taking in saltwater.

Ned eased around behind him as he began to go down again, reached out, and snatched him by the collar. Johanson spun and grasped Ned's wrists, pulling him in, kicking him repeatedly in the stomach as he tried to climb atop him. Ned managed to get his feet up between them and booted Johanson away, breaking his desperate grasp. The midshipman disappeared beneath the waves. Ned dove and got him by the collar. With all he could manage, Ned kicked to the surface—every joint aching with the deep cold, and lungs crying for air.

Johanson didn't fight this time. He was unconscious. Ned managed to roll him to his back and kick away to the cork float. Finally, after what seemed an eternity, they reached it. But Johanson wasn't breathing. As hard as he could, Ned drove a fist into Johanson's gut. The boy coughed, then puked up foaming water. Again and again he retched, then, eyes pressed tightly closed, clung to the float.

Ned managed to keep a hand on it while he treaded water—afraid to stop kicking even if he could, for he already could not feel his hands. In the distance, a quarter mile away, he could see the *Independence* hove to, her sails furled. Then he spotted the longboat.

He gained new strength from the sight of her prow cutting through the water.

In a half hour they were back aboard—shivering and soaked, but alive. As the crew hurried them both to the hospital, Ned noticed the great splotch of brown-dried blood on the deck, and two common sailors scrubbing at it with brushes. He knew he had lost a bunkmate. But Horace's body was already at the sailmaker's, being given a shroud of canvas.

Later, in his bunk, after the whale oil lamps had been snuffed, Ned lay awake. In the darkness, John Specter stepped on his lower bunk and stood next to Ned.

"You shouldn't have bothered saving the son-of-a-whore," John said quietly into the darkness.

Ned didn't answer.

"I saw him kick Horace's feet out from under him, just as he did to you."

Still, Ned remained silent in the darkness.

"It was all his fault," John continued.

Finally, when he got no response, he climbed back down and into his blanket. But the distance between the two boys' bunks, the empty space Horace had occupied, seemed a terrible void.

Ned dreamed of Bloomingdale for the first time in many nights.

The next day, between duties, Ned stood by the rail and stared out, thinking about Horace's quick death and his own vulnerability.

"'Tis hard ta lose a shipmate," a voice behind him said.

Ned turned to Rosco Handley, who knelt beside a cannon restraining block and tackle.

Ned nodded.

"Was he a good friend, young Beale?"

"As good as a man can make in a few days."

"The talk at the scuttlebutt 'tis he was kicked from the shrouds by that smart-ass, Johanson."

Ned eyed the man carefully, but his ruddy features showed only concern.

"I can't speak to it, Mr. Handley, as I did not see it happen."

"But I understand 'e tried the same with you."

"I'll not speak to that."

"Admirable, Mr. Beale." A faint hint of a smile tugged at the corners of the gunner's mate's mouth.

"I know ye had little time in the service, Beale, but ye'll find such matters have a way o' taking care of themselves. If Johanson does not come around on 'is own, he'll never know what bumped him over the rail on some godless dark night."

Ned looked at the kindly gunner in surprise.

"No threat, Mr. Beale"—the bosun looked at his work as he talked—"just fact. As I said, these things have a way o' taking care of themselves."

"Should I pass that on to Mr. Johanson?" Ned asked.

"Mr. Johanson will be told by the crew at the right time, Mr. Beale. No need for you ta worry yourself about it. Young middies learn from the instructors, from the epaulets." When Ned gave him an inquisitive look, he added, "the officers, boy." then continued, "and even"—the bosun glanced up and gave Ned a wink—"'occasionally from the likes o' the common sailor."

That night, Johanson returned from the hospital to the middies' berth. He passed Ned's bunk and paused. "You know I needed no help, Beale."

"You're welcome," Ned said without looking down from his bunk.

"And you're a smart-ass."

45

John Specter climbed out of his lower bunk and stood chest to chest with the senior middy. "And you're just a plain ass, Johanson. And a dumb, unappreciative one at that. "

Johanson, his fists clenched at his sides, started to respond, but was taken with a fit of coughing.

"Go to bed, Johanson," Specter said, "before you cough up a lung." A number of the other middies took up the admonition, and Johanson moved quietly to his bunk.

That night, none of the boys heard Johanson being taken from the cabin, nor knew of his being gagged and suspended from a line bound to his ankles for half an hour over a foredeck rail while the bow wake lapped at his face. If the officers far away on the poop deck knew of the crew's actions, they did not interfere. Johanson said nothing the next morning, but the hate in his eyes testified to his fury at the crew's not-so-gentle prodding—and the fact that he blamed Ned Beale for the whole incident.

The next time the boys were piped into the rigging, Ned was ordered to join them again, and soon was the first man up, taking the place of honor at the furthermost end of the yard from the mast.

The matter of teasing Ned Beale about his buttons was settled once and for all when Ned finally lost his temper and whipped Thomas Tucker soundly in the middies' wardroom during supper, to the pleasure of the other middies and the wardroom boys.

For the next two years, Ned Beale studied on board the *Independence*, making one voyage across the Atlantic. The trip was to transport George M. Dallas, the American minister to the court of the Czar of Russia, to Kronstadt, the Russian port on the Bay of Finland. Her first stop was Portsmouth, England, then Copenhagen, then Kronstadt, where she received a visit from the Czar. The ship then sailed south for Rio de Janeiro, to join the Brazilian squadron as its flagship.

Rosco Handley took a liking to young Ned Beale, and Beale found that he learned the practical side of the Navy from the older man. He learned to be decisive and damn the cannons, and to take advantage of his leisure. For as Rosco advised, "For each day of shore time with the mellow wine and hopefully not-so-mellow ladies, they'll be a month of hard weather and killing work."

During all this time, Ned Beale and Norvell Johanson maintained a respectful if wary distance. But Ned knew he was destined for great things, and would let nothing and no one stand in his way.

CHAPTER THREE

Shortly after the *Independence* crossed the equator, for the first time in the two years Ned had been aboard, Captain John B. Nicholson gathered the men on deck after Sunday's sermon.

The doldrums precluded all but busywork. The sea rose and fell in great silent slabs of glass-slick gray. Heat reflected off the water and deck and burned down from above. The cold wind of the North Sea seemed only a fond memory. The only creatures displaying vitality were bugs, which proliferated in great numbers from every crack and cranny of the vessel, called forth by the humid heat of the tropics. Bedbugs bred in the cracks of the walls, weevils in the flour and hardtack, worms in the salt pork, roaches everywhere, and all served as feast for the mice and rats, whose population grew in direct proportion. They in turn served as sustenance for the ship's cats—who grew fat and lethargic with full bellies and the heat.

"Gentlemen," the captain addressed the assembled men, "now that we have entered the Southern Hemisphere, I want to take a moment to tell you why the *Independence* is here. First and foremost, we are to serve as flagship of the Brazilian squadron. We will take the commodore aboard in Rio . . . An honor we should be proud of." The captain paused to wipe away, with an already damp hanky, droplets of sweat that tracked his cheeks. "France is at war with Argentina and Mexico," he continued, "and has blockaded the ports of her enemy. France, of course, is our friend, while Argentina and

Mexico are our neighbors in the Americas. We are to remain neutral in this conflict."

Captain Nicholson cleared his throat. "We do have another reason for our presence here. As you men know, in 1808 Congress outlawed the importation of Africans into the United States. Although slavery is, in my opinion, a blight on the country, it is a legal institution . . . . However, the importation of slaves is not. Our brothers in England have finally become enlightened, and have recently outlawed slavery in the empire. The good Lord has seen fit to show the Portuguese the error of their ways, and that longtime propagator of the sin has also outlawed it.

"However, slave ships still operate, and it is our responsibility during the course of our patrols to intercept and board any vile vessel suspected of that heinous trade." Most of the crew applauded, but many did not.

"For this duty, the home port of our operations will be Rio de Janeiro." At this, all the crew members applauded. Rio was well known as a sailor's haven.

Ned Beale stood near two black loblolly boys, freedmen, one of whom, Theonious Miller, he had become friends with. He watched Theo's reaction to the captain's talk. Though the two blacks kept their eyes down and resisted the urge to look at their white shipmates, both did applaud enthusiastically when the crew did.

The question of color aboard ship had not been one Ned had given much thought to. Three of the officers kept black slaves who slept on the floor in their cabins, and a number of black freedmen had positions of some responsibility aboard the ship as common sailors—though certainly none was an officer or a midshipmen. Ned had worked side by side in the rigging with black seamen and found them competent, and he had enjoyed his friendship with Theo.

When the captain gave the men their leave, Ned walked over to Theo and his friend.

"Theo!" Ned called. The two men stopped and turned back. Ned extended his hand to the other loblolly boy. "Ned Beale."

With obvious hesitation, the man shook. "Joshua," he offered.

"First name or last?" Ned asked.

"Only," the man said, cutting his eyes away. Ned turned his attention to Theo.

"I'd think this a duty station you fellas could get enthused about," Ned said, planting a foot up on a deck box and leaning his elbows casually on his knee as they talked.

"I gets enthused about dinner and shore leave, Mr. Beale," Theo offered, giving Ned a suspicious glance.

"And doing your job, Theo. *I've* watched you work in the orlop." Ned turned to the other man. "You're a loblolly boy, too?"

"Jus' transferred to cook's helper."

"How about you, Mr. Joshua . . . . You looking forward to the opportunity to cross swords with a slaver?"

"'Bout all we'd get ta do is haul slops and change beddin', Mr. Beale," Theo cut in.

"Still, you might have the chance."

"Beggin' your pardon, Mr. Beale, but you should look around."

Ned gave him a questioning look.

"If we picked up a cutlass against a white man, we'd be likely to get one in the back from one of our own shipmates."

"Thas' right, Mr. Beale," Joshua agreed. "Unless, o'course, the slaver was manned with men of color. Then the epaulets would be happy to send us over the rail to glory. "

"You mean to tell me there are men . . . officers . . . on the crew of the *Independence* who would fault you for doing the ship's good work?"

"If it meant spilling the blood of a white man, yes," Theo said with such conviction that Ned couldn't doubt him.

50

"Well, gentlemen," Ned said with a smile, "rest assured that if it's my blood about to be spilled, *I'll* not fault you for stepping in and lending a hand."

"Let's hope it never comes to that, Mr. Beale," Theo said, finally warming to Ned's attitude.

"If it does," Joshua said, "and my blood or Theo's here is spilled along with yours, ya'll find out we all bleeds the same."

"I don't understand your point," Ned said.

"Pool a' my blood, pool a' your'n, pool a' Theo's here, they all stand red. Not an epaulet aboard can tell you which of us was cut."

"One of the better arguments *I've* heard, Mr. Joshua," Ned agreed. "All blood does run red, whatever the color of the skin."

The two loblolly boys merely nodded.

"We'll, I gots mendin' to do." Joshua tentatively extended his hand. Ned shook it warmly.

"Nice to make your acquaintance," he said to Joshua. The two men nodded and turned away.

When Ned started back to the foredeck where a number of the middies had gathered in a lively chantey sing, he noticed Norvell Johanson and Thomas Tucker watching him from a position near the rail.

Ned ignored them.

"The Bantu are recruiting, Mr. Beale," Norvell called out.

"The Bantu?" Ned gave him a glance.

"The Kaffirs in South Africa, fighting against the British. They can use another nigger like yourself."

Ned stopped short, then slowly turned to face Johanson, who laughed with Tucker.

"*I've* known you for more than two years now," Ned said, his voice ringing with disgust. "You seem to get more stupid as time goes on, Johanson."

"And you get more brazen, Beale. We'll see how brazen you are when you face the cold steel of a slaver's blade."

"A situation I would relish, I assure you. But one in which I would much rather have Mr. Miller there, armed with his surgeon's scalpel, or his friend Mr. Joshua with his kitchen knife, at my side, than you and Tucker with cutlass and carbine."

"I, for one, am not surprised at your choice of comrades," Tucker said, and hocked and spat over the rail.

Ned continued on his way, but gave them a disgusted look.

Johanson watched Ned walk away. "That bastard," he said, his voice low but controlled. "*I've* had about enough of him. I'm going to make a pastime out of making his life miserable."

"You've tried in the past," Tucker reminded him.

He got a hard look for his efforts. "Not in earnest, I haven't. You'll see. He'll be mustered out before this tour is over."

"Mustered out?" Tucker said, giving Johanson a doubting look. He knew Beale, who had grown almost as big as Johanson, stood among the top in his class in cutlass and firearm drills, and was close enough to the top in Mr. Tallywacker's class that he had no reason to leave voluntarily.

"Mustered out," Johanson said with a growl, "or over the rail."

"Sometimes," Tucker said, grumbling, "I think you talk just to hear yourself."

"You'll see, Thomas Tucker. You'll all see." Johanson spun on his heel and stomped away.

Tucker shrugged, and went to join the sing.

"Sail off the starboard stern!" The cry echoed from the mainmast watch.

Ned reclined in a coil of line on the foredeck, reading his twenty-fifth volume since he had been aboard the *Independ-*

ence—he had kept careful track in his journal. Shelly, Cooper's *The Pilot*, Irving's *Tales of a Traveler*, Byron, Scott's *Talisman*, Plato, Cooper's *Last of the Mohicans*, and on and on. Books he borrowed from the officers and crew. Books in addition to his normal class work. He closed the copy of Captain Marryat's *The Pirate and the Three Cutters* he had borrowed from Lieutenant Conners, rose, and joined three other middies at the rail. From their vantage point they could barely make out the outline of a square-rigged vessel on the horizon.

Ned made his way aft, where the officers had gathered around Captain Nicholson, who studied the ship through his folding glass.

He handed it to Sean Conners, who glassed the ship for a moment before commenting.

"She's a bark under full sail. Can't make out her colors. Looks to be heading north-northwest, probably for the West Indies."

"It'll take us all night to run'er down if she holds true to course," Nicholson said tentatively. "Damn the flies, I'd hoped to make Pernambuco by day after tomorrow."

"She's on a proper course to have originated in Africa," Conners offered.

"Aye," Nicholson agreed, walking forward to the edge of the poop deck. "All right, gentlemen," he yelled to his three topsail bosun's mates, who were gathered, along with the sailmaster, in a game of whist on the quarterdeck, "prepare to come about!" He took the glass out of Conners's hands and studied the direction of the bark in the distance. "Make it three hundred degrees, Mr. Conners."

He handed the glass back to his first lieutenant. "I'm going below to get some rest. I'll relieve you at oh four hundred."

"Aye, sir, eight bells," Conners answered, then almost to himself added, while Nicholson made his way to the aft ladder, "I hope to God she is a bloody slaver."

Ned listened and felt the stirring of excitement as he shaded his eyes from the late-afternoon sun and tried his best to make out the ship in the distance. They had been twenty-seven days without a landfall, eight of which they had spent in the doldrums. The men were in need of a little excitement, and Ned hoped that this would be it. He had read and heard much about the slave trade, and knew that generally the slavers would run for it. Seldom would they fight unless they outgunned their pursuer. And a bark certainly could not out-gun the frigate *Independence*.

No, there would be no fight—unless her captain was a bloody fool—but at least there would be the excitement of a chase and the possibility, however slim, of a conquest. Odds were she was a harmless merchantman, but still, he could hope.

He went back to his coil of rope and to the adventure tale he had been reading. Whatever happened, it would not occur until morning.

He awoke in his bunk after sleeping to the serenade of a squall and pulled on a slicker before he made the deck. The slap of warm rain met him. The *Independence* shuddered under full sail in the gusting wind, with the lines and sails alternately chattering in luff then pulling ardently. In the morning darkness they could not make out the bark—if she was still out there and had not turned tail and made a new course. Ned heard the ship's bell strike its four sets of two, and true to his word, Captain Nicholson made the poop deck to relieve Lieutenant Conners. Ned followed the captain up the poopdeck ladder.

"You're at it early this wet morning, Mr. Beale," Nicholson said without looking back.

"Didn't want to miss the action, Captain," Ned answered, surprised the ship's captain even knew his name.

"Well, I hope we see some. Nothing I'd like better than to foil the actions of the lowest form of life on the planet."

"Any sign of a light from her?" Nicholson asked Conners, who stood at the wheel.

"No sign all night, Captain. She shows no running lights. We've made forty or fifty miles against this quartering wind. If she hasn't come about, we should be two to ten miles off her port stern and closing at about a half knot per hour. Should put us alongside by the time the bell rings eight again, if we're truly only two miles away."

"I'll take the poop deck. Get some sleep, Mr. Conners. You'll be leading the boarding party."

"Aye, sir." The redheaded first lieutenant gave Nicholson a casual salute and started for his quarters. Almost as an afterthought, he turned back to Beale, who stood alongside Nicholson, both of them staring over the rail as if they could see the bark in the pre-dawn darkness.

"Mr. Beale, shake Bosun Handley out of his hammock and pass the word that I want crews on their guns and ready for action by six bells."

"Aye, sir," Ned said and hurried for the midships ladder.

"You be topside, Mr. Beale," Conners called after him, "and you'll serve as coxswain on my boat."

"Yes, sir." Ned felt the surge of impending action as well as pride at being offered a position of trust and responsibility. As always, it had paid for him to be ahead of his peers and near those who decided the fate of the ship—as well as his own. He swelled with more pride when, after he had roused the gunner's mate, he returned to the poop deck and Captain Nicholson handed him the glass.

"At break of dawn, Mr. Beale, search the horizon and find that bark for me with your young eyes. I'm going below for a cup of coffee. Fetch me at sunrise . . . As soon as it's light enough to make out a sail in the distance."

"Yes, sir." Ned walked to the rail as Nicholson went below, and furtively searched the darkness through the glass. Impatiently, he paced the rail and awaited the graying of the eastern horizon. A younger lieutenant, Ezekial Mathiason, made the poop deck and snatched the glass out of his hands. "I'll have that," he said with a bark.

Ned gave him a look that would curdle milk, but handed it over. He was the ranking officer on deck.

"Captain Nicholson assigned the glass to me, sir. Please return it when you're through."

The young officer smirked at him, but after sweeping the black horizon, handed it back and walked aft to the wheel and checked their course. Ned dutifully waited through the occasional squalls for the sun. Finally, at what seemed like twice the hour that it was, the sun began to color the eastern horizon orange under scraps of billowing clouds.

Again the young lieutenant came to the rail and took the glass out of his hands, but returned it without Ned having to remind him. The captain had given Ned the order to fetch him when the sun came up, so Ned decided to search for the bark until its bottom edge cleared the distance. He scanned and scanned the horizon for the bark but could not make her out through the occasional passing squall .

Damn, he thought, she slipped away in the darkness. Ned sighed, handed the glass to Mathiason, and headed for the ladder to fetch the captain. He glanced back over his shoulder, then stopped and stared. He thought he made out the outline of a sail in the distance—in the east with the sun at their back. Then the squalls closed like wet gauze curtains and he could no longer see it.

He hurried below and first tried the officers' wardroom on the deck below the captain's cabin. The boy working there told him the captain had retired to his quarters, so Ned hurried back up a deck and rapped on the captain's door.

"Enter," Nicholson called out.

It was the first time in over two years aboard the *Independence* that Ned had been inside the spacious cabin. At first he was taken aback by the size of it. A deep cubicle on the starboard side housed a double-wide bed with what Ned assumed were closets fore and aft, a cherry wood chart table occupied the center of the room, and chart cabinets the port or larboard side. Two glassed-in windows—the only ones aboard the *Independence*—faced aft. Chinese rugs covered the deck. A hanging brass lantern swung quietly over the chart table where Nicholson worked, and cast deep, swaying shadows on the intricate carpets. The table, which stood solidly in front of a caneback swivel chair, was shared by charts, the ship's log, a lazy black tomcat with a white blaze on its nose, and a cut crystal brandy snifter and four crystal glasses on a silver tray.

"Trying to determine if we're getting any help from the current," Nicholson said without looking up. He plotted with a pair of dividers, received a deep-throated meow from the tom when he disturbed him, then eyed Ned over the chart. "Is she still out there?"

"I turned the glass over to Lieutenant Mathiason, sir, but had a look myself first. No sure sign of her that I could see."

"Damn, that's good news and bad. If she's not there, it means she changed course in the night. Has the wind shifted?"

"No, sir. It's gusting, but still generally out of the south."

"Then there's no reason for her to change course unless she's trying to avoid us. If she is, that could be good news." He scratched the old tom's ears while the big cat stood and stretched; then he pulled an oilcloth slicker from a cabinet, tugged it on, and headed for his cabin door. Ned took one more look at the spacious quarters, reaffirmed his goal of his own ship someday, and followed.

"I thought I caught a glimpse of a sail off the starboard stern, sir."

"Thought?"

"Yes, sir. I couldn't be sure, as the squalls closed in before I could be positive."

They topped the poop deck, and Nicholson took the glass from Mathiason and searched the northwest horizon, now bathed in golden light but still broken by the billowing black-lined clouds and the gauze of falling rain that blended cloud, squall, and sea into a haze.

"Where is she?" He asked as he swept the glass.

"If I were she," Mathiason offered, "and wanting to avoid us, I'd run due west."

"But no sign of a sail to the west?" The captain queried.

"No, sir," the young lieutenant admitted. "Still, through these squalls—"

"East, sir," Ned offered, and got a silencing look from Mathiason for his effort.

"The wind has been bearing northerly to northwest, sir," Mathiason assured him. "She would be running to the west to the Indies and the cover of the islands, with the wind quartering to her advantage."

"He knows we'll run him down long before he reaches the Indies. . . . If I were her captain," Ned said unsurely, "I'd know that's what we would think, and I would do just the opposite. . . . If I were hiding something."

"Don't you have other business, Mr. Beale?" Mathiason snapped in a harsh whisper while Nicholson walked aft, raised the glass, and searched the eastern horizon over the starboard stern rail.

"No, sir," Ned answered quietly, risking offense to the young lieutenant but hoping against hope that Nicholson would catch the sight of a sail in the east. Unfortunately the sun had climbed high enough that it would not be back-lighted, and squalls lined the eastern horizon, obliterating any chance of a sighting.

Nicholson sighed and returned to where Ned and Mathiason waited.

"The bastard is running, I can feel it in my bones," Nicholson said while other young officers joined them on the poop deck.

"Gentlemen," Nicholson informed them, "as much as I hate to do so, since we're running away from Pernambuco, set a new course, east." He turned to Ned, "Due east, Mr. Beale?"

"Due east, sir," Ned said, but his tone lacked confidence.

"Due east, gentlemen."

Mathiason shot Ned a killing look, but retreated to the wheel and informed the pilot. Gathering up a hand trumpet, the pilot walked forward to the poop deck rail and shouted the orders to the topsail bosuns to prepare to come about.

Sean Conners topped the poopdeck rail to join Mathiason after Nicholson returned below to his cabin. The two officers joined Ned and the others at the rail.

"Are you sure you saw a sail, Mr. Beale?" The redheaded first lieutenant asked doubtfully.

"I saw something, Mr. Conners," Ned said, but his voice had lost what little confidence it had harbored.

"A by-God goose chase," Mathiason said with a snarl. "We're losing our only chance at a little action because this wet-behind-the-ears mid*shit* thinks he saw something."

Ned felt heat creep up the back of his neck and tickle his temper. "*I've* got a dollar, Mr. Mathiason, says we spot her before four bells this afternoon."

Conners's mouth curled in a half smile. Mathiason studied the young middy derisively and smirked. "Make it five, Mr. Beale, and you've got a bet." Ned almost choked. Five dollars was half his savings.

"It's a bad bet, Mr. Beale," Conners offered quietly, knowing the odds of running down the retreating ship by two o'clock would be slim-and-none even if she were out there. "Even if she's running east, the odds are we'll miss her in these bloody showers."

"Five it is," Ned said, extending his hand to Mathiason to seal the bet. He wished he felt as confident as he had mustered his voice to sound.

"Sail ahoy!" Rang from the foremast just after the ship's bell sounded two bells.

Ned, who had taken up a position on the bowsprit, felt a surge of relief as he made his way back to the poop deck. He caught Mathiason's eye but got only another smirk.

"If she's not a bark, you still owe me," Mathiason mumbled to Ned when he passed. They were due aft of the retreating ship, and there was no way to tell her configuration yet.

"She's a bark, and the one we're after," Ned said with authority. "And I'll bet you another fiver she's a dirty slaver."

But he got no takers. The deck was suddenly busy with the trimming of sails and the preparation to come alongside. Still, it would be at least another hour before they overtook her even with every available sail set and trimmed and constantly adjusted to take maximum advantage of the fickle winds.

Captain Nicholson had returned to the wheel, and he stepped forward. "Mr. Beale, you've got a good eye. As Conners suggested, you'll serve as coxswain on one of the boarding boats. Pick a crew of eight good oarmen, cutlass and carbine. Mr. Conners, you'll lead the party. Please inform Captain Walton to prepare a contingent of his Marines."

"I'd like to go, sir." Mathiason stepped forward out of the group of junior officers.

"As you wish, Mr. Mathiason. You'll serve as coxswain on the Marine boat."

Ned hurried forward to find his oarmen. Each of the longboats aboard was assigned a permanent normal crew, and Nicholson had given Ned a pat on the back by allowing him to pick his own. He received glowering looks from Norvell Johanson and Thomas Tucker when they realized what duty Ned had been assigned, and when Nicholson did not select them.

Ned returned to the quarterdeck boat with John Specter as the only other middy selected, and to the surprise of the officers on deck, with Theonious Miller, the black loblolly boy who would serve as an oarsman.

As they closed with the ship, which proved to be a brig, they were disappointed to note that she had cask and case in haphazard manner on her topdeck, and appeared in every way to be a hard-at-work merchantman.

When they got within hailing distance, Nicholson took the hand trumpet and moved forward to the rail. "Where are you bound, and who be your ship?" He called, for the vessel's name was so obliterated by grime that it could not be read.

"We be the *Fairwind*, out of Barbados, bound for the Azores, loaded with sugar and 'emp! 'Ow 'bout you?" The voice, with a strong cockney accent, rang back in a friendly manner.

"Azores?" Nicholson glanced at his officers, shook his head in doubt, then turned back to the trumpet. "Then why where you headed northwest only yesterday?''

"Mistaken,. Captain!" The voice answered. "Must have been another vessel!"

"Hove to!"

A voice boomed out in answer. "We're a peaceful merchant-man, British registry, in international waters! You've no right to give us orders!"

"If you're peaceful, then hove to, before I cut ye in half with a volley of thirty-two-pound balls!"

CHAPTER FOUR

Nicholson turned to Conners when the brig failed to heed his warning.

"Mr. Conners," was all the captain said.

Conners put the horn to his mouth and called to a bosun who waited near the midship ladder. He in turn called down to the gun deck below.

The thirty-two-pounder boomed with authority, and the ball sang across the bow of the bark, sounding as if an iron stove had been flung there. The men on board hit the deck and waited until the echo of the blast faded and they were sure the big frigate was not going to fire again before they rather sheepishly peered over the rail, then hesitantly stood again.

"You're violating international charters!" the voice from the brig called out after the officer had regained his feet.

"Hove to, or the next round will demast you!"

The officers on the aft of the bark stood staring in indecision. Nicholson turned to Conners.

"A bit closer this time, Mr. Conners, but no chain yet." Conners forwarded the order below, and the frigate bared her teeth with a vengeful roar. This time the ball holed a jib. The smoke of the cannon drifted well aft before the ship's crew furtively peered over the rails.

"By the good Lord!" the voice rang out in anger. "You're no better than pirates! I'll have the whole English Navy on your blackguard hides!"

"The next round will bring down your foremast! Now hove to!"

The crew of the bark sprang into action, and within minutes her sails were backed, then furled, and she glided to a standstill, bobbing quietly in the sea. The squalls still marked the surface in the distance, but the two ships were untouched by the intermittent storms for the moment.

Ned directed the launching of one longboat and Mathiason the other. Nicholson carefully kept his ship where he could bring a full broadside of thirty eight guns against the bark, across their fifty yard separation, if she tried any mischief—but was confident she would not be so foolish.

As the longboats, two tentative feelers from one ship to another in the wide open sea, made their way across the open water, Ned's shoulders and stomach tightened in anticipation. This was the first time in over two years aboard the *Independence* that the frigate had been involved in any action even close to hostile. It was a feeling he would not soon forget, and it charged him with new fervor for his chosen profession. While he steered the boat, he kept the other hand on the cold shank of the cutlass at his side or on the solid assurance of the butt of his pistol—and decided not to speak to the others of the dry state of his mouth. The crew of the bark, amid snarling complaints and insults, dropped a rope ladder overboard.

Conners was the first to board. The Marine officer, Captain Phinias Walton, and eight of his troops in the boat below stood away where they could bring the fire of their musket carbines to bear if need be. All the men from Ned's boat, save one oarman assigned the watch, ascended the ropes. Then Captain Walton and the Marines came alongside and followed suit. Ned stared about the filthy, untended vessel and shook his head in revulsion.

"State yer business," the captain of the bark snapped at Conners.

"Lieutenant Sean Conners," he said, not offering his hand.

"I'm Captain Severn Doer, and again, state yer business." He kept his own arms crossed in front of him. Conners placed his gnarled, red-freckled hand to the hilt of his sheathed cutlass, and his expression hardened.

"We're empowered by the United States Congress to intercept and search any vessels suspected of trading in Africans. "

"You damn fool, can't ye see we're simple merchantmen 'eaded east with a full cargo? Yer interfering in free trade on the open sea; your bloody Congress 'as no power here . . . they'll be 'ell to pay."

"As there may be," Conners said. "Still, Captain Doer, we're searching your holds."

"I'll be damned if ye will, we're merchant—"

Conners stepped aside, and nodded to the broad-shouldered Marine, Captain Walton, who shouted an order to his men. The Marines had formed two lines of four, and the front four dropped to a single-knee position, and all eight brought their short, wicked-looking bayoneted carbines to bear on the four assembled officers of the *Fairwind*.

''We're going to search your holds,'' Conners repeated. "Have your crew stand the hatches aside."

As they moved to open the maindeck hatches, Conners waved Ned over to join him. They were disappointed to note that the holds were packed to the deckline with cases marked to be sugar and bales of hemp. He reached for the bayonet of a Marine, pried the cover off a case, picked out a cone of sugar, and studied it in frustration.

Conners dropped the cone dejectedly, received a snide comment from Doer, then moved aft to the quarterdeck ladder, followed by Ned, who waved Theonious Miller over to join them. Theonious had not said a word since Ned had invited him to come along, and his eyes were wide with the anticipation of finding a group of his African brothers chained below. As they descended the ladder, Captain Doer followed, still loudly vocalizing his complaints in the hard-to-understand cockney.

"It's not bad enough that ye violate the sanctity of this vessel on the 'igh seas, but ye bring a bloody kaffir... an armed kaffir—which should be against the law—along to sully me fine ship."

Ned glanced around him. The belowdecks were no cleaner than the maindeck of the vessel, littered with trash and food scraps, infested with far more bugs, roaches, and rats than the *Independence*. Suddenly Ned was very proud of his own vessel.

But he was disappointed as he searched below. They worked their way all the way to the filthy bilge and found nothing. Captain Doer led the way back topside. When Ned cleared the deck, he realized that Theo was not behind.

He looked back down the ladderway, and Theo appeared below, waving him back down. He joined him on the lower deck.

"When we moved down the ladder to de' bilge, we went too far."

"What do you mean, Theo?"

"They was three extra rungs on that bottom ladder. "

"So?"

"So, I tinks de be a 'tween decks—a partial deck, room enough to put some poor souls if you don't care how many died. I heard about such things the last time I talked to some escaped slaves." He glanced at Ned guiltily as if he had done something wrong by even talking to slaves on the run.

Theo leaned close to the bulkhead and listened. Then with a fervor, he beat out a rhythm with the flat of his palms against the hollow-sounding wall. It echoed through the narrow confines of the passageway.

He waited. Finally, when no answer came, a look of abject disappointment sagged across his face, then suddenly turned to gleaming joy as the rhythm echoed back. Faint, but definitely answered. He looked up at Ned with a look of triumph.

"Either de Brit bilge rats know de drums, or der is Africans aboard dis sorry excuse for a ship."

"Hold on a minute." Ned hurriedly returned to the deck, where Conners, with an apologetic air, and the boarding party were preparing to disembark the *Fairwind*.

''Lieutenant!''

He whispered to him, gaining the glare of Captain Doer and the crew in the process.

"You don't have a 'tween deck on this filthy pigsty, do you, Doer?" Conners asked, his look again hard.

"She's a standard bark, proudly built on strong oak ways of Scotland. And I'll be pleased to see ye and yours off 'er, now!" The captain's voice rose an octave.

''Watch them closely,'' Conners commanded Captain Walton, who happily backed Doer up with his bayoneted carbine.

Conners followed Ned below to where Theonious was searching for an access to the suspected 'tween decks. But they found nothing from the aft end of the ship. They returned to the deck, where Conners puzzled over the problem, while Doer and his officers stood and glared in triumph. Theo walked to the open holds and began banging on each crate.

"Get that bloody wog away from my hold!" Doer yelled, starting forward in a rage, only to be met by Captain Walton's bayonet firmly creasing his mid-section.

"Your bile would not even be noticed among the other slop on your filthy deck." Walton spoke for the first time since coming aboard. He gave Doer a hard enough smile that the cockney captain knew he was in deadly earnest.

Theo continued banging until he found a crate that rang with a hollow thump. It rested against the aft bulkhead. He fiddled with the crate top until it swung away, then looked up with light in his eyes and grinned.

"I found me a crate wid a single ladder. Funny you should be shippin' a crate wid a ladder." Before he finished, he slipped down inside, like a rabbit into a warren, and out of sight. Ned and Conners followed into the dark opening. They descended down the narrow ladderway deep into the hold, until they reached a slippery floor. By the time Ned got to where Theo worked—there was only room for two of them to stand, so Conners had to wait on the ladder above—Theo already had a two-by-two-foot hatch cover swinging aside.

The odor struck them like a flat-handed slap across the face. Both men covered their mouths and noses with a hand. Conners involuntarily moved three rungs back up the ladder, his eyes beginning to water.

"What the hell is that?" the lieutenant called down to them.

"We gonna need forge tools," Theo said, his face a mask devoid of emotion. Ned started up the ladder, and Conners hurriedly led the way out. They reached the deck and both men took a series of deep gasps, filling their lungs with fresh air. Then Conners looked at Ned expectantly.

"They're in there, alive," Ned said quietly, "and it's a wonder. Chained neck to neck, arm and leg to deck, side by side on their sides with not even room to lay flat, no more than eighteen inches headroom, packed like sardines in a slime of their own filth. There must be a hundred in a space ten by forty feet."

Ned felt like retching over the rail. Instead, he walked over to the snarling Captain Doer, and with the power of broad shoulders gained from two years' work in the rigging, exploded with a punch that dropped the barrel-chested captain flat on his back. No one on the deck made a move, including the captain, who bled profusely from a gash over his eye, but lay out cold on the deck.

Conners feigned Ned a hard look. "Mr. Beale, if you do that more than three or four more times, I'll have to put you on report." The Marine captain guffawed, and the other *Fairwind* officers backed away a few respectful steps.

Ned turned to one of the other officers, who looked as if he expected the same, but Ned spoke quietly. "Get the proper tools and free those people below." With a glance at Captain Walton, who motioned with his carbine, the man hurried to the ladder. "You, too," Ned instructed the other two officers.

"I'm not going down into that filth," one man mumbled, jutting his chin out adamantly.

"If I had anything to say about it, you'd make the rest of your voyage in that filth," Ned told him. "Now get below and help free those people." Hesitantly, the man obliged.

Ned took a deep steadying breath, and with Captain Walton and three Marines behind him, followed the three *Fairwind* officers back down the hidden crate ladder, armed with extra hammers and chisels the officers had brought.

Theo had crawled into the narrow space and was moving from man to man, ladling water to the stark, sunken-eyed prisoners.

"As God is my witness," Ned mumbled as he tied a wet kerchief over his mouth and nose, then set to work with hammer and chisel, "I never would have believed. . . ."

Theo glanced over at him in the dim light. Man's a predator, Mr. Beale, and he preys on his own."

"Let's get these people out into the air," Ned said, trying not to breathe.

He knew for as long as he lived he would never forget the stench of that narrow space, nor the unspoken gratitude in the eyes of the first black-skinned man he freed from his shackles. Nor the hate in their eyes as they glared at the officers of the *Fairwind*, whose fear you could almost smell over the stench. But the black men were far to weak to do as their eyes said they wished.

Ned gladly accepted the five dollars he had won from Lieutenant Mathiason in the form of a solid gold piece, and more happily gained a pat on the back from Captain Nicholson. A prize crew delivered the *Fairwind* to Barbados with eighty seven new freedmen, fresh from repeated dousing with buckets of saltwater, lounging on her decks and her officers chained in her holds—to Ned's chagrin, Nicholson would not allow them to be confined in the terrible conditions they had created—and turned the slavers over to the authorities there.

Ned, and the *Independence*, sailed on to South America.

Pernambuco was Ned's first taste of Brazil.

Although he had studied and mastered Spanish—thanks somewhat to Mr. Tallywacker's able instruction, but more so to the half-dozen Spanish, two Peruvian, one Chilean, and two Mexican sailors who sailed aboard the *Independence*—Ned had no knowledge of Portuguese, the national language of Brazil. At Pernambuco Ned enjoyed a shore leave on shore, but the less than four hours he spent in town gave him only a slight flavor of the country and little more than a glance at its beautiful women.

During his almost continual service aboard the *Independence*, women were something his life was all but devoid of—but a subject he seemed to be thinking more and more about as he grew older. He'd spent time ashore in Finland, in Russia, in England, but at his young age his interests were monopolized by education—formal education. And the sermons by the captain and the ship's chaplain were to be taken seriously. Of course, he had listened to the other boys talk, most of which he put off to wild imagination, fiction like most of his off-duty reading. But the older men of the crew, particularly the man who had taken Ned under his broad-shouldered wing, Chief Gunner's Mate Rosco Handley, he listened to with more respect and sometimes with awe as they eulogized the virtues, and lack thereof, of the gentler sex. The pleasures of women were extolled by Handley and his fellow gunners in great detail during the long tropic evenings.

During a free shift after the *Independence* had corrected course from south-southwest to due west—their final wind-abaft run into Rio's well-protected port—Ned found himself on the lower gun deck, where Rosco and a half-dozen gun captains were gathered for a smoke after supper.

Ned walked quietly over to the group of older men and settled himself on the deck, where they sopped the last of a lintel and bean soup from their wooden bowls with hardtack full of weevils.

"Tomorrow night we feast on churrasca," Rosco said as he fished his pipe out and packed it. "No more weevils ... and fresh vegetables."

"Churrasca?" Ned questioned.

"Carne churrasca, meat roasted over open fires. No one does it better than the Cariocas."

"What are Cariocas? Ned pressed, interested In this exotic port and its fascinating people.

Rosco's ruddy face broke with a knowing smile. "The citizens of Rio call themselves Cariocas, and they be the most fun-loving people in the world." He took a deep draw on the pipe as the rest of the men chuckled.

Ned was anxious to be in on the joke. "Fun-loving?"

"The roast meat be the best, but it books no comparison to the raw Brazilian treats," Rosco said, his eyes twinkling with humor.

"Raw," Sam McElervy, a gunner's captain with a painted but slightly faded wooden ball where his right eye should have been, added, "but served hot and a'plenty."

"Raw but hot?" Ned wrinkled his nose in disgust as he watched Sam's left eye dance from man to man while his right eye stared straight ahead.

"Don't be so sure you won't like it, young Mr. Beale," Rosco teased. "You happen to get leave when we do, and Mr. McElervy and I will tour the town with ye, and take ye on a long, or short as the case may be"—he chortled and was joined by the others—"stroll up cock alley.''

Ned began to understand that he was the brunt of the teasing when Rosco used the sailors' slang for a lady's private parts. He leaned back against the cannon and decided to listen rather than question. But McElervy was not quite ready to let it rest.

"And we'll save ye from the wrath of the epaulets," the one-eyed gunner's captain said with a laugh.

Ned wanted the men to know he understood the term and to get his own digs in. "Why would the officers be unhappy about my visiting cock alley? Is there a Navy law against women? I'd think all you old cobs would be rottin' away in the brig if there was such." Ned got a laugh out of the men with this.

"No law against that, young Beale. In fact"—Sam guffawed and slapped his thigh—"that will keep you young firebrands from breaking the ship's strict rule against boxin' the Jesuit." All the men laughed hardily, except gunner's captain Jose Cabrelino, a Chilean Catholic. He found no humor in the reference to the rumored sexual self-abuse of supposedly celibate priests.

But the men meant no offense, and his lack of joining in went unnoticed. Ned's slightly red face did not. The boys were continually teased about their youth and inexperience. Ned decided he had better quit while he was ahead. He sat back against the thirty-two-pounder and securely buttoned his lip.

For the next hour he enjoyed the men's reminiscences about the wonderful food and women of Rio, while the *Independence*, her spankers and jibs spread wide, wing-and-wing, with the wind at her back, split the waves in a rush toward that destination.

John Specter jostled Ned awake at daybreak. "Get dressed and topside, Ned. We're in the middle of a sea battle!"

Without socks, Ned pulled his boots on and ran through the milling boys, following John topside. It took a moment before Ned realized that the battle was a distant one. A French cruiser almost a mile away maneuvered for position as two faster but much less heavily gunned Argentine schooners tried to cross her bow and stern and catch her in a crossfire.

The *Independence* put her topsail men in the rigging and shortened sail, but Nicholson would not hove to. He wanted no chance of the battling ships on either side mistaking his frigate for an enemy. He would keep men in the rigging so they could bring the *Independence* under full sail the instant any of the distant ships made for her. Besides, his crew could get a better view of the action from there. Ned and John climbed to the first crossarm of the mizzenmast and watched.

One of the schooners was soon demasted and, when the cruiser turned its full attention to the other, ran for a distant rain squall. As the French ship approached the wounded smaller vessel, the Argentine captain wisely lowered his colors.

Later that afternoon, Captain Nicholson and his sail-master, an ex-Brit sailor named Henry Throckmorton, made an appearance in the middies' wardroom and gave a lecture based on the tactics the opposing captains in the sea battle, so fresh in the middies' mind, had utilized.

At no time had the middies paid more attention to a lecture, particularly after Nicholson informed them of the servitude the captured Argentine crew would be subjected to.

That evening, surrounded by towering basalt domes protruding out of the dense velvet green jungle of Rio, the *Independence* dropped her hook in the shallow, quiet bay off the fabled city.

The odors of the jungle and town wafted across the quiet water, cloying smells of vegetation and humanity and heat. Islands, like wads of floating green moss, dotted the bay in the distance, and billowing clouds, reaching with tentacles of

73

mist into their canyons, occluded the higher mountains beyond the placid water. Closer to the thatched and tiled roofs
of the city itself, near a wharf crawling with bright-shirted,
dark-skinned stevedores, a French frigate quartered an Argentine cruiser, and both rocked in blissful peace less than a cable's length apart, their shore boats nuzzling against each of
them like piglets suckling a pair of sows—a peace that would
disappear instantly when they left the neutral harbor.

No shore leave was given the crew of the *Independence*
that night, but in the morning Ned discovered that the larboard half of the midshipmen—his shift—would go ashore at
the end of the day. He did notice that the Argentine cruiser
had slipped out of the harbor under the cover of darkness.

Ned did his day's work with the fervor of one eager to
finish—and wished he could hurry the clock. Finally, at four
bells in the afternoon, Rosco Handley approached Ned, who
hurried below to change clothes.

"Are ye ready for that stroll we talked about?" Rosco
asked, the gleam of mischief still in his eye. Sam, his painted
wooden ball still in his, approached a few paces behind.

"I appreciate your looking out for me, Mr. Handley," Ned
said tentatively, "but I really should take my shore leave with
the other middies."

Sam stopped beside Rosco and leaned on the bigger man's
shoulder in a familiar manner. "It seems the lad fears the
short-heeled wench. Should we leave him to his brother suck-
lings?"

"Short-heeled?" Ned asked. Almost immediately he regretted showing his ignorance again.

"Short-heeled, lad, easy to rock to her back."

Ned started to feel the heat rise, but the truth was, even
though being with a woman was an experience that gripped
his curiosity, he feared being in the company of older men
when he had the opportunity. What if he didn't do it well?

He mumbled, "It's not that at all, just—"

"You needn't come with us, Mr. Beale," Handley said with a laugh, but his eyes had gone from glint of humor to compassion. Rather than the opportunity to back out, Rosco's understanding attitude gave Ned the rush of courage he needed.

"Don't mind him," Rosco continued, shoving his friend Sam away. "He's a seven-sided lout."

Sam shoved him back playfully.

"Seven-sided?" Ned asked, seeming continually to be at the disadvantage of these older men and their slang.

"Ya! A right side, a left side, a fore side an' aft, an outside, a bloody black-hearted inside . . . an' a blind side." With this Rosco again laughed and slapped his thighs, but Sam merely shook his head.

"I've only heard that bloody bad joke on four stinkin' continents," Sam said with a growl, then clapped Rosco on the back. "Are we ashore?"

"Wait," Ned said suddenly. "Let me change. I'll be but a minute."

Rosco laughed. "This is liable to be a rough ride, sailor. Meat raw and hot, demon rum to scorch yer gullet, and the devil'll be holdin' his hand over God's eyes till the sun rises again. By then, you may be wishin' it never does."

"I'll be but a minute." Ned turned and started below, then hesitated. "Can I bring a mate?"

"If he's quick of wit," Sam yelled, "game for hot meat, and has his own full purse, bring him!"

Ned ran below, hoping he could find John Specter, and wondering again if he really wanted to do this.

CHAPTER FIVE

The four sailors made their way among the *carreras*, gig-like carts filled with jungle fruits and firewood, and among herds of stock—pigs and fowl and a few scrawny cattle—and working Brazilians. They climbed a long, low hill from the bay past the warehouses and storage yards of the waterfront to the tenderloin area of the town. The sign outside a stone building said simply *Salao* or Saloon, but inside another said *Salao Papagaio*, and its two words, painted in a variety of colors, bracketed a brightly illustrated parrot with green body, red wings, yellow beak and feet, and bright yellow eyes set in its blue head. Hanging from the low ceiling were a number of parrot cages, each with a preening bird, and on each end of the bar a T shaped dowel stand held a brightly colored two-foot-tall macaw whose slow movements and occasional squawks, as it moved from side to side disdained the more raucous saloon customers.

"Maria Tres Dedo," Sam introduced the girl to Ned and John with a sweeping gesture. Ned was amazed at how pretty she was except for the reason she had her nickname. Rosco had already explained, when he recognized the girl across the crowded saloon, that she was infamous with the sailors. Three-Finger Mary was English, emerald eyed, and redheaded, with skin like cream sprinkled with paprika. She shone like a gleaming ruby amid brass tokens as she moved among her bean-brown and dusky sisters of the night.

Ned snatched his hat off, but John Specter merely stared at the girl, unable to keep his eyes from wandering to her hand and its missing third and little fingers.

"You had an accident," John mumbled, his eyes on the hand. She wore large rings set with colored stones on the two remaining fingers and thumb, as if she wanted the world's gaze to be attracted to her lack.

''You're very pretty," Ned said quickly, his own eyes meeting her gaze, and John turned red at his indelicate comment.

"*Obrigado*, " the girl said. "That's thank you, if you don't know the Portuguese. Thank you, Ned. My good friends call me Dedo. Have you gentlemen gotten a drink?''

"Not yet, Dedo," Rosco's voice boomed across the table.

"Then what is your pleasure?" she asked.

Ned, too, reddened and he felt the heat on his neck—but also in the pit of his stomach. It crept down his thighs when her eyes swept him up and down with the boldness of a hostler appraising a new horse. Rosco and Sam sat with arms folded, enjoying his nervousness.

"*Vinho* all 'round!" Rosco boomed, "then the pleasure of yer company, missy. "

Her laughter tinkled, and Ned could not keep his eyes from studying her from the nape of her slender neck to a well-tapered calf as she worked her way back through the crowd to the intricately carved bar where three bartenders in bright colored shirts poured almost as quickly as they could move.

Mary moved gracefully, dressed in a soft-flowing red skirt that ended just below the knee and a low-cut scoop necked blouse that showed the swell of her freckled breasts—pushed into a pair of mounds by some contrivance that Ned could only imagine. Her hips swayed enticingly when she moved away on sandaled feet, causing the skirt, flaring from a waist Ned thought he could get his hands around, to sweep from side to side.

The sun wasn't down yet, and already the saloon was packed with men. Sailors from a dozen countries, townsmen

77

and merchants, Brazilians, Argentines, Frenchmen off the frigate, a group of German miners. But even with the large numbers of whites, for the first time in his life Ned sat in a room where men of color drank freely. From Mary's pale, speckled white to a dusky black, the complexions were as varied as the languages.

The girl, whom Ned guessed to be in her early twenties, returned balancing four mugs between her good and not-so-good hands.

"Keep the silver flowing, boys, and I'll keep the *vinho* coming your way." She scooped a few coins off the plank table and started to move away.

"Join us, Mary, and bring three of yer mates," Sam suggested so hungrily that Ned expected him to lick his lips when he finished.

"It's a full house tonight, gents," she said. "When yer ready ta see the inside of a crib, I'll bring a few of the ladies 'round."

"After a mug or two, missy," Sam managed as she moved away. "But don't get too tied up in the meantime!"

"Now, *that*, lads," he said to Ned and John, "is enough to loosen purse strings tied with the tightest bowline."

Neither Ned nor John had a comment, but rather continued to look from girl to girl while the ladies moved among the men.

A dusky black girl, whose breasts pushed at her tight blouse, caught John's eye. Self-consciously, he cut his gaze away. Undaunted, she laid her chubby hands on his shoulders and began to knead his muscles.

"A stallion fresh off de boat," she said, and John turned his head so he could see her.

With a strength belying her short but wide figure, she spun the chair so his knees faced the side. John's eyes widened when she flipped her bright blue skirt up and sat astride him, one well-rounded hot thigh on each side of his, her knees exposed below the pushed-up hem line—more of a woman's leg than John or Ned had ever seen—her warm brandy breath inches from John's face.

"I am called Chapa. Are ya ready for a back room, and de ride of ye life, young stallion?"

"I . . . I . . ." John stammered. But Chapa threw her head back and laughed. Running a hand behind John's neck, she buried his face in the cleavage between her ample, bouncing brown breasts. His face almost disappeared in the chocolate mounds strongly scented with rose water. When she let him loose he glanced around gasping for breath and his dignity. Sam and Rosco guffawed loud enough to turn heads in the noisy room.

"Best ye wait till the colt has drunk a bit more courage," Rosco said with a laugh. Rising with a deep throated giggle, Chapa pinched John's cheek. When she moved away, breasts and hips straining at her cotton garments, he took a deep breath, snatched up his mug, and, with the whites of his eyes showing around his pupils, downed it in three gulps. A trickle of red wine found its way down the side of his mouth and formed a drop on his chin.

''I think John needs another," Rosco said, and yelled for the barmaid across the room.

Mary cut her eyes away from the five rugged French sailors she stood among, and made her way over.

"It's the cribs, is it?" she asked, and her green eyes settled on Ned's.

Sam clapped John on the back. "So is it milk, lad, coffee with a bit of cream, or coffee as God made it . . . hot and black?"

John flushed and glanced at his mug. "I'll have an other wine."

Sam and Rosco laughed. "Do ye want a light-skinned wench, one that can hide from ye in the dark, or somethin' in between?"

"Milk-skinned and carrot-topped!" Ned said quickly, and Mary moved beside him. She rested a hip against his shoulder and casually wrapped an arm around his neck.

"You've a good eye for a mare, young Beale. She's a red-spotted brindle, but pretty as a speckled pup," Sam said with an envious look. "In fact, I believe I'll have some of yer time, lass, when you've finished with the young middy."

"You never minded a buttered bun," Rosco said to his friend, his tone derisive but his eyes twinkling. "I don't imagine Beale here will wear it down to the nubbins, will you, Ned?"

Before Ned could answer, Mary bent low next to his ear and whispered a throaty invitation. She rested her hand on the back of his neck and tickled his hair, then winked at Sam. "If yer purse has the dollar, I have the time." Sam turned to John, seemingly anxious to get the boys on their way.

"What'll it be, young Specter?"

"Whatever," John mumbled. His eyes, wide with apprehension but beginning to warm with interest, moved around the room.

"And who would ye suggest for the young stud?" Rosco deferred to Mary.

"We've a new girl, not much more than a child, and fresh from Sao Paulo. Let me fetch her."

Mary moved away, and Ned's eyes assessed her up and down until she disappeared among the men.

"How did she lose her fingers?" he asked without taking his eyes off the spot where she disappeared.

"Stepped into a fight among the rabble that frequents this fine establishment, and a blade took them. Should have minded woman's business," Sam said, as if it were a daily occurrence; then he fixed his eyes on Ned. "A bit of advice, lads. When ye get in the cribs, keep one hand on yer purse and an eye peeled on the door. You wouldn't want a couple of the local lads to knot yer head while yer interest rested else-where."

"And keep yer mind on something other than the business at hand," Rosco advised. "Yer dollar will go farther.''

Ned had no idea what he was talking about. His eyes remained on the spot where Mary had disappeared, and his face broke into a smile at her return. The young girl she had in tow was the color of mocha, wearing a black skirt and white blouse, with a bright green sash around her waist and with long, braided black hair hanging below it. Her eyes, in the round face of an Indian, flashed like black pebbles in the bottom of a stream bed, and she kept them down, demurely staring at the matted straw on the earth door.

"Gents," Mary said, "this is Theresa."

John stood.

"Take the lad's hand, Theresa, and show 'im to yer cubbyhole," Mary said.

Without looking up, the girl reached out and took John's hand.

"And you're mine, bucko," Mary said. Hooking her three remaining fingers into Ned's hand, she pulled him to his feet and started to lead him to the rear of the saloon.

Before they reached the curtain hanging across the exit through which John and Theresa had disappeared, a hand snaked out of the crowd and encircled Mary's arm in a steely grip. Ned stopped and turned to eye the man who had jerked Mary to a halt.

"You said you were returning, cheri'," a tall, thin-faced man chastised her.

"And I will, as soon as I've spent some time with this handsome, anxious man," Mary said with a tight smile, and tried to pry the man's thin, iron-like fingers off her upper arm.

"Surely the man will not mind if Henri goes in his stead," the dark-haired Frenchman said without bothering to glance in Ned's direction. His cold-gray eyes burned into Mary's.

Ned appraised the Frenchman. He stood a head taller than Ned, but thinner. His forearms were slender, but corded with muscle. Ned judged him to be a topsail man on the frigate anchored in the bay. Alone, Ned would have jerked Mary out of his grasp, but four other rugged-looking French sailors—two Ned's height but thicker of chest, and two as tall as the talker but more heavily built—stood in a semicircle behind the man.

"Let me go," Mary said, her face a mask, but she winced as the Frenchman tightened his grip.

"Do not insult Henri, ma cheri." His eyes shone flat and cold as pond ice.

Ned stepped forward and spoke quietly. "Pardon me, but the lady is in my company."

Slowly, the Frenchman turned his head. The other four behind him turned to face Ned and all eyes burned into him.

"Are you speaking to me?" the man asked.

"The lady is in my company," Ned repeated.

The Frenchman began to laugh, at first a small chortle, then an insulting roar. Ned stood, perplexed. The other Frenchmen joined in laughing and holding their sides. Ned cut his eyes to Rosco and Sam, but saw them immersed in conversation.

Finally, Henri stopped laughing. He wiped his eyes, then spoke in a low voice to Ned.

"Return to your friends and you will live to be old and gray-headed with stories to tell your grandchildren, and I will take care of the real man's work for both of us."

Ned felt the muscles in his arms and back begin to bunch. He had to look up to see the Frenchman's face, and he was close enough to smell his rancid breath.

Mary moved around the Frenchman. "Follow me," she instructed Ned.

The Frenchman brushed by Ned and up behind her as she moved away. "As you wish, cheri'," he said. She stopped in her tracks and turned to face him.

"I said," Ned snapped, "the lady is with me."

The Frenchman turned to face him, and Ned caught the glint of the knife that had appeared in his hand.

''M'sieur, " Henri said, his tone as sharp as his knife, "unless you wish to become a capon, and forever after have no need of the beautiful mademoiselles, I would suggest you go back to your Yankee friends—" Just as he started to step forward, Three-Finger Mary snatched a heavy mug full of wine off a table and smashed it over his head, driving him to his knees.

Before Ned could react, blows pummeled him from behind and he crashed forward into a table full of Cariocas.

Two of the men managed to snatch up their drinks and scrambled out of the way, but two others slammed to the floor.

Ned rolled to his back and kicked an attacking Frenchman in the stomach, driving him back with an audible "oof," but one of the Brazilians who had been knocked from the table jumped him, trying to get in a blow. Ned rolled across the floor with the man, then found himself snatched to his feet, his arms pinioned at his sides.

Two of the Frenchman held him while another stood in front of him, driving powerful blows into his midsection. Then the Frenchman flew to the side—Rosco and Sam had entered the fray. Ned slammed himself back, crashing the man at one side into the stone wall of the saloon. He freed his arm on that side and smashed his fist repeatedly into the other man, who covered his head with both arms and spun away as blood from his smashed nose splattered across the stones.

Sam, Rosco, and Ned managed to get their backs to the wall, and the four Frenchman and four Brazilians formed a semicircle around them.

Ned glanced at the front door, wondering how they were going to get out of this, and saw two stripe-shirted sailors enter. Norvell Johanson and Thomas Tucker stood gaping at their shipmates and the eight men around them. They spun on their heels and left.

"Bastards," Ned swore under his breath, then found himself swinging and kicking at charging combatants.

Suddenly he fought only one man. The Argentines had jumped in. Five of the men had relished the opportunity to join the battle, as long as they were fighting against the French. Fists, elbows, bottles, knees, and an occasional chair flew and smashed into brawling men.

Then the room filled with soldiers. Brazilians in uniform and shako hats jerked men to their feet and shoved them against the stone walls. No man remained unmarked; many bled from blows, flashing knives, or bottles.

The *comandante* of the Brazilian troops strode forward into the center of the saloon, a quirt in his hand. Angrily, he slapped the stiff leather against his leg.

"Who is at fault here?"

No one among the two dozen men answered. Mary stepped out of the curtained rear door with John Specter.

"The Frenchmen started it," she said.

"No—" Henri stepped away from the wall, but a barrel-shaped Brazilian soldier slammed him back with the butt of his carbine.

"The Frenchmen," she repeated.

"Thank you, Dedo," he said in a familiar manner.

"All of you others go about your business . . . back to your ships if you are wise," the *comandante* ordered. "You gentlemen from the French frigate, I'll return you to your ship as soon as I get a damage estimate from the proprietor. We'll see how valuable you are to your *capitao*. I suggest the rest of you find your way back to wherever you belong or you'll find yourselves *cadasrrados*."

"What did he call us?" John asked defensively.

"Jailbirds, lad," Sam answered, rubbing his bleeding knuckles. "Let's fly out of here before he gets serious about it."

"Let's go," Rosco said, brushing himself off and mopping the blood from his forehead where a bottle had creased his pate.

"But—" Ned glanced at Mary.

"She'll be here the next leave you get," Sam said. "Any chance to stay out of a Rio *cadeia*—jail—should be jumped on like a gull on a clam.

But Ned was not so sure. As they made their way back to the ship, he wondered if a night with Mary might be worth a stint in their *cadeia*.

The next day, Ned, Rosco, and Sam were called into the officers' wardroom, where Lieutenant Conners waited.

"We've had a report that you gentlemen were involved in a brawl at Papagaio's."

"Not exactly a brawl, sir," Rosco said.

"Mr. Beale?" Conners asked.

"There was a fight, sir. Not started by us, however."

"You're confined to the ship for a week, Beale. Handley and McElervy will forgo grog rations for three days."

"Yes, sir," Rosco mumbled. "That it?"

"That's it," Conners said. "Beale, stay a moment."

Rosco and Sam stomped out. Ned waited, his hat in his hand.

"What the hell is the matter with Norvell Johanson, Mr. Beale?"

"The matter?"

"Between you and him. He ran straight to Nicholson with a report of the trouble at the saloon. For the past year, every time I speak to him, he has a complaint about you. What's between you two?"

"I have no idea, Mr. Conners."

"I suggest you settle your grudge."

"I have no grudge."

"Then I suggest you settle his. The service is no place to harbor ill feelings."

"Yes, sir. But it's his problem, not mine."

After Ned left, for the first time since returning to the ship, he remembered Johanson and Tucker coming in the door of the saloon and leaving without helping their shipmates.

John Specter enjoyed a week's worth of teasing Ned about his adventures with the pretty Indian girl, and Ned's missing his chance to retire to the back room with Mary. Ned had to grit his teeth and bear it.

True to Sam's word, Three-Finger Mary was there a week later, and every night and every spare dollar Ned could save was invested, each time they were in port, in furthering his education.

Again, with the pressure of studying and learning the ship and the excitement of new ports, Ned forgot about Norvell Johanson, deciding that letting the other midshipman stew in his own juice was the best retribution. His father had told him many times that temper was a valuable thing, and a wise man spends it with respect and never loses it. He decided to forget about Johanson.

Finally, after almost a year in the Brazilian Squadron, where Ned received his warrant as full midshipman, the *Independence* set sail for home. For the first time in almost four years, Ned would see Bloomingdale and his family, and would finally have the opportunity to attend the Naval Asylum and take his. exams. With any luck, he would become a passed midshipman, and then, with luck, an officer of a ship-of-the-line. But he would have to part company with his good friend and mentor, Rosco Handley.

From the back alleys of Rio and the Caribbean to the Naval Asylum in Philadelphia seemed a much longer trip than the six thousand miles it was. If Ned had not spent a month's leave at Bloomingdale with his mother, he wondered if he would have been able to stand the intense study during his six months at the naval school, a good deal of which time he remained cloistered in a dank, dark room. He wrote his brother, Truxtun, saying he "lived like a monk but felt like the devil."

But he did survive it—barely, since a smallpox epidemic broke out in Philadelphia during Ned's tenure in the naval school. Although all the middies and professors were treated with the latest scientific hope—vaccination—some did not take, and Ned lost a professor to the dreaded disease. The Navy closed the school for six weeks, and Ned went back to Bloomingdale.

Shortly after his return to the Asylum, on June 23, 1842, Ned Beale stepped before six examiners, five of them officers of the line and the sixth a professor. Ned presented his journal and letters of support from Nicholson and Conners, and answered a number of questions regarding seamanship. To Ned's relief, he passed. Again he wrote Truxtun and described his passing as "the most extraordinary event of my life."

But a passed midshipman was not yet an officer. To become one, he had to receive the coveted lieutenant's epaulets—which might take three to eight more years.

Ned was assigned to the *Columbus*, commanded by William C. Spences, and sailed to join the Mediterranean squadron. The *Columbus* spent two years in Europe.

Norvell Johanson also passed his exams, but unlike Beale, was assigned to shore duty. Due to his family's political connections Norvell became a clerk, a secretary assigned to the office of the Secretary of the Navy.

Ned hoped he had seen the last of Norvell Johanson.

During his tenure in the Mediterranean, Ned discovered its disparate religions and began a comparative study of them. He read the Koran, and though he adopted some of its advice and extolled in his journal that men should "excel each other in good works," he did not adopt its cautions against alcohol, gambling, or pork.

He did, however, temper his "French" leaves, visits to shore that took him among the base and depraved.

In 1845, Ned returned to Bloomingdale and a long-awaited six-month leave. He was reassigned to the naval squadron commanded by Commodore Robert F. Stockton, and was immediately impressed with the man. He was what Ned considered the epitome of a naval officer.

Ned found himself scheduled aboard a peculiar vessel, the *Princeton*, a steam-powered, screw propelled warship developed by Stockton himself. Before becoming a naval officer, Stockton was an industrialist and inventor—and an intimate of politicians. The steam-powered vessel was about to set sail for the Mediterranean so the United States could show off her technology, but unexpectedly, Stockton and his command received other orders. James Polk had just been inaugurated as president, and wanted to know what the Republic of Texas had in mind regarding the Mexicans. He had received overtures that Texas wanted statehood, and extended his invitation to have them apply.

Ned Beale found himself re-assigned. He wrote a friend suggesting that the real reason for the voyage of his newly assigned vessel, the *Porpoise*, part of Stockton's Texas-bound squadron, was "to investigate the annexation of Mexico."

The *Porpoise*—where Ned met up with his old friend John Specter—was a hermaphrodite brig, much smaller than the *Independence* at eighty-eight feet in length and only twenty-five feet in beam. Since she carried an intimate complement of eighty men, Ned found himself with much broader duties.

Stockton's squadron entered Galveston Harbor on May 13, 1845, with the *Porpoise* in the lead. The warships fired a salute to the Republic of Texas, Stockton immediately went ashore to meet with Texas officials, and all the officers and middies were invited to a great ball as guests of the town officials. Ned, John, two lieutenants, and Captain Hubert Paxton, who in actuality was a lieutenant also, set out, as the sun touched the western horizon, aboard a longboat to the low salt grass shore of Galveston to attend the ball. With over a hundred officers and an equal number of townsmen, the eighteen women in attendance found their dance cards full. Two dozen black slaves served food and drink, and stayed as obscure as possible.

Ned and John stood near the refreshment table, sipping a punch of fruit juice spiked with a fiery home brew made of whatever sweet fruit the locals could crush and distill. John Specter eyed the tough men of Galveston and its surrounding lowland farms and ranches.

"So far, what I've seen of Texas, she's no prize," he mumbled in a low tone to Ned.

"I trust," Ned answered, "there's a bit more of her than we've seen. She stretches from the Red River on the down to the Brazos on the south, and if these Texians have their way, will one day stretch all the way to the Rio Grande."

"'I've not seen the Red, nor the Rio Grande, so I can't judge."

"Nor have I"—Ned smiled and clinked mugs with John—"and I trust, as a naval officer, I never will."

A tall man in a cutaway coat—but one that had seen some wear—contrasting with his frilly new stock and cuffs, mounted the podium where the band played, and silenced them.

"Ladies and gentlemen, for the sake of those whom I have not yet had the pleasure of meeting, my name is Dr. Anson Jones, and I'm the president of this fine Republic of Texas."

The crowd politely applauded.

"I'm pleased to announce . . . step up here, Commodore," he directed Stockton to join him. "I am pleased to announce that I'll soon be out of a job. Commodore Stockton here will carry back with him, to Washington D.C., the news that we are accepting the invitation of the United States of America to join that Union."

The applause and shouts of the crowd drowned out his voice for a long while. Finally he got the crowd to quiet again. "Commodore Stockton will carry with him a copy of our recently completed state Constitution. God willing, Congress will accept us into the Union in time to circumvent any action by the Mexicans, whom we are sure will take this news as a personal insult. But I think I express the feeling of all Texians when I say . . . damn the Mexicans!" The crowd roared their approval.

Ned glanced around him, a bit surprised to see a number of dark-skinned men, obviously of Mexican ancestry, also applauding and cheering with the best of them.

"Pardon me, ladies, but strong times call for strong language," Dr. Jones said to the women near the podium, then looked back at the crowd. "I'll not belabor this and will let you return to the festivities, but I would like Commodore Stockton, as President Polk's emissary, to say a few words first."

Stockton, tall and handsome in full commodore's regalia of blue uniform and gold braid, with a shock of wavy brown hair, stepped forward.

"Welcome, Texas, to the Union, and God willing, Congress will move swiftly. But rest assured, my squadron will, brook no interference by the Mexicans so long as we're in Texas waters." The crowd roared and stomped their feet. "And as soon as Congress does confirm Texas as a state, if necessary we'll deliver a force of Marines to the heart of Mexico City, should they insult our sisters and brothers of the proud State of Texas."

Both Stockton and Dr. Jones stepped down from the podium to the thunderous approval of the crowd. The band began again, and the hundred and eighty men without dancing partners resumed their drinking.

Ned and John kept an ear cocked to a nearby conversation. A buckskin-clad frontiersman with a salt-and-pepper beard fanned across the middle of his chest stood regaling the half-dozen men who circled him.

"By God, the Alamo will be a cakewalk when Santa Ana hears of this."

Another man, obviously a supporter of the action, hoisted his mug. "Let him come. With the full support of the British, the French, and the U. S. of A., we'll knock his frilly uniformed cloak in the mud and put his tail between his legs worse than Houston did . . . and this time we'll hang the peacock."

The first man shook his head. "I hope so, because he'll come, and he'll come feathered out in full regalia and folderol like the cock of the walk. Keep yer powder dry, boys, keep an edge on those blades, and be ready to get yer hackles up." Reaching over with a knife the size of a small sword, he forked a roll off a platter on the table, then took a gnaw out of it.

Ned watched and listened, then turned his attention across the room to Commodore Stockton, who stood talking with a group of well-dressed Texians in cut-away coats whose ladies wore the latest in Paris gowns. He moved across the room where he could listen in to the conversation of the man he'd already come to admire more than any other since his father.

"Polk will stand for no mischief from Santa Ana," Stockton reassured the men. "The real question is whether or not the British will support any action against the Mexicans by the United States. The feeling in Washington is that the Brits want the territory the Mexicans call Alta California—enough they just might fight for it—and it's for sure they covet Oregon and will brook no interference from the Americans there."

Dr. Jones listened intently, then offered, "Personally, I hope Santa Ana does make a move. We'll drive him back to the Rio Grande and claim the river as our border, where it naturally should be."

"That would suit me also, Mr. President. However"— Stockton had the gleam of the hunter in his eye—"would suggest to President Polk that we take all of Mexico, or certainly New Mexico and California in the bargain. Damn the British, they already have enough of the world. Manifest Destiny, Mr. Jones. America, from the Atlantic to the Pacific, and a strong Navy on both seas to defend her. And someday you'll see a road, an all-weather wagon road, connecting the Atlantic and the Pacific all the way across the western wilderness." Stockton raised his glass and the rest of the men did also. "To Manifest Destiny.''

Ned listened to Stockton, and again was proud he served under the man. A road! A road all the way from the Atlantic to the Pacific. It was a grand thought. One fitting a man of destiny. A road across the wilderness. Ned wondered if it would come in his lifetime, and if it did, would it lead to a British Pacific state?

"I would settle," Dr. Jones said after they drank, "and, if I may speak for our constitutional convention, we will settle for the Rio Grande."

John Specter nudged Ned quietly. "We'll both make lieutenant a hell of a lot faster on the deck of a wartime ship. I, for one, hope to hell this Santa Ana does make a sashay into Texas."

"Sounds to me like there's no doubt about it. He'll be coming." Ned raised his mug to John, "To making lieutenant in record time, Mr. Specter." They drank. "And to living through it," Ned added quietly, and got a smirk from John for his trouble.

The fleet, with Stockton carrying the Texas Constitution, set sail for Washington, D.C.

Already convinced that Congress would resolve the issue of slave or free regarding Texas and its acceptance into the Union, the only real stumbling block to its annexation, President Polk had ordered "Old Rough and Ready," General Zachary Taylor, and four thousand dragoons to march to Texas.

CHAPTER SIX

While Ned was home on leave in Bloomingdale, after his return from Texas, he was called to the front parlor by his mother's houseman, Sampson, where a naval officer and his midshipman-orderly awaited him. He was surprised to see Norvell Johanson, already a lieutenant, standing with his hands folded behind him, staring out the window. Ned, though dressed in farm clothes, snapped to attention when Johanson turned to face him.

"No need for that, Beale," Johanson said, a tight smile on his face. 'Since you're out of uniform. I'll be happy to accept your salute when you're properly attired in your middy's dregs. I've only brought your orders over. Thought I'd take the opportunity to visit an old shipmate."

Ned ignored the "middy's" remark, momentarily disarmed by Johanson's almost playful attitude.

"Why, thank you. I see you've already made lieutenant. Congratulations."

"As we talked about many times, Beale, the cream always rises."

"Yes," Ned reluctantly agreed, then remembered his manners. "Would you care for coffee or tea?"

Ned's mother, who had hurried to her room to freshen up, entered behind the two visitors.

"Of course they would, Ned. Good morning," she said. "I'm Emily Beale."

Johanson turned to the attractive but graying middle-aged woman and nodded politely. "Thank you for your offer, Mrs.

Beale, but I'll only be a minute more." The orderly, not having been introduced, remained silent. Emily Beale, a longtime Navy wife who knew protocol better than any of the young men in the room, did not press the issue. Johanson's abrupt manner disturbed her, and instinctively she excused herself and left the room.

"I noticed in your file that you've been serving under Commodore Stockton," Norvell said, regaining the tight smile.

"I was on board the *Porpoise*. As you know, she's part of his squadron." Ned felt sure Johanson was here for some reason other than using Ned's orders as an excuse for a social call.

"And you enjoyed serving under him, I presume, since you asked for duty aboard his flagship, the *Congress*."

"Stockton's a fine officer," Ned said quietly, concealing his true enthusiasm for the man.

"True. Of course, there are many fine officers."

"True." Ned eyed the folded documents Johanson carried, slightly wadded, in his left hand.

"It's good you think so, Beale." Johanson thrust the orders forward, his eyes glinting in triumph. "You're to report to New York in two weeks, then on to the Great Lakes, where you'll be assigned to a coastal cutter patrolling those waters."

Ned's mouth went dry. A war about to start with Mexico, and he'd been assigned as far from that duty as possible. He wanted an opportunity to see action.

"I'll be leaving now, Beale," Johanson said as he walked toward the front door. His orderly trailed him, still silent.

Ned unfolded the orders and stared at them. "What's your duty at the department?" Ned asked without looking up.

"Duty rosters, Beale, duty rosters. It's a gratifying job. I assign middies, such as yourself, and junior officers, to their respective duties. It's a real opportunity to help my deserving friends." Johanson's eyes absolutely shined in triumph.

"Then I can thank you for this assignment?"

"I try to take care of old friends, Beale. But, of course, I don't have the final say. All I do is prepare the rosters. The commodore has to approve and sign them."

Ned walked past Johanson and his orderly and opened the front door. With absolute control, he smiled pleasantly. "It's been good to see you, Norvell, and, again, I'm happy to see that you've made lieutenant so quickly. You certainly must have wonderful connections." Ned could not help inferring that his promotion could not have been from merit.

"Thank you, Beale," Johanson said with a gloating smirk. "You should follow along soon, with such a wonderful opportunity as the Great Lakes." Norvell nodded, and without extending his hand, walked out into the morning sunlight and headed for his waiting gig. "Enjoy the freshwater sailing," Norvell called, then guffawed loudly without looking back as he climbed into the gig.

"I will, old man. And you enjoy shuffling papers."

Norvell cut him a hard look, but the orderly whipped up the dappled roan and the gig lurched away.

"Bad news?" Emily Beale asked Ned, who stood glaring out the door after Johanson.

"The worst. There's a war about to start, and the only man I can honestly say I've made an enemy of is in charge of cutting my orders. I've been shipped to the boondocks."

"Not a bad place to be, son," Emily said, a glint of hope in her voice, "when the possibility of a war is at hand."

Ned turned to his mother and gave as hard a look as he could muster to the woman who had always supported him. "If I want to end my career as a midshipman, it's fine. You need to help me, Mother. I've got to get my requested assignment aboard the *Congress*."

When her husband had been alive, Emily and George Beale were vitally active in Washington politics, and since his death, Emily had seen fit to continue those contacts.

96

Unlike most widows, she called on senators and *Con-gress*men and offered her assistance in campaigns and causes. And now it was time for that assistance to be repaid.

"Let me get dressed," she said, a defeated but proud smile on her face. Then her look hardened like a she-wolf defending her young. "I've assisted in more than one campaign while you've been seeing the world." Her mood lightened as she warmed to the challenge.   "I guess it's time to see if it did any good, other than keep a crazy old woman busy."

"You're not old, Mother, and certainly not crazy. I'll get into uniform and have Sampson harness up and bring the carriage around."

Before noon, Ned and Emily Beale were socializing with senators and *Congress*men at the Willard Hotel, where they were invited to a luncheon. Before the day was out, Emily Beale had a letter of introduction in hand, and she and Ned sat waiting to squeeze in between appointments to see Secretary of the Navy George Bancroft.

Two days later, Johanson's orderly—with Johanson's absence glaringly apparent—delivered Ned's revised orders. Again, he was to report to New York City, but this time to the *Congress*, being outfitted at Gosport Navy Yard. He had beaten Johanson this time, but he wondered how much trouble he might have with the man in the future. An officer of the line with an enemy in Washington might never know where his promotion barriers, or worse problems, lay.

But he had the duty he most wanted and would serve under a man with vision. A man who believed there would one day be a real road across the wilderness, and a reason to have one.

The *Congress*, like the *Independence*, was a full-rigged frigate. One hundred seventy nine feet in length and forty nine in beam, she carried forty two long thirty-two-pounders and eight shell guns on a single-gun deck. Only four hundred eighty men manned her. She was to serve as the flagship of the Pacific Fleet, with Stockton as the fleet's commodore, and Samuel F. DuPont as her captain. Ned was pleased to find Lieutenant Sean Conners aboard, and even more pleased to meet up on the gun deck with Bosun Rosco Handley and Gun Captain Sam McElervy. Ned was not particularly pleased to be aboard with Lieutenant Ezekial Mathiason, who had never warmed to Ned since the incident tracking the slaver.

Shortly after his arrival on board, Ned found himself called to Captain DuPont's cabin. He knocked quietly.

"Enter."

"Passed Midshipman Ned Beale, sir." Ned stood at stiff attention.

DuPont spoke without looking up from his journal. "Beale is a name I'm not unfamiliar with. You're related to George Beale?"

"My father, sir," Ned said proudly.

DuPont raised his eyes.

"I see the resemblance. Since you haven't had time to settle in yet, I'm sending you to Philadelphia. The Navy's received a shipment of hemp line at the yard there, and I've requisitioned several thousand feet. You do recognize sound line when you see it, Beale?"

"Yes, sir."

"Then report to stores purser for the requisition, a travel voucher, a freight voucher to get it back here, and some traveling money. Then be off with you. It's imperative that the line . . . sound line . . . be aboard in a fortnight, as Commodore Stockton is returning from Washington and we'll be sailing."

"Yes, sir." Ned snapped another salute, then spun on his heel to leave.

"Sound line, Beale," DuPont called after him. "The safety of this ship depends on it."

When Ned arrived in Philadelphia after a trying three-day coach ride, he went straight to the Navy Yard. He was glad he did know sound hemp line when he saw it, for the line in the Navy yard was anything but. He puzzled over the problem while the stores officer at the Philadelphia yard tried to convince him that the line was the best available—even though he could not guarantee its arrival in New York for two weeks.

That night, at his bunk in the Navy yard, Ned studied the hemp line requisition order. It made no reference to the Navy yard as the source.

The next morning, he roamed the docks until he found a chandlery with several thousand feet of what he considered sound hemp line. He negotiated with the proprietor, and received the man's assurance that he would place it on his own coastal schooner and sail as soon as it was loaded. Ned could accompany it back to New York. Using the requisition form, Ned boldly filled in the amount and signed it "Edward Fitzgerald Beale, requisition officer, the *Congress*."

"You are authorized to sign this?" the chandler quizzed him.

"Would I do so if I were not?" Ned replied with authority. The chandler studied him for a moment, and Ned returned the look with a glare.

That afternoon, Ned, who knew that Captain DuPont resided in Philadelphia, called on his captain's home and informed Mrs. DuPont that he was returning to the *Congress* and inquired if he could carry anything back to her husband.

"My, what a thoughtful young man." Mrs. DuPont gave him a pat on the cheek. While they dined, she had her servants prepare a crate full of packages for her husband. The next morning, Ned, sitting atop Captain DuPont's crate amid bales of hemp rope, rode out of Philadelphia Harbor aboard the schooner *Barbara Ann*.

Two days before the *Congress* was due to sail, bales of hemp line swung up and over the rail and into her deep hold. Ned reported to the purser with a copy of the requisition.

"I thought this line was coming from the Navy yard." The old prune-faced purser's mate furrowed his brows as he studied the form.

"The line was inferior," Ned said simply.

"Whose scrawl is this?"

"Mine."

"You bought twelve thousand feet of hemp line from some private vendor over your own signature?" "Captain DuPont ordered me to return here with sound line before we sailed. The Navy didn't have sound line."

The man furrowed his brows even deeper and studied Ned again. "You better start thinking about your second career choice, young fella," the purser grumbled. "I gotta report this to the captain."

"Give him my regards," Ned said. Turning, he headed for his cabin.

"I imagine you'll have the opportunity to do that yersef, soon enough," the man said behind him.

Ned got a sinking feeling in his stomach for a second. Then, knowing he had done the right thing for the ship, he threw back his shoulders and strode away.

He hadn't been in his cabin, shared with three other passed midshipmen, for more than enough time to introduce himself to the two men who lounged in their bunks, when a sound rap brought him back to the door.

A young midshipman stood there.

"Captain wants to see Midshipman Beale, on the double."

Ned took a deep breath, excused himself, and followed the young man topside, then aft to the captain's cabin, located under the poop deck.

The young middy rapped on the door, then stood aside and didn't follow Ned in.

Captain DuPont, Commodore Stockton, Lieutenant Sean Conners, and the sail master stood around DuPont's chart table. When DuPont looked up, Ned felt a sharp shudder in his backbone from the captain's glare, but did not show it as he stood at attention.

"At ease, Beale." Left standing, Ned folded his hands behind his back. DuPont finished the point he was making to the other men, then turned and strode over to face Ned.

"You got back on time," DuPont said, his face expressionless.

"Yes, sir."

"And with as fine a load of hemp line as I've had the pleasure to see aboard."

"Yes, sir. I hope so."

"Beale, who the hell gave you permission to acquire that line from a private chandler?" The captain folded his hands behind his back and seemed very interested in Ned's response.

"You, sir."

DuPont looked puzzled. "I did? I sent you to the Navy yard in Philadelphia."

"You sent me with orders to be back on board with sound line within a fortnight, sir."

"That's true."

"The Navy line wasn't sound, sir. And the stores officer informed me that it would be two weeks before the Navy could deliver, sir. The *Congress*, if your instructions were clear, would be somewhere off the coast of the Carolinas by then, sir."

Stockton turned from his chart, bemused by the conversation behind him, and stepped up beside DuPont. Ned snapped back to attention.

"Is this the young man who used a Navy requisition to buy line from a private vendor?" Stockton asked harshly. Ned cringed involuntarily.

"Yes, Commodore," DuPont said with a doubtful shake of his head.

"Damn Navy stores people ought to learn to buy the best. I sometimes wonder if there's not a little money passing under the table in our yards. Well done, young man." Stockton laid a hand on Ned's shoulder. "However, I wouldn't like to be that merchant, trying to collect from the Navy." He smiled. "But I'll send a dispatch authorizing the purchase."

"Thank you, sir," Ned said, remaining at attention with his eyes forward.

"Excused, Beale," DuPont said, with only the slightest indication of a smile on his face.

Ned about-faced and headed for the door.

"Beale," Stockton stopped him in mid-stride. Ned spun again and tucked his chin in. "At ease, man. How's your penmanship?"

"Fine, sir."

"Are you fast with the pen?"

"Fast as the next man, sir."

"With your permission, Captain DuPont, may I suggest that Mr. Beale is hereby made ship's master, and will, in addition, serve as my personal secretary."

"Of course," DuPont said, moving back to the chart table as if nothing spectacular had happened. Ned's chest expanded until his buttons strained.

"Thank you, sir," Ned snapped.

"You're excused, Mr. Beale," Stockton said. "Be in my cabin at oh eight hundred, prepared to take some dictation for dispatches, including the one that will keep you from being railroaded out of the Navy." He chuckled as Ned saluted, then pulled the door closed. When DuPont quickly called out to him, Ned stuck his head back in the doorway.

"Thank you for calling on Mrs. DuPont, Mr. Beale," the captain said with a smile. "And for fetching my trunk. That was thoughtful of you."

"My pleasure, sir." Ned saluted again.

Ned stood on the quarterdeck, and to the surprise of a group of sailors heading for the mizzenmast, jumped up and clicked his heels. He let out a yell that snapped all heads on the aft end of the ship around, then collected himself, straightened his blue jacket, and with the utmost dignity, strolled to the midship ladder and descended to his cabin.

Ship's master was responsible not only for keeping the official ship's log; but also for the shipping and stowage of her stores; the inspection of her rigging, spars, and sails; and for supervision of her anchoring. It was a position of trust, and one that should assure him a quick shot at lieutenant's epaulets. He considered himself on his way.

The next day, without informing the crew of their destination, the *Congress* set sail. A half-day at sea, and Captain DuPont called all hands. He informed them that the *Congress* was on her way around the Horn, to become the flagship of the Pacific Fleet.

DuPont also informed them that President Polk had taken a hard stand against the British and that he stood fast on his claim for all of Oregon. Britain would not take the president's action lightly. The captain cautioned that General Zachary Taylor and his dragoons were in Texas and that the War Department fully expected to be at war with Mexico soon, an action that would effectively shut the Pacific Fleet off from the command centers in Washington, D.C. The Pacific Fleet would soon be on its own.

But it was information Ned already had, for as the commodore's secretary, he was privy to all but the most secret of Navy dispatches. He worked at the absolute nerve center of the squadron.

As the *Congress* plowed her way south to the West Indies, Ned settled into his new duties. His position as ship's master was still not that of an officer, the lieutenant he hoped to become soon, but it was one of respect and substantial responsibility. He had just become familiar with his myriad jobs when the *Congress* put into Barbados for water and fresh stores, the last stop before the long run to Rio.

To the surprise of Stockton and Captain DuPont, while in port they learned that the British fleet had sailed from Bridgetown less than a week before, also bound for California. It was news critical to the government, news that seemed to confirm the fact that the British were not going to stand for Polk's decision to make the line between the United States and Canada the fifty fourth parallel. News that must be relayed to the secretary of war and the president.

The *Congress* sailed from Barbados with full casks of water and stores of fresh fruit and meat, on to California, but with the insecurity of leaving behind a U. S. government that had no way of knowing the Brits were moving to California in force. Stockton could not turn back, but he had to find a way to inform the Navy Department and the president.

Ten days out of Barbados, Stockton found the solution to his problem.

The Danish ship *Mariah*, bound for Antwerp, appeared on the horizon. When close enough, the ship signaled a request for the *Congress* to hove to. Stockton and DuPont took a longboat to share a table with her captain, who reported to Stockton's inquiries that he had not seen any sign of the British fleet moving south, that they had lost their navigator to a fever, and, he was embarrassed to say, that they were themselves lost.

Stockton immediately offered to provide them with a skilled navigator to get them back on course if they would agree to drop him in England.

Ned Beale found himself and his meager belongings in a longboat headed for the *Mariah* within the hour. Strict and secret unwritten instructions from his commodore burned in his mind: Find out the British intent in California and Oregon, but above all, report the British Fleet's movements to President Polk and Navy Secretary Bancroft with all possible haste.

From his promotion to ship's master, to what he considered exciting duty as a spy—on his own, off the ship, and away from his comrades—all within a few weeks.

With trepidation, Ned climbed the rope ladder to the deck of the *Mariah*, and among the strange guttural chattering of blond-haired, pale Danes, set sail for England.

CHAPTER SEVEN

The *Mariah*, a brig of just over one hundred feet, wallowed along loaded to the gunnels with hogsheads filled with cones of fine Brazilian sugar, bales of sisal for the rope factories, and bundles of jungle woods, hard as the hubs of hell and heavy as a whores heart, for the makers of furniture in Denmark. Ned, only twenty-two years old, was greeted by the skeptical scowls of the captain and first mate, but within the hour had taken two sightings and given the captain a new position, confirming the one the ship, unbeknownst to Ned, had been given by Stockton. Captain Anselm Bronck's face split in a broad grin, and he sailed on with confidence.

With the ship's cabins already full of her officers, Ned was relegated to the forecastle and an existence equal to that of the most lowly crewmember for the duration of the voyage, during which time they sighted no other ships until they entered the Irish Sea. They headed for the northwestern English shipping port of Liverpool.

Ned happily departed the *Mariah* onto a dock, among many, on the northern shore of the mouth of the Mersey River, twenty eight days after he'd boarded the ship, on the first day of a particularly cold and foggy December. He headed straight for the harbormaster's office, but to his disappointment found no vessel booking passengers was scheduled to leave Liverpool for the United States until late in the winter. Neither December nor January were months of preference for sailing the North Atlantic. And the next ship that would book passengers was bound for Boston, and sailing out of London, not Liverpool.

Ned decided to try to fulfill the second objective of his trip—find out what he could regarding the British intent in Alta California. He inquired innocently where he might get a mug of grog among other men of the sea—military men, he stressed—and got directions to a nearby pub.

He neared a waterfront inn and paused long enough to rent a room, a private room, to the inn keeper's joy, as most of the small rooms were shared by four or more. He stowed his duffel, having left most of his gear, including his uniforms packed in his trunk, aboard the *Congress*, since Stockton's plan was for him to meet up with the ship in Callao, Peru.

The Grampus Tit was not a place for a cautious or prudent man. Ned pushed open the door and took a last deep breath of cold evening air before he braved the heavy smoke and acrid, sweaty odor of the dark pub. Men in oilskins and boots to their thick thighs lined the bar in the low-ceilinged room and sprawled among tightly packed tables. As Ned's eyes adjusted, he made out, by the light of smoking whale oil lamps, a few British Navy uniforms among the commercial sailors and stevedores. Shouldering away from the door until he found a one-foot space at the bar, Ned slapped a silver dollar down with feigned authority and bravado.

A barman with a soiled shirt barely covering his protruding belly glared at him with pig eyes under hooded brows. "Aye, mate," he managed with a stub of an unlit cigar clamped in his yellowed teeth.

"A mug of ale," Ned ordered. The man started to move away, then noticed the American coin. He picked it up, tested its weight with the studied look of a London banker, then moved away and pumped a dark, foaming ale from a small keg.

"Yer a Yank?" the barkeep asked, sitting the mug on the bar.

"A sailor is a sailor, a citizen of the world after he's been at sea," Ned said, purposely playing down any connection with a country this one might soon be at war with. "I'm off the Danish brig, *Mariah*, just in from Rio, and lookin' for a berth on any ship bound anywhere." Ned raised the mug, toasted the barkeep with a motion, and drank the warm, thick beer half down before returning the mug to the well-worn bar, where the barkeep had spread his change.

"Well, mate, the Grampus Tit's the place to pick up the 'arbor scuttlebutt. Ye'll 'ave a beggar's spot aboard some rat-ridden scow in a few 'ours if ye spend your Yank silver 'ere. Of course"—his voice lowered—"ta' level with ya', the money 'tis sparse, since the bloody stinkin' Irish'll work for 'eads and trotters an' are tak'n most the jobs."

Ned just nodded; then, turning to face the room, he purposely nudged the uniformed man next to him a little harder than necessary. The man almost slopped his drink, and flashed him a hard look.

"Pardon," Ned said. "It's crowded in here."

"Aye," the sailor agreed with a growl, returning to his conversation with another sailor.

"You off a frigate?" Ned pressed, and the sailor eyed him a little suspiciously. His scowl turned to a grin when Ned added, "Can I buy you gents a mug?"

Waving the barkeep over, Ned motioned for him to fill the sailors' mugs.

The larger of the two, whom Ned had bumped, extended his callused hand. "I'm Connie Carey, recently of the *H.M.S. Bon Homme Smithson*. And what be yer name?''

"Beale, Ned Beale, just off the good Danish brig *Mariah*." Ned shook and was introduced to the other man, Pat Fitzhenry.

"You say recently?" Ned pressed Connie.

"Aye, she's sailed and I've had enough of the king's Navy. I'm mustered out an' headed back to Kilkenny and me folks . . . by and by, as soon as I've downed enough of this English sludge to get me there."

"And the *Smithson* will fare well enough without you?" Ned said with a good humored smile.

"The bloody English Navy wouldn't be fit to sail the pond at Buckingham Palace without the help of the Irish, lad. And don't ye be forgettin' it." Connie Carey gave Ned a wink and a slap on the back that would have felled a smaller man, then turned back to the bar.

"Are there many Irish sailing men?" Ned asked, wanting these men to get used to his inquisitive manner.

"Only the finest of all the world's sailing men, lad," Fitzhenry offered with the same confident tone Connie had used. "Though," he added with a confidential air, "they be obliged to sail her bloody majesty's ships when they would better be spreadin' Irish canvas."

"Tell me about sailing aboard a frigate?" Ned said, wanting to avoid the age-old Irish/English animosity. He waved the barkeep over, motioning him to refill their mugs.

Ned became the barkeep's best customer for the better part of the next two weeks, and made at least a half hundred friends among the regulars. Each night he moved among the uniformed men with particular ease, buying round after round of drinks. Each day Ned prowled the docks and shipyards, inquiring as to what ships were under construction or repair, and particularly about those that carried the preface H.M.S.— Her Majesty's Ship.

At the end of two weeks, Ned boarded the latest in English transportation, the steam train, and four days later found himself frequenting the pubs of London on the southeastern shore of England. Already England had six thousand miles of track. The country was teeming with activity and seemed to be thriving under the reign of Victoria.

This time he found himself near Parliament, and generously began to buy mugs, but now for pages and messengers, cleaning men and hack drivers—any who worked in or around Parliament or for the members of the House of Commons or of Lords. It was amazing, he decided, how much one could glean from disgruntled employees, particularly those whose tongues were loosened with ale. They bellyached about their employers, and in the process gave up all they knew about their business.

Ned spent a lonely Christmas "savoring" a greasy roast duck and chips in a drafty corner of a small pub. He was asleep in his tiny room over the pub dreaming about Bloomingdale before Big Ben struck ten.

By the time he was ready to board the first ship he could find for America, he had collected a wealth of information in addition to the one gift he carried. A milkglass container of aged brandy, finely blown and formed in the image of the beautiful young Queen Victoria and carefully painted by true craftsmen, was tucked under Ned's arm. His mother, though she would deny it to her gentle friends, enjoyed a dollop before retiring and would enjoy the glass container long after she had finished its contents.   The *Hound* was a full-rigged ship, and pushed by the February winds of the North Atlantic made Boston in eighteen days. In the privacy of his cabin, Ned put pen to paper, and all details of his two and a half months in England were painstakingly reduced to writing. He boarded the first coach south from Boston, and three days later, soiled and rumpled from his arduous trip, called directly at the White House—not even stopping at Bloomingdale to be fitted in a new uniform or to clean up.

The Marine who greeted Ned in the late afternoon at the White House door glared at him and his rough, common sailor's clothes with skepticism when Ned informed him that he had been sent to deliver a dispatch to the president from Commodore Robert F. Stockton.

"Wait here, Mr. Beale," the Marine commanded, leaving Ned, hat in hand, standing on the White House steps. The guard's counterpart on the other side of the door stared at Ned unblinkingly until Ned retreated a few steps to the walkway in front of the stoop and laid his duffel aside. Ned pulled his greatcoat closer around his neck and tucked in his scarf to keep the chill out and waited.

The first Marine returned to his position bracketing the door. "Wait," he snapped, returning to his stiff stance.

It was the better part of half an hour, with the wind beginning to howl through the barren trees on the White House lawn, before the door opened. A man in a well-tailored brown frock coat, and a gleaming white shirt with stiff cuffs and collar stood just inside the door, out of the wind, and motioned Ned up on the porch.

"Mr. Beetle," the man inquired as Ned stopped at the threshold, where the man blocked his entrance.

"Beale, sir," Ned enunciated clearly, a little irritated at the error, and more so at being left in the cold after so long a journey. "Passed Midshipman Edward Fitzgerald Beale, recently from the *Congress*, and even more recently from Liverpool and London. My orders are to report directly to President Polk and Secretary Bancroft."

"Humph," the man managed. "Whose orders?"

"From Commodore Robert F. Stockton."

"May I see them?" The man extended his white gloved hand.

"And who might you be, sir?" Ned asked, beginning to take umbrage at the man's manner and growing more irritated at being kept standing in the cold.

"I'm the president's personal secretary." The lean-faced man would have glared down his long nose had Ned not been taller. As it was, he raised watery eyes to Ned. "Your orders?"

"My orders are verbal. My mission was such that it would have been unwise to carry penned orders."

"Humph."

"Are you having trouble with your throat, sir?" Ned asked. "Perhaps if we both went in out of this cold wind, your condition would improve."

"Lieutenant"—the President's secretary turned to one of the guards—"step inside and wait with this impertinent young man while I find someone to speak with him."

"The president, sir," Ned repeated as the Marine lieutenant pulled the tall door shut behind them.

"I doubt that, young man." This time the secretary did manage to look down his nose.

"Either the president, or the secretary of the Navy, sir. No . . . one . . . else," he said emphatically.

"Wait here," he barked, then disappeared out of the foyer.

Ned removed his greatcoat and his scarf, then his hat. He eyed the room uncomfortably, searching for a place to lay them down or a coat tree to hang them on. He found no tree, and dared not place them, wet and soiled as they were, on the fine furniture lining the walls. Instead, he draped them over his forearm and moved along the papered walls, studying the paintings that hung there. Hard eyes of unsmiling men and women studied him in return, locked as they were inside gilded frames.

Finally, after he began his third round of the room—to the displeasure of the glowering Marine lieutenant—the secretary returned.

"You're to report to the Naval attaché's office and ask for Captain Harold B. Timmings. He will talk with you regarding your 'orders,'" the secretary said, giving Ned a superior glance before he spun on his heel and started away.

"I will be happy to do as requested," Ned called after him. "However, I am under direct orders to report to no one other than the president or the secretary of the Navy." Ned's voice crept louder as the secretary got farther and farther away. "Neither Captain Timmons nor any of the commodores in

Washington will get this report. Only President Polk or Secretary of the Navy Bancroft."

The officious secretary stopped in his tracks but did not turn for a moment; he seemed to be considering Ned's words and weighing the effrontery of the brash young man.

"Wait here," he said wearily, still without turning, then continued on his way. After a few moments, he returned.

"The President is expecting Secretary Bancroft among his dinner guests. He can give you five minutes at seven p.m. Be here, young man."

"Yes, sir," Ned said with a snap in his voice. The presidents personal secretary sighed in resignation as Ned, followed closely by the Marine lieutenant. headed for the door.

It was as dark as the *Congress*'s bilge by the time Ned gathered his duffel and made his way back to Pennsylvania Avenue to find a hack to carry him to Bloomingdale. He would have time to visit with his mother for an hour before his return.

To Ned's surprise, he found the private lane to the two-story white farmhouse at Bloomingdale lined with carriages. The house stood brightly lit, and he made out a group of drivers gathered around a bonfire, warming their hands and backsides, in the carriage house as the hack driver dropped him off. He could hear the strains of a string quartet and the occasional sound of laughter wafting from the tightly closed house.

Unshaven for two days, soiled and rumpled from his trip, and out of uniform, he had no desire to attend a party.

Carefully, he made his way around to the back of the house, entered the kitchen, and received the greetings of the servants and a rough embrace from old round-faced Sampson, the black houseman who had taken Ned and his brother hunting and fishing many times while they grew up. Ned entreated them to heat him some water but keep silent about his being home until he could change and clean up. Then he made his way up the servants' back stairs.

Dressed in clean if somewhat out-of-style clothes from his father's closet, shaved, washed. and combed. Ned made an appearance in his mother's drawing room, where he found over three dozen guests.

"Ned!" his mother said in wide-eyed shock. He crossed the room and hugged her. "I thought you'd be halfway to California by now!"

*Congress*man Samuel Edwards. an old family friend from Chester, Pennsylvania, stepped forward and extended his hand. "Young Ned, good to have you back in Washington. Has the *Congress* returned to port?"

Ned worded his answer carefully. "No. sir. I have special dispensation to return. Acting as . . . as a messenger for Commodore Stockton."

"Messenger? Is there something at hand the Congress of the United States should know of?"

"I doubt it, sir. But I'm not privy to Commodore Stockton's communiqués." Ned was not accustomed to lying, even though ordered to do so.

Edwards looked at him questioningly, but dropped the matter for the moment. His son, Harry, whom Ned had spent many pleasant days with as a boy, stepped out of the crowd, extended his hand, and shook warmly.

"Ned, let's get you a cup of your mother's spiked punch while you tell me of your adventures."

Ned kissed his mother on the cheek, whispered, ''We'll talk later,'' then followed Harry to the punch bowl.

He received the greetings of several other guests as he crossed the room, but his eyes were locked on the table. Three young ladies stood head to head whispering excitedly at Ned's approach, but he had eyes for only one of them. He remembered Mary Ingalls Edwards from years before, but at five years younger than he, Ned certainly did not remember her looking as she did now.

Seldom at a loss for words, Ned felt tongue-tied at Harry's introduction.

"Have you resigned from the Navy, Ned?" Mary asked, her eyes passing over his civilian clothes.

"No . . . no, I just had to return from the ship with communiqués."

"A messenger boy?" one of the other girls teased, and she and her other friend giggled, but Mary did not.

"I'm sure that it is a very important job, if the captain assigned it to Ned," Mary said reproachfully to the other girls, but her eyes never left Ned's.

"The commodore assigned it, actually," Ned managed. "Special communiqués to the president from Commodore Stockton. I'm his personal secretary as well as master of the *Congress*." He burned with the need to tell this beautiful young lady more, but could not.

"An assignment from Stockton?" The question came from behind him.

Ned turned to find Samuel Edwards close, his empty punch glass in hand.

"Yes, sir. Dispatches from Commodore Stockton."

"To the president?"

"And Secretary Bancroft," Ned managed, but he could feel his ears burning in embarrassment. He had already said too much.

"And what news is so exciting?" Samuel Edwards pressed.

"No idea, sir." Ned smiled and turned his attention back to the *Congress*man's daughter.

"And if he did know"—Mary's smile almost took Ned to his knees—"he wouldn't say. Would you, Ned?"

"Not if you pulled out my fingernails and held my feet to the fire . . . if I was ordered not to, of course."

"Father," Mary admonished, "don't you dare keep pulling Ned's fingernails."

"Humph," her father grunted, and passed on to the punch bowl.

Ned talked with Mary Edwards until he knew he could just make it back to the White House by seven.

Again, the astute Samuel Edwards noticed Ned as he excused himself from his daughter's company. "Leaving   so soon, Ned?" he asked with an inquisitive smile.

"Yes, sir. Business," Ned said simply.

"I see the gig is waiting at the door. Going into the city, are you?"

"Yes, sir. Military business. It's good to see you again, Congressman Edwards."

"And you, Ned. I hope to see more of you."

"Yes, sir. I hope so, too." He glanced at Mary. "I truly do hope so, sir."

Ned hurried upstairs to retrieve his notes, then headed back down and out the door, but overheard the Congressman speaking to his mother, Emily.

"Bright boy, that Ned. And closed-mouthed. A good trait in a military man."

Ned couldn't help but smile. He was pleased that he had managed to keep silent without offending Mary's father.

Sampson had the gig awaiting him at the front door, and Ned whipped the sorrel into a trot. The mist had become a soft rain, and the road began to cradle puddles. The gig's narrow wheels arched a stream of water behind them. He arrived at the White House, handed his reins to a groom, checked his watch by the light of a whale oil driveway lamp, and seeing he had three minutes to spare, hurried to the tall front door.

This time, dressed as he was, the guard greeted Ned with a smile and an extended white gloved hand. "Your invitation, sir."

"No invitation, Lieutenant. I'm to see the president by special appointment."

"I'll check with his secretary."

Ned again was relegated to waiting on the White House porch, but this time the other Marine guard did not look at him as if he were ready to impale him on his bayonet.

In a moment, the guard returned. "You're to wait in the south drawing room, Mr. Beale."

Once more Ned found himself admiring the gilded framed oil paintings on the walls, but at least this time he had been served a cup of hot tea. He anxiously glanced at his pocket watch as the minute hand swept through the hour of seven, then eight, then nine. If you couldn't wait on the president of the United States, who could you wait on? Ned justified. But he had had hopes of seeing Mary Edwards again before she and her family left Blooming dale. He had already devised his battle plan.

Though she was a small target, he would sail along side and give her a full thirty cannon broadside, no quarter would be given or asked, until she became his. With the vision of her face vivid in his mind's eye, he heard the door swing wide.

The man who entered stood less than medium height, but he had an upright bearing that made him appear larger. He brought deep-set gray eyes to bear on Ned, and swept shoulder-length gray hair back with an ungloved manicured hand as he crossed the room. His black stock, at least three inches wide, circled a stiff high collar and complemented the finely cut black frock coat he wore. Ned snapped to attention and saluted. The president extended his hand and shook Ned's firmly as another man entered the room. "You're Edward Beale." The president smiled tightly, then motioned to the other man. "Do you know Secretary Bancroft?"

"No, sir. I've not had the pleasure."

117

Bancroft, too, extended his hand, shook, and nodded. "I hope this is important, young man."

"Commodore Stockton thought so, sir. He dispatched me to return on the first available vessel to make this report."

"Then get on with it, young man," Bancroft said a little wearily.

"The British Fleet sailed via Barbados in late October, on their way to the Pacific. It's Commodore Stockton's belief that the British are stepping up their strength in that ocean as a direct result of their interest in Alta California, and as a result," Ned turned to the president, "of your position on the Oregon border. sir."

"You say 'fleet,' young man." The president's interest focused on Ned. "What was their exact strength?"

"We could not ascertain that information in Barbados. However"—Ned pulled a sheaf of papers from his inner coat pocket—"I was forced to take a Danish ship to England in order to get transport here, and have gleaned the following information during my stay. You will find a detailed description of each vessel in Commodore Sir George F. Seymour's Pacific Fleet, including backgrounds on most of their officers, with particular emphasis paid to his flagship, the *H.M.S. Collingwood*, an eighty gun frigate, the *Talbot*, and—"

"I'm sure it's all in your report," Bancroft said with a deep sigh.

"Don't interrupt the young man," Polk admonished his secretary of the Navy. Bancroft noticeably reddened. "Join us in the dining room, Edward. I'm interested in where and how you obtained this information and. more so, in the general attitude of John Bull."

With some trepidation, Ned followed the president of the United States and the secretary of the Navy into an intimate after-dinner brandy with the senior members of Congress and the Cabinet.

It was two a.m. before Ned, his head swimming with the import of the people he had met, reined into the lane at Bloomingdale, the rain now hammering down. He unharnessed and grained the sorrel without bothering Samson, then, exhausted, made his way up to the guest room that at one time had been his. But his dreams were not of presidents and military service, or of glory, but of a brown-eyed, diminutive girl.

The next morning, to his great disappointment, his mother informed him that the Edwards were on their way back to Chester, Pennsylvania, that day.

"Do you think Mary would mind if I wrote her, Mother?" Ned asked over a bowl of porridge.

"You've known Mary Edwards for most of your life, Ned. Why shouldn't you write her?" his mother asked innocently, but she smiled knowingly.

"Not like she is now," Ned managed, "not like she is now."

His mother laughed, and refilled his coffee cup.

Ned, at Bancroft's direct orders, spent almost a month in debriefings with several naval officers, all several ranks above him.

Harry Edwards, Mary's brother, had not returned home with his family, and Ned suddenly developed a new interest in his old friend. Most of Ned's spare time was spent with Harry. The two young men met at the Willard Hotel with the intent of having a final night out before Ned's scheduled departure on the steam-driven U.S. mailship *Falcon*.

After a few drinks, Harry sat back in his chair. "Ned, you've got a long and exciting trip ahead. Hopefully, a long and exciting life."

Harry had been subjected to Ned's unending questions regarding his sister and had enjoyed ribbing Ned somewhat. Now he saw another chance. "Not much of a life for a married man. A man should remain unfettered if he's to be the adventuring kind."

Ned eyed his old friend with speculation. "I would think adventure would only whet a man's appetite for becoming settled . . . with the right woman, of course."

"Of course." Harry smiled, then his face lit with boyish excitement. "Let's find out what is in our future."

"You have a crystal ball?"

"No, one better. I know where a phrenologist is plying his trade. Professor Phinias Von Fiffeberg or some such. Let's go." Harry rose, a bit unsteadily after the drinks.

"Hold on, Harry. What in the devil is a phrenologist?"

"A doctor of lumps."

"Pardon me?"

"A doctor educated in the halls of Europe's finest universities, or so said the newspaper article."

"And he foretells your future?"

"By reading the hills and valleys of your cranium."

"You need another drink to clear your cranium. Harry, sit down and let's have another glass of this fine bourbon."

"No!" Harry said enthusiastically. "I've been wanting to do this, and now seems the time. I need to relay this valuable information to my sis—to my family, regarding your illustrious future." Harry dragged him to his feet.

"What if it's not so illustrious?" Ned asked skeptically.

"Then," Harry said, ''I definitely need to relay that. Samuel Edwards would tolerate no son-in-law with a cranium not suited to an illustrious and highly profitable future."

"No one said anything about becoming your brother-in-law," Ned mumbled as Harry led the way out of the Willard and hailed a hack.

The hack bounced across Washington to Georgetown and reined up in front of a brownstone, one with a broad banner— PHRENOLOGY, THE FINITE SCIENCE OF FORETELLING YOUR FUTURE, PROFESSOR PHINIAS

FARNSWORTH—stretched across its width above its windows.

Harry, with a reluctant Ned in tow in the darkness of early evening, made his way to the door.

They pulled the bell string, and in a moment the door swung aside. A short, wizened man in a white Van Dyke beard and gray hair that splayed from the sides of his partially bald head like wings of victory on a mottled goose egg, answered. Stepping aside with a gallant bow, he ushered them in.

He extended his thin hand, as liver-spotted as his brow, and again bowed.

"Professor Phinias Farnsworth at your service, gentlemen."

Harry negotiated a price of two dollars each, down from the horrendous amount of five the good "professor" began with, by assuring him that both he and Ned were undoubtedly destined for short, uneventful lives, and the professor's job would not take long. Farnsworth led them into a drawing room smelling of chemicals, just off the foyer. Jars of various scientifically labeled substances and slimy creatures lined a bookshelf, and a mortar and pestle rested in readiness. Engravings of surgeons performing their art over screaming patients lined the walls, giving Ned a squeamish turn of the stomach.

A high-backed pivoting wing chair, with metal clamps where the subject rested his neck, was the focal point of the room.

"Who's first?" The professor took a position behind the contraption.

"Ned!" Harry proclaimed with a slightly drunken giggle.

"No . . . no, Harry, this was your idea."

Displaying only a little reticence, Harry took the seat. With gentle but firm movements, Farnsworth clamped his head in position.

"That hurt?" Ned asked.

"Silence!" the professor brayed before Harry could answer. "I must have absolute silence for utter concentration."

He began fingering Harry's head and muttering. "Occipital lobe, parietal lobe, occipital, glenoid fossa," then as quickly as he began, he unclasped him and Harry sat up, turning with anticipation.

"A long life, Mr. Edwards." Farnsworth paced, hands folded behind his back, head bent in concentration. "You will have some travail, but generally you will be happily engaged in a worthwhile occupation and be successful."

He paused, and Harry waited in anticipation. Then, when the professor did not continue, he asked with some irritation, "That's it?"

"What more would you like?"

"Who am I going to many? How many children will I have? Will I die rich and respected? What, exactly, will I accomplish?"

"I am not a fortune teller, Mr. Edwards. Phrenology is the science of predominance, not prediction nor predestination. I can only tell you what you should accomplish, not what you will. That is up to you."

"You're a faker." Harry jumped up from the chair.   "I am a trained—"

"Hold on, Harry." Ned stepped between the two, facing his friend. "Hold on. I've paid my money, and I want Dr. Farnsworth to read my noggin . . . and without prejudice, if you don't mind." Ned promptly took a seat.

"You wait outside," Farnsworth said with a snarl at Harry.

"The hell I will," Harry snarled back. Farnsworth glowered at him a moment, then resigned himself to his task. He stepped behind Ned, clamped him in, and began.

"Interesting frontal eminence," he mumbled, then moved his hands to the sides. "The temporals are pronounced . . . that's good." Ned was astounded at the strength of the man's fine hands as he continued naming another dozen pans of the skull.

"Hum!" the doctor said as he finally unclasped Ned, after spending twice as much time as he had on Harry. Ned turned in anticipation.

"Strife, struggle, success, failure, it's all there, young man."

Ned couldn't help but smile. "Is it there for a long time, or am I going to be struck down by a beer wagon when I walk outside?"

"You have no tendency for unreasonable risk, and if that happened I would be surprised. However, you are a man who will accept all reasonable risk. I would guess that you will not die in your bed, and when you do die, you will carry the scars of a great deal of confrontation. Strangely, I see you leading thousands down a path to . . . to their future."

"Thanks . . . I think," Ned managed.

"Let's get the hell out of here," Harry groused and headed for the door.

"Mr. Beale," Farnsworth said, stopping Ned, "do what you are capable of, do not worry about what others do or think. Strive to do your utmost, and you will outshine those around you . . . if you don't catch a stray beer wagon." He smiled, then cut his eyes to Harry, who had the front door open. "Unlike your impetuous friend."

Harry slammed the door behind them hard enough that the oval cut glass pane in its center shook. "He says you'll carry scars . . . . I should have scarred that charlatan," he grumbled as they reached the street.

They had to walk five blocks before they caught a hack back to the Willard. A great path, Ned mused as they walked and Harry fumed in silence. *A road?* Maybe Stockton's road across the wilderness. No, I'm a Navy man, and a Navy man I'll stay. Roads are Army business, engineers' business. Ned put the professor and his prognostications out of his mind.

123

Mary Edwards did not return to Washington until two days after Ned had left to catch the *Falcon* for Panama, where he planned to cross the Isthmus to the Pacific and find a ship to carry him south to Callao. Mary and Ned each wrote the other a letter during Ned's short stay in Washington, and both carried the promise of continued writing.

Though happy with his newfound interest in Mary Edwards, Ned left Washington saddened. His old friend and icon Andrew Jackson had died at seventy eight at his home in Nashville while Ned was at Bloomingdale. The old man's last words were that he wished to meet all his friends, both black and white, in heaven.

Even though he had always harbored great trepidation regarding Jackson's treatment of the Cherokee's, and other Indian tribes, the old man's last words were a desire, and a quality of thinking, and character, Ned admired.

CHAPTER EIGHT

Ned traveled by coach from Washington to Charleston, where a launch carried him and the mail out to meet the *Falcon*. A stop at Savannah, then not another in the United States, as she stayed well offshore of Florida. They rounded the lighthouse of St. Augustine and ran for Havana.

From the placid beauty of Cuba, the Falcon returned across deep blue seas until they suddenly showed an almost iridescent, then muddy-green where the influx of the Mississippi clouded the gulf. Finally they entered the wide river herself, where roils of brown water like dirty soapsuds continually pushed against their progress and where the odor of fetid swamps wafted from the low shores a half mile on either side.

Ned had no desire to spend time in New Orleans, he had visited the fabled city once when fighting the slave trade. Instead, he was anxious to get back to the *Congress* and deliver his important dispatches, hopeful that he would get his job as ship's master back. But the Falcon was scheduled to take on fuel and firewood, and an adequate load was not on the wharf yet. It would be two days before they would sail, the captain informed Ned and the three other passengers aboard. Ned went ashore and checked into a hotel. At least he would get the opportunity to gain his ground legs again after so many days at sea. From the hotel, he mailed three letters he had written to Mary while aboard the *Falcon*.

He dined that night in the hotel, feeling no need to take advantage of the city's reputed "French" night life, and rose early the next morning, eager to see if the city had changed and determined to see it all and make the time pass as quickly as possible. The trees of the city, particularly the cypress and oak, hung with gray moss, and the windows were lined with lacy wrought iron. Ladies in fine gowns of the latest French fashion reaffirmed the city's close affinity to Europe.

Ned decided to walk rather than take a hack on his sight-seeing, and was enjoying himself immensely, taking a mid-morning coffee in an open-air cafe near one of the city's many parks. But as soon as he left the cafe and approached the older commercial section, full of livestock and ware-houses, his mood soured.

A long line of slaves, shackled neck to neck and ankle to ankle, eyes down, passed him, many of them bearing fresh crisscrossed lashes of the whip. Two overseers walked front and back of the dozen bronze-skinned, muscular blacks, and another sat astride a tall, coal-black stallion. He carried a club and a coiled blacksnake whip—and Ned knew it was not to clear the road of the flocks and herds of livestock that occa-sionally blocked their progress. His morbid curiosity over-came a worry that he might lose his temper with the three scruffy-looking men herding the blacks, and Ned fell in be-side the overseer bringing up the rear of the cavalcade.

Unlike his mounted friend, this one carried not only a stubby club but also had a pair of pistols stuffed in his belt.

"This a chain gang from the prison?" Ned asked the man, who gave him a disinterested glance. The guard spat a long stream of tobacco juice into the cobblestone street and back-handed its remnants from his lips before he answered.

"Nope, just a bunch of runaways going to market. They won't fetch much, being as how they're no account."

"How'd you come by them?"

"You from up north?" The man glared at Ned.

"Heading for the Pacific via Panama." Ned feigned a smile at the man.

"Never been there," he said, and splattered the cobble-stones with a brown stream. A herd of swine driven by pair of black youths blocked the path of the line of men, and they hesitated, some of them stumbling into those in front. The overseer in the lead berated the swineherds as they hurried the stock along, popping them with long willow switches

In the moment's respite, the man gave Ned his attention. "We make our way fetchin' back runaways to their owners. The bad ones we bring in from the plantations and sell for a portion of the proceeds...if'n the owners don't want 'em no more. These are the bad ones."

The swine were cleared and the procession began again. One of the blacks, cloudy eyed, gaunt, and looking as if he had not eaten in days, stumbled and sank to his knees.

The runaway behind him, shorter and more thickly built, quickly reached down and dragged the man to his feet, and just as quickly, the blacksnake—as fine as a lizard's tongue at its tip—whistled through the air and opened the man's shoulder with a two-inch gash that yawned pink as a maiden's mouth, then flooded with blood.

The black grabbed for his bleeding shoulder and gave the man with the whip a fleeting but withering glance.

The man Ned had been talking with leapt two strides and raised the club. Ned strode right behind him, and grabbed the attacker's wrist before the bludgeon could begin its descent.

"No need for that," Ned snapped.

"Neighbor," a cold voice rang out, "y'all's about to mess the streets of this fine city with your stinkin' guts . . .and offal on N'orlans' streets is again' the law."

Ned cut his eyes from the icy stare of the man he held to the overseer astride the stallion; the man trained a large caliber pistol on Ned's middle.

"All I said was that there's no need to strike this man—''

The mounted man waved him back with the barrel. "None of yer affair, and if y'all be wise, it'll stay that way. Suggest

127

y'all head back to Boston, or wherever y'all slithered in from." The overseer cocked his weapon with a nonchalance belying the situation. The sound was among the loudest Ned had ever heard.

The guard he had grabbed shoved Ned roughly away.

"Don't ever lay hands on me again, friend," he said with a snarl, then spat another stream of tobacco juice, splattering some on Ned's boots.

Ned felt the heat surge up his backbone, straining his tolerance like the whipping of the man had done, but he was facing three hard men, and one already had a pistol trained on him. He prudently kept his lip tight.

The mounted man motioned with the cocked big bored pistol, and the line of blacks started slowly forward, chains rattling in rhythmic dejection.

"Where's this auction?" Ned asked suddenly.

"Blighton's," the mounted man said, uncocking and stuffing his pistol back in his belt. "But don't come less'n y'all's fixing to bid on meat. We don't cater to no spectators, and we're already packin' a grudge agin' one dumb Boston sailor—y'all!" He and his two associates laughed.

''What'll they bring?" Ned pressed, watching as they worked their way on down the road.

"Grief, to the fools what'll buy 'em," the mounted man called over his shoulder, laughing again with his friends. Then he reined up and eyed Ned as if he might just per chance be a buyer. His voice suddenly rang dead serious. "Thousand fer some, maybe nothin' but what gator bait's worth for others. Bring yer purse, pilgrim, and y'all can at least help run up the price."

Ned caught the first hack that came along and instructed the driver to deliver him to the Falcon. He had saved only a few hundred dollars in the years he had been in the Navy, and most all of it, except what he had in his pockets, rested in the Falcon's safe.

Within the hour, he was back at Blighton's Auction Yard.

He inquired as to the time of the auctions and found they ran all day and oftentimes well into the night.

Patiently be waited until finally the swine, cattle, and horse auctions were complete. The first of over a hundred slaves to be auctioned took a podium next to the corrals the livestock had been displayed in. Children, old men, and old women were presented in that order; then came spirited bidding for the young women. Finally, strong young men took their place alongside the auctioneer. Many brought as much as four thousand dollars from the crowd well primed with free liquor.

But the bidding fell off drastically when the final group was herded up on the podium. Some of them looked unhealthy; all of them bore the marks of the lash and the clubs the three overseers still carried. The majority of the hundred men and women who had been in the crowd had left, not bothering to wait to view this group of dangerous malcontents.

The dozen men still bidding were given the opportunity to mount the podium; to prod and poke the inspect the dozen blacks chained and assembled there.

Ned locked eyes with the overseer—the same man who had leveled the pistol on him—as he approached the podium. The man tipped his hat and gave Ned a crooked-toothed grin. Ned ignored him and worked his way among the men, observing and investigating the blacks.

He overheard one of the men speaking to a defiant appearing black man almost twice his size. "If'n I buy you, boy, and you give me the slightest cause, I'll feed your balls to the hogs . . . you understand?"

The huge slave gave no indication that he did understand; he just stared straight ahead. The threatening white man grunted and moved on.

Ned stopped in front of the powerful black who earlier had bent to help the man in front of him. Broad-featured and wide-shouldered, with a neck knotted with muscles, the man stood in stolid silence. Flies lined the gash in his shoulder, but the man made no effort to shoo them away. He stared stone-faced, straight ahead.

Ned whispered, "I brought money, but—I want no slave." The man gave no indication that he understood. "I'll bid on you and give you your freedom, but you'll owe me. Consider it a loan." Ned saw only the slightest flicker of his pupils. "You'll have to work it off." Nothing.

Ned retreated at the auctioneer's signal for the bidding to begin. He knew he would be taking a risk. Beyond that of the loan of the money, it was against the law to buy a slave for the express purpose of freeing him. And New Orleans, like the rest of the South, was very serious about its slave laws.

Hell, Ned thought, watching the line of slaves, then centering his gaze on the one with the flies buzzing around his shoulder, if I did buy him and give him his manumission, he'd probably cut my throat on the first dark night. He seems little more than a savage. Just as Ned was about to turn and leave, deciding that he was a damn fool for even coming, he eyed the black a last time with a degree of pity for his ignorance. The man suddenly broke his straight-ahead stare, and his eyes began searching the bidders. The instant he locked gazes with Ned, he gave an almost imperceptible nod, and hope seemed to flicker somewhere deep in his hard countenance.

Within ten minutes, two hundred twenty eight dollars poorer, Ned walked out of the building with his man close behind.

They stopped in the street..

"You owe me two hundred twenty eight dollars," Ned said, standing eye to eye with him. The black had not said a word while his chains, against the advice of the overseers, were being removed, nor during the time Ned settled with the auctioneer and received the bill of sale for a male slave known only as Jourdan.

Now the man looked Ned straight in the eye, and for the first time spoke. "Money take long time to pay back. You want interest? Trading post at Brazos charges what white man calls interest. Cost money, borrow money, or borrow goods."

Ned began to laugh. "Is five percent fair?"

"Five dollars on each hundred, each year! Fair." The man stared at Ned for a moment, then at Ned's extended hand. He shook, but without meeting Ned's eyes. "If it all right by you, I'd soon get far from this place as I can, fast as I can."

Ned spun on his heel and strode away from the building. He found a hack with the driver, as wide as the swaybacked nag who pulled the gig, asleep in the front seat, and shook the obese man awake.

Jourdan wore only a ragged pair of homespun trousers, shredded around the cuffs and tied at the waist with a piece of hemp rope.

"Take me to a general store," Ned told the driver, who was rubbing his pig eyes under a floppy-brimmed hat, then turned to Jourdan. "I'll advance you a little more for some decent clothes . . . all right?"

"All right." Jourdan nodded.

"Hold on, there," the driver said with a snarl, his fat jowls shaking. "No nigger rides in my rig."

Ned eyed the man with a glance of contempt, then turned to Jourdan, who had made no move to climb aboard.

"It's fine. I can outrun broke-down nag not fit to eat." The driver looked Jourdan up and down but decided to keep his comment and not attempt to tongue-lash the deep-chested man. Jourdan simply ignored the fat man. As the driver popped his whip over the back of the swayback gray, Jourdan, raw marks of his former restraints on his neck and ankles, laid a hand on the buggy rail and, barefooted, trotted

131

easily alongside, with Ned expecting him to bolt into each clump of brush or side street on the
way.

By nightfall, since the hotel had no provisions for slaves, even in the stable, Ned and Jourdan went aboard the Falcon, where Jourdan was well and comfortably situated among some coils of extra line, and Ned back in his cabin. The first thing Jourdan did on boarding was remove the lace-up, ankle-high shoes Ned had purchased for him. Most of the time on board that evening, they hung around his neck, their laces tied together.

Ned fully expected to find the shoes lying alone on the deck and the man gone the next morning when he wandered out, but Jourdan, shoes back on, was busily helping the crew cast off from the wharf. Ned watched the man work and wondered what exactly he was going to do with a servant. He would be the youngest man in the Navy to have one aboard a ship-of-the-line—if Stockton and DuPont allowed Jourdan aboard. And that was a big if.

It took seven days steaming to Charges, Panama, where he would begin his crossing. The Falcon passed between Cuba and Yucatan, crossed the mouth of the Bay of Honduras, where she picked up the southeastern trades, ran the gauntlet of a cluster of coral keys, then chugged into the deep water of the Caribbean Sea. The weather remained generally pleasant, with an occasional squall to keep things cool—and sometimes make them exciting.

Ned tried to get to know Jourdan during the voyage, but found him to be generally uncommunicative. He decided that the man probably came along just to get the hell out of Louisiana and, as Ned discovered during their limited conversations, away from his home state of Texas. Jourdan let him know that he was not only black African, but Kiowa. A zambo, as half-black half-Indians were known. Jourdan, though the son of a slave, thought himself a free man until he had

132

been captured by the slave chasers hunting others and brought back to New Orleans from the badlands of West Texas.

Most of the time Jourdan remained silent, and when not helping the crew, stared overboard as if he could not wait for the next port of call—and escape, Ned decided.

The mouth of Rio Charges was so narrow it could easily be missed, lost in the high, rugged shore of eastern Panama. Cut with heavily jungled ravines, so green they seemed to reverberate in his vision, the most seaward slope was crowned and the river mouth marked by the seaside Castle of San Lorenzo on a militarily impregnable point alongside where the river reached the sea. The other side of the river, away from the castle, lay flat, marshy, and uninviting. Even so, Ned noted a few stilted huts among the trees there.

As soon as the Falcon swung into the protection of the point, an immense canoe, formed from the trunk of some giant tree and manned by six paddlers, set out from shore, and by the time the Falcon dropped anchor in the muddy bottom, clattered alongside.

Ned, his money and dispatches in a sewn belt around his waist, accompanied the captain and first mate ashore while Jourdan rode quietly in the stern. The mate was kind enough to arrange quickly for transportation inland--another smaller canoe—and two guides to take Ned and Jourdan upriver.

At the first mate's advice, Ned visited what passed for the general store in the tiny village, and purchased two broad-brimmed woven hats, a pair of machetes, and two canvas bedrolls for him and Jourdan. With two Navy-issue Aston pistols at his waist, a ten inch knife in his belt, a machete strapped to his back, a broad-brimmed straw hat on his head, and the Marston pocket pistol hidden in his boot, Ned mounted the canoe between two dark-skinned natives and with his even darker-skinned traveling companion in front of him. They set out from Charges into the brown, jungle-bracketed Rio Charges in the late afternoon. Ned had asked the first mate if the native canoe paddlers and guides could be trusted, and received this discomforting reply: "As trustworthy as a New England preacher." Then the man, a bottle of whiskey in hand, laughed heartily.

The Indians paused long enough to line the canoe bottom with a covering of sugarcane. All of them sucked pieces of the sweet joint grass as they moved into the river.

Sometimes the foliage from the riverbanks entwined above them, forming a dark canopy. Alligators hit the water with a splash when the canoe neared their basking spots on the vine-covered shore. Monkeys did acrobatics through the branches and clinging vines, moving freely from one side of the river to the other, and scolding the interlopers for disturbing their chattering business. An occasional snake, ignored by the paddling natives, hung in the branches or swam in the muddy, brown river. Ned tried to be as nonchalant as the locals about them but could not help but eye them carefully and clutch the machete when the boat passed under hanging or beside swimming reptiles. Insects plagued them, testing their flavor silently until slapped away. Only jungle sounds, buzzing insects, and the lap of the paddles broke the silence.

The river seemed to branch a hundred times during the first two hours of paddling, and Ned marveled at how surely the helmsman steered the craft into selected channels, which seemed identical to their myriad forking neighbors.

At dark, with a thousand tiny flying creatures buzzing around them and lighting on every square inch of exposed skin to place a new bite on already swollen and irritated bumps, they pulled the canoe into a side channel and nosed it into what passed for a clearing. A low fire in the green-dark distance signaled a village, and thatched huts and a few nearly naked natives appeared at their approach.

The natives ignored them, as if visitors were a common occurrence. Ned and Jourdan were assigned a hut just large enough for the two of them to lie down in, and they "enjoyed" a handful of jerky Ned had traded out of the cook of the Falcon before they had disembarked, and finished the meal off with a joint of sugarcane.

Jourdan borrowed flint and steel from Ned and built a small fire at the open doorway to the hut, explaining that it would help keep the bugs out. The cabin filled with smoke, and though it added somewhat to the heat, the bugs did leave. Finally, with no light other than the tiny fire, Ned unrolled his canvas and stretched out. He looked at Jourdan questioningly.

"I watch, you sleep. You watch, I sleep," the man stated quietly.

Somewhat suspicious of his intent but knowing he would have to trust him sometime, Ned went to sleep quickly.

When he awoke before dawn, Ned eyed the bedroll next to him, and though it appeared at first glance that someone occupied it, Jourdan was gone. Ned quickly sat up and realized that one of his .50 caliber Aston pistols was also missing.

"Son of a bitch," he whispered aloud.

"Quiet," the whispered word came through the thin walls of the thatched hut. Jourdan's voice.

Ned lay awake for an hour, his remaining Aston clutched in one hand, the machete in the other. Then the sun began to turn the jungle from darkness to dark green shadow.

Finally, Jourdan appeared at the opening. Casually he entered, handed Ned the Aston, and lay down. "Men nearby in the night. I sleep a few minutes now."

"You were supposed to wake me."

"Don't trust guides. They like pistols too much. I stay awake. Sleep now till time to go."

As servants went, Jourdan was not much of one. He was content to carry his share, but never infringed on Ned's willingness to carry his own. If Ned picked up one of the spare paddles and helped with the canoe, Jourdan did like wise, carefully watching what Ned did. He stayed close by, occasionally eyeing the Astons with interest but never demanding one. The machete he carried seemed enough, at least for the time being.

On the second day, they passed the village of Gatun, even less impressive than miserable Charges. The river flowed swifter and sweeter, and lay brightened by many colored lilies among the walls of green-shadowed foliage on either side. Brilliant butterflies circled the air like blossoms set free from the trees and vines. By the second night, they reached a village called Dos Hermanos, and just as they dragged the canoe ashore, the sky blackened and rain hammered down as if it were a waterfall on the river. But that night, Ned and Jourdan found a room in the back of the only cantina in the town, and slept dry under a well-thatched roof, their bellies full of pork and jungle fruit.

The river roiled high the next day, and the current hurried rather than meandered. Ned and Jourdan were obliged to take up the paddles themselves or little progress would have been made. They passed several ranchos, seen in distant clearings since the jungle thinned the farther they got away from the sea.

Ned's Spanish was good—for the classroom and shipboard variety—and he continued to improve it with the natives who accompanied them. On the third night, they stopped at the rancho of a Padre Dutaris. He possessed a herd of fine cattle, and they dined on beef and enjoyed his hospitality. All and all, to Ned's surprise, he was enjoying this crossing that he had heard so many horror stories about.

On the fourth day, after hours of arduous poling, they reached the end of the canoe ride: Gorgona.

Ned paid the Indians, complimented them in Spanish, and gave them a little extra. Then he and Jourdan went looking for mules to rent or buy for the continuation of the trip over the spine of the isthmus. They found a saloon with a couple of comely, dark-skinned barmaids, one of whom immediately took a liking to Jourdon, and paused long enough to enjoy a glass of the local poison. Finally, after Ned freed Jourdan from the girl's attentions, they found a hostler and livery but no mules. Three mustangs, so small you could almost step aboard, were rented for a single reale each. They were to be turned over to the hostler's brother in Panama City at the end of the crossing, only one day's hard ride away—if they could leave an hour before dawn.

For a few extra centavos, they bedded down on the outskirts of the small village in the tack room of the makeshift barn belonging to the livery man. Again Jourdan insisted on staying awake while Ned slept. And again Ned awoke a little before dawn to find Jourdan missing. This time he heard no voice from outside the walls. He rose and searched for his boots, then stepped out of the tack room. Still nothing.

Checking his money belt and his guns and supplies, he found everything intact.

At least the black had not stolen everything—only the two hundred twenty eight dollars Ned had spent to free him, and the clothes he had bought him, Ned groused to himself as he began to saddle the stock. He decided against finding the hostler and getting back the reale for Jourdan's horse. It would be more trouble than it was worth.

By the time the sun colored the eastern sky, Ned sat easily in the saddle, and the village lay far behind. His gear, hardly a decent load even with the weight of a substantial mail bag, bounced along on a pack horse. The horse he had rented for Jourdan still stood in the corral .

The trail wove up onto a higher plateau, where he reined up, and in the distance saw the welcome blue of the Pacific. He plunged down into the jungle canopy, following a trail deeply grooved by passing travelers over many centuries. The heat and the filtered light of the jungle made it difficult not to doze on the easy-gaited little horse. Ned's head hung on his chest, and only when a bug bit him or crawled into his ear or a droplet of sweat rolled down his cheek did he look up.

"Amigo!"

Ned snapped his head up, startled by the voice. Three men, wide straw hats shading their dark, mustached faces, stood in a narrow, rocky spot in the trail. Ned recovered his composure, smiled, and tipped his hat. The horse halted, dropped his head, and began to nibble at green shoots on the trail's edge.

"Buenos dias," Ned answered in his most polite Spanish, for the men who blocked his way were rough-looking, and each of them had a musket hanging at his side and an ugly machete in his belt. Ned felt more than foolish for riding up on them while inattentive.

"Not a good day for you, amigo," the one who had spoken said, a gap-toothed grin on his stubbled face.

Becoming truly alarmed, Ned casually rested his hand on the butt of one of the Astons. "Why's that, amigo?"

"You are on my road, and you have not paid."

"Oh. I thought this was a public road."

"This is Aleandro's road, and I am Aleandro."

"And what does it cost to pass on Aleandro's road?" Ned asked, his own tight smile drawing into a thin line.

"Everything you have, and your life if it's not quickly." Aleandro laughed with a great guffaw. By the time he had finished, Ned had the Aston out of his belt and in hand.

"I think not," he said with a snarl.

"I think so," Aleandro said as his smile faded to a glower. With a flip of his shaggy head, he motioned to Ned's side, and Ned glanced quickly, letting his eyes stray only a moment. Even though the three men in the trail had not bothered to shoulder their muskets, the two men flanking Ned had, men Ned had not seen before, and their muskets centered on his chest.

"Don't you now think so?" Aleandro asked, his smile returning.

138

"I have a silver Americano dollar to pay you for passage," Ned said, not moving, keeping the Aston leveled on Aleandro's chest. "And that is all you get."

"Your pistolas are worth much more than that, amigo." Aleandro took a step forward. Ned ratcheted the hammer of the cap-and-ball Aston back.

"I will spend the dollar, or I will spend one lead ball—into your chest, amigo."

At the sound of the pistol cocking, the bandido froze in mid-step, then regained his balance and backed up a step. He placed his hands on his hips, glowered not a half dozen paces away, and studied Ned.

"You are a foolish gringo. You will die in this jungle, the small creatures will feast on you, and your blessed madre will not have a grave to mourn over."

"Do you feel better knowing that your madre may soon have a spot to mourn your death? Somehow, the placement of flowers does not satisfy a man's need." Ned managed a tight smile, though his stomach swarmed with tickling butterflies and the sweat trickled down the back of his neck, tracking his backbone. "As soon as you take another step, or one of your men fires, this Aston will blow you into next week."

"You would not be so foolish," Aleandro said, but his smile wore thin on his face, and his eyes reflected no humor.

"Why would I want to die alone, amigo?" Ned asked despite the dryness of his mouth.

"And many of you die with him," a voice shouted from the distance behind Ned. He wanted to turn but was afraid to take his eyes off Aleandro. With a flood of hope, he realized the voice was Jourdan's.

Aleandro's face turned to stone.

Ned announced, "There are another dozen or so gringos behind me who have killed many foolish men who wanted our poor possessions. All armed to the teeth and wanting stories to tell their grandchildren, of course."

Aleandro began backing up until he stood almost out of sight in the jungle. "Pasa, amigo, my compliments," he called out, fading from sight into the deep undergrowth. Ned turned and searched the trail behind him where the voice had come from but saw nothing. All of the bandidos were gone before the mustang on the trail behind broke from the cover of a thick patch of jungle and, hooves flinging mud, galloped up beside Ned.

"Give me gun," Jourdan demanded.

Both angry and relieved, Ned snarled at him, "Where the hell have you been?"

"Pistol!" Jourdan snapped impatiently, and Ned handed one of the Astons over to him.

Gun in hand, he seemed to relax, but he continued to scan the undergrowth. "Women. Took long time."

Ned started to growl at him but decided he would keep quiet—at least until his stomach stopped doing flip-flops. "Let's go," he said, and gave his heels to the little mustang. "Before they realize we're nothing but a dumb, lazy sailor and a roaming Romeo." He was so mad at himself for dozing along on a dangerous trail that he found it difficult to find fault with anyone else.

Shortly after dark, they arrived at the wharf in Panama City where they were to wait for the brig Chile, due in three days.

That night, lying in his bedroll on the planked wharf, Ned decided that he had been very lucky. He would never, he swore, allow himself to be unaware of his surroundings or confident enough, in a strange place, to doze. Next time the zambo might find a half-dozen women and be a week in catching up—if he bothered to at all.

Twice in one month Ned had looked at the business end of a gun, and he damn sure didn't like it.

CHAPTER NINE

When the *Chile* reached Callao, the *Congress* lay at anchor, waiting.

Ned convinced the *Chile's* captain to dispatch a boat to take him and Jourdan to her, and for the first time in six months he stepped back aboard a ship he could call his own. Passed Mid shipman John Specter, after greeting him warmly and welcoming him "home," brought him the message that Stockton and DuPont were with non-Navy personnel, tied up with last-minute preparations to sail. Ned would be expected in the commodore's cabin at seven to dine with Stockton; Commander Samuel Francis DuPont. executive officer of the skip; and Lieutenant Sean Conners. a new transferee to the Congress as first lieutenant.

That gave Ned several hours to arrange his thoughts, and to deliver crew mail he carried to the purser for distribution. For a while he would be a very popular member of the crew, since he carried not only mail but also the latest newspapers from New York. Boston, and Washington. D.C.

Ned situated Jourdan in his cabin where he would sleep on the floor, to the skeptical inquiries of the three passed midshipmen he shared the cabin with, then shook out his uniform and did his best to make it presentable prior to his command appearance. By seven, when he waited at Stockton's door, he looked fresh and shaven.

Stockton himself answered the door and greeted Ned with a warm handshake and the question. "What news of war with Mexico?"

"No declared war, at least as of the time I left New Orleans. Taylor is deep in Texas, believed, if rumor in New Orleans can be trusted, to be bivouacked in Corpus Christi. By now he may be in Matamoros, but I can't testify to that."

"Damn, I had hoped to have definite word." Stockton's broad shoulders seemed to slump. He returned to the table where his personal man stood pouring tea.

The commodore's table, where Ned greeted Commander DuPont and his old friend Conners, was set for four. Ned handed the dispatches over to the commodore, and when invited, took his seat.

"Well, gentlemen," Stockton said as he carefully unpeeled the wax from the dispatch carrying the secretary of the Navy's seal, "this should tell us our fate for the next few months." He read in silence, then excused Molo, his Kanaka personal servant and groom. The big man nodded and left the cabin. DuPont, Conners, and Ned waited anxiously.

"Let me read it word for word." Stockton said. " 'It is the earnest desire of the president to pursue the policy of peace, and he is anxious that you and every part of your squadron should be assiduously careful to avoid any act that could be construed an act of aggression. Should Mexico, however, be resolutely bent on hostilities, you will be mindful to protect the persons and interests of citizens of the United States, and should you ascertain beyond a doubt that the Mexican government has declared war against us. you will employ the force under your command to the best advantage. The Mexican ports on the Pacific are said to be open and defenseless . . . you will at once blockade or occupy such ports as your force will admit."

Stockton sat back in his chair and took a deep, contemplative sip of hot tea.

"What about Ten Eyck?" DuPont asked. Ned had no idea who they were talking about and listened with interest as Stockton addressed the problem.

"My original orders were to deliver Commissioner Ten Eyck and Consul Turrell to the Sandwich Islands, and since these rather nebulous orders do not contradict those, I will do so. . . . Besides"—he smiled for the first time since greeting Ned at the door—"Molo would be disappointed if we didn't call on his home port." Stockton rose and crossed the cabin to the door. "Speaking of Molo, let's eat while we review the other dispatches."

"Wait, sir," Ned interrupted. Stockton returned a few steps. "There's more." Stockton started to sit, but hesitated as Ned continued. "For your ears only.''

Stockton glanced from DuPont to Conners, who rose and started for the door.

"I'm sorry, gentlemen," Ned said. Both men waved him off.

As soon as the door closed behind them, Ned turned to Stockton. "I truly am sorry, sir. Should I have waited?"

"They're naval officers and understand. Go ahead," he said, obviously eager to hear what Ned knew.

''The president sent this message verbally, for your ears only. He cautioned that it could not be written down."

"The message, Beale."

Ned collected himself, then carefully began. "If you err during these next few months, before you have the opportunity to learn if war has been declared, then err on the part of aggression. Mexico, the president believes, will go to war. Mexico owes the United States some thirty million dollars, and the president has already offered to settle that debt for the territory between the Brazos River and the Rio Grande, with California and New Mexico thrown into the bargain. Mexico has refused. Santa Ana crows like a fighting cock, and we are to believe he means to do battle."

"Good." Stockton began to pace, his hands behind his back. "Go on."

"There is an Army topographer, John Fremont, in California or Oregon, with a hard crew of mountain men. Maybe as many as forty. The president says to use them in whatever manner you see fit in the event of a conflict. In the event of a declared war, a land force will be immediately dispatched. By the by, Senator Benton also called upon me . . . or should I say, insisted I call upon him—"

"I know Benton, and his beautiful daughter." Stockton smiled, obviously pleased with the private information Ned conveyed. "He's a bit pompous, but effective."

"Fremont is his son-in-law, and any consideration you can give him would be appreciated by the senator.

"Senators can be handy to have in your debt," Stockton said, almost to himself, then flushed when he realized how much he was beginning to trust young Beale.

"The president said," Ned continued, "and I quote his exact words: 'If you have even a minimal reason to believe that war has been declared, secure California first, and he said—'l mean secure'—and then, if absolutely certain California is ours, move on to the western coast of Mexico.' "

"That's it?"

"That's it," Ned assured him. "Word for word."

"Politicians always leave it for the military to make the mistakes ... and become the scapegoats," Stockton grumbled, suddenly sullen. Then he brightened. "Well, the next few months should be exciting, at the least. Fetch the others and call Molo back to the table. I'm famished."

Ned hurried to the door and called to the commander and lieutenant who lounged on a deck box near the mainmast; then he walked to the private mess between Stockton's cabin and Commander DuPont's and asked Molo, who could barely squeeze his big frame into the narrow space, to serve. As the commander and lieutenant reappeared, Molo arrived in Stockton's cabin with a steaming bowl of vegetables in one hand and a generous platter of roast chicken in the other.

144

The officers never mentioned the topic they were precluded from hearing, but rather discussed with Ned the political situation at home in some detail, and continued to question him about the state of affairs in England. By the time they had finished a snifter of brandy, Ned still did not have the information that interested him most: regarding his position as ship's master.

When Stockton had finished his brandy, he yawned and stretched—a sure sign that the officers had overstayed their welcome. Ned rose with Conners, and both expressed their thanks for the fine meal and asked to be excused. Ned reached the door before Stockton called out to him.

"Mr. Beale." Ned turned, hoping against hope he was to be informed that he had his old job back. "Report to me here at oh seven hundred in the morning. I want to get some dispatches out."

"Yes, sir," Ned said, not allowing the disappointment to show in his voice. At least he had his position as Stockton's personal secretary. He waited stiffly as Stockton yawned again. "Is that all, sir?"

"No, come to think of it. You did a fine job, Mr. Beale, and I've decided to turn in your papers for promotion to lieutenant. You will conduct yourself as such, and shall be entitled to display that rank even though your promotion will not be confirmed by the Navy Department for some time. Congratulations." Stockton rose and extended his hand.

"Thank you, sir!" Ned saluted smartly even though they were below decks and it was unnecessary. Stockton smiled and casually returned the salute, then Ned shook hands with him.

Ned could hardly contain himself. It was the only thing he could have heard that would have made him happier than getting his master's job back. Then Commander DuPont added, "And you can return to your master's job as soon as we are at sea. The commodore will keep you busy until then."

"Yes, sir." Ned spun on his heel, happy to be excused. It was all he could do to maintain his decorum and not jump up and kick his heels in front of Conners, who offered him his hearty congratulations as they made their way to the midship ladder. But as soon as Ned and he parted, Ned did leap, and shout a yell that caused a number of the middies and officers to come to their cabin doors to see what the commotion was.

When they cornered Ned, he found himself in a long discussion with the men in the officers' wardroom regarding the situation in England and at home. It was well past midnight before he rolled into his bunk.

The next morning, he broached the problem of Jourdan with the commodore. Stockton ran a hand through his thick, curly brown hair.

"Now that you're a passed midshipman, practically a full-fledged officer, you're entitled to have personal property aboard ship ... but you say you have arranged for the manumission of this man?"

"Yes, sir."

"Then he's no longer personal property. You must either claim him as your slave, or convince him to enlist. Otherwise there's no place for him aboard the Congress."

"I can't claim him as a slave, sir. He's not. And knowing Jourdan"—Ned smiled—"he would take this ship apart timber by timber if I attempted to make anyone believe otherwise. I'll convince him to enlist."

"A wise choice. I would have been disappointed . : . Stockton let the matter drop and went on with his dictation.

After thirty minutes, Stockton glanced at his pocket watch, then looked up. "Mr. Beale, the tide has turned and, with it, we're bound for the Sandwich Islands. Would you care to take your position at the quarterdeck rail?"

"Yes, sir. I believe I'm not out of practice. At least I can get her out of this wide harbor. "

"Then do so. I'll see you back here when you've got her on the wind."

Ned hurried on deck, eager to get back to the skills he was trained for. He yelled a greeting to those he knew and moved to the sailing master's position at the rail, excused the young lieutenant there with the explanation that the commodore himself had instructed Ned to take her out, then signaled the drummer. who began to beat general quarters.

The *Congress*'s stern anchor had been hoisted first thing in the morning, and now she rode on her larboard bow hook only.

Ned watched the topsailmen mount the ratlines, and the various sections man their positions on deck. The hustle and bustle, yet well-planned and orchestrated movements of the men on deck and going aloft on a sailing vessel had become second nature to Ned, and he loved it. But for the first time in his sailing career, he felt a twinge of regret as he prepared the ship to move farther and farther from home—and from Mary Edwards. He put her out of his mind and continued with his orders.

Twenty broad backs stood ready to put muscle to the capstan rails. "Stand by to cast off," Ned ordered, then quickly followed up, "Break and heave the larboard hook."

A bosun with a mouth trumpet relayed his order, and the creak of gears, the taut snap of the anchor rode, and the ringing of the men's voices proved he had been heard and obeyed.

> Yo, heave ho!
> Heave hearty ho!
> Heave with a will!
> Heave and raise your dead!
> Heave and away!
> Yo, heave ho!

Over and over the song rang from the capstan position on the lower cannon deck, and the creak of pumps began as a crew hosed down the rode and then the chain, clearing it of mud and weed as it was stored below.

"Square away the main yard!" Ned shouted, and the thrill of bringing the hundreds of tons of dead-anchored ship alive and under control surged through him.

"Let fall the fors'l and mains'l! Lively does it, lads. . . . Be handy! Be handy!" Ned glanced to the side and saw Jourdan watching with rapt interest.

The sails dropped away and luffed for a few seconds before they filled with wind, and the lazy ship became a thing of beauty as she captured its latent power.

Ned glanced up on the poop deck and noticed two well-dressed strangers standing beside Commander DuPont at the rail. It must be Ten Eyck and Terrell, the representatives from the State Department, he decided.

As soon as the ship lay on course, Ned signaled the drummer to beat the order to stand down, and his duty was complete.

"You are the bossman of this ship?" Jourdan asked. Ned turned and gave his friend a smile.

"No, Jourdan, only the sailing master. I also plot the course and keep track of the stores. Do you think you might enjoy duty aboard a beautiful vessel such as this?"

"I am a man of the chaparral. If man made to be in ocean, he would have fins," Jourdan said, a dark and very serious look on his face. Ned decided he would wait a while before he broached the problem of convincing Jourdan he must enlist.

Ned took Jourdan below and found his old friend Chief Gunner's Mate Rosco Handley, and told Jourdan that Rosco would teach him to be a gunner and that he would bunk with his gun crew. Jourdan nodded, only slightly interested in his new assignment, but stayed when Ned left.

Partly because he loved the work and partly because he wanted to keep his mind off Mary Edwards, Ned paid particular care to the trim of the sails and his navigation on the passage to the Sandwich Islands. He checked and rechecked his position; trimmed and re-trimmed this sails; and, as if to repay the faith the commodore had again placed in him, the passage was made in a record thirty days.

The men of the *Congress* were more than pleased to be greeted by a bevy of brown-skinned girls, as naked as the day they were born, who swam from the many canoes that followed the ship into the harbor. Stockton and DuPont convinced them to depart, with the promise that the men would soon be granted shore leave. And their promise was kept. Rosco Handley reported to Ned that Jourdan did not return to the ship from his first liberty, and though he had never officially enlisted, he had been named on the roster and was declared absent without leave.

Ned requested special permission to go ashore and find Jourdan, but after a full day's search was unsuccessful .

A few days later, a merchantman brig flying the Stars and Stripes anchored nearby. The *Brooklyn* sent word that her officers, and a gentleman by the name of Sam Brannan, would like to come aboard, and Stockton agreed to receive them for supper. Ned received an invitation, and a dozen officers gathered in the officers' wardroom to greet the four visitors.

As soon as Brannan sat down, he offered a toast. "To the United States of America, and to General Zachary Taylor, may he prevail in the present hostilities—"

"Hostilities?" Stockton interrupted.

"You haven't heard?"

"Heard what?" Stockton demanded.

"We got word when we put into Juan Fernando Island: Taylor and his dragoons have met the enemy at Palo Alto and Resaca de la Palma and drove them out. He was at Matamoros, and from what I've heard about old Rough and Ready, he'll be in Mexico City before the Mexicans can prime their muskets."

"Then war is declared?"

"I cannot confirm that, but we can presume—"

"The hell we can," Stockton snapped with an uncharacteristic curse. "Only fools rush in. Still ..." He contemplated a moment, then shook his head in frustration. "I wish to God that we had definite news of a declaration by Polk." Deciding he had said too much, Stockton raised his glass. "To Zach Taylor and Manifest Destiny.''

The officers drank, but the rum didn't quench the fire of the promise of forthcoming action that burned in each man's belly.

Ned found himself fascinated with Brannan, a big, engaging man who regaled the men with stories of his newfound religion and his mission with the other two hundred twenty-five Mormons aboard the *Brooklyn*—a group dedicated to establishing a colony in Alta California, whether or not the Mexicans agreed.

Stockton; too, seemed convinced that the Mormons meant business, and agreed to sell Brannan and his group one hundred fifty muskets and fifty Allan's pepperbox revolvers from the armory of the Congress.

On June 20, with the ship due to sail in three days Stockton had hurried the re-provisioning and concluded his business after he got Brannan's news—Ned again asked for leave to see if he could locate Jourdan. He had been missing for almost two weeks, and Ned was worried that he had met with foul play. When the longboat delivered Ned and a group of officers and midshipmen to the wharf, Ned set out on his own and immediately began questioning every native he came across.

By the third saloon, a comely barmaid in a loose-fitting blouse that exposed her ample breasts informed Ned that her cousins, who lived in a village on the other side of Diamond Head, were entertaining a sailor from the *Congress*, and had been for two weeks. Ned rented a wiry piebald mustang and followed her directions.

The village squatted on the edge of tall, copra-bearing palms in a quiet cove. Gentle waves lapped the sand, and children played at the water's edge. Ned sat the horse, shaded his eyes with a hand, and searched the village with his gaze. He had almost decided to turn the little horse, ride away, and leave Jourdan to this newfound idyllic life when he spotted his friend's thick-chested frame sitting between two bare-breasted native girls who were busily engaged weaving mats from palm leaves. Ned sat the mustang, undecided, until Jourdan spotted him and stood and waved him down enthusiastically. Ned spurred the little horse into a trot, reined up, and tied him to a slender coconut palm.

"I have missed you," Jourdan called as he trotted over and laid a hand on Ned's shoulder.

"You needn't have, Jourdan. All you had to do was return to the ship."

Jourdan looked at Ned, then at the two girls, then back and Ned. He shrugged, as if it should have been obvious to Ned why he had been more than happy to remain ashore. Ned broke into a smile, then a guffaw. Finally he calmed himself as Jourdan dragged him over to where the girls continued to weave.

Jourdan introduced Ned, who still had a bit of a silly smile on his face. Both of the girls had a fresh beauty and the innocence of an adolescent, although their bodies indicated their maturity. They eyed him with interest, and soon began laying a feast of fish steamed in a wrapped leaf, poi, and fruit on one of the mats they were in the process of weaving. While they worked on the meal, Ned regained his composure.

"Are you coming back to the ship?" he asked Jourdan, who lay comfortably in the shade of a palm, his bare feet in a trickle of a stream that meandered into the village from the

151

jungle, then disappeared into the sand before it reached the sea.

"What does Jourdan owe you?" he questioned.

"Still just under two hundred dollars."

"Then I come back, until you are paid."

"Jourdan, you can't just come and go from a ship-of-the-line as if you were still out in the chaparral."

"Why not?"

"Because you have duty on board."

"There are many men on board to do duty. Jourdan had been a long time without a woman, and these women . . ." He admired the two who were nearby shucking a pair of coconuts. As if to confirm his opinion, one of the girls walked over and offered Ned a half shell, still filled with sweet, succulent, clear milk. Ned drank, eyed the girl whose black eyes flashed with interest, and decided that there was no need to chastise Jourdan. He would do what he wanted nevertheless, and if he came back to the ship, Rosco would see he got a taste of discipline. "We have to go soon?" Jourdan asked.

The girl who had served Ned wrapped an arm around his neck and settled one of her full brown breasts against his biceps. He had seen the beautiful girls of these islands since he had sailed the *Congress* into port, and the warmth and softness of her breast against his biceps and the privacy and beauty of the spot were just too much.

"No, Jourdan," he said quietly. "We don't have to be back until midnight."

"Good. Then can properly say good-bye to womans."

"Yes, we can say good-bye to the women." Ned settled back on the mat and allowed the girl to put in his mouth a piece of fruit, sweet and moist on his tongue. She ran her fingers through his hair and laughed, then pulled him to his feet and led him into the darkness of the jungle.

It was just before midnight when they returned to the wharf, riding double on the little mustang. Ned had paid the

152

man in advance for the use of the horse, so he tied his reins to the saddle horn, slapped him on the rump, and watched as he trotted off toward the livery. Ned was sure he would be all right; everything on this island seemed to be self-sufficient.

The next morning, when Rosco Handley realized that Jourdan had returned, he requested permission to clamp him in irons for five-day penance. Jourdan at first got his back up; then when reassured by Ned that it would only be five days and that it was a standard punishment for any man absent without leave, Jourdan went below peacefully.

He had been in irons before, but when the five days were over and he saw Ned again, he informed him that he would never be placed in irons again.

"I hope not, Jourdan. You must learn the rules."

"No rules in chaparral," he said simply, rubbing the marks on his wrists.

"Maybe not, but there will be someday."

"When Jourdan even with you, he go back to the chaparral. He not have fins, anyway."

Ned laughed, and Jourdan managed to thin his lips, the closest thing he usually did to smiling.

"Well, we're on our way to Monterey to meet up with the fleet. Maybe they have chaparral there," Ned said.

"Maybe, maybe not. Somewhere, they have it, and then Jourdan will be gone . . . if you are paid."

"As you wish."

"I wish we were back on island with women," Jourdan said, and turned to go below to see what job Rosco had for him.

Ned did not reply, but he, too, wished he was with a woman. The island girl had only made him think of Mary Edward's, and wonder if her white skin was as smooth and cool as that of the native girl she would never hear about.

Ned went below. He had borrowed a copy of a book by a popular poet, *The Raven and Other Poems*, and decided he would read a while. Maybe it would cheer him up.

CHAPTER TEN

On July 15, 1846, after a comfortable crossing, the mainmast lookout spotted the high mountains of the Sierra Madres above a cloud bank, but by the time the *Congress* made the point, fog rolled in so thick you could not make out the lowest yardarm—even the gulls took to the sea's surface, hove to. The *Congress* took their lead, hove to, and waited.

It was late afternoon before they dared round the rocky point into Monterey Bay, where the capital of Alta California rose up out of the quiet waters. Wind-flagged cypress, weaving lanes lined with frangipani and wisteria, and thatch- and tile-roofed dwellings were scattered along the hillside above the largest building in the village, the customhouse, which lay at the waterside. And the news buzzed through the crew regarding the flag that flew over it. The Stars and Stripes waved in the afternoon breeze, the simple rectangle of cloth sending a tremor of pride and wonder through the American sailors.

The *Congress*, with Lieutenant Edward Fitzgerald Beale commanding the deck as sailing master, smartly took her place in the line of American warships alongside the *Savannah*, the *Cyane*, and the *Levant*.

To his surprise, Commodore Stockton noted the banner of Commodore John Sloat, the acting commander of the Pacific Squadron, flying from the masthead of the *Savannah*. As Stockton prepared to pay his respects and deliver his orders, relieving Sloat of his command, Stockton wondered why Sloat was not aboard his flagship, the *U.S.S. Constitution*, affectionately known to the sailors as *Old Ironsides*.

Stockton dispatched Ned to see to the launching of a long-boat, and informed him he would accompany, in his capacity as secretary, to pay respects to the commodore.

Commodore Sloat, with his own personal secretary, Lieutenant Erin O'Connel, in attendance, received Stockton and Beale in his cabin—in his nightshirt.

"You'll pardon my appearance, Robert," Sloat said in a low voice after being introduced to Ned, "but I've been ill for months."

"Of course, John." Stockton took a seat, and Sloat returned to his bed. "Since you've been ill, you may be happy to know I carry orders to relieve you."

"Thank God," Sloat replied.

The preliminaries aside, Stockton asked, "What of the war?"

"As you can see, we've raised the flag over Monterey. She also flies over Yerba Buena, Sonoma, and Sutter's Fort on the American River."

"Then you've received word that war has been declared?" Stockton asked with a tight and anxious smile.

"I wish it were so easy, Robert," Sloat answered weakly. "No, I've received no word, but did hear that General Taylor has engaged the Mexicans in Texas."

"We heard the same."

"Anyway, the settlers around Sonoma, north of here, rose up against General Vallejo, took him and his family prisoner, and raised their own flag, declaring California a republic. I could not condone that, and promptly moved to establish the United States as the rightful possessor of Alta California. Mr. O'Connel will read you copies of my edicts. I had to move quickly, Robert."

O'Connel cleared his throat and picked up one of many parchments scattered over Sloat's desk, while Sloat tried to clarify the situation.

"This first communiqué was my note to Commander Montgomery, commander of the *Portsmouth* . . . who was in Yerba Buena when news reached me about what they are calling the 'Bear Revolt' in Sonora . . . a month ago, on June fourteenth." Sloat managed an exhausted smile. "The settlers there raised a ridiculous flag with a bear crudely drawn on it. We're told it looked more like Rosey's pet pig than the gallant beast California is so well known for." He weakly waved a sallow hand for his secretary to begin. "Go on, Mr. O'Connel."

Officiously, he began, "Dispatch, Sloat to Montgomery, July sixth: 'I have determined to hoist the flag of the United States at this place tomorrow'—the dispatch originated here in Monterey—'as I would prefer being sacrificed for doing too much than too little. If you consider you have sufficient force, or if Fremont will join you, you will hoist the flag at Yerba Buena, or at any other proper place, and take possession of the fort and that portion of the country."

"Well and bravely done," Stockton offered when O'Connel paused, but thought, bold, but possibly career suicide.

O'Connel continued, "Then the commodore informed our ships here via this communiqué 'July seventh, we are about to land on the territory of Mexico, with whom the United States is at war; to strike their flag and hoist our own.... It is not only our duty to take California, but to preserve it afterward as part of the United States, at all hazards—' "

Sloat interrupted him and offered a weak smile. "I used the term 'war' in its broad sense, not its legal one. It goes on, with instructions to the occupying force, but you will have copies to review later. Read the proclamation.... I posted this with each flag raised in order to inform the Californios of our position."

O'Connel dug through the pile of parchments, came up with the proper one, and began, "Although I come with a powerful force, I do not come as an enemy of Californians. On the contrary, I come as their best friend, as henceforth California will be a portion of the United States. Inhabitants not disposed to accept the high privilege of United States citizenship will have the option of leaving the country or may remain, observing strict neutrality. "

"Well said, John," Stockton congratulated the commodore. The man has declared his own personal war on California . . . and given me leave to continue with little risk to my own reputation. "Yes, John, well done indeed."

"And somewhat well received," Sloat graciously accepted the praise. "I've had the *Savannah*'s purser, Daingerfield Fauntleroy, and a volunteer force of thirty five on shore. They've set up regular communications, via horseback, with San Juan Bautista, Yerba Buena, San Jose, and Monterey. He's in San Juan Bautista now, officially taking possession of the city and raising the flag. By the way, I made sure General Castro, who was in charge of the presidio here in Monterey, has received a copy of my edict. It had to travel all the way to Los Angeles"—Sloat smiled triumphantly—"as he and his army have fled there. Now he has a choice of embracing our flag, or continuing to rant and rave about opposing us. So far that's about all he's done, other than confront Fremont. . . . You know of Fremont?''

"I understand he's here with the topographical corps," Stockton offered, but said nothing about the messages Beale carried from both Polk and Senator Benton.

"Yes, and he and his force of sixty so-called Bears confronted Castro and several hundred Californios at a hill called Hawk's Peak. Captain Fremont, with his normal bravado, raised the flag there long before my orders to do so. Castro had already sent him word to get the hell out of California, but Fremont thumbed his nose at the Mexicans. Then when the general charged the hill the next day, he found Fremont

Rush to Destiny – L. J. Martin

and his men had slipped out in the night. I guess Castro figured they were leaving the country, since he did not pursue."

"So Fremont has been active," Stockton said, as much to
himself as anyone else.

"He's caused his share of trouble," Sloat managed, seeming to weaken again. He lay his head deep on the pillow.

"I hate to badger you when you're feeling so poorly, John,
and I promise I'll get out of your hair soon, but I need a little
more information. What about the British?"

Before Sloat could answer, a sharp rap on the door sounded across the room. O'Connel answered it, and a young midshipman stood erect in the hallway.

"The *Collingwood* has entered the harbor, flying Admiral
Seymour's banner," the middy stammered in excitement.
"The commander requests the presence of the commodore on
the poop deck."

"My uniform," Sloat commanded his secretary. Stumbling
to his feet, he tried to struggle into his braided coat, then collapsed back to sit on the bed, his face pale and drawn. "This
may be your answer," he said shakily. "Goon up, Robert. I'll
be along."

Stockton and Beale hurried after the young midshipman.
When they reached the poop deck, Commander Armstrong,
executive officer of the ship, stood with his first lieutenant
glassing the *Collingwood*, the eighty-gun pride of the British
fleet, under full sail with white water off her bow—and heading directly for the American fleet as if with a purpose.

"Well?" Stockton asked.

Armstrong glanced over his shoulder. "Her gun ports are
closed, but she has plenty of crew topside." He returned to the
telescope.

"I suggest you load and stand by," Stockton said quietly,
"but keep your ports closed also."

Armstrong turned from the glass long enough to nod to his
first lieutenant, who hurried forward. The drummer began

159

calling all hands, and soon the ratlines were shaking with top-sail men going aloft, and all guns were being loaded and primed.

When the men reached their positions and the guns were loaded, the ship fell deathly quiet. Tension mounted as the *Collingwood* neared

"What of it, Armstrong?" Stockton asked again.

"No sign of activity at her guns. I believe she's going to hove to."

''Have your men stand down, but stay at the ready."

Armstrong nodded to the first lieutenant, who had re-turned to his post. "And have the band welcome them," Armstrong added. The lieutenant hurried to signal the drummer. The other ships of the American squadron did not have to be signaled; they were close enough to hear and observe the action of the *Savannah*, and they, too, busied themselves in readiness.

But the *Collingwood* gave no sign of hostility. She turned into the wind, backed her sails, and before she had shuddered to a complete stop and dropped her hooks, a longboat was launched.

Admiral Seymour stood ramrod straight in the bow of the long-boat, his hands folded behind him. The *Collingwood's* captain and first lieutenant rode seated at his back. Before he was halfway to the *Savannah*, its band was playing "God Save the Queen," and by the time he reached her deck, the *Collingwood's* band had answered with "Hail Columbia."

But as Seymour and the officers climbed over the rail and his eyes swept the 'at ready' condition aboard the *Savannah*, his face did not echo the goodwill portrayed by the ships' bands.

"Who's in charge here?" he barked.

Commander Armstrong, who has descended the poop deck ladder ahead of Stockton and Beale, answered. "Com-modore Sloat will be on deck soon, sir."

"I'm in charge," Stockton growled with authority and a little irritation as he strode up. He extended his hand to Seymour. "Commodore Robert Stockton at your service, Admiral. Welcome aboard."

Seymour made no move to accept the handshake. Rather he cut his eyes back and forth from Armstrong to Stockton. "Am I to be kept standing here on deck while the American Navy makes up its mind who's in charge?"

Stockton folded his hands behind his back and spoke very deliberately. "I'm in charge. Commander Armstrong is not aware that I've relieved Commodore Sloat of his command, as we've not formally passed the sword as of yet. If you'd care to accompany me below." Without awaiting an answer, Stockton led the way aft. The Englishmen followed, and were in turn followed by Ned and Commander Armstrong.

Stockton seated the men in the officers' mess, got the mess boys busy with coffee and tea, then excused himself and personally went to Sloat's cabin. He wanted a moment to think. Sloat informed him that he was just too ill to meet the Englishman and asked him to relay his regrets. Stockton assured him that he could handle the situation.

While Stockton was gone, Seymour turned his attention to Ned Beale. "I see your gunners were busy at work."

"Gunnery practice," Ned said, then quickly changed the subject as the mess boys entered with trays. "Tea or coffee, gentlemen?"

Stockton reentered and took a seat at the head of the table.

"I was just informing Admiral Seymour that we were engaged in gunnery practice...." Ned cautioned his boss.

"Yes, gunnery practice," Stockton said, and smiled at the admiral.

"And I also noticed a strange flag flying over the customhouse." Seymour's manner was abrupt, his eyes hard.

"A proud banner, hardly strange to this squadron, and one that will fly there forevermore." Stockton's eyes were equally hard and never flinched from the admiral's gaze.

"And what would you have done, Commodore, had you entered this harbor and found another banner flying there? One totally strange to the norm ... one, shall we say, alien to that of the country who had invited you to visit?"

"Never having been a prudent man, and had I not been a friend of both the former and latter parties, I would have gotten in one broadside against my enemy no matter how outnumbered I might have been, possibly have gone to the bottom, and left the politicians to settle the matter.'' Stockton smiled, blunting Seymour's reddening face, then quickly continued, "Our flag not only flies over Monterey, Admiral, but over Yerba Buena, Sonora, Fort Sutter, and soon over all of California. But to seriously answer your rhetorical question, I would have backed my sails, struck up the band, and my captain and first lieutenant and I would have made a social call on the other party's ship, just as you did."

The two men assessed each other for a moment while the other junior officers in the wardroom fidgeted in their seats or stirred their coffee or tea. Finally, Stockton continued.

''Of course, any other nation who would have raised her flag over Monterey would not have had substantial land forces on the eastern borders of California as we do . . . three armies of dragoons, to be exact, and unless I lack news, and England and Mexico are at war, would not have the claim against California that we do ... Mexico, the party who invited you here. Since Mexico is no longer in possession of California, let me extend the invitation of the United States. Anchor where you may in California, Admiral. The English are always welcome. Enjoy our fine harbors."

Again he got no reaction from Seymour, so he continued .

"The conclusion of this war is only a matter of a short time. So you see, Admiral, the Stars and Stripes, not the Union Jack, flies over California for good reason, and we have claimed her as the sovereign property of the United States."

"Then your claim to Monterey is based on other factors?" Seymour was beginning to waver under Stockton's barrage.

Stockton smiled. "Many other factors. And, of course, possession is nine tenths of the law. Good English law, passed to us by your own courts, I believe."

The admiral hurrumphed but said nothing more.

Stockton raised his cup and eyed each man in the room as he toasted. "God save the queen, and God bless the United States of America."

The English captain and first lieutenant watched the admiral carefully before they raised their cups. Seymour cleared his throat. "Bless Her Beautiful Majesty Queen Victoria, and the bloody States."

Stockton laughed and drank, as did each man in the room, then rose. "Mr. Beale and Commander Armstrong will be pleased to conduct you gentlemen on a tour of the *Savannah*, while the mess boys make the wardroom ready for supper. I trust you gentlemen will accept our hospitality?"

"Why not?" Seymour agreed, and the situation relaxed even more.

With a gesture of familiar goodwill, Stockton patted Seymour on the back as he followed Armstrong out of the wardroom.

"Admiral, I've a good bottle of Napoleon brandy, hauled all the way from New York for a special occasion. I trust we can toast the 'bloody States' more properly after supper." Even Seymour smiled at that.

Stockton stopped Ned and spoke to him in the privacy of the wardroom after the Englishmen were out of earshot.

"Check with Sloat and find out who we should invite from Monterey to attend this event. We might as well make political hay while the sun shines. I want the Mexicans to know that the English are not to be their saviors."

"Yes, sir," Ned said, then mischievously added, "I was unaware we had three armies entering California."

"Sometimes, Mr. Beale, even a commodore can be excused for stretching the truth, twisting it, or even publicly believing an untruth as long as he knows it's such and his action is for a good and noble cause."

"Yes, sir," Ned said.

After the tour of the ship and a quick meeting with Sloat, Ned found himself on a shore boat, a written invitation in hand for the captain who was acting commander of the Mexican presidio of Monterey; one for the alcalde of Monterey, its highest civilian position; and one for the padre of the mission. He was also instructed to call on Thomas Larkin, the American consul to Alta California.

Sloat had fully endorsed Stockton's plan, and suggested to Ned that the supper would serve to convince Monterey's civil and military bodies, and her soul, in one fell swoop.

That night, Ned had a chance to meet with a true politician. Thomas Larkin gained his respect immediately as the man listened, offered few opinions, involved the Mexicans in conversations between the English and the American officers whenever it was of benefit to the United States—beating home the point that the English had no interest in attempting to lower the American flag—and generally charmed and impressed everyone at the supper.

As Ned escorted the English officers back to their longboat late that night and watched them set out for the *Collingwood*, he wondered what would have happened had the English ship-of-the-line entered Monterey Harbor when only one or two of the American ships had been anchored there. The *Collingwood* was no match for four vessels; the Americans knew that and Seymour knew it. But Ned was sure of one thing: Had only one or even two ships been in the harbor, this incident could have become the beginning of a war with England, rather than merely a repercussion of a "possible" war with Mexico.

The next day, Stockton, with Ned in attendance as secretary, spent hours with Thomas Larkin. Each man made forays to discover the exact nature of the other's orders and presidential relationship. But neither offered the other any confidentiality's. Rather, they parried back and forth, and Stockton only managed to gain general insights into the average Mexican's nature and the condition of Californio politics. He was pleased to learn that the Californios—Mexican Californians—were divisive, with each general looking out for his own interests above that of California.

It was a disunity Stockton would put to good use.

The following day, at Stockton's orders Ned was in Monterey trying to buy or requisition stock for a land force Ned would command, when he looked up to see a major force of riders entering the pueblo.

At first he thought the ragtag bunch were Californios, then realized that one of the riders wore the field dress of a United States Marine. Ned walked to the middle of the road and watched the riders, over a hundred, approach at a brisk walk.

The spare man in the lead wore buckskins and sat straight and tall in the saddle; there was no question he was in command. Five Indians followed. Behind them rode the Marine, then a group of trappers. Stretched in no particular order behind them rode men in all manner of dress, carrying all manner of weapons. The man in the lead touched the wide brim of his felt hat as he passed Ned, recognizing the uniform, but didn't bother reining up. The Marine turned his mount out of the column and dismounted, offering Ned a casual salute.

He extended his hand. "I'm Lieutenant Archibald Gillespie."

"Lieutenant Ned Beale." Ned studied the wide-shouldered Marine with interest. His dark red hair and freckles gave him a boyish look, but his callused, powerful grip conveyed another impression.

"I take it that's Fremont?" Ned asked.

"Captain John Charles Fremont," Gillespie said with a nod. "Those are his Delaware Indian scouts behind him. The little fella who doesn't look like much is Kit Carson, behind him is Alexis Godey, then Joseph Walker. Those fellas have seen about as much of the West as any men alive. "

"How did they tie up with a Marine?"

"Special envoy from Washington." Gillespie offered no more and Ned didn't press, although he was burning with curiosity. "How about you?" Gillespie asked.

"Serving aboard the *Congress*. We just arrived day before yesterday, delivering Commodore Robert Stockton, who's taking command of the Pacific Squadron."

"Then Sloat's out of it?"

"I imagine he'll sail soon."

"We're camping on the point. If you're heading back to the ship, you might inform the commodores that we'd like to come aboard this afternoon."

"Done," Beale said. Gillespie remounted and reined away. Ned watched the column pass. So these are the Bears, he thought. An undisciplined bunch of louts, but they look hard and mean. The Mexicans had better be tough and resolute. Ned hurried back to the longboat to convey Gillespie's request to Stockton.

That afternoon, Fremont and Gillespie met with Sloat and Stockton in the *Savannah*'s wardroom. Ned and Erin O'Connel also attended.

It was the first time Sloat had personally confronted the topographer. "You've taken bold action," Sloat said, but his tone conveyed neither compliment nor condemnation.

"Only that action necessary to protect the lives and property of Americans," Fremont answered.

"At whose authority?" Sloat asked.

"Authority? I need no authority to protect American citizens... women and children."

"Then you're telling me you have no orders to instill revolution in Alta California." Sloat was beginning to look distressed, in addition to ill.

"I acted in response to the news that the citizens of Sonoma had raised a flag over that pueblo and declared California an independent republic. Castro ordered all Americans out of California, and those settlers couldn't stand another trip over the Sierras . . . even if they would have considered leaving."

"And I acted," Sloat said, his face beginning to redden, "in response to that revolt and my reports that you, and a force of Army topographers, were engaged in warfare with the Californios."

"And you acted properly."

Sloat turned to O'Connel, who busily took notes of the meeting. "You're getting this down, word for word?" he asked, and received a nod.

"Look, Commodore"—Fremont rose from his chair—"history will judge us both. Neither of us will be condemned by anyone for protecting Americans."

"I hope you're right, Captain Fremont. But again, I must insist on asking you, and Lieutenant Gillespie, you have no orders from the War Department?"

"I'm on a mapping expedition," Fremont said, but cut his eyes away. He walked to a porthole and stared out at the bay, which shimmered in the late-afternoon sun. "And you?" Sloat demanded of Gillespie.

"Commodore, if I carried orders, they would be for the ears of the orderee only."

"That's not an answer."

Gillespie, too, rose to his feet. "At the risk of seeming impertinent, sir, that's the only answer you'll receive to a question I deem improper."

"And you, sir, are impertinent."

167

Gillespie's face reddened. It was obvious he was not used to being called names by any man. "And you, sir, are my superior officer. Still, that gives you no call to be demeaning."

Sloat seemed to consider this, and Fremont turned from the porthole, his face a mask but his eyes amused.

"True," Sloat finally admitted, and sank back into his seat. "You'll forgive me, but I've been ill, and this whole business. . ." He waved his hand in a gesture of uncertainty.

"Well, gentlemen," Stockton finally stepped in, his eyes glinting with self-assurance, "whatever the reason, the gauntlet has been cast. As the new commodore of the Pacific Squadron, I'll not see a flag of the United States lowered from any staff in California. It's my intent to see it fly from every staff, over every pueblo, before this month is out."

"And I, sir"—Fremont stepped forward and extended his hand to Stockton—"assure you that you will receive the absolute cooperation of one of the finest groups of fighting men ever assembled. The California Bears!"

Stockton shook, but cautioned Fremont. "This 'Bears' thing is fine as a regimental standard, Mr. Fremont, as long as your men know it's just that. California will never be an independent republic."

"Of course, Commodore," Fremont said, but Ned got the distinct impression that the captain would have been just as pleased to continue his conquest of California—be it for the benefit of the new "republic" or the nation.

"Well," Stockton added, "the faster we defeat Castro and his hundred or so rabble lancers—"

"Hundred?" Fremont interrupted. "My reports say four hundred, and I must tell you, sir, the Californio is no rabble. He's the finest horseman I've ever seen, and though he's basically not political, he will fight. We've not seen the last of Castro, nor his cavalry."

"One hundred, four hundred, it makes little difference." Sloat waved a hand in indifference.

Little to you, as you are on your way east, Ned thought. These men have faced the Californios and the Indians, and I think I'll listen to those with experience Stockton, too, looked at Sloat with some pity. His eyes seemed to reflect Ned's feeling that the quicker Sloat sailed, the better.

Stockton invited Fremont to accompany him back to the *Congress* for supper. Ned happily accompanied Gillespie to the Bears' camp to dine with the rugged group of scouts and mountain men.

Ned decided he liked Gillespie, who, like Ned, had been sent on a special mission from the president and the War Department. He also enjoyed the company of Kit Carson, Alexis Godey, and Joseph Walker. Ned and Godey talked for hours about the interior of California, an area called the Tulares by the Mexicans, and Ned decided he must see the fertile valleys Godey described. He wondered if he would do it at the head of the land force in pursuit of a group of Californio *soldados*. It never occurred to him, after hearing tales of their confrontations with the Mexicans, that he might be pursued by the festooned lances of the Mexicans.

CHAPTER ELEVEN

Ned kept busy the next few days. His mounted force of carabineers was organized, and he spent some time drilling his
sailor volunteers, including Jourdan—who needed no drilling—in horsemanship. He enlisted Alexis Godey's help, with
the permission of Fremont. Sloat sailed aboard the Levant,
and Stockton promptly made several reassignments in the
squadron. He appointed Captain Mervine of the *Cyane* as
commander of the Savannah; Commander DuPont, executive
officer of the *Congress*, was advanced to captain and given
command of the *Cyane*.

Stockton and Fremont had been spending a great deal of
time together without benefit of a secretary as the commodore
kept Ned busy ashore. It was obvious Stockton admired the
explorer. He told Ned, "Fremont is of the same ilk as I. The
man charges forward, damning the consequences." Even so, it
surprised Ned when Stockton gave Fremont a commission as
lieutenant colonel in command of his newly formed Naval
Battalion of Mounted California Volunteer Riflemen, allowing them to retain the Bear flag as a regimental standard.
Fremont was an Army officer, and Stockton's commission
was stretching his authority—at least to Ned's way of thinking. Fremont immediately entreated Stockton to send the battalion to San Diego, where he would secure horses and drive
the Mexicans out of Los Angeles, and Captain DuPont soon
received Stockton's orders to carry Fremont and the Bears
south .

To Stockton's disappointment, Fremont, aware of the va-
garies of politics, requested written orders. Stockton up until

then had not thought Fremont the kind who would protect his political backside—but then, his father-in-law was a senator. Stockton dictated the following to Ned: "You will please embark on the *U.S.S. Cyane* with the detachment of troops under your command on Saturday afternoon. The ship, at daylight on Sunday morning, will sail for San Diego, where you will disembark your troops and procure horses for them, and will make every necessary preparation to march through the country at a moment's notice from me; . . . The object of this movement is to take or get between the Colorado and General Castro. I will leave Monday on this ship to San Pedro so as to arrive there about the time you may be expected to have arrived in San Diego."

On the last day of July, Sam Brannan and his band of Mormons aboard the *Brooklyn* sailed into the expansive San Francisco harbor, prepared to take over California. They found the Stars and Stripes already flying over the fort at Yerba Buena.

Ned, acting as sailing master again, with his carabineers back to their old jobs for a short time, took the *Congress* south and landed in San Pedro. The few Mexicans there, working among the old hide warehouses, looked on with curiosity as the sailors-turned-soldiers disembarked the ship and formed a unit of marching men. Ned was dispatched to round up mounts, but most of the stock seemed to have disappeared. The ship's carpenters had been busily constructing wheels and carriages for a few of the ship's cannons, and caissons for the shot and powder, and the finest mules Ned could find were harnessed to them.

Stockton, mounted on a tall sorrel stallion, took the lead, and the band struck up a lively marching song as the party set out. Just south of Los Angeles, Fremont and his party caught up with Stockton.

Fremont, too, rode a fine bay Mexican stallion, only his horse had its mane and tail festooned with ribbons decorated by the friendly Mexicans of San Diego. Pathfinder Fremont reined up beside Stockton, and Alexis Godey fell in beside Ned, who rode just behind.

"Damn few horses," Fremont reported. "Most of the men of San Diego rode out before we landed. . . pushing the local livestock out in front of them. Seems they joined up with Castro."

Stockton gave him a worried glance, then studied the flat, sandy terrain between his force and Pueblo Los Angeles in the distance. "Wherever they are, it's not on this Bat field. Seems we have clear sailing into the pueblo."

"Don't think so," Godey said, surprising his horse up beside Fremont and Stockton, who looked at the buckskin-clad mountain man curiously. They followed his gaze.

"Shade of that scrub oak grove up yonder." Godey pointed the long musket he held in one hand. Stockton raised his hand, and the body of men following came to a halt. He reached behind his saddle and fished a telescope out of a tolled blanket tied there, brought it to his eye, and studied the spot over a mile away where Godey had pointed.

"By God," Stockton mumbled without lowering the glass. "Damned if there's not a hundred or more men among those oaks."

"Hun' an' twenty-five. . .be my guess," Godey said. He spat a stream of tobacco juice into the sand.

"Should we ride on and act as if they're not discovered?" Stockton asked, but before he could get an answer, two riders broke from the oaks and, at an easy lope, headed straight for the advancing troop of Americans.

"No need," Fremont answered, but he and his men continued to search the plain for signs of other Mexicans.

Stockton dismounted and walked forward as soon as he realized the riders flew a white flag from a lance one of them carried. He stood with hands folded behind his back, the picture of nonchalance, but spoke back over his shoulder.

"Keep your carabineers at the ready, Mr. Beale," he instructed.

But Ned already had his group of mounted riflemen spread in a long line in front of the force—most of whom were afoot. Stockton looked as if he would retreat as the hard-riding Californios got very close before they jerked rein, dismounted, and hit the ground in front of him in a cloud of dust.

The taller of the two vaqueros, in leather trousers decorated with silver conchos, a flat-brimmed hat pushed back off his head, and a short, snug-fitting jacket, stepped forward and extended his hand. The shorter remained mounted, his eyes nervously searching the army of men. The tall man drew himself up to his full and impressive bearing.

"Welcome to El Pueblo de Nuestra Senora la Riena de Los Angeles de Porciuncula. I am Jose Maria Flores, formerly an officer of the Army of Mexico."

Stockton accepted his hand. "Commodore Robert Stockton, currently of the American Navy. . . . I presume you are surrendering your forces?"

The tall man, eye to eye with the commodore, studied Stockton for a moment, then smiled.

"General Castro and our governor. Pio Pico, have departed Alta California for Mexico. We, the citizens of this pueblo, see no reason why we cannot receive you in peace, if peace is what you desire."

"Then you are surrendering? I see you have a considerable force of men in the trees."

"Peaceful men, men of the land who wish to return to their farms and ranchos."

"Then, sir," Stockton pressed, "are you surrendering your forces?"

"My men will lay down their arms if allowed to go home in peace."

Stockton seemed satisfied with that. "Bring your officers into Los Angeles this evening. We will draw an official document of surrender—"

"We will be pleased to reach an agreement with you, but surrender sounds as if we dispute your presence. It seems an admission of some kind. A peace agreement, if you don't mind, Commodore, with all men and officers free to return to their work."

"We seek no prisoners, Senior Flores. We consider all citizens of California to be citizens of the United States. . .until they demonstrate otherwise. There will be stipulations, such as no armed aggression against the United States, but as my predecessor wrote in his proclamation, you are all welcome as citizens."

Flores again extended his hand. "My men will return to their homes, and my officers and I will be in the pueblo at sundown." After they shook, Flores swung easily up into the saddle. Almost as an afterthought, he added, "Los Angeles is a peaceful pueblo, Commodore. Her people go about their business with no mischief in their hearts. Please ask your troop to bear that in mind. I would hate to hear of an accidental shooting, or of mistreatment of any kind."

"As would I," Stockton assured him. "We want business as usual."

Flores resettled his flat-brimmed hat, gave the stallion a touch of his big roweled spurs, and rode away as easily as he had approached. The other man, who had not uttered a word, followed. Stockton watched as Flores spoke with his own men; then they dispersed in every direction.

Stockton returned to his men, and in a voice loud enough for the troops in the lead to hear, announced, "That, gentlemen, corks it. Pueblo Los Angeles is ours, as well as all of Alta California. Her governor and the head of her armed forces, such as they were, are on their way to Mexico."

Fremont looked disappointed, but joined in the hip, hip, hoorays that followed.

The little army marched into Los Angeles with the band playing.

That evening, seated around the desk of the former governor in the pueblo's government house, Flores and his officers, including the short man who had been with him, and who turned out to be Pio Pico's brother, Andres, signed a parole agreement. They agreed to return to their homes, keep the peace, and not bear arms against the Americans. The agreement was sealed with supper and many toasts with the pueblo's excellent red wine.

Fremont spent only a few days in Los Angeles, then left recently promoted Marine major Archibald Gillespie and a force of fifty men in charge of the presidio with orders to maintain martial law, and returned to San Pedro and the *Congress*. Fremont, still looking for some action, convinced Stockton that he should ride in pursuit of Castro and Pio, just to make sure they had really left Alta California. During the pursuit, he found eight buried cannons Castro's force had elected to hide rather than attempt crossing the desert with, but no sign of the governor or general .

Once back aboard ship, Ned returned to his normal duties, and his first was to take a dispatch from a confident and ebullient Commodore Robert Stockton.

"Address this to Secretary Bancroft . . . in your best hand, Beale," Stockton advised, sitting back in his desk chair. Ned took pen in hand and waited. Stockton paced the floor.

"I entered the famous city of Angels . . . and took unmolested possession. The flag of the United States is flying at every commanding position, and California is in undisputed possession. Thus, in less than a month after I assumed command of the United States forces in California, we have chased the Mexican Army more than three hundred miles along the coast, pursued them thirty miles in the interior of their own country, routed and dispersed them, secured the territory of the United States, ended the war, restored peace and harmony among the people, and put a civil government into successful operation."

When Ned had finished taking the dictation, a midshipman informed them that Fremont had returned from the desert. Stockton sent word he wanted to see the lieutenant colonel, then told Fremont he wanted him to send his best scout to Washington with the dispatches immediately. Fremont sent Kit Carson, who was pleased to carry the message, as it meant he would see his wife, Josefa, in Taos along the way. He set out immediately with a force of fifteen men, carrying not only Stockton's dispatches but also letters from Fremont to his wife and his father-in-law, Senator Thomas Hart Benton. Carson also carried three letters from Ned Beale—one to his mother and two to Mary Edwards.

Stockton sent Fremont and his Bears north along the coast with the order to confirm the American occupation and possession, and raise the flag in every pueblo along the way. The *Congress* sailed for Monterey.

Stockton began disbursing his officers to various pueblos, bringing military government to California.

For the next two months, Ned Beale found himself as military governor of San Jose, where, attending many gracious fiestas and fandangos given by the local dons, he began to learn about and appreciate the Californio way of life. In the meantime, Stockton, in Monterey, appointed Fremont as provisional governor of the newly acquired Territory of California, and, this matter behind him, prepared plans and equipment for an invasion of Acapulco. The news of a formal declaration of war had been received, and Stockton felt more confident than ever—and he wanted to strike at the heart of the enemy, Mexico City. His "field" victories made him believe that the Navy was far more versatile than had ever been believed before.

Fremont and his Bears had made it north along the coast, raising the flag, spreading the word, until they reached Monterey. Stockton immediately sent them inland in northern California to do the same.

On September 21, Ned had returned to the capital to report his progress to Stockton, when a rider stumbled off a horse that collapsed in front of the customhouse in Monterey.

The purser immediately brought the exhausted man to Stockton on board the *Congress*. Ned and the commodore received him in Stockton's cabin.

"I'm John Brown," the tall, slender rider offered. "Five days ago, I hightailed it out of Los Angeles—"

"Five days!" Stockton exclaimed, staring at the man in disbelief. "Why, man, that's five hundred miles."

"Five days, Commodore! I killed me more'n one mustang on the way, and had to travel shank's mare thirty miles to boot, carrying my tack, after the Mexes shot my sorrel out from under me—damn good horse, too!"

"My God, man, sit down." Stockton pulled out a chair for Brown, who collapsed into it, then nodded his thanks to Ned when handed a mug of rum. He downed the drink in one long swallow, backhanded the dribble away, and continued.

"Major Gillespie and the men of Los Angeles were under siege when I rode off. He'd been negotiatin' with the Mexes, who want him to leave with his men. But they want him to leave his arms and the money you left him to run the pueblo. . . reparations, the Mexes say. He says to tell you he won't lay down his arms nor give up the money. He says if he gets out of it, he's headin' for San Pedro. Over three hundred Mexicans there got 'em surrounded, an' more comin'... leastways I spotted more on the road."

"Who's at the bottom of this?" Stockton's eyes had hardened, and his jaw clamped tightly.

"Don Juan Flores an' a bunch o' others."

''The lying, deceitful scum; he's broken his pledge,'' Stockton sputtered.

"Truth is, I didn't much cotton to Gillespie's policies none myself."

''What do you mean?'' Stockton asked, taking a seat.

"Martial law, he called it."

Stockton noticeably flinched, for it had been his own order.

"Curfews, no cantinas for the men, no firearms to be displayed, no public gatherings, including parties, and the Mexicans love their parties. Arrested several men for being out after dark. Mexican way of life wouldn't tolerate such. He deported one man to Old Mexico for stealin' . . . then the rumor flew that he was gonna hang a few. That wrapped it, an' ol' Flores put the bow on it. I got ta tell ya', Commodore, he coulda did better with those folks. As it was, they was shootin' the hell out of the government house when the major sent me out, and tried to shoot the hell outta me—and me what's been with 'em for more'n five years. I even got me a Mex name, Juan Flaco."

Stockton turned to Ned. "Mr. Beale, prepare to sail on the morning tide. Where's Fremont?"

"Still in the central valley or Sonoma."

"Then take a ship's boat. . .in fact, take three rigged to sail and twenty of your carabineers, find him, and bring him back. I'm dispatching *Mervine* and the *Savannah* to San Pedro in case Gillespie and his men have reached that port and need evacuation. As soon as Fremont and his men arrive, we'll sail to San Pedro. This time, Flores and his band of traitors will rot in jail."

"I could sleep right here, Commodore, but a bed would be more to my likin'." Brown stretched and yawned.

"As soon as you eat, Mr. Brown, we will find you a place to rest."

"I don't know if I have the strength to eat," Brown said, and rested his head on his folded arms on Stockton's table. He was snoring before Ned shut the door behind him.

In three days, Ned returned with Fremont and his officers on the boat, with Fremont's Bears following on horseback.

When Ned presented himself to Stockton, the commodore was shocked at his condition. Ned's eyes were almost swollen shut, and his body was covered with welts.

"You look like you've been rolling in a hornets' nest," Stockton said with concern.

"I learned a little California woodsmanship ... the hard way," Ned said sheepishly. "I built a signal fire from oak branches to bring the other boats to an island the colonel and I had selected as a night camp. . .only I used poison oak. I've never been more miserable.

Fremont attempted to convince Stockton that he needed the stock they had transported aboard the Navy ships, as he had had so much trouble locating horses in San Diego, and that he and the Bears should make the trip on horseback. Stockton disagreed, and had the Bears board the merchantman *Sterling*. On October 13 that ship and the *Congress* sailed. On route, the two ships became separated in the fog, and the *Sterling* encountered a merchant ship, *Vandalia*, and learned that Captain Mervine, who had sailed earlier on the *Savannah*, had attempted to retake Los Angeles without awaiting Stockton and been soundly defeated by the Mexicans at Dominguez Rancho. Mervine had buried six and had scores wounded.

Fremont, using this change in events as an excuse to ignore Stockton's orders, decided to go back to Monterey, get his stock, and continue south on horseback.

When Stockton and Beale, aboard the *Congress*, arrived in San Pedro, they found the *Savannah* anchored well offshore. Captain Mervine had a boat launched and alongside as the *Congress* dropped her hooks. Major Archibald Gillespie

179

climbed the ship's rope ladder behind the captain. Stockton, with Ned in attendance, received them in his cabin.

"Major Gillespie," Stockton began, "I'm glad to see you made it safely to San Pedro. No losses, I trust?" Stockton's look made it clear he was displeased at the turn of events.

"You mean at Los Angeles ... only six wounded. At Dominguez Rancho, I'm afraid it was much different.'' Gillespie cast a look at Mervine that would have wilted a smaller man.

"Dominguez?" Stockton asked, confused.

Mervine stepped forward. "If you don't mind; Major . . . ? Commodore, we decided to strike quickly, and took a force of three hundred men to retake Los Angeles—''

"I specifically ordered you to San Pedro, to relieve and evacuate Major Gillespie and his men. and instructed you to await us!" Stockton began to redden, his fists clamped at his sides, his jaw thrust forward. "How many men did you lose at this Dominguez Rancho?"

"Nine; six there, and three have expired since."

"You lost nine men as a direct result of disobeying my orders?"

"We. . .we lost nine men, and had over thirty wounded as. . .as a result"—Mervine began to stammer—"a result of taking what we consider. . . considered propitious action. Action taken after acquiring intelligence you had no way of knowing. Events had changed drastically. It was reported that the Mexicans were low on powder, and we didn't want to give them time—"

"Not so low they couldn't kill nine good American boys!" Stockton's voice rang through the room, and Molo peeked out from the pantry. The look he received from Stockton sent him scurrying back.

"The damned Mexicans had a cannon, and kept firing and dragging the damn thing away with those leather lines before we could attack. They were well mounted, and rode like bloody demons."

"And you had no cannon?" Stockton asked with an incredulous look on his face.

Mervine did not answer, but Gillespie cleared his throat and offered, "Captain Mervine, against my field advice, elected not to wait on the mounting of ship's cannon."

Mervine looked at Gillespie as if he were a traitor and spat his own invective. "However, Major Gillespie encouraged the attempt to retake Los Angeles, and provided the obviously incorrect information that the Mexicans were low on powder. And all of us had been told they were cowards.. .."

"Enough!" Stockton stood red and quivering. He took a moment to collect himself, then turned to Ned. "Mr. Beale," he said with slow deliberation, "later today I want you to take statements, individually, from each officer involved in this debacle. Full and complete statements, witnessed and signed by each man." Stockton turned back to the two officers. "You two. . .are. . .excused."

Both men saluted and turned to leave. Ned noticed as they moved away that Mervine's shoulders slumped and he shuffled from the room, while Gillespie's were thrown back and he strode out, the picture of confidence.

Stockton paced the cabin for a moment. "This drastically changes our plans, Ned." Stockton spoke aloud as he thought things through. "I'm sure that a field force is on their way here, if not already in California's borders. . .unless that force was circumvented by my apparently premature dispatch. We must, as we indicated in that damned dispatch to Washington, must have California under control." Stockton hung his head, uncertain for only a moment. "We'll look like such fools if we don't." He walked to the port and recomposed himself, then turned back to Ned, his eyes full of fire again.

"I want you personally to take charge of getting a major field force ready. And this time, I mean ready. Cannons and caissons properly mounted. Cavalry drilled to perfection."

"Do I begin here in San Pedro?" Ned asked.

"Why not—"

The door rattled as someone knocked, and Ned answered. A young midshipman stood nervously, and addressed the commodore. "The exec requests you on the poop deck, sir."

Ned followed Stockton topside, and they stood looking at the scene onshore. Up a ravine leading away from the bay, and between two large stands of live oaks, they could see horses galloping by, visible only through a narrow space.

A longboat with a wood-gathering shore party clattered alongside the *Congress*, and the sailors created a clamor as they scrambled aboard. The bosun in charge of the party hurried aft and saluted Stockton, handing him a small piece of folded parchment.

"A dog showed up where we were cutting wood and had this tied to his collar," the bosun offered.

Stockton unfolded the piece of cigarette paper and read aloud:

> Gringos:
>   Have the coffee ready, we will soon be
> in your camp.

Even as Stockton read, a group of a dozen Mexicans rode down the beach at a gallop, waving their flat hats and using their quirts on their high-stepping horses.

"Gunnery practice, gentlemen," Stockton suggested, and the ship's officers jumped to. Soon the deck rocked with the repeated shock of cannons and nostrils stung with the pungent odor of gun powder as the ship's gunners fired round after round at the galloping Mexicans.

The Mexicans kept appearing out of the scrub oak, riding like the wind down the beach and in and out of the few hide and tallow warehouses, then disappearing back in the brush. Frustrated, the gunners fired until they knocked the corner off a small hide warehouse, splintering its timbers and knocking the building off its foundation. The Americans tired of the fruitless game at about the same time the Mexicans did. Still the stream of horses and an occasional rider showed, passing between the oaks up the draw. The officers on board came to the conclusion that there were thousands of horses, and hundreds of riders pushing them—all pouring into San Pedro to bring the full force of the Californios against the Americans.

Stockton waved to Ned to join him below, and decided as they returned to his cabin, "There's too big a risk to drill ashore here. We'll sail to San Diego, and you can train your force there. I don't know where the hell Colonel Fremont is," he grumbled.

Andres Pico, Pio Pico's brother and now the second-in-command of the newly formed Mexican forces, sat on a hill overlooking San Pedro. He watched the American forces sail away. He allowed himself a loud guffaw, to the joy of the vaqueros who rode with him. He had kept his one hundred men in shifts, driving a hundred head of horses around and around a small hill, knowing that the Americans, watching the "huge herd" gallop by, must think the horses were thousands and the men at least several hundred.

CHAPTER TWELVE

In San Diego, Stockton found that the small garrison of Americans had been overrun, and had retreated to a merchantman in the harbor. He landed a force that far outnumbered the few Californios, and the Mexicans withdrew. He immediately began building a fort on a rise overlooking the harbor, Presidio Hill. Within days, Fort Stockton was a formidable log and dirt structure.

Stockton was surprised to find the town almost devoid of horses and cattle—the Mexicans had driven them out ahead of them. By the third day, the beef was gone, and foraging parties drove in swine, goats, and even chickens from the nearby ranchos. Stockton was wise enough to know that he would soon incur the wrath of the whole populace if he took the very food off their tables.

Ned spent his days visiting nearby ranchos, requisitioning riding stock and searching for cattle. Despite all his efforts, the Americans were desperately short of horses and mules, animals necessary to mount any field operation.

After the fort was finished, Stockton called Ned to his makeshift headquarters there.

"I received word," Stockton said, "that Fremont met a merchantman when we were separated in the fog, and returned to Monterey for his riding stock." Stockton began to pace. "To be frank, I was angered at his action, but now that you're having so much trouble rounding up horses . . . maybe he was right."

Ned was unaccustomed to seeing the commodore doubt himself. Ned put it off to the hard and desperate work of finishing the fort. Noting the deep circles under the commodore's eyes, Ned attempted to raise his spirits.

"You had no way of knowing the Mexicans would drive their stock out in front of them—"

"Don't patronize me!" Stockton snapped. He turned away to stare out the gun slots of his roughly constructed headquarters building, rubbing the back of his neck.

"I wasn't patronizing, Commodore," Ned said quietly. "If Mervine had obeyed your orders, we would have had no losses and could have retaken Los Angeles by sheer force of numbers."

Stockton turned back apologetically, but then his look hardened. "Bandini says there are hundreds of horses and thousands of cattle at Warner Rancho, fifty miles inland. Take your carabineers and see if you can collect them . . . at least as many as your thirty men can drive."

"Yes, sir." Ned was pleased to see Stockton's confidence return. "However, I've only got forty head of riding stock, and two thirds of them have been ridden hard for the past three days. They'll be crow bait if I make a hundred-mile round trip with them."

"Then take only ten men." Stockton ordered quickly, then seemed to sag under the weight of his decision.

Ned had seen no real action. Others had been in firefights with the Californios, but he had not ... and he secretly envied them. War meant battles, but his had been only with the technical aspects. Now he had a chance to ride into the heart of the country he knew lay controlled by Andres Pico and Jose Maria Flores.

"The ten horses still in good shape are the best of the lot, Commodore. We'll have no problem riding out of trouble if we find ourselves facing a superior force."

Stockton still seemed apprehensive about the order, but they needed the stock if they were to do anything other than hold the ports of California. And they needed the cattle if he was going to avoid starving the citizens of San Diego and his own men. He hated the thought of the army arriving and doing the real work of conquering California, particularly after he had sent that damned dispatch to Bancroft—a dispatch that now seemed to Stockton to be full of braggadocio. And worse, one that was incorrect. He certainly did not have control of California, nor did he have an effective government set up. He had to have horses if he was to control California.

He put a hand on Ned's shoulder. "I apologize for being snappish. I'm a little weary. Be careful, Ned."

"Yes, sir, and I'll return with stock if there're any there."

Ned selected Alexis Godey and Jourdan among the men who would accompany him. William R. Manchester was also in Ned's selections. Manchester was a man who had distinguished himself repeatedly. Ned named him second-in-command and appointed Godey and Jourdan as scouts.

The little force set out an hour before dawn and rode the first day without any sight of Californios, other than a shepherd and a couple of vaqueros who were busily cleaning out a spring. They waved good-naturedly as the Americans passed. That night they camped on a brush-covered hillside, careful to find good forage for the stock. By noon of the second day they passed through San Pasqual, an Indian village of several hundred, where they received information that Andres Pico and over a hundred *soldados* had been in the village only the day before. Ned was convinced that luck was with them on this trip and that they would find the stock they needed.

They reached Warner Rancho on the third morning, driving two dozen head of prime horses they had come across on the way. As he had done each time he had requisitioned stock, Ned issued a chit to the segundo, the foreman, at Warner's, for three dollars a head for horses--the number to be determined later—and for a dollar and half a head for cattle—the value of their hides less fifty cents for the skinning and treating that had not been done. They enjoyed the hospitality of the rancho that night, and set out at dawn with directions to two meadows where they would be sure to find both cattle and horses.

By noon, they drove over two hundred head of stock in front of them. Ned was elated at his success, but now the problem was to get them back to San Diego. The trip going, with only ten riders raising dust, was easy compared to the return. He sent Godey and Jourdan to scout, even though it left him with only eight men to drive the large herd, and instructed them to range more than a mile ahead on the port and starboard, and to hotfoot it back at any sign of Mexican *soldados*.

By late that afternoon Ned, riding point, saw Godey returning at a gallop. The scout jerked rein and slid to a stop. "Twenty or so Mexes, Lieutenant. Just over that next rise."

"Did they see you?"

Godey flashed him a hard look but ignored the slight on his woodsmanship. "Hide the stock in that draw yonder. I don't think they be headin' this way. Jus' settle the dust and we won't be found out."

"Where's Jourdan?"

"That zambo is a hand. He'll take care of hisse'f."

Godey reined his horse around and glanced back over his shoulder. "I'll keep an eye on 'em."

"Don't be seen," Ned said without thinking.

"Jus' get the stock quiet and out of sight." Godey gave spurs to his mount.

As Ned gave the orders to turn the bawling and neighing herd, he was convinced he could hide them well enough; the draw was narrow and deep. But keeping them quiet was another thing. He left William Manchester at the canyon mouth as sentry. They settled down in the narrow canyon, its walls covered with chaparral poked through with an occasional rock ledge, the bottom with cottonwoods watered by a little trickle, and waited.

Within an hour, the herd had finished off the few sprouts of green grass along the trickle, and were trying the patience of the riders by attempting to wander up the steep banks or up or down the canyon. Finally, after two hours, Godey returned.

"I think they're moving on. We can sit tight another hour, then it should be safe—"

His report was interrupted by William Manchester, running up the draw. He shouted before he reached them. "Jourdan coming, and a bunch of Mexes right behind him." Manchester turned and started back down the draw at a run.

Ned quickly assigned two men to stay with the herd, and directed his remaining men to take the high country along the deep draw.

"Don't fire until I do," he commanded, then ran in Manchester's footsteps, with Godey at his side.

Before they reached the mouth of the canyon, Jourdan pounded through, hunkered low in the saddle, his mustang dripping with lather. He did not see William Manchester in the rocks as he galloped by, but did see Ned and Godey, who ran down the canyon's narrow bottom. Before he reached them, the force of Mexicans, twenty strong, carrying muskets and long, festooned lances, reined into the canyon's mouth. Manchester, still fifty yards in front of Ned and Godey, now joined by a panting Jourdan, rose up from the rocks with his carbine at his shoulder.

His shot echoed up the canyon and knocked the *soldado* in the lead from the saddle, causing the others to rein away in confusion. A Mexican rider dove from the saddle as his horse took the steep bank and went over backward.

The others spun and spurred out of the canyon, their afoot comrade scampering along behind, their wounded man rolling in the dust in pain.

Ned breathed a sigh of relief until a half dozen Mexicans returned, their horses tattooing the trail at a dead run, their lances poised in front of them. William Manchester madly attempted to reload his carbine; Godey and Ned slammed theirs to their shoulders. Both rifles barked before the Mexicans galloped down on Manchester, and one of the riders in the lead doubled in his saddle. Ned snatched the Allan's revolver from his waist and snapped off two shots, but the distance was too great. Musket balls whined over his head as the men up the canyon behind did their best to come to Manchester's aid.

William Manchester abandoned any hope of reloading in time and grabbed the carbine by the barrel to use as a bludgeon. He leapt from the rocks, swinging the carbine at the nearest rider—but another *soldado* lunged with his lance, and the bloodied point appeared out the front of Manchester's abdomen.

Jourdan's rifle spat fire, and the *soldado* grabbed his shoulder and released the lance, but it stayed with Manchester as he staggered forward. The Mexicans reined away. One of them hooked arms with the dismounted wounded man and swung him up behind. Ned and Godey fired after them.

Jourdan, Ned, and Godey scrambled to reload, then ran forward to help Manchester, who had gone to his knees in the canyon bottom. Ned reached him first, moved around behind him, and grabbed the lance while Jourdan and Godey grabbed the wounded man's shoulders to hold him steady. Ned jerked the lance from his back and felt the sickening rasp of metal against bone. He ripped his own shirttail away as Godey pulled Manchester's up, exposing the ugly puckered wound in his back—a wound pumping blood. Ned tore another width of shirttail and tied them together to make a bandage that encircled the man, binding the wound front and back.

When they finished, he glanced at Godey, who caught his eye and shook his head in resignation—but Ned bowed his neck.

"He's going to be all right. Get up where you can watch out," he instructed Godey, who spun on his heel and began climbing the canyon side to watch for another attack.

"Two of you make a drag," Ned ordered. He saw the two men he had left with the horses and cattle galloping down the draw toward them. He waited until they reined up. "I thought I told you two to stay with the stock!"

"We heard the shootin'—"

"That stock is the reason this man sheds his blood. The next man who disobeys me will spend the rest of his enlistment in chains. Do you understand?" Ned's eyes flashed fire.

The two men nodded, spun their horses, and galloped back up the canyon. Ned pointed at two more men. "You two stay here with Godey until we're ready to pull out." He glanced up the canyon wall to where Godey sat casually in the crotch of two rocks, but his eyes busily searched the area outside the canyon's mouth.

Ned yelled up to him. "Godey, you're second-in command now!"

Alexis Godey gave a casual nod of the head, unimpressed with Ned's confidence.

They were able to make the last day, pushing the herd at a trot—no longer burdened with the drag. After hauling him in a travois for a half day as he continued to fail, they had buried William Manchester along the trail under the shade of a laurel grove in a green meadow looking up at the taller mountains in the distance.

They saw no more of the Mexicans and arrived at Fort Stockton, to the welcome greeting of Stockton and the hungry troops, at nightfall the next night.

That night, after a meal of beef stew, Ned gathered around the campfire with Godey, Jourdan, and the other scouts. Uncommonly quiet, Ned listened to the men retell glories of the trip. Each time he was asked about the exploits, he managed only a shake of the head and a tight smile. And each time he thought of what happened, he again felt the rasp of iron on bone when he pulled the lance from Manchester's bloodied back.

Lying in his bedroll that night, staring up at the thousand stars, he decided that there was only one glory in war: finishing it with good purpose. He hoped he had seen the last of bloodshed, but somehow he sensed it was just beginning.

The next morning, one of the local Indians, whom Stockton had employed as scout, rode in with the news that Andres Pico was in San Pasqual with fifty or more men. It was the first week of December, and San Diego was experiencing a rare overcast. The smell of rain lay in the air, and an unusual chill permeated the bones.

Stockton called his officers together. Major Archibald Gillespie had been kept busy with building the fort and reconnoitering supplies. Stockton had avoided assigning him to any duty that would bring him into contact with the citizens of the pueblo of San Diego, for Bandini had informed Stockton that Gillespie was the most hated of Americans. His name became the rallying cry for the *soldados*.

But Ned had just returned from a strenuous trip where he had lost a man and gathered almost three hundred head of horses and cattle. He assigned Gillespie the task of raiding Pico's camp.

Gillespie's sixty men were almost ready when another rider arrived at Fort Stockton with, at least to Commodore Stockton, disappointing news. Edward Stokes, an Englishman with a rancho near Warner's, carried a letter from U.S. Army brigadier general S. W. Kerany. Stockton called his officers together and Ned read the letter aloud:

> I, this afternoon, reached Warner's Ranch, escorted by a party of First Regiment Dragoons. I come by orders of the

president of the United States. We left
Santa Fe on the twenty-fifth of September, having taken possession of New
Mexico, annexed it to the United States,
established a civil government in that territory, and secured order, peace, and qui-
etness there. If you can send a party to
open communications with us, on the
route to this place, and to inform us of the
state of affairs in California, I wish you
would do so, and as quickly as possible.
Your express by Mr. Carson was met on
the Del None, and your mail must have
reached Washington at least ten days
since. You might use the bearer, Mr.
Stokes, to conduct your party to this
place. The fear of this letter falling into
Mexican hands prevents me from writing
more.

The news was disappointing in that Stockton wanted the Navy to conquer California, and it was by no means accomplished. While Stockton absorbed this new state of affairs,
another rider entered camp. Rafael Machado had deserted
Pico. He brought the disturbing report that another hundred
men had joined the general's ranks. Stockton breathed a sigh
of relief. Had he gone ahead and sent sixty men against one
hundred fifty, it could have been another disaster.

Stockton pondered the message and discussed it with his
officers.

"I get the impression that Kearny is in some kind of distress. But, by God, I would think the man would have stated
the same, or at least given us a hint of his problem."

"The reference," Ned offered, "to the letter falling into
Mexican hands would seem to indicate he was not telling all."

"Whatever the problem, let's get a force of men out there with a dispatch." Stockton turned to Gillespie. "Take the best of the horses and a flying force of twenty-five of the best men and go on to Warner's. I'll have a dispatch written by the time you've gathered your force and mounted. . .and Gillespie"—Stockton's voice hardened—"don't try to take on the whole damned Mexican Army by yourself. Just get the dispatch through and lead the dragoons back here."

Gillespie saluted as if it were a legitimate order, offered in earnest—since his commander undoubtedly knew he would try the whole Mexican Army, alone if necessary.

Stockton dismissed the rest of his officers, and Ned took a seat at the small folding table used as a desk and took pen in hand.

The commodore dictated: "Captain Gillespie is well informed in relation to the present state of things in California and will give you all the needed information. I have this evening received information, by a deserter from the rebel camp, of the arrival of an additional force in the neighborhood of a hundred men, which makes their number about one hundred fifty. I send with Captain Gillespie, as a guide, the deserter, that you may make inquiries of him, and if you see fit, endeavor to surprise them."

"Usual closing?" Ned asked without looking up.

"No," Stockton said. "Sign it . . . let's see . . . sign it . . . Robert F. Stockton, commander in chief and governor of the Territory of California."

This time, Ned did raise his eyes. Stockton's look brooked no argument, and Ned did as told. But he could not help but offer a comment at Stockton's bold move.

"That should make conditions in California clear to General Kearny. I imagine you've given some thought to the fact he may carry other orders?"

"Perfectly clear," Stockton said, but his tone did not carry the confidence of his words, and he did not address Ned's question.

Ned folded and sealed the parchment, then rose and changed the subject.

''Commodore, I would like to carry this personally."

"You only just returned, Ned. Don't you think—" "I'm well rested, and I've got a bone to pick with Pico's men. Manchester's death rests heavily on my shoulders."

Stockton put a hand on Ned's shoulder, and his eyes softened. "Men will fall under your command, Mr. Beale. You cannot personally avenge every one."

"I understand, sir. But allow me the opportunity to avenge this first one."

"All right. But with luck, Pico will turn tail and run at the sight of a platoon of dragoons."

"Somehow, I don't think so, Commodore. Not this time. This time the wolf will fight. He tasted blood at Dominguez Rancho . . . and the taste of victory whetted his appetite."

"Take a few of your best with you," Stockton said. Turning, he folded his hands behind his back and stared out the gun slots as Ned left with the dispatch in his pocket.

Ned found Jourdan and Alexis Godey, who immediately insisted they accompany him, and the three of them joined with Gillespie, the deserter, Machado, and Gillespie's twenty-six volunteers—this time with a four-pound cannon in tow. By the time they were ready to ride out, another ten men, Anglo citizens of San Diego and Mexican Californios sympathetic with the American cause, joined them.

As they rode out of Fort Stockton, it began to rain. Ned reached behind him and dug his spare powder out of his bedroll. He checked the cotton bag for dampness, then pulled out a piece of oilcloth he used to cover the wet ground under his bedroll, wrapped the two cotton bags carefully, and re-stowed them. The men turned their collars up, pulled their hats low, and girded themselves for a long, wet ride.

The afternoon of the next day, they loped into Warner's Rancho and dismounted in front of a squat, wide-shouldered General Kearny and his exhausted and trail-worn officers.

Kearny's men were enjoying the first meal of fresh beef in over six weeks, other than the Missouri elk—mule—they had been relegated to eating.

Ned introduced himself and handed the parchment to Kearny, who wrinkled his brow and motioned for Ned and Gillespie to follow him into his tent.

The general whipped his hat off and wiped the water from his face with a kerchief, then unfolded the parchment. He read silently, grunted, and flung the parchment aside unceremoniously.

"This Commodore Stockton has declared himself king of California?"

Ned cleared his throat. "Commodore Stockton has been at this for some time, General. It was necessary for him to establish some command for the Californios to look up to."

"Fill me in, gentlemen." Kearny motioned for the two officers to take seats in folding chairs surrounding a small map table, and sat down. "I'd offer coffee, but we've been out for three weeks."

Ned rose and stuck his head out the tent flap to yell at Jourdan, "Break out the coffee! These men look as if they could use some!"

The other dragoon officers who had gathered outside the tent smiled at the thought of hot coffee, their breath white in the cold as they blew into cupped hands. Ned returned to his chair.

"I notice your stock is broken down and sorry-looking."

"It's been a rough trip on men and stock," Kearny agreed. Then a short man in buckskins and fur hat stuck his head in the doorway.

"Kit!" Ned said. He and Gillespie rose and extended hands. "I thought you'd be in Washington."

"General Kearny here turned me 'round in New Mexico. Broken-Hand Fitzpatrick carried the commodore's packet on. I'm sure it's been a'gatherin' dust in Polk's office for several days. I just wanted to howdy you boys." He nodded and backed out of the tent after an uncharacteristic full paragraph of speech—it was normally yea and nay with Kit, and little more.

"We'll come jaw with you as soon as General Kearny's through with us," Ned called after him, then turned his attention back to Kearny, and was surprised to note his obvious antagonism toward Kit.

"The man actually had the effrontery to argue with me regarding leading me back here," the general groused.

"He's an independent sort," Ned said, not bothering to inform the general of a fact he already knew, that Kit Carson was beholden to no man or army.

Gillespie and Ned filled the general in on the past few months' activities in California, including the news that Pico and his *soldados* were rumored to be nearby—just outside of San Pasqual. When Ned related Fremont's appointment as provisional governor, Ned could see the general's hackles rise.

"Governor! A shavetail colonel in the topographical corps. And a colonel by the grace of a Navy commodore. A commodore who only yesterday signed a dispatch as 'governor.' Pardon me, gentlemen, but this whole thing's a laugh." But he was not laughing.

"I'm sure the commodore did what he thought was right, and, General, he was acting on the orders of the secretary of the Navy," Ned managed, as the general reached over and pulled a slightly damp cigar out of Gillespie's pocket.

"You don't mind," the general said. Oblivious to whether Gillespie minded or not, he bit the end off and spat it on the din floor. He lit the cigar, having to work at it to quell the dampness, and puffed a few times in deep thought. Then he rose.

"And I am operating on the direct orders of the president of the United States. You're dismissed, gentlemen," he brayed. "The Army is here now, and I'm acting on the orders of the president to establish a civil government, and things will soon be under control. What's past is past. The commodore's attempts will be noted and appreciated . . . such as they were."

Ned and Gillespie rose and followed as Kearny walked out into the rain. Kearny turned to his men.

"Pack up, gentlemen. Sleep in your slickers tonight, ready to ride before dawn. We've got word of a considerable force of Californios nearby." Kearny yawned and stretched nonchalantly. "And we're going to rout the bastards."

Kearny called to one of his officers, "Mr. Hammond." The man walked over, his eyes ringed with dark exhaustion. But he nodded enthusiastically at Kearny's order.

"Find the Mexican camp without being found out, and get back here well before dawn."

Beale stepped forward. "I know something of the country, General. I'd be happy to accompany the lieutenant."

Kearny looked Beale up and down and damped his teeth on the stub of the cigar. "We don't need any more damned Navy interference."

Without the formality of a salute, Ned spun on his heel and stomped away. Kit Carson rose from a nearby fire and joined him.

"He's mule-headed," Kit said, his short legs working to keep up with Ned.

Ned strode to the shelter of a yawning live oak before he paused. His jaw muscles worked. Kit stood a minute, smiling.

"I don't figure you got any chewin' backy?"

"Not a chewin' man, Kit. Sorry."

"Been outta chaw most of a month.'' He studied Ned with a glint of humor in his eye. "You're gonna wear your chompers down like a twenty-year mule, you keep a'gashin' 'em thataway."

Ned, realizing he was working his jaw like a dog worrying a bone, gave Kit a tight smile. "You've been putting up with the general for two months. Is he always this hardheaded?"

"One thing I've learnt 'bout Kearny. He's seldom wrong."

Ned jerked his head up, then realized Carson was being sarcastic.

"I notice the more brass a man totes, the righter he is," Carson added.

Ned clapped the little scout on the back. "Let's go find Godey. He's got a chaw for you."

"I don't imagin' ol' Alex might have a dollop of cactus juice?"

"I wouldn't be a damn bit surprised, Kit, not a damn bit." They turned their collars up against the cold rain and strode out from under the cover of the oak into a heavy rainfall to hunt for Alex Godey.

CHAPTER THIRTEEN

Kearny, dreary-eyed and open-collared, stood warming his hands outside his tent where his orderly had a fire going. Lieutenant Thomas Hammond was soaking wet from his night's foray, but stood erect at the general's side, his voice ringing with excitement.

"I found them, General. Must be most of a hundred of them."

"And did they find you, Lieutenant?"

"I'm not positive," he said uncertainly." A sentry challenged us, and we turned tail. I'd guess they figured we were unfriendly, the way we lit outta there."

"Still, there's a good chance. . . ." Kearny folded his hands behind his back and paced.

In his oilcloth nearby, Ned, with a group including Carson, Godey, and Jourdan, watched and listened as the general turned to his orderly.

"Have reveille sounded. We ride out in twenty minutes."

Long before dawn, the column formed up.

Dragoon captain Abraham Robinson Johnson rode in the lead with an advance guard of twelve. Kearny rode close behind with Lieutenant William Hemsley Emory of the topographical engineers and five other surveyors, and with Lieutenant William Horace Warner. Captain Benjamin D. Moore and Lieutenant Hammond followed with fifty dragoons. Another fifty followed in no particular order: some rode with the baggage, some formed up with friends, whether in their particular unit or not. When Kearny met up with Carson, he had more than four hundred men with him, but hearing that the

California situation was well in hand, he had sent the majority of his men on to Mexico to help with the war effort there.

At Kearny's direct orders, Ned tailed far in the rear with Major Thomas Swords and the baggage. Kearny must have considered the cannon baggage since the four pieces, including the small four-pounder Gillespie had dragged from San Diego and that earlier had been hauled all the way from Sutter's Fort, were spaced among the pack mules. Jourdan had elected to ride with Ned rather than with the other volunteers.

The column, whose decrepit horses and mules hung their heads in exhaustion, began to string out almost immediately after leaving Warner's Rancho, and Captain Henry Smith Turner, on a fresh mount obtained at Warner's, continually rode back and forth trying to keep the ranks closed up. The rain pounded down, hampering horses and men and caused the cannon to slip and slide on the narrow road, a road not much more than wagon ruts and often much less.

After a few hours on the trail, Ned unrolled his oilcloth, rode along under the protection of its cover, and reloaded the Allan's revolver with dry powder from the cotton sacks that had been tightly rolled in it. He carried his saber, his single-shot muzzle-loading cap-and-ball carbine, and his Allan's. He knew neither firearm was worth a tinker's damn if the powder was wet. Jourdan also carried a carbine and an Allan's but no cutlass.

Re-holstering his revolver, Ned commented to Major Swords, "Shouldn't the order be given to have these men recharge their weapons?"

Swords cast Ned a sideways glance. "You want to ride forward and suggest to General Kearny that he may have forgotten something so basic?"

Ned would have laughed if it weren't so important. "Your good general suggested I keep my position here with the baggage. It might come better from you."

"General only listen to general," Jourdan quietly put in.

Swords ignored the zambo's remark. "Suggestions in this outfit originate from the general's as indisputable orders." Swords shook his head in disgust, but as a good officer he would not directly condemn his superior. Nevertheless. Ned saw that Swords promptly pulled his own revolver and, without further comment, began recharging it. Jourdan followed suit.

"The hell with it," Ned said, and spurring his horse out and around the column. He knew that just ahead the road forked, and with of the condition of these men and their animals, he decided he had to put his two bits in with Kearny. As he passed Gillespie, the major, too, spurred his horse and followed.

They reined up beside the general.

"Something the matter in the rear, Lieutenant?" Kearny snapped to Ned, who now rode directly beside him.

"No, sir" Ned answered as politely as he could. "The road forks just ahead. General. If we take the left, we bypass San Pasqual. These Mexicans will be mounted on fresh stock. The finest horses I've ever seen, ridden by the finest horsemen in the world—"

"Poppycock. I don't suppose you've ever seen the Apache ride?"

"No, sir," Ned admitted. "Still, all in all, I'd say the Californio is among the finest."

"And I concur," Gillespie offered, to Ned's surprise. "So, what are you suggesting?"

"I'm suggesting that we avoid San Pasqual, give your men and animals a chance to recover from the desert crossing and get their strength back, and give us a chance to provide the men with fresh mounts."

"You have fresh mounts at San Diego?" Kearny asked, obviously already tired of Ned's suggestions.

"Possibly, by now. We brought in a herd of horses, and even now they're being broken."

201

"So you want me to avoid contact with the enemy in order to obtain horses that are unbroken ... or at best green. That's good Navy reasoning, I suppose." Kearny shook his head in disgust. "I suggest you return to the rear of the column, and don't move forward again unless ordered."

"Yes, sir." Ned saluted without enthusiasm. He started to spin his horse, then hesitated. "My own powder was getting damp, General. Shouldn't you have your men—"

"By God, man, you can be infuriating!" Kearny brayed, red in the face. Ned gave the spurs to the horse. Gillespie stayed beside the general for a moment but did not gain even a glance from the thick-set man. Finally the major quietly reined his animal around and returned to his Marines.

Ned reined up between Jourdan and Swords. They did not bother to ask him about his success with Kearny—the look on his face was enough.

They rode in silence for another half hour, the rain now a drizzle but still dampening the men's interest in conversation. Rather, faces remained buried as deeply as possible in up-turned collars. On the crest of a rise up ahead, the forward section of the column halted.   "What's up?" Swords asked.

"San Pasqual is just over that rise," Ned pointed. The mountains, climbing steep on either side and covered with chaparral, were clouded in mist. Ned saw Kearny, over a quarter mile ahead of him, raise his cutlass in the air in an enthusiastic motion and saw the small troop—Captain Johnson's lead guard—joined by a number of surveyors, spur their horses and disappear over the rise.

Unable to contain himself, Ned dug heels to his own horse. He was damned if we would be caught guarding a bunch of pack mules if the action was about to begin. Besides, he knew he was one of the few men well enough mounted to do any good against the Mexicans. Swords stayed with his cannon, but Jourdan galloped close behind. By the time they reached the head of the column, which had crested

202

the rise, Ned could see the troops strung out in front of him, including Kit Carson and some of the San Diego volunteers who had left Gillespie's band—and a group of Mexican *soldados*, thirty strong, riding easily away in front of them. A few straggled shots echoed up the canyon when the dragoons fired after the *soldados*.

As Ned passed Kearny, he heard the general shout after him, victory ringing in his voice, "Avoid this, eh, Beale? It's a rout . . . a bloody rout, you Navy slacker!"

But as far ahead as the men rode. Ned could see that the Mexicans were not earnestly riding away. If they had been they would have quickly outdistanced the dragoons.

Apprehension flooded Ned, and almost instantly he saw another group of lancers sweep down onto the trail out of the deep chaparral behind the strung-out dragoons. Reatas sung in the air, and the men were jerked out of their saddles. Many were able to unsheathe their heavy cutlasses, but they were no match for the long lances of the mounted *soldados* when carbines misfired from damp powder.

Ahead, Carson and the volunteers caught up with the uneven fight, but Kit's horse stumbled, and the little scout flew forward, rolling deftly into the chaparral. Ned saw him rise and pick up his carbine—broken in half at the breech. As Ned and Jourdan pounded by, Ned unclipped his own carbine, yelled "Carson!" and flung it to Kit, who caught it on the fly and turned to make his way up into the chaparral, where he could find a vantage point.

His cutlass unsheathed in his left hand, Ned began firing his Allan's from his right when he got within range. His chest surged with anger when he saw the numbers of dragoons lanced and dying on the canyon floor.

He sensed something to his right, and ducked just as Jourdan yelled a warning. The loop of a reata whistled its deadly song over his head. Dropping low in the saddle, he reined the mustang and faced two *soldados* charging down on him with lances at the ready. The Allan's bucked in his hand and one of the men grimaced and grabbed his side, dropping the lance, but the other came on. Before Ned could recock, a lance ripped through his right side. He swung the cutlass from low on his left and caught the surprised Mexican a glancing blow across the head. The cutlass buried in his horse's neck just in front of his saddle pommel, and was almost jerked from Ned's grip when the horse wildly plunged away.

Ned took a fleeting second to survey the scene around him—and saw Gillespie and his Marines charging into the fray. Gillespie rode well in the lead of his men and directly into a group of five *soldados*. Even over !he roar of battle, Ned could hear the Mexicans calling out Gillespie's name in anger. They fell on him when his carbine misfired. His cutlass flashed, knocking lances aside.

Ignoring the pain in his side, Ned hunkered low in the saddle and drove his mustang forward into the nearest of the mounted *soldados* just as another's lance drove into the Marine's face, knocking Gillespie from the horse. Ned kicked free of his horse, and a Mexican went to the ground—but Ned landed on top. He smashed the handguard of his cutlass repeatedly into the Mexican's face, leaving him covered with blood and unmoving, then spun to find Gillespie.

Ned fired into the mass of men surrounding the Marine and swung his cutlass, beating his way through. He heard Jourdan's yelled warning, and turned to see a Mexican flying out of the saddle, a victim of Jourdan's empty swinging carbine.

A barrel-shaped *soldado* held his broken lance like a sword and lunged at Ned, who turned aside at the last desperate moment. The lance pierced his tunic, and he smashed the heavy Allan's against the man's head. His eyes rolled up as he went down in a heap.

Gillespie staggered out of the men, his teeth smashed out and his lips flinging blood. He was screaming in anger at his enemies, cutlass waving in one hand, holding his chest—where a gaping wound lay open under the sliced uniform—with the other.

The Mexicans suddenly retreated, and Ned glanced over his shoulder to see Kearny and fifty of the dragoons gallop into the battle. They crashed past Ned, who madly searched for his horse. He had to get Gillespie to the rear if the mortally wounded man was to have any chance at all.

Ned watched Kearny gallop by as the Mexicans fled in front of the onslaught. Ned caught his horse's reins and, with Jourdan's help, pushed Gillespie into the saddle; then, realizing the Marine was about to lose consciousness. climbed on behind him and galloped to the rear. Jourdan followed, turning in the saddle and firing at two pursuing *soldados* who had come out of the undergrowth swinging reatas.

Ned reached the rise where Swords aligned the cannons and shoved Gillespie out of the saddle and into the major's arms. He caught him and lowered him gently to the ground.

"Get him some help!" Ned yelled, giving spurs to the mustang again.

By the time he had covered the quarter mile back, he could see that Kearny and his dragoons had charged into the jaws of hell. The Mexicans had used the same trick, allowing the dragoons to string out deeper into the canyon, then circling again.

Trick me once, you're a fool, trick me twice, I'm a fool, Ned thought in anger as he looked for the general.

Jourdan, galloping behind, screamed at him, "Reload while time!" Ned reined up and reloaded the Allan's. He could see Carson on the hillside, picking targets carefully, but almost every time he tried to shoot, the carbine misfired. Again, Ned gave heels to the mustang and charged into the battle. Kearny was surrounded by *soldados*, and Ned saw one of them drive his lance deeply into the general's broad backside.

With the irony of men in battle, Ned laughed. If he or any of them live through this, the general will carry a wound with a scar he could not show to his grandchildren. Ned carefully picked targets, nudging the mustang forward. Jourdan, by his side, did the same—driving the Mexicans away from the general. Kearny, suddenly finding himself out of it, staggered around, his hands hanging at his sides. Then he dropped to his knees.

At the roar of Swords's cannons, the Mexicans swung their horses away and retreated at a dead run.

The hillsides above the battle exploded with the four and six-pound shells. Ned, his battle-weary horse heaving in exhaustion, saw the general being picked up by his men and hoisted onto a horse. Ned looked back up the rise to see a group of Mexicans leaving through the chaparral on the hillside, pounding down on the cannons and their few defenders. This time it was he who yelled at Jourdan, who stood searching the chaparral for a target. Ned caught his attention, then spurred the lathered mustang back up the road. When he passed, he hooked elbows with Kit, who had moved back to the road, dragging him up into the saddle behind him. Before they reached the cannon's position, Ned's stomach filled with dread—afraid all would be lost, as the cannoneers fought in hand-to-hand desperation, surrounded by lance-armed Mexicans.

To Ned's surprise, Archibald Gillespie was back on his feet, long cannon swab in hand, manning his little four-pounder when not using the swab to parry the thrust of a mounted *soldado*. Another group of twenty *soldados* who had circled back were descending the hill at full charge, weaving through the heavy brush to join those already attacking the cannoneers.

Alone, Gillespie calmly adjusted the cannon to meet their charge. At less than twenty yards, he touched off the load of grapeshot. Smoke and fire billowed from the four pounder and horses and riders tumbled end over end down the slope, almost rolling into their own fighting *soldados* and cannoneers—and the cannon shot seemed to break the spirit of the Mexicans Those still mounted reined away from the battle and back up into the chaparral. Ned and Carson leapt from the saddle to help Gillespie reload while Jourdan recharged both his and Ned's revolvers, firing with either hand as groups of Mexican riders challenged from the hillsides. Again Jourdan reloaded, and flipped Ned's revolver back to him just in time to meet another charge brought on when the cannon's wet powder misfired. Two lancers galloped into them, and Jourdan sidestepped one when his revolvers, charged with the same powder as the cannon had been, misfired. When a *soldado's* horse reared, Jourdan managed to jerk the lance out of the man's hands, but not before he had taken its blade across his shoulder.

Ned's pistol fired and he saw the *soldado's* leg jerk. After reining away in desperation, the Mexican slid from the saddle—his mustang wisely running on, seeking the solace of the heavily brushed hillside. While the battle continued to roil around the cannon, Ned scrambled forward and, with Jourdan's help, dragged the wounded Mexican soldier back and bound him. Prisoners might come in handy, Ned figured. Then he reloaded and awaited another attack.

When the dreadfully wounded Major Gillespie realized that the cannons lay in good hands, his knees buckled and he crumpled to his back.

The cannoneers—when the powder didn't misfire—began an intermittent fusillade into the surrounding hillsides, more discouraging than deadly. The dragoons below realized that the Mexicans had retreated. With the Mexicans well out of pistol range, Jourdan began helping one of the cannon crews.

The dragoons in the cleft ahead quickly began collecting their wounded and dead and made their way back up the hill.

The roar of battle ended even more quickly than it had begun. The smell of gunpowder hung in the mist, and the quiet moan of the wounded seemed close in the dampness when the exhausted horses staggered back, carrying their grisly loads, their hooves sucking at the mud. Ned, Jourdan, and Carson surveyed the scene below.

"That, Mr. Carson," Ned said disgustedly, "was the worst show of battle planning I have ever even read about, much less been witness to."

"Mexican lance longer than cutlass. Powder wet," Jourdan offered sagely reducing the battle analysis to the bare bone as he inspected the wound where his homespun shirt was ripped at the shoulder.

Ned watched the dragoons get Kearny off his mount and strip away his pants. They laid him down, and a surgeon began tending his torn buttock. Ned glanced over at Kit. "Looks like the general is done for," he said seriously.

"Done for?" Kit studied the general for a moment. "Poked in the butt looks about all."

"Far too close to his brain, Kit," Ned said without a smile, but his eyes glinted with humor. Carson guffawed. "That just might be a true thing, Ned boy," he said. Then his tone turned serious. "You'd better have your side looked after . . . and Jourdan's shoulder could stand some fancy tattin'." Carson pulled the torn tunic apart to examine Ned's wound.

"Let's see if we can get the last of Gillespie's bleeding stopped first," Ned said, kneeling beside the fallen Marine, who seemed to be unconscious. His ripped mouth hung open, and his throat rattled when he sucked in air. His torn chest oozed blood and lymph. Ned grimaced as he realized he could see pink lung in the gaping wound.

Gillespie opened his eyes. Ned tried to clean the dirt and grass from the bloody mess that had been Gillespie's chest. "Did we win?" the Marine asked, his words slurred through torn lips and missing teeth.

"We didn't lose all, Arch," Ned answered the best he could.

"Good," Gillespie slurred. "Damned Mexicans don't have the heart for a good fight."

"Keep quiet, Arch, and get some rest. Let's just hope the 'damned Mexicans' don't decide to come back."

"I'm ready, bring the bastards on," Gillespie said with a gargle but didn't open his eyes.

Ned managed a tight laugh and shake of his head. A surgeon, having treated Kearny, arrived and began suturing Gillespie's wounds.

"Som' bitch," Carson said, shaking his head at the fallen Marine—who clamped his eyes shut tighter and made no sound as the surgeon worked. Kit turned his attention to the regrouping dragoons and Marines.

"Where's Godey? I need a chaw an' a suck on that coon's bottle." He wandered off in search of his fellow scout, and Jourdan followed. Ned started to move away, but the surgeon grabbed him by the sleeve.

"Not so fast," the surgeon said. "I've got enough of this catgut left to close that side up."

"You sure?"

"Sit your rump down, soldier." Ned complied. The surgeon worked quickly. His tunic sleeves had turned the color of old iron from all the dried blood on them. Ned watched, and winced, and wished he had Godey's bottle.

They made camp the best they could on the rise where the cannon line had been organized by Swords. Carson and the scouts built travois, and sewed and bandaged; Ned walked from group to group, studying the situation. Captain Johnson, who had bravely led the initial charge, lay dead, as did Captain Moore. Eighteen others suffered the same fate, and as many more lay wounded. To Ned's consternation, there was no sign of any Mexican dead, though there were many reports of wounded. They had two Mexican prisoners, Pablo Vejar and Francisco Lara, whom Beale had blown out of the saddle.

Ned walked to where Kearny rested on a pallet among his officers and found that the general had sustained two lance wounds Ned hadn't known of. His attitude toward the general softened. Foolish he might be. Ned decided, but he certainly is no coward. He had stayed in the midst of it as long as he stood on his feet.

Ned paused a while to listen to the conversation of Kearny's remaining officers, who claimed that the dead Johnson had charged without Kearny's order. They claimed Kearny had yelled "Trot!" and Johnson, in the excitement, had thought he heard the general yell "Charge!" Ned offered nothing to the conversation, for he had been too far in the rear to hear anything. But he understood how the order could have been misunderstood, with Kearny waving his cutlass in the air like a wild man ready to ride into the fires of perdition itself.

With Gillespie gravely wounded, Ned took charge of the Marine and Navy forces, including the volunteers from San Diego. He gathered his men around him in late afternoon and, with the approval of Captain Henry S. Turner, who had been given command of the dragoons by Kearny, sent four three-man patrols out to reconnoiter the hillsides and make sure the Mexicans were not forming up for another attack. As soon as they reported back that the Mexicans were nowhere to be found, Turner dispatched Alexis Godey and Thomas Burgess, a San Diego volunteer, to San Diego with a message to Stockton. He wrote:

> Headquarters camp near San Pasqual. At early dawn this morning General Kearny, with a detachment of United States Dragoons and Captain Gillespie's company of mounted riflemen, had an en-

gagement with a very considerable Mexican force near this camp. We have about
eighteen killed and fourteen or fifteen
wounded, several so severely that it may
be impracticable to move them for several
days. I have to suggest to you the proprie-
ty of dispatching, without delay, a considerable force to meet us on the road to San
Diego. We are without provisions... General Kearny is among the wounded, but it
is hoped not dangerously; Captains Moore
and Johnson, First Dragoons, killed, Lieutenant Hammond, First Dragoons, dangerously wounded.

Dr. Griffen, the surgeon, spent the rest of that December 6 moving among the wounded. Besides Ned, Kearny, and Gillespie, they were Captain Gibson of the San Diego volunteers, scout Antoine Ribidoux, Lieutenant Warner of the engineers, Sergeant Cox, privates Kennedy and Streeter, and ten other dragoons.

That night. under cover of darkness, the eighteen were buried. Before dawn, Cox and Kennedy died, and their graves were added to the line while the sun grayed the overcast to the east.

Turner decided to move on toward San Diego, and the group staggered out at midmorning.

They realized the Mexicans were flanking them along the way when a lighting strike by swift riders drove off a half dozen of the packhorses. Turner didn't bother to give chase. By mid-afternoon, exhausted, their mules and horses collapsing around them from wounds and exhaustion, they staggered into a dilapidated rancho. A few shots rang out from a rise overlooking the adobe buildings, but Carson and the scouts routed the Mexicans quickly. Turner camped on the hill they had driven the Mexicans from, overlooking Rancho Bernardo. The only stock available at the rancho were a few skinny chickens, and they divided them among the men, who ate mostly stew made of Missouri elk, tough as rawhide, for the mules had died of starvation and exhaustion.

Before they had finished their mid-afternoon meal, the American force found themselves surrounded by Mexicans again. The Mexican *soldados* rode in and out of the chaparral, showing themselves but always staying out of range. Only when a party rode to the bottom of the hill to a small stream for water did the Mexicans attack in earnest to drive them back. Now, when they needed it, the rain had stopped. After a few shots were exchanged, Turner noticed a Mexican riding out of the chaparral with a white flag flapping from his lance, and yelled at the men to stop firing.

Ned moved to join Captain Turner, pacing him while they walked down off the hill.

''I don't need Navy help,'' Turner groused, trudging, slipping, and sliding down the wet hill.

"You speak Spanish?" Ned asked tersely.

"No ... no, I don't." He flashed an irritated look, then conceded. "You can interpret, but let me do the primary talking."

The Mexican buried the lance point in the mud at their feet at the bottom of the hill. Sitting astride his prancing Andalusian stallion, he sneered at the weary Americans. "General Andres Pico wishes to inform you he holds two gringo prisoners. Seniors Burgess and Godey. He would like to exchange them for the men you hold."

Ned listened, then translated for Turner, who mulled it over a minute. In English, Ned reminded him, "Godey was sent to San Diego. It might be nice to find out if he got there."

"All right. Tell the greaser we'll trade."

But when he returned to the hilltop, Turner decided to keep the wounded man. Lara, who pleaded with him not to be moved. He was happy to be under the care of the American surgeon. Ned, Turner, and Vejar, his hands bound behind him, descended the hill, but Ned was not happy.

"You made a deal," he argued. "You should have forced Lara to go."

"We may need more trading material later," Turner said with a snarl. "I was trading horses before you were born, and I'll get both men for this one miserable greaser.''

As it happened, he got only Burgess, who knew nothing of Stockton's return message. But Burgess did relay that Stockton had no horses to carry a relief force, or even the carretas Godey had pleaded for.

Dejected, Ned returned to his riflemen and reported that they were surrounded by Mexicans, could not get to the stream due to the snipers, and would soon be eating their riding stock. At darkness he called Jourdan over away from the others.

"Can we sneak through their lines?" Ned asked.

"You and I could make it."

"Then I'm going to see Turner." Ned stalked away. Kit Carson rested among the scouts, but seeing that something of interest was happening, left his group and strode up beside Ned.

"You thinking of a way out of this pile of Army road apples!" Kit asked.

I'm going to get Turner to let Jourdan and me go for help. Something is seriously wrong at San Diego, or Stockton would have been back with Godey. They're probably on their way on foot, since they're short of stock . . . unless they, too, are under attack."

"I'm going with you," Kit said, brooking no argument, and Ned offered none, for he was glad to have the scout's help.

Ned confronted Turner. "I want to get out of here and get to Stockton."

Turner. leaning on a scrub oak trunk, glanced up. "We need to rest. We'll fight our way out of here in the morning."

"You've got wounded who will die if moved. They need carts. Stockton needs to be informed of the gravity or the situation here. Obviously, your note did not do that."

"More Navy help!" Turner said sarcastically, but his own fatigue kept him from expressing it as he might have.

"Any hep' would be obliged by those wounded," Kit cut in. "I don't give a fiddler's fart 'bout Army. Navy, Marines, or any of that gol'darned goat dung. Those men over there need hep'. Beale and his zambo and me is a'goin'."

"Go to hell, as far as I'm concerned. The rest of us are going to have a chunk of greaser ass on our way out of here come dawn."

Ned started to say something, but Kit grabbed his arm and led him away. "Don't labor it, man, you done got what you wanted. Get Jourdan, and I'll be meetin' you at the surgeon's camp."

They regrouped at the surgeon's campfire, got a list of what the doctor most needed, agreed that they would have a much better chance on foot—as the Mexicans could easily hear horses and would ride their tired animals down quickly—made a quick plan to stay together until they had broached the Mexican lines, and waited until the overcast seemed the thickest and the night the darkest. Just after midnight, they started out with the moans of the wounded the most encouraging of all possible good-byes.

Ned carried his carbine and had his Allan's at his waist. He left the cutlass behind, as it was too clumsy to move with through the brush.

They worked their way to the bottom of the hill, where Kit stopped and silently pulled his boots off. Even in the wetness, twigs from the scrub oak snapped under foot. Ned and Jourdan followed his example. With the advantage of feeling the branches before they put their weight on them, another safe footfall could be found when the twigs were detected. They moved on, slowly and silently picking their way like buck-skinned toe dancers.

They fell to their bellies and crawled across an open field that had been grazed clean by the rancho's former stock, and breathed a sigh of relief when they reentered a scrub oak thicket on the other side. Ned was about to whisper for them to put their boots back on and split up when he heard the voices of several Mexicans.

The three of them froze in position, pressed low in the brush. A Mexican laughed nearby. Then they heard approaching footfalls.

CHAPTER FOURTEEN

A Mexican *soldado* moved closer to them, the crunch of his steps like a regimental drum corps in the darkness.

Ned could make out his outline against the overcast sky and smell the odor of his glowing cigarillo. Just as Ned was about to spring out and throttle the man, the *soldado* stopped, unbuttoned his breeches, and urinated in the bush. He hummed a fandango tune as he finished his business, then buttoned up and returned the way he had come.

Silently, Ned and the others slipped away, backtracked to the open field, moved a hundred yards along the thicket, then re-entered and crossed it again.

They came up against a rocky slope. Kit had stopped and begun to slip back into his boots when a voice rang out, "Apeadero, hombre!"

Kit ducked lower, and Ned and Jourdan, behind him, moved back into the brush a step or two.

From the side another voice said, "Que pasa. Gaspar?"

A movement appeared on the ledge above Kit's head, and the scout's hand snaked up, caught the sitting man by the collar, and jerked him off his perch. He yelled in alarm, "Gringos!," then "oofed" as Carson cracked his musket across the man's skull. Ned dropped the boots he carried and charged forward, Jourdan close behind, just as four other Mexicans rounded the rock outcropping. A shot rang out. Fists, feet, and muskets, used as bludgeons, flew.

A blow glanced off Ned's head, and he saw stars for a moment; then the man who had leapt on him was jerked away. Jourdan pummeled the man with powerful fists and yelled, "Run, Ned, run!"

Ned rolled to his side and staggered to his feet, and ran without finding his musket. He rounded the rock ledge and ran into another, passing an ember-glowing campfire where the men must have been camped. He scrambled up a shale slope, slipping and sliding, tearing his hands and bare feet on the sharp outcropping, but made his way to the top and into a thick laurel stand. Still he raced on, out of the laurel and into shoulder-high chaparral. Only when he reached a grasping stand of cactus and stepped directly onto the prickly pine was he painfully reminded he had no boots.

He paused and plucked the spines from his feet as best he could, and continued on.

No one knew the stars better than Ned Beale, but the stars lay hidden behind the thick overcast. He stopped and listened for pursuit but heard none—not even the footfalls of Kit or Jourdan. Finally Ned thought he could make out the glow of the moon. He sat for the better part of an hour, collecting himself, orienting the faint glow with a fixed branch in a scrub oak above him, resting, and digging at the thorns in his feet with one of the full needle-sharp thorns he had plucked out of his pants.

He decided that yes, the slight change in tone in the sky above was the moon, and he set out in the direction the blur traveled: west. The pain in his feet and lower legs and the throbbing ache from the blow to his head worked at him until he reeled with dizziness. He had not eaten the day before. Finally, he stumbled onto a trickle of water, drank, and used its coolness to smooth his feet and legs and wash away the dried blood from the hundreds of punctures. As he sat by the stream in the darkness, listening to the night sounds of coyotes and owls, he wondered about the fate of Kit and Jourdan—but knew the most important thing for any of them was for one of them to get through.

Then he felt a warm, sticky trickle on his side. The lance wound had opened and was bleeding freely. Ripping away a piece of his shirttail, he made a compress, but feared it would do little good.

Dawn crawled over the countryside, and he found himself on a long, sloping flat, one thick with chaparral. He wondered how far he was from the sea, but the overcast and mist precluded him from seeing for more than a half mile, even when he found a high spot above the heavy brush. He stopped and tore apart his shirt and bound his bloody feet, now not only punctured by the spines but also torn and bruised from the many rock outcroppings he had stumbled over in the darkness. The padding around his feet offered some relief. Once, he almost stepped on a small rattler that buzzed in angry defiance. Afterward, every branch became a viper to his exhausted eyes. He stumbled on.

It must have been noon when he came upon a field where two vaqueros worked a tiny herd of cattle. From the cover of the brush, with blurred vision, he studied them. He attributed his exhaustion to the loss of blood from the wound in his side. He wondered if he dared approach them, then decided he must not risk it. The horses they had would hurry his journey, but one of the men was armed with a musket, and both carried reaias. Even though Ned still carried his Allen's, he was exhausted and would be easy prey for two alert vaqueros. Could he shoot them down from the brush and take their horses? No. They were peacefully working their cattle. Instead, he moved back in the brush, skirted the field, and proceeded on foot.

By late afternoon, he reached the sea. Stumbling into the surf, Ned soaked his bloody feet in the stinging but healing salt water and washed away the blood from the wound in his side.

He turned south, and continued on in the darkness. Exhaustion tried to pull him down into the deep salt grass, whispering that he would be better after a few hours' rest. No! He refused its enticing tug. Making his way up above the surf line, he let the sounds of its gentle roll guide him south—but it, too, whispered, lie down and rest.

He drove himself on, each step a supreme effort.

He had lost all track of time when he saw a light in the distance. Coming to the water's edge, he realized it was either the anchor light of a ship or a shore light across a bay. Lurching, barely able to go on, he struggled to put one foot in front of the other along the rugged shoreline with renewed vigor granted him by the teasing, distant light.

Dawn of the second day grayed the eastern cloud-muddled sky when he stumbled alongside a hide and tallow warehouse on the outskirts of San Diego. Now, he prayed to himself, let Stockton be in control of the pueblo. I've not come this far only to fall into the hands of the Mexicans. With the dedication of one within moments of his goal, he climbed Presidio Hill to Fort Stockton.

"Who goes there?"

He had to think for a moment. Was that English or Spanish? Ned collected himself, knowing he must look worse than the lowest wallowing drunkard. "Lieutenant Edward Fitzgerald Beale," he said with precise enunciation, then pitched forward on his face in the mud.

He awoke on his back on a cot with Commodore Robert Stockton standing over him.

"Ned." The commodore lifted his head, and he tasted the warm, sugared tea Stockton held to his lips. "Jourdan got here before you. We're putting together a marching force now. We've got a hundred twenty-five men leaving on foot . . . and we'll get your men and the dragoons back."

"Carson?" Ned managed to ask.

"He just came in a few moments ago."

All three of them had made it. Now if only there were anything left on the hill overlooking Rancho Bernado for the relief force to find. But that was no longer his job. As a surgeon worked over him, he fell into a deep sleep, sick from the loss of blood and his injuries.

Ned awoke hours later and wondered if his memories of two nights of barefooted, blood-shedding hell was a dream. The room in which he lay on fresh, clean cotton sheets was whitewashed, open, and airy. Above him a crucifix, arms stretched wide in supplication, stared down at him. Wide shutters revealed a beautiful patio and flowering bushes and vines. Sunlight streamed into the room, and the smell of food cooking made his mouth water.

He heard the creak of hinges, and turned to focus on a dark-eyed girl wearing a white blouse and dark skirt with a red sash binding her narrow waist, and hair to her rounded hips—a Mexican girl, he realized, wondering if he had been captured. But her flashing smile reassured him quickly, and he decided if he was a prisoner, this was the way to be imprisoned.

"You are awake! I thought you might sleep through La Navidad." The girl's laugh tinkled like the Christmas bells of the holiday she referred to.

She crossed the room and smoothed the sheets on his bed. "1 am Rosalia Bandini, and you are a guest of Don Juan Bandini, mi padre. Are you hungry?"

"I could eat the south side of a northbound skunk," he rasped, then flushed at his sailor slang, but she laughed again, and her skirts whirled with pleasant starched rustling as she left the room. In less than a minute, she returned with a tray—followed by Don Juan Bandini and the rest of his large family. Ned drank fresh coffee and feasted on tortillas filled with chocolate. He was introduced to Senora Bandini and her four daughters, then realized he had met Don Juan at a social function before.

In the days 'hat followed Ned found himself more and more attracted to Rosalia Bandini and to the Californio way of life.

He was snapped back to reality when he was visited by of-

ficers of the *Congress* and handed mail—including three letters from Mary Edwards. In the third and last one he was in-
censed to read that she was busy in the Washington social
scene and had recently attended a reception where she was
treated to several dances with "a very old and dear Navy
friend of yours," Norvell Johanson, now a newly elected congressman from his home state of Pennsylvania and due to
assume office in the spring.

Mary closed by asking Ned why he had never mentioned
"such a wonderfully handsome Navy chum."

Over two weeks passed before Ned, desperately weak and
twenty pounds lighter than he had been before San Pasqual,
returned to the Congress and the care of its surgeon and loblolly boys. On the first night of his homecoming, his fellow
officers held a reception in is honor and informed him they
were awarding him special gifts for his recent action. They
read the following proclamation:

> Dear Beale,
> We your friends and brother officers have
> ordered from England a pair of epaulettes
> and sword to be presented to you by the
> hands of Lieutenant Tilghman, in testi-
> mony of our admiration of your gallant
> conduct in the bold and hazardous enter-
> prise of leaving General Kearny's en-
> campment, after the Battles of San Pas-
> qual and San Bernardo of the 6th of De-
> cember, 1846, for the purpose of bringing
> information to the garrison of San Diego
> and obtaining relief for the suffering
> troops. Your bravery in the field of action
> and cool determination in the service
> above merits our warm applause and we
> congratulate you on the opportunity of

distinction which you so handsomely improved. . . . Hoping that the President of
the United Slates will not overlook your
merit and that you may speedily wear the
epaulettes and sword as the mark of your
legitimate rank, we remain. Yours Faithfully,

It was signed by twenty of Ned's fellow officers of the Pacific Squadron.

Though elated and complimented by his peers' acclaim, he
was saddened to know that twenty-one men had died at San
Pasqual and that many more had been wounded. The only
Mexican seriously wounded—at least as far as the Americans
could ascertain—was Lara, the man whom Ned himself had
shot. Senor Lara's leg had been amputated, a fact that saddened Ned deeply.

General Kearny, with only fifty-seven dragoons remaining
in his Army of the West, allowed himself to be relegated to
the position of head of the occupying army, and did not argue
with Stockton's self-proclaimed position as governor of the
Territory of California. And Stockton prepared to march on
Los Angeles, the last bastion of Californio control in the territory.

Stockton had received reports that Fremont was marching
south, and the *Cyane* had arrived and supplemented his force
with powder, guns, and men. Two days before New Year's
Day, close to six hundred men, this time welt drilled and carrying pikes as a defense against the Mexican lances, set out
for Los Angeles up the El Camino Real. Five cannons were
mounted, and the men had practiced with them for days.
Stockton had appointed Lieutenant Stephen C. Rowan of the
Savannah as troop commander of the sailor army, but Kearny
adamantly objected.

Kearny had been treating the "governor" of the Territory

of California with deference until this insult, seemingly aimed at him.

Stockton immediately assembled his men and stated that the general had "volunteered" to take command of the troop but that he, Stockton, was retaining his position as commander in chief—and General Kearny continued to address him as such.

Stockton selected Lieutenant Andrew F. V. Gray as an aide-de-camp. Gray had commanded the relief force to rescue Kearny and Turner from the hill—now known as Mule Hill, due to the animals being the only food left--that overlooked Rancho San Bernardo. Stockton also made a strategic political appointment of Midge Pedrorena, a Mexican volunteer from San Diego, as an aide-de-camp.

Ned Beale, barely able to get in the saddle but adept at keeping that fact from Stockton, was appointed to lead a troop of mounted carabineers. Gillespie, with gaps where his front teeth had been and with his ribs still bound tightly, was not to be left out; he took command of the San Diego Volunteers. Kit Carson and his mountain men rode ahead as scouts, and by special request and permission of the commodore, made Jourdan a member of their party.

The column rested at Mission San Luis Rey, then moved on to Mission San Juan Capistrano and rested again. With the new recruits from the *Cyane* footsore after the first day, the march took most of a week. Surely Fremont would be in position outside of Los Angeles by now, Stockton figured. The battalion approached the San Gabriel River on January 7, 1847.

On the far side of the winter-swollen river, Mexican *soldados* moved in and out of the brush and willows, with streamers flying from their feared lances. Well mounted on quick Andalusian stallions, the elusive riders were never still, and it was impossible to determine their numbers.

Kearny and Stockton made camp.

After nightfall, Carson and the scouts were sent on forays across the river, but returned with little information other than that there were horse tracks everywhere and that the men had heard the hoofbeats of many horses in the darkness.

At dawn, Jourdan helped Ned into the saddle. His troop of carabineers sat on a bank overlooking the San Gabriel River. A small flock of sandhill cranes winged their way overhead, silently surveying the river for a quiet place to fish or frog for their morning breakfast. Bothered by the activity in the river-side camp, they wisely moved on. Ned watched the graceful birds and thought them more than merely wise, for a half mile across the river several hundred mounted, uniformed *solda-dos* and vaqueros moved across the long slope. It appeared the Mexicans had finally resolved their internal disputes and come together as a cohesive force.

Jourdan, who worriedly stayed at Ned's side, spoke for the first time that morning. "This worse than Pasqual."

"For the Mexicans, surely," Ned said, a bit irritated at Jourdan*s negative attitude. But the man's courage could not be doubted—and Ned feared he was right.

"You go back to camp. Stay with cooks," Jourdan grumbled at Ned.

"You just try to kill half as many Mexicans as I do," Ned retorted with bravado, and Jourdan only shook his head disgustedly.

At first in the gray dawn, the Mexicans kept no particular ranks but rather seemed to ebb and flow in groups of ten or twenty. But as the sun silvered the tops of the hills to the east, the Mexicans formed into along line four men deep.

Kearny sent the morning's orders to Ned via a runner "Take the right flank and encircle and destroy the enemy."

Ned eyed the hundreds of men across the river and wondered how a force of thirty carabineers could flank and destroy six hundred, but when Kearny gave the order to charge, wanting to broach the river before the Mexicans reached it,

Ned nudged the mustang into the strong flow. Only once did the tough little bay lose his footing and have to swim. Luckily the river was fast but not too deep where they crossed. Kearny had picked a wide spot to ford, for he wanted no problems with the cannons.

When Ned reached the far side, the horse plunged out through a stand of rules, got to dry ground, and shook like a dog. Ned had to take several deep breaths, for his head swirled more than the waters of the San Gabriel. He steadied himself and turned back to his men.

"Check your loads," he commanded, not wanting misfires, as so many men—now dead men—had suffered at San Pasqual. While he waited patiently for several of his men to reload and for his own dizziness to end, he watched Kearny and the bulk of the force's progress. As soon as the cannons reached the river's edge, they bogged down in quicksand. Ned could see the panic in the ranks as the men tied lines to the cannons. Even Kearny dismounted and took up a towline with his men, encouraging the workers.

Ned wondered why General Flores did not launch an all-out charge while the American cannons were obviously out of commission, but he did not. There had been some question as to whether the *soldados* had cannons, but that was soon answered. Just as Ned's last carabineer nodded nervously to Ned that he was ready, the roar of a cannon deep behind the Mexican lines snapped all heads, and all eyes followed the whine of the shell overhead. The plume of the shot in the middle of the river brought a nervous laugh from the troops at the Mexicans' marksmanship, but encouraged the men in their efforts, and the American cannons almost instantly were pulled free. Plunging and yelling, with muskets held high, the Americans hit the widest, shallowest spot in the river in a wave. Gillespie and his mounted San Diego Volunteers took the point and led the charge.

"We're after their cannons, lads!" Ned called out, reining

225

away into the chaparral and river willow above the tule line. As Ned and his thirty carabineers crested a small ridge, Ned again glanced back at the main force and saw a plume of sand on the hillside behind the Americans. The Mexican cannoners could not seem to get the range. Kearny already had his cannons in place on the Mexican side of the river, and the Americans began a steady fusillade against the hilt ahead.

Ned was sitting the nervous, prancing bay, trying to gauge exactly where the Mexican cannons were, when he was forced to other business. A squad of *soldados* broke out of the chaparral not a hundred yards ahead, and reatas spinning above their heads, bore down on Ned's riders. Every other man, teamed with the man beside him, dismounted and knelt next to his horse, firing from a prone position. Ned and Jourdan teamed up, each careful not to fire until the other man was almost reloaded.

The squad spread across the field, and each man picked a target. The Mexicans, some with lances lowered, some with reatas twirling, charged bravely—but this time American powder was dry, Ned let the riders get within forty paces before he fired; his shot was quickly followed by the volley of his carabineers. The mounted men took the place of those who had knelt to fire, while the first reloaded and remounted. Another volley quickly followed the first, and the Mexicans, many blown from the saddle, many others afoot as their horses had been downed, milled about and tried to reorganize. With the second volley, they scattered or spurred away. Ned's men gave a shout of triumph, and those who had fired the last volley reloaded and remounted. Chomping for another fight, Ned's force gave chase.

Across the field, hundreds of Mexican *soldados* charged the American force, but this time the well-organized dragoons were in position, not strung out on exhausted mules and horses. The forward line knelt, and another line stood behind. A deadly hail of shot dropped the Mexicans before they could get near enough to use their red-ribbon-festooned lances.

Ned and his force charged into the chaparral, looking for the Mexican cannons. He realized he was moving with the majority of the Mexican force. They scattered in full retreat.

He moved his squad away and up a low rise, watching and gaining his breath, as the *soldados* dissolved in disarray. He sent a rider back to tell Kearny, and continued to search the thick chaparral for the cannons. Soon he joined up with Carson and his scouts, who had been assigned the left flank. Kit reined up beside him.

"Mexicans are back to their old tricks," Kit said with a smile. "Retreatin'."

"Let's keep them on the run," Ned said, and Kit nodded.

"You all right, Beale?" The scout centered his gray eyes on Ned.

"Happy as a skunk in the henhouse," Ned answered, but he read the concern in the scout's perceptive gaze and knew he must look as weak as he felt.

They came across a Mexican cannon, abandoned, with its carriage blown apart by the accurate fire of the Americans. Encouraged again, they continued to harass the *soldados*, but soon the well-mounted Mexican riders outdistanced their pursuers. Ned and Kit decided to report to Kearny.

The dragoons made camp on the hill where the Mexicans had taken their stand, and Ned immediately rolled into his oilskin and fell asleep. Jourdan awoke him with a plate of beans, which Ned downed gratefully; then he slept again. But in the morning he had his carabineers in the saddle before dawn, and they all pushed on, without opposition for miles. They marched on toward Los Angeles and again the Mexicans took a stand, on a mesa, Canada de Los Alises, but were quickly routed.

The dragoons camped that night on the high ground, and the next day Carson and his mountain men had scouted the town, the dragoons entered an almost deserted Los Angeles, marching band blaring. But this time there was no one there to appreciate it.

To the gratification of the troops, the Mexicans had fled without their stores of aguardieme. By the middle of the afternoon, almost every American was in his cups, singing and reveling in their victory.

The Americans had lost another twenty killed or wounded, but estimated the Mexican losses at eighty. One of the wounded again was Archibald Gillespie, but this time his wound was slight.

Three days later, Fremont and his Bears rode into Los' Angeles, and with his grandiose flair, the new colonel announced to Stockton and Kearny that he had accepted General Pico's surrender at San Fernando without firing much more than a shot. He had-delivered to the officers the capitulation of Cahuenga, dated January 12.

Kearny stomped off in anger, amazed that Fremont had taken it upon himself to negotiate such a critical treaty, but said nothing to Stockton about the matter. Stockton busied himself setting up a civil government for California, again assuring Fremont that he was provisional governor of the Territory of California, at least until a confirmation by congress. Kearny kept a reticent silence. Within days the majority of the force moved south again to San Pedro and San Diego and enjoyed the Californio life again.

Ned was relegated to a hospital bed for almost a month. Then, finally, he was on his feet—but weak and suffering from a terrible loss of weight. Still, he joined the social activities of the Americans, now considered conquering heroes in San Diego.

But Ned was not to enjoy the Bandini and other dons' hospitality for long. On February 24, 1847, Stockton called him to his office at the fort.

"Are you fully recovered, Mr. Beale?" Stockton asked.

Ned took a deep breath and lied. "I'm ready for whatever

orders you have, sir," he answered, but even then was surprised when the commodore turned to actually gave him his orders.

"Good; you're riding overland back to Washington City with dispatches. Pick your squad and be ready to depart at sunup. Kearny is grousing about the fact he is not in charge, claiming that Fremont is an Army officer and under his command. I'm sure he's sent a dispatch to Washington via his own courier, with his own version of events in California. It's important—in fact, critical to all our careers—that we tell our side of the story, and no one can do that better than you."

Kit Carson and his fellow mountain men; White Elliott and Baptiste Perrot; the half-Negro, half-Comanche scout now known as Jourdan Zambo; R. Eugene Russell; Theodore Talbot; and six packers and muleteers were mounted and headed east before the rising sun began to make them squint.

They left a California where three men—Stockton, Fremont, and Kearny—were signing letters and documents as governor of the Territory of California.

As Ned rode out, he swayed in the saddle, weak and emaciated, no matter how he had assured Stockton to the contrary. He wondered if he could make it across the desert. But he knew that even if he didn't, Kit Carson would. Ned girded himself for a long tough test of his endurance against Indians and the elements—perhaps his greatest, and maybe his last.

Chapter fifteen

N ed sat high on a barren hillside overlooking the treeless expanse beyond the willow-bracketed Colorado, into which he would ride. He was. unsteady in the saddle, weak, ill, and unsure. Still, he signaled for his group to take the descent to the spot selected for their crossing. He had heard from Kit Carson that few places in the West were less hospitable than the stark country where the Gila River meets the Colorado. Kit had laughed at the term "river." Rivers in southeastern California and southwestern Arizona, he cautioned, generally mean beds of sand. They are cut only by the rush of water when scarce rainfall colors the desert with flowers after bursts of flooding torrents. Ned prayed they would encounter those rushes, or a least a few pools left by their passing.

For the first twenty days of the journey, Jourdan or Carson had to help Ned in and out of the saddle, but he insisted he ride on and "work his way through his weakness" as they followed the Gila. By the time they climbed high into the southern Rockies, looking for the nation's spine, the continental divide, he was stronger but almost cadaverously thin. Soon the snows made game even more scarce and travel all but impossible. Still, they plowed on. Kit Carson knew well the route they traveled, having crossed it twice in the past year, the last time leading the ungrateful Kearny back to California. And Kit knew its inclement weather and native occupants. Each night, to the grousing of the men who had seen no tangible sign of the Apache and believed there was no real threat, Carson would see to the building of their campfires, then, after cooking, would prod the men into moving away from the fires to sleep deep in the brush. With the constant whipping cold and the occasional but vigorous storms, the men were not happy about being denied their fires.

Arizona, though not so much so as California, was a contrast of scorching desert and lush, green mountains. Small islands of pines spotted the desert where the country rose into high mountains. Suddenly rushing streams--jubilant gushes of precious water, not sand—and green pines appeared as if the traveler had crossed through the gates of heaven out of the licking flames of perdition itself. It was on the edge of one of these islands, where the snows began, that Ned and his little band of travelers camped, near the continental divide.

Poked awake by Baptiste Perrot, Ned rubbed his eyes in the darkness.

"Up, Lieutenant," Perrot whispered.

"What's happening?" Ned asked, instantly awake.

"Carson says ze Apache are going to 'it us at dawn."

"Where is he?" Ned, having learned the propensity of scorpions to see their damp darkness, shook out his boots and pulled them on.

" 'E is out in the brush, on 'ees own, as usual. Says for us to about our business, but keep ze peestols at hand."

The party, some of them grumbling that Carson had had too much sun crossing the desert, were up, dressed, and had checked their loads long before the slightest hint of a graying eastern sky.

The mules and horses had been hobbled in an open grassy area with easy access to a trickle—one that disappeared into thirsty sand not a mile below where they camped. Ned helped with the packing of a big gray mule when the first shot snapped their heads around—and the mule onto which he had just hoisted a pack dropped to the snow as if it had been hit in the head with an ax. A rain of arrows buzzed the air.

Ned dropped with the mule, using its body as cover, and by the time he hit the ground had his six-barreled Allen's revolver palmed. He didn't have to wait long for a target. Two dozen savages, half of them mounted, half on foot, charged out of the brush, notching and firing arrows and swinging stone axes. Only two of them carried muskets. Another arrow thumped into the dead mule as Ned and the other men picked targets. Their firearms roared in the quiet morning, and gun smoke seared their nostrils.

Two Indians fell immediately. The savages quickly retreated, surprised at the preparedness of the waiting men. The fighting was over almost as soon as it had begun. As the men stripped the pack from the dead animal, Carson, unseen during the attack, wandered into camp with a wide grin and carrying something: a bloody scalp. He held it up to Perrot.

"Som'bitch didn't know this ol' coon was behind him."

Ned's stomach rolled; then he was even more surprised when Jourdan moved into the brush and began deftly peeling away the hair of another of the fallen men. By the time he had returned, Ned was ready to forgo his breakfast.

"Let's get on the trail and the hell out of here," he suggested.

"Yeah, let's leave, but were a'gonna circle back," Carson said, his look hardening.

"What the hell for?" Ned asked.

"They got what they wanted, and we got to punish 'em."

"They wanted to lose their hair?" Ned asked sarcastically.

"The mule . . . they wanted the mule," Carson answered patiently. "If we let them get off cheap, they'll jus' hit us 'gain and 'gain. When they comes back to butcher, it's Perrot, ol' White, and this coon who'll do the skinnin'."

"Jourdan go, too," the zambo said. Ned didn't object. In fact, Ned kept totally quiet. Carson and the other two mountain men had lived in this country' longer than Ned hoped he ever would and had managed to stay alive by adopting the ways of the savage. Ned mounted up, and they pressed on. But less than a mile out of camp, Carson and die mountain men wordlessly reined away.

Over an hour later, from far behind them, Ned and the mule skinners heard the echoes of distant shots. In another hour, Carson and the mountain men clattered up behind. Fresh scalps dripped from their saddles among the other folderol there.

By the time they reached the Rio Grande on the far side of the great divide, Ned considered himself a man of desert and mountain, not just sea. He had carefully paid attention to each task the mountain men had performed, and had learned well—though some of their habits he could easily pass. They paused at Taos for three days, and Carson happily visited with his wife.

Ned Beale, after reaching the relative safety of Santa Fe and Taos, spent a great deal of time reflecting on the crossing. He carefully reviewed the country in his mind and wondered if a road could be built across the Southwest—not a trail, but a full-fledged road with bridges and grades that horses and mules could climb and wagons could brake down without the use of rope restraints. He decided that it could, and that in almost every instance, it would have watering holes no more than a day's wagon trip apart. When this war was over, and California was a territory, when the rest of the country heard of the beauty of the Pacific Coast, when they discovered the potential of a country where living is almost too easy, then the clamor would begin and a road was bound to follow. The Panama crossing with its disease and jungle would not do for the women and children who would come from the East. They should be able to cross the country with the protection of American troops and American forts all the way. And the rutted wagon trails to the north took far too long and risked too much, like death from winter snows.

As Stockton had professed, there would be a road.

But the Southwest would have to undergo some great changes first. Like California, New Mexico, too, had had its troubles. After Kearny had left for California, thinking the

civil government was well in control, the Mexicans had revolted and hung Charles Bent, the man Kearny had appointed
provisional governor there—Kit's brother-in-law. Ned and
Carson, with Carson's wife Josefa, who had herself barely
escaped with her own life, watched in the town square while
frigid wind whipped around them as several of the rebels
were hung.

Yes, there would be a road, but many changes had to
come first.

After Kit had said his farewells, they pressed on along the
well-traveled Santa Fe Trail over another range of snow-
whipped mountains and entered the Great Plains, where the
continual frigid wind punished them almost as the cold of the
mountains had. At Fort Leavenworth, they boarded a flat-
bottomed boat and headed down the Missouri for St. Louis.
The boat was no palace, but with a potbellied iron stove and
plenty of wood, and water all around them, it was heaven
compared to the desert and mountains. At Westport they
changed to the luxury of a steamboat, the John J. Hardin, and
on May 16 reached the gateway to the West, St. Louis.

Before they had left California, Fremont suggested to
Beale that they visit his father-in-law's home. Senator Thomas Hart Benton was not in residence, but they were received
by his daughter, John Charles Fremont's wife, Jessie. Beale
delivered several letters to her from her husband in addition
to those he delivered to other residents of St. Louis from officers of the dragoons, including the truculent Captain Turner,
whom Ned had found so hard to deal with at Mule Hill.

Ned, and even more so Carson, were amazed at the reception they received in St. Louis. They were flooded with invitations and surrounded by an admiring public each time they
went out of the house—and houses were not to the liking of
Kit Carson. He had even pleaded with Jessie Benton to allow
him to sleep on the veranda, which, with her normal good-
natured laugh, she did.

Enchanted with Fremont's intelligent and attractive wife, Ned was pleased when she invited him to join her for tea in the bright sitting room on the third day of her hospitality.

"I've had a chance to read all of John's letters, Ned," she began as they sat across from each other in Demon's large river-view house. "And to be truthful, I'm seriously disturbed."

"The situation in California has been strained, to say the least."

"John thinks that this general, Kearny, has a vendetta against him."

"Kearny is concerned with his own reputation, and he's looking for any scapegoat. John acted admirably in California, and only did the bidding of his superior officer, Commodore Stockton."

"But Stockton is Navy, and John is Army. To be truthful, my husband's letters are more than concerned— if I didn't know him so well, I would say panicky—and John doesn't panic.",

Ned cleared his 'throat, wondering himself just how sticky the situation would become. Before he had left California, Stockton informed him that he would be sailing to Monterey to turn over the Pacific Squadron to Commodore William Branford Shubrick, who was due on the *Independence*. So control of California was soon, if not already, out of Stockton's hands. And Kearny seemed to be making more and more noise.

Still, he tried to console an obviously worried Jessie Fremont. "No matter what Kearny says, California was a Navy operation. Had Stockton not acted with vigor and purpose, as did your husband, Kearny would have met the full force of Californios and probably been wiped out at San Pasqual. Stockton had the situation all but under control by the time Kearny stumbled in from the desert. Don't worry, Jessie, John will be vindicated."

"After all he's done for this country, I hope so. John couldn't stand. . . ." She let it go unsaid, and instead poured Ned another cup of tea. "We're having a reception for you this evening at the Congregational Church. All the prominent people in the community will be there."

"For me?" Ned asked, and received a gleaming smile from the pretty Jessie, seemingly putting her worries about John aside.

"Yes. With an orchestra and everything. You must save me at least one dance."

"How about the other men—Kit, Jourdan, and the others?"

Jessie smiled a little defensively. "They are a little on the wild side. The ladies—"

"They're due more attention than I, Jessie. Had it not been for Kit and Jourdan—"

"Mr. Carson, then, if you insist. But ask him not to mention his pouch of scalps or his Sioux wife, please. But as for Mr. Jourdan ... St. Louis society just wouldn't stand to socialize with a Negro. Right or wrong."

"Kit no longer has a Sioux wife. Jourdan wouldn't come anyway." Ned returned her tight smile. He was back in civilization.

Suddenly his stomach filled with dread. Just what kind of a reception were they in for in Washington City? Hell, California was a territory of the United States, at least as far as the Americans were concerned, and that was a fact due to the direct efforts of his boss, Commodore Robert Field Stockton.

Still, Kearny claimed he acted on the direct orders of President Polk. If the president thought Fremont acted against his direct orders, there would be hell to pay. Reason was on the side of Ned, Stockton, and Fremont, but one thing he had learned in his years growing up in Washington, reason didn't always get a chance to put in its two bits' worth.

The rest of the trip to Washington was spent in the luxury of riverboat and train. Ned, with Jourdan and Kit at his side, went straight to his mother's home. Bloomingdale.

Without announcing himself, Ned found his mother in the kitchen. She turned at the sound of his entrance and dropped the pan of bread dough in her hands.

"Ned, my God, sit down." She rushed to him, gave him a quick hug, and pushed him into a ladder-back kitchen chair. She surveyed her son, gaunt and skeletal, and tried her best not to worry over him like a hen over one of her brood.

He could read her thoughts by the look on her face. "I'm fine. Mother. I've lost a lot of weight, but I'm fine. Are Mary Edwards and her family in Washington?"

"You sit down and I'll get something for you to eat." His mother turned to the stove and talked as she worked. "Mary and her family are in Chester. But we'll go there just as soon as you've finished your business here."

"I've got friends with me," Ned said, then rose and walked to the back door. He waved Kit and Jourdan in and introduced them, just as Sampson, his mother's houseman and Ned's longtime friend and mentor, entered from the carriage house at a run.

"Mister Beale!" he said and stood hesitantly, a wide grin on his black face. Ned crossed the room and engulfed him with a hug, now a little more of an armful than he had been the last time Ned had seen him. Jourdan watched with interest but said nothing until Ned introduced him.

Ned motioned to the men. "Get your things upstairs. . . . Sampson will show you to my brother's old—"

"No, sir," Carson said with a groan, and Ned remembered he hated to be inside. "I'll sleep out in the barn."

Ned laughed. "Then show Jourdan—"

"Ned?" his mother interrupted, a slightly shocked look crossing her face.

Jourdan did not miss the inflection in her voice, and quickly added, "No, sir, Ned boy. I be stayin' in the barn--"

"He can stay with me," Sampson, who slept in a room off

the carriage house, offered quickly, then Jourdan chimed in.

"I be stayin' with this man."

Emily Beale looked relieved, and Ned decided his own feelings were best left unsaid in his mother's provincial house. She was far more open-minded than most.

"I've got to get to the Navy Department, Mother," Ned added quickly, and turned to Sampson. "See these men are well fed. It's been a long journey." But a proud one, Ned thought as he exited the room and hurried upstairs to don his uniform. He had been traveling in buckskins. It was only May. They had completed the journey, fighting the rigors of late winter, in less than three months. He wondered how fast it could have been done had there been a road. From what he had heard of the northern trails to California and Oregon, the way they had come was obviously superior. This, too, he would report to the Navy Department.

By the time he was dressed, Sampson had the gig harnessed and waiting. When Ned entered the large brownstone Navy Headquarters building, he collided with someone, and looked up to see Norvell Johanson, who exited the building with two other men in high hats, black frock coats, and blue trousers, white stocks tied about their necks. Ned stepped back and surveyed the tall, blond ex-Navy man without smiling.

"Johanson! I thought you were on the other side of town now. Didn't I hear you were elected to the House?"

"That's correct, Beale," Johanson said rather contemptuously. "Still, I try to keep in touch with my good friends in the Navy Department. They need the help of Congress, you know." His look turned triumphant. "You look like hell warmed over. ... I see you are wearing the epaulets of a lieutenant? It was my understanding your commission had not yet been approved."

"Acting lieutenant, by special dispensation of Commodore Stockton."

"Stockton? Unfortunately, none of us has heard the last of Stockton. I'm personally introducing a petition to Congress to formally chastise Stockton and his whole contingency of Pacific Squadron officers for that disgraceful business in California. Had Kearny not arrived—"

Ned reddened. "Chastise? Stockton is a hero, you damn fool. If it hadn't been for Stockton—"

"Stockton wanted to be king of California. And Fremont . . . disgraceful. I'll be surprised if he's not court-martialed. And don't call me a fool, you lackey. I understand you've been glued to Stockton ... a true sycophant."

"Sycophant?" Ned roared, and stepped forward threateningly. "You know nothing of the California situation. Stockton and John Charles Fremont are both heroes!" It was all Ned could do not to knock Johanson on his back, and maybe some sense into him, but to do so in the lobby of the Navy Department would be career suicide at best.

"We'll see what Congress has to say about that," Johanson continued, and spun on his heel and started away. Ned, his jaw clamped, stared after him. Johanson paused at the door and turned back; the other men stood between him and Ned, as if expecting Ned to launch himself at the congressman at any second. A slow smile slithered across the congressman's face.

"I understand Mary Edwards has been communicating with you?"

"We write," Ned snapped, wondering what business it was of Johanson's.

"These ladies are sympathetic with servicemen. I imagine she will soon be bored of it." Johanson lifted his head and glowered down his nose at Beale. "You see, I've been calling on her quite often." He spun on his heel and disappeared through the door.

Ned stood rigidly, heat prickling his neck, trying to calm himself before he entered the office of John Y. Mason, the secretary of the Navy. After serving as acting secretary of war for some time as well as secretary of the Navy, George Bancroft had resigned to become U.S. minister to Great Britain. Ned had not met the new Secretary of the Navy, Mason, but had heard good things about him. The secretary did not keep him waiting.

Ned stood at rigid attention until the secretary raised his eyes from a parchment he was reading. "At ease, Mr. Beale."

Striding forward, Ned offered a handful of dispatches, then his orders.

Mason silently read the orders, which Stockton had addressed to Beale but suggested be presented to the secretary:

> I have selected you to be the bearer of the accompanying dispatches to the Navy Department in consequence of your heroic conduct in volunteering to leave General Kearny's camp, then surrounded by the enemy, to go to the garrison of San Diego for assistance and because of the perils and hardships you underwent during that dangerous journey, to procure aid for your suffering fellow soldiers. You will proceed without delay with Mr. Carson's party by the most expeditious route overland. On your arrival at Washington you will immediately deliver the dispatches to the honorable secretary of the Navy and receive instructions for your future government.

Mason looked up over his pince-nez glasses and adjusted them on the end of his nose. "When did you leave California, Mr. Beale?"

"February twenty-fifth, sir."

"Take a seat," Mason directed. "That is excellent time, particularly in the winter."

"We didn't tarry, sir."

"You come rather well recommended by Commodore Stockton."

Ned flushed, embarrassed by the manner in which Stockton had constructed his orders. "Thank you."

"Kit Carson accompanied you?"

"Yes, sir."

"I also want to speak with Mr. Carson as soon as possible. Is he with you?"

"He's at my mother's home . . . Bloomingdale."

"Fine. Later then. Now, Mr. Beale, please tell me from the beginning, what transpired in this fiasco the Navy is being so criticized over in California."

Ned looked a little surprised. The secretary continued, "And be precise and definitive; I'm going to ask a secretary in to take notes. We're in for political battle, Mr. Beale."

Suddenly tired of having to be wary, Ned collapsed back in his chair. The secretary walked to a side door and called out. A young midshipman, pen and tablet in hand, hurried into the room.

Ned sighed and clamped his jaw. He would almost rather be back in the wilderness worrying about savage Indians than here in Washington, worrying about politicians—they seemed a much more formidable enemy.

For two very intensive days—days Ned had hoped would find him on his way to Chester—Ned answered the secretary's and other officers' questions. Then for two more, he sat in silence in the hall outside while Kit Carson, properly attired and consequently uncomfortable in frock coat and high hat, did the same.

Finally, Ned and his mother—Carson and Jourdan having gone fishing with Sampson—left on the train for Chester, Pennsylvania. When they arrived, Samuel Edwards was in town. Ned found himself strolling the elm-lined street near Mary's home, arm in arm with her—the first time he had seen her in over a year. Ned, now twenty-five years old, had come to Chester with the intention of leaving betrothed to Mary Edwards. But his confidence had been shaken as she seemed somewhat distant and aloof, and also as a result of Norvell Johanson's parting comment about "calling on her." Ned wondered how many other young men were calling on Mary.

"You must have lost thirty pounds since I saw you," Mary said with concern.

"You find it unattractive?" Ned asked. "I'm sorry to disappoint you." Exhausted and still ill, he could not help but be a little defensive.

"No, silly. It's just that I'm worried about you."

"That's kind of you," Ned said, but his tone reflected his irritation. For the past several days he could not get Norvell Johanson's comments out of his mind, nor his own anger at not having knocked the congressman flat on his back. They strolled in silence for a few steps, Mary twirling her parasol, which matched the yellow gown she wore. Ned thought she had never looked so lovely. And that fact irritated him even more.

Ned said, hoping to broach the subject of Johanson and his relationship with Mary.

"Oh?" Mary answered, offering no enlightenment.

"He said he had been calling on you."

"I've seen him many times ... at receptions and other public affairs," Mary said, seemingly amused at Ned's probing. Again they strolled the pathway in silence, and Ned felt an uncommon and uncomfortable heat on the back of his neck.

"Only in public?" Ned quizzed.

"Are you jealous of Norvell Johanson?" Mary teased, with a sparkle in her eyes.

"Why would I be?"

"Don't be peevish with me, Ned Bcale." Mary picked up

the pace, beginning to become irritated with Ned's inability to get to the point.

"Peevish? I thought we were taking a walk and the opportunity to get to know each other again." Ned spoke without looking at Mary. Rather, he stared straight ahead, happy that the pace was faster so he could get back to Mary's house and out of this conversation.

"I thought we already knew each other rather well."

"So did I, but I'm beginning to wonder." Ned felt truly irritated, and he didn't really know why. This was not going the way he had planned.

"You've been gone two years, Ned," Mary said. "I've done all the normal things the daughter of a congressman would do. I've gone to church functions, to public receptions. . . . I've met hundreds of handsome young men."

"Not many of them newly elected congressmen—"

"You are jealous of Norvell?"

Again they walked quietly for a few steps. Ned cleared his throat. "I'm in the Navy, Mary. A Navy professional. I'll be gone, from time to time, for more than a year. . . possibly much more. I've hung my professional hat on Commodore Stockton's hat rack . . . and Stockton is about to come under the harshest criticism. Right now I don't feel like much of a bargain . . . marriage-wise."

"I didn't know I was fishing for a bargain," Mary leased, her voice again light.

"If you are, I hope you're using that worm Johanson for nothing more than bait."

Mary flushed. "Congressman Johanson—"

"You called him Norvell before."

She reddened. "Norvell is a contemporary of my father's. His occasional presence in my father's house is business, Ned Beale. I'm sure I will see him from time to time, but no more than you will see some lithe Indian maid or beautiful California senorita. I would like to go back now."

"As you wish." Ned spun on his heel, feeling a little guilty as the thought of Rosalia Bandini flashed though his mind. Still, with his long strides making one for Mary's two, he paced her back to the house. As they reached the step, he could not help but add, "1 thought you had seen him only publicly. You said his 'presence in my father's house' . . ."

"That, too, on the occasion of a party or during business, I consider public, Ned Beale." Mary opened the door, not waiting for Ned to do so, and stepped inside. "I'm going up now. I'm sure I'll see you at dinner."

Ned watched her cross the entry and ascend the stairs without looking back, and suddenly he felt very empty. He cursed himself, crossed to a porch swing, and plopped down in it. He was still creaking back and forth when Samuel Edwards arrived from his meeting in town. Seeing Ned on the porch, he turned the team and buggy over to a servant and ascended the porch, shook with Ned, and perched on the porch rail. Ned remained standing.

With gray pork-chop sideburns fuzzed out from his rosy cheeks, and penetrating dark eyes, the congressman was not an unpleasant man, if an inquisitive one.

After answering the congressman's seemingly endless questions about California and ignoring the tiff he felt between him and Mary, Ned finally got to the business at hand. "If I can convince Mary I'm worthy, would you consider my joining your family, sir?"

"You wish to be adopted?" Sam Edwards teased, reflecting his daughter's propensity to do so. Seeing that Ned was hardly in the mood to be amused, he chuckled, then added quickly, "If Mary considers you worthy, Ned, I certainly do. I do wish you would wait until this business regarding Freemont and Kearny is over—"

"I haven't asked Mary yet, sir. I thought I would ask your permission first."

"Mary seems to think your asking is a foregone conclusion. Ned."

"She does?" Ned's eyes shot up. "I thought Norvell Johanson—"

"That pompous ass, If I didn't need his support occasionally—"

"Then he has not been calling?"

"Mary wouldn't give Johanson . . . well, suffice it to say, Mary is a politician's daughter, and she well knows the value of good connections and decent relations with other politicians. Not a bad trait for a military officer's wife, I might add."

Two nights later, on that same porch, having made peace with her, Ned Beale kissed Mary Edwards for the first time.

Infused with new confidence, he asked her to marry him, and she consented. He and his mother returned to Washington a week later. He was betrothed to Mary Edwards, though they would not wed for at least a year, probably two.

Still, he could not wait to run into Norvell Johanson again. This time, without lifting a hand, he had done an even better job of boxing Norvell's ears than he had on board the *Independence*.

Now if he could just get the hell out of Washington before the cauldron that was the result of the Stockton/ Fremont/Kearny spat in California boiled over. The last thing he wanted was to be stuck in "civilization," grilled by politicians, when the war with Mexico raged in the South, and California, a place he had grown to love, awaited its destiny.

But his first night back in Washington, attending a reception at Senator Demon's Washington home, he was sucked out of the frying pan and into Washington's political fires.

CHAPTER SIXTEEN

You've got to help us," Jessie Fremont pleaded.

Almost as soon as Ned and Kit Carson had entered the senator's home, where almost a hundred people had gathered for a reception, Benton and his daughter ushered Ned into the senator's sitting room. Benton, cigar in hand, waistcoat straining at its buttons over his abundant belly, sat behind a finely wrought cypress desk—a gift made in South Carolina—and in a rather pompous manner informed Ned of the brewing situation.

Ned knew that Thomas Hart Benton and President Polk had been at odds ever since Benton had wanted to be appointed supreme commander of the forces fighting Mexico. When Polk had not done so, Benton had begun a campaign of discrediting Polk's administration.

"I don't know how I can be of help," Ned answered. He pondered the terrible news that John Charles Fremont was on his way to Washington, finding his own way as a prisoner-at-large, having been placed under arrest by General Kearny by letter for insubordination. A court-martial proceeding was scheduled.

"Well, sir," Benton said, his eyes narrowing as he carefully tapped the ash from his cigar into a solid silver ashtray, "I can be of help to you. The question you should ask," he said shrewdly, "is, will I?"

"I don't know what you mean, Senator," Ned parried. He knew exactly what the senator meant. "I will do anything in my power to help John. . .anything legal and truthful. He acted admirably in California, and to the best of my knowledge, always at the orders of Commodore Stockton."

"That, sir, is exactly the point this pompous ass Kearny is trying to make. John acted under Navy orders, ignoring his own commander."

"That's not correct, Senator. Kearny was present many times when Stockton was directing John's actions. Kearny never, at least in my presence, contradicted those orders."

"That's fine, Beale, but the real problem is to discredit Kearny. He was a coward at San Pasqual—"

"That's not true, Senator. Kearny may have been a poor commander, but never a coward."

Benton studied Ned for a moment, then rose and circled the desk and leaned on the edge, crossing his arms. "Then a fool, if not a coward. A bungling idiot who caused the death of two-score men."

"He did not conduct that battle as I would have."   "An idiot!"

"He did not deploy his forces as I would have."

Jessie spoke for the first time since she had informed Ned of the problem. "But you'll testify to the facts. . . ." She turned to her father. "The facts speak for themselves, and Ned, as the hero of San Pasqual, will have great credibility."

"There were many heroes," Ned offered. "Kit Carson and Jourdan, Archibald Gillespie, and a hundred others."

"Maybe," Jessie said with a smile, "but no others commended by their fellow officers and men."

"Kearny," Benton said triumphantly, "was at the Willard the other night when one of the other officers began telling a story about Carson. Kearny claimed he had never met the man and that Carson was not responsible for guiding him to California. And that he had no knowledge of Carson, or of you going to San Diego for help . . . and made no mention of your man Jourdan."

"Those are all lies," Ned snapped. "Carson, Kearny. and I did some pistol shooting in California together. Kearny was showing off his pistols and wanted Kit, particularly Kit, to fire them. He knew Carson well, and knows damned well . . ." Ned flushed and turned to Jessie. "Pardon me, Jessie, but this riles me." Ned calmed himself. "Anyway, he knows damned well what happened at San Pasqual. Kearny is angry because Carson reported to him when they first met that California was well under Stockton's control. Kearny sent most of his force south as a result of that report, then with his few remaining men exhausted, foolishly rode against Andres Pico."

"Then you see, Ned," Benton smiled knowingly, "the man is a liar and a scoundrel. His charges against John are totally false. Seditious, even. Typical of this administration, as a matter of fact." Benton launched into a long tirade regarding Polk. Finally, Jessie rose and saved Ned from the senator's onslaught.

"Father, there are almost a hundred guests outside, and all of them want to meet Ned. He's agreed to help. What more can we ask?"

The smile Jessie Benton flashed would have convinced any court of anything she wanted, Ned decided as he followed her out of the room. He could not believe the tale Benton had told about Kearny, but as the evening wore on, more and more stories were related to Ned about the reports Kearny and the dragoons gave of the Battle of San Pasqual, and more and more Ned began to believe that maybe Kearny had claimed he did not know Kit Carson. Politics, which to Ned seemed a word to cloak lies, began to sour his stomach.

Later that night, lying awake in his bed at Bloomingdale, Ned thought about the events of the evening.

Kearny had claimed he had saved the day at San Pasqual. At least the articles in the newspapers reported it that way. If Kearny was after John Charles Fremont and planned to make him a scapegoat, what was to stop him from going after Stockton? And his officers?

Ned rolled over and pulled the covers up, resigning himself to the Mexican way of thinking. *Poco tiempo*, he decided. There was time enough tomorrow to worry about it.

The next day, Senator Benton demonstrated to Ned just how much he could do for him. He read into the Congressional Record, a glowing report of Ned's action in going to San Diego through the enemy lines for help and of his heroism, a report in contention in every way with the story Kearny had relayed of the events in California.

Without question Ned was aligned, as far as all of Washington and the Polk administration was concerned, with the Fremont side in the Fremont/Kearny argument.

Benton fought hard to get the matter resolved without a trial. In his pompous way, he continued to threaten the president and the cabinet. He swore he would see Kearny and his three underlings—Turner, Emory, and Cooke—brought before their own court-martial proceedings. All he really succeeded in doing was causing Kearny to spitefully bring two additional charges against John Fremont: mutiny, and disobedience of the lawful commands of a superior officer.

The Fremont trial kept Ned and Carson in Washington for most of the year. When Ned was finally called to testify, after hearing the self-serving testimony of Kearny and his dragoons regarding their action at San Pasqual, he was terribly disappointed to have his testimony declared inadmissible even before he could give it. The action of Kearny at San Pasqual, the court ruled, was not the issue in Fremont's courtmartial. The only issue was whether Fremont disobeyed a superior officer. After a great deal of political infighting, two of the three charges against Fremont were dropped. Finding him guilty on one charge, the court remanded him to the clemency of President Polk. Polk told Fremont to pick up his sword and return to duty after the trial. Instead, Fremont resigned.

By the time the trial had ended, Ned was thoroughly disgusted with Washington and politicians. Among other things, Kearny had claimed under oath that he did not know Kit Carson, just as Benton had said he would.

Ned was still engaged to Mary Edwards, but even that seemed tenuous as the trial, and his continued poor health, took almost everything out of Ned. There was little left for anyone else—he felt like a shell whose innards had dried up or been eaten away by worms. Ned refused all invitations to Washington's many parties and receptions. He wanted nothing to do with a government that would allow a man like John Fremont to be punished for acts Ned considered heroic, while Kearny went on with his career and was assigned even more responsibility, after acts Ned considered incompetent at best.

Time and again, Ned asked for duty carrying dispatches back to California. He wanted out of Washington and away from politicians. Finally, he received his orders. He parted ways with Mary Edwards with a hollow feeling in his stomach.

Nothing in his life seemed to be going right.

With dispatches in hand, Ned, Carson, and Jourdan reached St. Louis, but shortly after leaving the next stop, Fort Leavenworth, Ned fell ill again. Carson and Jourdan, at Ned's insistence, went on without him. Ned felt Jourdan would be better off in California. He had long ago paid his debt to Ned, and though he had seen thousands of miles of mesquite and chaparral, he had elected to stay with him. It was difficult for Ned to pan with Carson and Jourdan, but the dispatches had to be delivered. Jourdan was his own man, and belonged in the mountains and deserts.

It took Ned two weeks to recover from his relapse, during which time he received new orders. Again he was bound for the Isthmus of Panama, and on to Callao, where he was to join the *Ohio*.

By the time he started down the Mississippi, the war in Mexico was over. But it was just as well, for Ned was also soured on his military career. He was sick of politics and politicians and now realized that high-ranking officers were many times only politicians in fancy gold braid. He wanted to get back to California, and wished there were a road so he could clomp along on a good horse, or the way he felt, in a comfortable buggy. But there was no road, and again, he fought the Panama crossing.

Secretly he wondered, if he did get to California, if he would ever return to the East. He did his best to put Mary Edwards, Washington, and even his family out of his mind.

When he reached the *Ohio*, he reported to her captain, Commodore Thomas Catesby-Jones. And Catesby-Jones, to Ned's regret, proved as stiff as his name.

"Lieutenant Edward Fitzgerald Beale reporting for duty, sir."

"Lieutenant? It is my understanding you are a passed midshipman." Catesby-Jones spoke without looking up from his paperwork, nor extending his hand in welcome.

"Acting lieutenant, Ned offered, "by special dispensation of Commodore Stockton."

"Stockton is no longer commander of the Pacific Squadron, as you well know. Stow those marks of command until you get confirmation, Passed Midshipman Beale. Do you understand?"

"Yes, sir," Ned responded too quickly, his tone churlish.

For the first time since Ned had entered his cabin, Catesby-Jones raised his eyes. "That doesn't set well with you, Beale?"

"You are the captain, Captain."

"That's true, and it would serve you well to remember that. I brook no insubordination aboard my vessels, Beale, and prior accomplishments mean nothing here. What you do aboard the *Ohio* is all that counts with me."

"And what will I be doing aboard the *Ohio*, sir?" Ned questioned, but he was truly uninterested.

"I didn't ask for a new officer, Beale. In fact, I don't need one. You will not have a specific assignment, but rather will operate in sort of a floating capacity, what, when, and where needed. Do you understand?"

"What and where needed. Certainly, sir." Ned saluted, and spun on his heel to find the first lieutenant and get his bunk assignment. He was sure of one thing: Having his privacy was not a likelihood on board the *Ohio*. And he was right: He was relegated to bunking on the gun deck, and given a tarp to separate his quarters from those of the common sailors.

But he found that to his liking. He suddenly felt no interest in making friends, and this way it was easier to stay away from the officers' wardroom. Even when approached by other officers or midshipmen, Ned remained snappish and unfriendly. He did his work and didn't bother to comment on that of others. The *Ohio* made her way north to her new assignment in the port of Mazatlan. He made no friends, he wrote Mary Edwards no letters. He kept to himself, and for the first time in his life, did not even bother to read. Rather, he sulked.

When the *Ohio* reached her new homeport. Ned was among the first to draw shore leave. Within minutes, he had visited the ancient town's five cantinas and settled on one. And there be began to drink. *Aguardiente* was the drink of choice in Andolfo's Cantina. and by the time Ned was due to report back to the quay for the midnight boat, he had consumed his share, and the share of several others.

He awoke, lying in an alley, staring into the unblinking eyes of an iguana, one longer than Ned's arm. Ned leapt !o his feet, then reeled in dizziness, his head knotted from whoever had seen him leave the cantina in his drunken condition. With the sun beating down on him. he tried to find his bearings, then sat back down in the dirt alley. Unable to get his directions, he struggled again to his feet, wondering for a moment where he was. He remembered Andolfo's—and that he had been due back aboard the *Ohio* at midnight. He searched for his purse. It was missing, a fact that didn't surprise him under the circumstances.

Making his way to the street. he turned downhill, a good bet, for he could see the harbor at the foot of the long street. Pigs and chickens rooted and pecked in the road, ignoring him as he stumbled by. Finally he made his way to the shoreline, and then stumbled along the quay until he stood abeam of the *Ohio*, moored two cable lengths out in the harbor. He sat on the edge of the stone wall and waited, then lay back. and in a heartbeat, was asleep.

Someone nudged him with a toe, and he bolted upright. He rubbed the sleep from his eyes and realized he was staring into the hard gaze of Catesby-Jones.

"You're absent without leave, Beale," the commodore barked. Ned surveyed the men behind him and realized all of the ship's officers were staring down at him. "I was rolled and robbed, sir."

The commodore wrinkled his nose and stared him up and down. Ned realized he was covered with mud, or something worse, and struggled to his feet. "Rolled in pig dung, I would guess."

"Possibly chicken shit," Ned offered.

"Don't be smart with me," Catesby-Jones snapped. Ned wondered what possible difference it made what he had been rolled in, and shrugged his shoulders.

"Get down to the ship's boat and have the bosun row you aboard! Clean yourself up! You're confined to quarters for a fortnight!"

"Aye, sir," Ned said and yawned.

"You find that information less than exciting, Beale?" Catesby-Jones was beginning to redden. "Let's make it a month. Would you care to try for the brig?"

"No, sir," Ned said, but it was all he could do to keep from yawning again. Catesby-Jones spun on his heel and stomped away, followed by his officers, many of whom continued to glance back at Ned, Wondering how this could have been the man who gained the plaudits of his fellow officers during the California revolution.

Ned stretched and wandered down to the ship's boat. He fell asleep during the short row to the *Ohio*, and was prodded awake by the bosun with one of the oars. He made his way up the ladder, managed to shed his clothes, and rolled into his hammock.

When he awoke, his head ached in earnest, and the first lieutenant, a thin-faced chap as stiff as his captain, stood over him. "Catesby-Jones wants to see you, Beale."

Ned rolled out, managed to find a clean shirt in his duffel, but did not bother to comb his hair. He found his own way to the captain's cabin, knocked, and entered without awaiting an invitation.

Catesby-Jones stared in wonder at him. After buttoning up his own tunic, the commodore took a seat at his chart table. Ned, head throbbing horridly, looked around for another chair, spotted one, and started for it.

"No one said for you to sit, Beale," Catesby-Jones said with a growl.

Ned sighed and turned to face the seated commodore. "As you wish," he mumbled.

"What I wish is that you were the officer I was led to believe."

"I'm Passed Midshipman Edward Fitzgerald Beale," Ned managed, and again stifled a yawn.

"Are you ill, Beale?" the commodore asked, and seemed truly concerned.

"Not particularly."

"What does that mean, 'not particularly'?"

"We're all ill, aren't we, Captain?"

"What the hell are you driving at, Beale?"

"Nothing. I'm fine."

"Then begin acting so. I reacted harshly and out of anger when I gave you a month in your quarters. I'm reducing that to a week."

"Thank you, sir," Ned said. "Is that all, sir?"

"That's all," Catesby-Jones said, obviously still miffed at Ned's attitude. "You're dismissed."

Ned did his duty for a week, and confined himself to quarters each night and during his off time. The day his confinement was over, he received a letter from Mary Edwards. The brig Nova Scoria, a merchantman with a load of missionaries on their way to the Orient, had arrived and delivered mail. Catesby-Jones had invited the passengers ashore to join the crew of the Ohio, and requested the locals to put on a real Mexican fandango. It was to be an event.

Ned pocketed the letter, wanting to read it in private, and did not do so until he retired to his canvas room and pulled the tarps tightly shut. He lit a taper and lay in his hammock.

She began with the usual niceties, but Ned, to his surprise, began to fill with dread as he read on. In the final paragraph of the rather distant letter she said:

> I would be less than truthful if I did not tell you that I was disappointed with our relationship during your last months in Washington. I know that the trial was a great disappointment. That, and the fact that you seemed to be ill most of the time was a strain on you. Perhaps it would be better for you if you did not have to worry about our betrothal for a while? Perhaps you could concentrate on

your career, as you have always said was of
great importance to you. If you wish, you can
recant your offer, and I will understand.

In anger, Ned tossed the parchment aside and dressed for the
reception. It was obvious that Mary understood nothing about
him. She had no empathy for him nor John Fremont. She, like
the politicians she surrounded herself with, was only concerned with herself. Now that his career was on the skids, she
was off like a rat leaving a sinking ship. The hell with her, the
hell with the Navy. He buttoned the last buttons on his tunic
and headed for the longboat.

The fandango was held on the quay with the bay on one
side and a wide stretch of beach on the other. Among the
Methodist missionaries off the *Nova Scotia* were sixteen
women, four of whom were young, shapely, and appeared
ravishing to men who had been shipboard for many months.
To the surprise and pleasure of Commodore Catesby-Jones,
Ned was the picture of Navy pomp and ceremony—and a
gentlemen who went from lady to lady, dancing in the most
gracious manner to the *mariachi* band's attempts at the latest
eastern dance tunes. As the evening grew on, and torches
were lit around the portion of the quay used as a dance floor,
the Methodists thought Ned to be the most gallant of all the
officers.

The succulent odor of a roast pig turning over a pit in the
sand wafted over the crowd, and all of them awaited its removal from the spit. Even though the fruit punch provided by
the local dons was as virginal as the unmarried Methodist
ladies in attendance. Ned resolved that situation by making
friends with a group of vaqueros whom he found were to be
pan of the later evening's entertainment—and he found that
they were more than willing to be part of his at the moment.
Each *caballero* had a quart of pulque to help them kill time
until the riding exhibition and was eager to share it with the

256

marinero who spoke their tongue like one of their own. Each time he had the opportunity, Ned slipped out of the group of officers, local dons and their ladies, and wide-eyed Methodists, to take advantage of the vaqueros' hospitality, until finally he began to slur his words.

Catesby-Jones studied him suspiciously as Ned bowed low to the prettiest of the Methodist women and stood chatting with her in a most familiar manner while the Mexicans began a local dance. At the conclusion of the song, the announcer asked for the torches lining the sand to be lit while the next dance was being performed. Afterward the vaqueros would demonstrate the *carrera del gallo*, where they would bend low off their galloping mounts and pluck the heads off buried roosters. The women swooned with a combination of fascination and disgust. Then the announcer proudly announced that they would eat the pig that had been turning over the coals all day as soon as the riding demonstration was finished. It was even now being placed on the table already laden with dishes of fruit, frijoles, corn roasted in the shuck, and the inescapable tortillas.

Ned was greatly attracted to the young daughter of the Methodist leader and decided he would impress her and the Navy officers with his own riding skills. In San Diego he had participated in just such a display of horsemanship and had, one time out of many tries, managed to end up with a rooster's head in hand.

Without Catesby-Jones seeing him, he slipped out behind the band and meandered down the sand to where the vaqueros were gathering, while other young men buried roosters in the sand in front of the gathering. He drank with the men while some of them began to ride to drum rolls from an *Ohio* drummer who had brought his instrument ashore. The first two riders missed their marks, and Ned laughed and chided the men—and drew deeply on their bottles. He turned to one of the better-dressed vaqueros, who had introduced himself as Navarro Vega.

"Senor Vega, I thought the vaquero never mished ...missed?" Ned slurred.

"Have another drink, *marinero*." The tall vaquero studied Ned with interest and tolerance. "You speak our language well. Have you ridden the *carrera del gallo*?"

"One time, and found it eashy. . .easy to do. I'm surprised your men—these vaqueros you claim can ride—have not been success. . .successful."

"They do not ride as well as I," Vega said simply. It did not seem a brag coming from him.

"Nor I," Ned said, then guffawed loudly. "I am the *marinero* vaquero. Are you a betting man?" Ned knew that all vaqueros loved to bet, particularly when it came to horses and riding skills.

"Of course. What is it you would bet?"

Ned studied the man for a moment, then turned his attention to the man's stallion staked nearby. "Tha. . . that's a fine headstall," he said, admiring the silver adorned bridle on the horse.

"True, as fine as any made."

As they talked, the crowd roared its approval at one of the men, who came up with a rooster's head. Jealous, Ned pressed on.

"I has'. . .have two American silver dollars against your poor headstall."

"Never. However, I do admire the brass buttons on your jacket."

"You would bet brass against silver?" Ned said with a drunken laugh.

"No, I would not be so foolish. But I would bet the head-stall against your jacket and shirt."

"Done," Ned said. "I will ride first, and use your horse. . .until one man misses."

258

"He is a great deal of stallion, *marinero*," Vega cautioned. "A bit more difficult to ride than your rowboat." Vega and all the vaqueros laughed.

"You will not lass. . .laugh, when I return to my ship with your headstall, senior." Ned moved to un-stake the stallion.

"Hold on, *marinero*," Vega said, stopping Ned. "You will leave the jacket and shin with Pablo here. He will hold the stakes."

"How can he hol. . .hold the headstall?"

"You will have the headstall with you," Vega said, again demonstrating his tolerance.

Ned laughed and removed his jacket and shirt. Bare-chested, he mounted.

Vega handed him the bottle of *pulque*. "For luck," the vaquero said, and all the men laughed.

Beginning to be offended at their amusement, which now seemed more like derision, Ned glowered at the men, but took a deep draw on the powerful liquid. He quelled the urge to cough and handed back the bottle. He turned the stallion facing the course stretching fifty yards down the sand to where, in the light, the crowd awaited the next rider.

Ned concentrated, wondering if they had set out more torches—there seemed to be twice as many. He could not see the head of the rooster, but knew it was there. He steadied himself on the dancing stallion and lost a stirrup. Chuckling, one of the vaqueros stepped forward and shoved Ned's foot back into the *tapadero*. Again Ned concentrated on the course ahead of him. Before he could give the big horse his heels, the vaquero who had helped him with the stirrup brought his quirt hard across the horse's flanks, and the animal leapt forward.

As Ned galloped out of the darkness to the accompanying laughter of the vaqueros behind, he saw the look of surprise on Captain Catesby-Jones's face. Ignoring him, Ned tried to locate the rooster as the horse reached a dead run, bearing down on the crowd. But everything was reeling, and the spot he was sure was the gallo's head would not stay still. It seemed to skitter across the sand. He kicked the port side stirrup away and bent low. Ned's head swam. The rooster's head seemed to roll away. Ned jerked rein violently and saw the crowd scatter in front of the charging stallion; then felt himself falling.

Head over heels, he flew off the stallion, now bucking violently as it knocked flaming torches aside. Ned lofted through the air, skidded across a table covered with bowls of food, the punch bowl, and a golden-roasted pig, all of which scattered from his attack. He rolled to the sand flat on his back. He tried to rise but could not, falling back to caress the sand-covered pig the announcer had been so proud of. Catesby-Jones leaned over him just as Ned, covered with beans and chunks of melon, managed to roll to his side—and pass out.

He awoke, eye to eye with a rat the size of an English terrier, locked in the bilge. The rat scampered away but Ned could not, as much as he wanted to.

Two weeks later, after subsisting on bread and water, he was taken before Catesby-Jones.

"Beale, you are a disgrace to the uniform," Catesby-Jones said disgustedly. "It would be better for all of us if you would tender your resignation."

"Never, sir," Ned, now stoic and ashamed managed quietly.

"Then I have some special duty for you. You seem to manage to carry dispatches with some ability. God knows I don't need you aboard the *Ohio*"—his voice rang with derision—"but I do need a courier to go to San Francisco with a dispatch."

"San Francisco?"

"Yerba Buena. . .they've begun calling it San Francisco, like the bay. You're to see for yourself proof of the rumored gold discoveries, then proceed back to Monterey for dispatches from Consul Thomas Larkin."

"Fine, sir," Ned said, hiding his enthusiasm at being ordered to return to California and at getting away from the *Ohio*. "When do I leave?"

"There's a Mexican *goleta*, the *Campeche*, sailing north on the morning tide. Be aboard her."

"Yes, sir." Ned saluted and about-faced.

"And, Beale," Catesby-Jones called after him, "don't fail me."

The commodore's words seemed to work into Ned's backbone as he moved below to the gun deck and his duffel. Failure was something with which he was unaccustomed. No matter what his personal problems, his health, or his opinion of the Army, Navy, and politicians, he would not fail again, nor give anyone a reason to doubt him. But as he walked below to his makeshift room to gather his things, his knees felt weak under him and his head swam as if he were still intoxicated. His two-week meager diet had done nothing to bring him from the ill state he had suffered so long.

The next morning, shaven and property uniformed, he was again called to Catesby-Jones's cabin. He presumed it was to receive the dispatch and was surprised when the commodore handed him another folded document, which carried the seal of the Department of the Navy.

"I was not going to deliver this to you, Beale. I considered writing the Navy Department with a recommendation that they reconsider. . .but here's a dispatch that arrived during your stint in the bilge. Your commission as lieutenant."

Finally, after a little more than ten years of service aboard ship, at age twenty-five, he was a full-fledged officer.

"Don't insult those epaulets," Catesby-Jones cautioned him sternly. A feeling of true regret at his recent actions gnawed as his gut as he saluted and left the room.

Along with the dispatch from the Navy Department, a communiqué Ned had waited years to receive, was a packet of letters from his mother, from Mary, and to his surprise, one from Senator Thomas Hart Benton. Mary's letters were cool, but nothing more was said about letting him out of his offer of matrimony. Benton's offered his congratulations at becoming a commissioned lieutenant and explained that he had interceded with the Navy Department and with President Polk to obtain Ned's appointment—but assured him that Ned's own record had been the deciding factor.

Later that morning, Ned sailed on the Mexican schooner for San Diego, where he would catch an American coastal vessel north. The first thing he did after the vessel cleared the harbor was find a flat spot atop a scuttlebutt to write. He apologized to Mary Edwards for acting the fool, and swore that he would never give her reason to doubt him again. And more importantly, he swore it over and over to himself as the schooner plowed up the coast of Baja California.

Never again, he resolved, would he disappoint himself, never again would he disappoint Mary.

There were things that needed doing, and, Ned decided, he would be the one to get them done.

CHAPTER SEVENTEEN

On the morning of the last day of June 1847, Ned stood at the taffrail behind the ship's churning side wheel and marveled at the contrasting images of San Francisco. In the distance he would see the old Mission Delores surrounded by new structures, redwood-planked walls with shake roofs, adobes with tile roofs, and tents. As the steam-driven *Pride of Mobile* dropped anchor near a half-finished wharf, Ned hoisted his duffel onto his shoulder and descended the ladder into the ship's longboat. But not without trepidation. He couldn't help but notice the remarkable lack of people.

There must be a plague of some kind in San Francisco, he decided. Otherwise why aren't there people on the streets and working the wharves and landings?

Without so much as an Indian to meet them, they pulled the longboat onto the mud flats, then to the greeting of clamoring gulls, smacked across the muck to the sand.

An old vaquero, his face creviced by years of wind and rain and dust from trailing cattle, sat on a willow branch crab trap, watching Ned stride away from the longboat. The old man lit a clay pipe and sucked at it as Ned paused nearby and yelled to him. *"Viejo! Donde esta los hombres del ciudad?"*

The old man puffed at the pipe. He eyed Ned as if he were a little loco for not knowing. "They have all gone to the goldfields, senor."

So they were true—the rumors they had heard in Mazatlan, and continually on the way north. He had expected to see a city with the hustle and bustle of new business, a city responding to a gold strike, not one as devoid of life as the shells that littered the beach. He had sensed something strange as soon as they entered the harbor. Over a dozen ships—barks, brigs, schooners, and two steam-driven side-wheelers rested at anchor in the bay. But none of them had anyone on board.

Ned hoisted his duffel, resigned himself to walking to the presidio—then dropped the duffel quickly and spun toward the *Pride of Mobile* as two shots echoed across the water.

Her captain stood at the rail, two smoking pistols in his hands. But he was not reloading. Rather, he cursed and waved his arms. Half his crew was swimming ashore—and the half who weren't probably couldn't swim.

Ned hoisted the duffel and headed up the road along the bay to the Presidio. The ramparts of the old fort were green with moss, the old Spanish cannons still pointing out to sea, although they had been spiked years before. The Stars and Stripes, reflecting the admission of Texas into the union, waved in the sea breeze.

But so did something else.

As he neared, somewhat winded from the walk but feeling far stronger than he had in over a year, he shook his head in disgust. Two men, still wearing the uniforms of dragoons, hung from a scaffolding in the center courtyard of the presidio, their eyes bulging as if they had hung there for some time. The bodies swayed back and forth in the quickening breeze.

Ned paused at the gate, where only one guard stood. "Where's your commanding officer?"

"Third door after you turn right," the private said with little enthusiasm. Ned moved inside and rounded the heavy stone wall to the right, found the door, and entered. He dropped his duffel on the floor and moved to a desk, where a mutton-chop sideburned sergeant glanced up from his paperwork; then returned his attention to it without a greeting.

"What did those two do?" Ned asked, gesturing with his head to the courtyard.

The sergeant disdained to look up, then appraised Ned a moment before he answered. "They died a' throat trouble. Captain thinks a rope collar's a good treatment."

"Serious, Sergeant?"

"Same thing ninety-five percent of the city's done, but when those two did it, it's called desertion."

"And what was that?" Ned asked even though he had already guessed the answer.

"Headed out to the goldfields."

"Why haven't you gone?"

"Because he's a good soldier," a voice came from an interior doorway before the sergeant could answer.

Ned turned to face a tall, well-tailored officer standing there. Despite his youth, the man's reddish hair was receding, and his eyes bored into Ned in critical appraisal. Striding forward, Ned extended his hand and introduced himself.

"Captain William Tecumseh Sherman," the man replied, with a handshake that convinced Ned he was firmly in command of the fort.

The captain dropped some paperwork on the sergeant's desk; then Ned followed him into his Spartan office and sat across the desk from him.

"I've been sent by Commodore Catesby-Jones to verify the rumors of a massive gold discovery," Ned began.

"Not rumor, Mr. Beale. I've seen it myself. Tell the commodore if he's wise, he'll keep his ships out of California."

"Why's that?" Ned asked, a little offended at the Army giving advice to the Navy.

"Relax, Beale. In fact, call me Cump, my friends do, and I've got friends in all the services, even the Navy." Sherman smiled, and his smile was infectious. Ned returned it, and the captain continued. "If the commodore doesn't stay out of the bay, he might as well sell his sails for tent canvas. He'll have his ships here for some time. Crews'll jump ship and head out for the goldfields like everybody else. Stories are coming out of the fields that a one-legged blind mute can get rich overnight." Sherman paused to fish a cigar out of his tunic pocket; he extended it to Ned, who shook his head. Sherman dug for a match and continued, "And they're not all stories. I've seen a man with several pounds of dust and nuggets. In fact, last night I saw a man at Gaspar's Cantina with an eight-pound nugget. I watched them weigh it."

Ned sat, awed at what the captain was telling him, but did not respond.

"What's the commodore's interest in all this? You coming all the way from Mazatlan an' all."

"General interest, I'm sure." Ned rose and walked to the captain's glass-paned window to stare out across the bay. "But someone should get confirmation of this to Congress, Cump. It will help California be confirmed as a state."

"I didn't know she had asked to become one, Edward," Sherman said between puffs on the cigar he held the match to.

"My friends call me Ned. If California hasn't, she will."

"Well, Ned, don't worry about Congress. I've dispatched a messenger. Last week, ten men rode out of here on their way over the Sierra. Congress will know in short order.''

Ned visited with the man for a while, then excused himself and headed for Gaspar's Cantina. As sure as Sherman's word, a miner stood at the bar, well into his cups, with several pouches hanging from his waist. Laying on the bar, surrounded by the few patrons left in town, rested the biggest chunk of gold Ned had ever seen.

Ned sidled up among the men and ordered a drink. As it was poured, he nodded to the grizzled miner with the newly acquired wealth.

"That's on me," the man with a wispy pate spotted by dark sun stains instructed the bartender, who handed Ned the *aguardiente*.

"Don't fret, friend," the bartender admonished Ned when he pushed his own coin across the bar. "He hasn't let another man buy a drink in two days ... an' he can afford it."

"Yeah, Navy, do not fret."

Ned turned quickly at the sound of the familiar voice. Jourdan stepped over and, laughing loudly, clapped Ned on the shoulder.

Ned assessed him up and down. With two pistols at his waist and dressed like a vaquero, he looked like a *pistolero*. Ned shook his head in wonder. "I thought you and Carson would be staring at the world with your heads on the end of a Shoshoni lance," he said with a laugh.

Jourdan bellied up beside him at the bar. "Carson stayed in Taos. I came with scouts who hear about gold," he said. Then his expression turned serious. "But no women in gold-fields."

Ned grinned, then glanced around. "I don't exactly hear the rustle of calico around here."

"A few. But most leave with miners. Now I go with you. Where you go?"

"I'm headed back to Mexico and the Pacific Squadron." Ned eyed the nugget on the bar. "Then, with luck, back east again. It would be good to have you come with me. Besides, you still owe me eleven dollars and eighty cents. "

"Good. I go with you," Jourdan said. It was settled.

Ned turned back to the bar and waited for a break in the conversation, then asked the miner, "Why haven't you turned that chunk to cash?"

"Ain't that much cash in Frisco," the man said with a laugh.

"Might be," Ned offered. The conversation quieted as the men weighed what he had said.

"You look more like a commodore than a banker," the miner said with a drunken chuckle.

"Both." Ned smiled back. "You got a price on that nugget?"

"Gold's sixteen dollars the ounce," the man said, and his eyes narrowed. "But that's for these here pouches of dust and lil' baby nuggets. Ol' king nugget here'll bring more'n that . . . from some fool who wants to stand proud with the ownin', while he lies about finding it his self." He guffawed at the thought.

"I heard you telling these fellas that there's more of these out there, just for the picking."

"If Everett Champness, emperor of these here Californy goldfields, says there is, then they be, son."

"Then why not sell the big one, Mr. Champness?"

A little irritated, the miner turned his attention to the bartender. "Hell, no Navy man has enough to buy ol' king nugget anyhow."

"I might know of one who'd give you ten dollars an ounce," Ned said quietly.

Again the miner appraised Ned.

"That's some kind of braying for a blue-coated donkey!" he said loudly, and his cronies laughed along with him. Jourdan had said nothing, but stepped forward and eyed the miner without breaking a smile.

Ned was beginning to feel the heat on his neck, but he had a higher purpose than teaching the man manners.

"Ten dollars an ounce, in gold coin," Ned offered forcefully. "Coin you can trade anywhere."

He had been saving his money for years, and carried a money belt loaded with Spanish, Mexican, and American gold coins. He had rapidly calculated the weight of the giant nugget in his mind and, if eight pounds was the true weight, had come up with one hundred twenty-eight ounces. He carried almost two thousand dollars in his belt and hidden in his duffel.

"Bray away, man," the miner taunted. "This here chunk is eight pounds."

"Ten dollars," Ned barked, knowing everyone in California wanted gold coins.

"Fifteen," the miner said, "but I want to see the shine of your money."

Ned unbuttoned his tunic, pulled the belt from his waist, and dropped it on the bar with a thump that betrayed its weight. The miner reached for it, but Ned grasped his wrist in a steely grip. The miner jerked his hand back.

"You want the ten or not?" Ned asked.

"I said fifteen, but if you'n not just honkin' like a gray goose, I''ll take fourteen, and make up your mind ... you'll get a sore crotch from fence-straddlin'." He got another laugh from his whiskey friends.

"Twelve," Ned said, his eyes never leaving the miner's. "Without an assayer here, who's to say what the real value is?"

The miner cut his eyes shrewdly. "How do I know you're not just a'cacklin'?"

"Now it's you with the sore *cojones*. Twelve, in gold coin right now. That nugget'll do you no good if you're headed back to the fields. If he hears about you carrying that monster, some ol' boy not so lucky'll split your gullet from ear to ear while you're sleeping the whiskey off."

"That's been tried by a couple of fellows who're now buttons on St. Peter's coat, or Satan's. Thirteen," the miner said, understanding—no matter what he said—the logic of Ned's argument.

"Thirteen's an unlucky number," Ned countered, knowing he had the nugget but wanting the best price he could get.

"Thirteen and a half ain't." The miner smiled sincerely for the first time.

"Neither's twelve and a half, so get off that fence rail."

"An' you'll buy the house a round a' good nose varnish?" the balding miner asked, beaming.

"And I'll buy the house a round of the best whiskey in the house," Ned assured him, reaching for his money belt.

Another familiar voice rang out behind Ned.

"Mr. Beale!" Ned turned to face the captain of the *Pride of Mobile*. Under a floppy-brimmed hat he had traded his officer's cap for, he stood dressed in canvas pants, linsey-woosley shirt, and lace-up boots, and he wore a heavy pack on his back with crossed pick and shovel showing over the top of his shoulders. On his hip he carried a pistol and an Arkansas toothpick, as well as a belt hatchet. He was weighed down like a donkey.

Ned shook his head in wonder. "I take it you're off to the diggings?"

"The *Pride* is well battened down, and I couldn't raise a crew for love or money. Actually," he said with a laugh, "I guess love of money is the reason I can't raise a crew. I've written the owners a letter explaining. You headed for the fields?"

"No, sir. But good luck to you."

"Count out your coin, Navy," the miner pressed, and Ned did .

Ned left Gaspar's Cantina with the biggest nugget he had ever seen or heard of in his duffel, and with Jourdan close on his heels. They didn't even bother to try the harbor for a ship—the ships in San Francisco Bay were one-way vessels. Instead, they rode double on Jourdan's horse, straight back to the Presidio, where they talked Cump Sherman out of another mount. Before nightfall, they were heading down the peninsula for Monterey. Ned wanted to be far from San Francisco by the time the news of the nugget he carried got around.

With Larkin's dispatches added to his duffel, and the loan of Larkin's personal schooner with two Mexicans and Jourdan as crew, Ned rounded the end of Baja California on the first day of July. They met a *goleta* coming north, and the Mexican schooner had informed them that the *Ohio* and Commodore Catesby-Jones had moved north into the Sea of Cortez to La Paz. Ned sailed north and three days later, to the surprising accompaniment of the band on board the *Ohio*, dropped his hooks within a few yards of her.

Even with the Fourth of July celebration under way, Catesby-Jones retired to his cabin and received Ned privately.

Ned had gained almost twenty-five pounds and was beginning to look like the same man who'd ridden out of San Diego to help Kearny fight the Battle of San Pasqual.

"You look well, Beale," Catesby-Jones said. "Much better than you did when you left. Traveling is good for you. We're having a celebration ashore later, due to the holiday. The locals have invited us ..." Then the commodore seemed to remember the last fandango Ned had attended. "But I'm sure—in fact, I insist—you're too tired to attend." Catesby-Jones gave him a wry look.

Ned smiled, but didn't answer or argue, so Catesby-Jones continued.

"What of the rumor of gold?"

With a bit of a flourish, Ned rolled the nugget out of a cloth he had wrapped it in onto the commodore's chart table. It clunked to a stop in the center. Catesby-Jones studied the bulbous chunk of yellow metal for a moment without touching it. Then he lifted his doubting gaze to a smiling Ned.

"That cannot be!"

"Lift it!"

The commodore hoisted the heavy load, and pushed a thumbnail into a protruding section of it.

"I'll be damned!" he said with an uncharacteristic curse.

"My reaction exactly," Ned said. "And the tales of these are rampant. I saw bags of dust and smaller nuggets. Every

271

able-bodied man in San Francisco and Monterey has gone to the diggings. We must get this news to Washington."

Catesby-Jones weighed Ned's statement for a moment, then his look soured. "I have no budget, nor the inclination, to send another man to Washington."

"Commodore," Ned said quietly, "this is news that Washington must have. California is only a territory. If my guess is right, she'll see the biggest influx of people the world—at least America—has ever seen. She'll need law enforcement. She'll need supplies of all kinds. She'll need men. And she'll bring millions of dollars of trade to the United States and her merchantmen."

"I have no budget, Beale."

"I'll go, and pay my own way."

The commodore seemed to consider a moment, but shook his head. "No!" he said with finality. "The next ship 'round the Horn will take the news. A few months'll be soon enough."

Ned took a steadying breath, anxious that he was not convincing the commodore. Then it came to him, and he cut his eyes slyly at the man. "The captain at the San Francisco Presidio, William Sherman, has already dispatched a squad of dragoons to Washington with the news. Cump Sherman and the Army will see that Congress is informed . . . and, of course, get the plaudits for doing so." Ned watched Catesby-Jones screw his face into a growl .

"The Army! The blasted Army has done enough in California!"

"I could beat them there, Commodore," Ned said, his excitement contagious. "I know I could, if I crossed Mexico. It'll be a lot faster than sailing all the way to Panama and back up. I talked for hours with Archibald Gillespie about his trip here across central Mexico, and all I have to do is backtrack it. I'll pick up a ship for the States in Veracruz."

272

"Out of the question," Catesby-Jones said, but Ned knew he was weakening. "The county is wild with *ladrones* now. Since General Paredes has disbanded his army, the bandit ranks have swelled. It is impossible to get through. . . particularly for a man carrying a chunk of gold that would make a decent anchor."

Ned pulled off his tunic and pushed up his sleeve. He extended his arm so the commodore could see it. "I'm brown as any Mexican after my days at sea, and I speak Spanish like a native. I'll dress Mexican and take Jourdan with me. We'll get through the highway thieves. They'll mistake us for one of them. In fact, they'll be lucky if Jourdan doesn't steal their horses."

The commodore studied him, his hands folded behind his back. "It wouldn't do for the damned Army to take this proof to Congress. Still, I can't spare men for an escort."

"If any vessel at all sails south and can get us across the Sea of Cortez, we'll leave in the morning." Ned saluted and spun on his heel to head for his duffel before the commodore changed his mind.

"Ned"—the commodore stopped him at the door, using his given name for the first time—"write your will and make your peace with the Lord before you attempt this crossing."

"Get me another five Allan's revolvers, sir. The pepperboxes'll serve as my escort and do the Lord's work along the way." Ned grinned. "He, too, wants the news of His bounty to reach Washington."

Ned hired a fishing boat, and he and Jourdan headed south on the ketch on the morning tide. Both men leaned on her rail dressed in *calzonevas*, *charros*, and wide-brimmed hats—and both carried a pair of Allan's revolvers. In addition, Ned had four more revolvers and holsters in his duffel. They would have to find riding stock in San Blas, where Ned planned to move inland to Tepic, then to Guadalajara, then on to Mexico City, where Catesby-Jones had instructed him to call on the

U.S. minister, Nathan Clifford, and pick up any dispatches Clifford might want carried on to Washington.

The storms, *chubascos*, hit them with a vengeance before they passed the tip of Cabo San Lucas, and beat them all the way southeast to Mazatlan, where they lay over for three days to let the weather quiet down. Jourdan did not smile for the whole trip. He still hated the sea. Finally, after twelve days, they reached San Blas, the busiest and oldest port on Mexico's western coast. Ned bought four small but mountain-tough *caballos* from a Mexican hostler, who advised them not to ride into the mountains. They were deep in the jungle-covered mountains, well out of the city, four hours after hitting the port.

Each man carried two six-barreled revolvers at his waist and two in saddle holsters. In addition, Ned carried two in the bedroll tied behind him. It was said of the Allan, "If she didn't get what she went after, she would fetch something else." The little stubby pepperboxes, as they were affectionately known, were inaccurate but single action—a single pull of the trigger would rotate and fire the next .36-caliber barrel. They could put a lot of lead in the air. They were feared.

They met only one other mounted party on the road. A guarded Mexican coach, known locally as *diligencia*, rolled by them with ten mounted guards flanking, its windows tightly shut. The guards eyed them carefully, and Ned was almost pleased to note that they considered them to be *ladrones*. The disguise was apparently working. The rain began to pelt them before nightfall.

Ned reined off the rutted, muddy road and found a campsite under the spreading branches of a jungle tree. They built a fire and fried the last of the salt Pork Ned had carried from the *Ohio*. While it was still light, they rolled out their bedrolls near the fire; then, as soon as it died down and darkness closed over the jungle, they reasoned to one of Kit Carson's old tricks and rolled up and moved their horses deeper into the undergrowth. After staking them, they continued even deeper, where they rolled out again. The jungle rang with a thousand insects and animals, and both men were soon covered with bites of flies and tiny no-see-ums that bit before their presence was known. The night passed without incident, but the tracks of a half-dozen mounted men surrounded their dead fire as they rode out the next morning. Ned and Jourdan said nothing, but eyed the tracks and each other knowingly. That night, without having to discuss it, they rode on without stopping. The sky had cleared and the moon lit the trail enough to follow. By the next afternoon, having switched horses a dozen times to keep up the pace, they reached Tepic.

They found sanctuary, and feed and stable for the horses, at a small Catholic mission on the outside of the old city, and rested. The next morning they rode out again. High in the mountains, they began to get relief from the insects as the jungle thinned. That night one man stood guard while the other slept, a regimen they would continue.

Twice they passed rough-looking riders on the trail. One group of four eyed them greedily, but both Ned and Jourdan palmed the nasty-looking little pepperboxes as they passed, and the *ladrones* settled for a *"Buenos dias."*

Both men and horses were beginning to feel the pressure of the continued pounding of the trail, and the hit-and-miss rations and sparse grass. Jungle grasses carried little nourishment for their bulk, and the horses had had no grain. Their ribs were beginning to show. Then jungle gave way to higher, conifer forest.

After miles of hard climbing, Ned was glad to hear from a traveler that the next pass would crest the mountains and they would begin descending into the high valley that sheltered the capital of Mexico. The sun dropped toward the western horizon and the shadows stretched long as, high into the pass, they approached a narrow, rocky, climbing ravine.

Jourdan reined up ahead of Ned. "This is bad spot." He studied the cleft ahead and the deep shadows of the rocks lining it.

"Hopefully the last one before we drop into the valley of Ciudad de Mexico,'' Ned said. His eyes were bloodshot. He yawned and stretched widely—but he, too, was wary at the tight pass and its hundreds of hiding places. "We ride far apart?" Jourdan suggested.

"You first or me?" Ned answered, looking not at Jourdan but rather scanning the rocky hillsides.

"No matter, man in lead gets shot in belly, man in rear gets shot In back." Jourdan spurred his horse. It was clumsy trying to hold one of the revolvers, rein your horse, and hang on to the lead rope of the spare mount. Ned pulled his second horse forward and tied its lead rope around its neck so he could let it run free, and it would not drag. He watched Jourdan clatter up the trail ahead. Before he followed, he glanced back. A half-dozen riders had formed up in the trail fifty yards behind them. They had not been there before and must have come down out of the rocks. He whistled, but his mouth went dry and dread flooded his stomach. Jourdan reined up and looked back, seeing them also.

Jourdan spurred his horse, already twenty-five paces ahead of Ned, and Ned gave his roweled spurs to the little mustang's side sooner than he had planned to, following Jourdan to the crest above. But before they reached it, another half-dozen riders clattered out of the rocks, blocking their way.

Jourdan threw aside the lead rope of the drag horse, dropped his own reins to the saddle horn, then snaked another Allan's into his hand. He spurred the mustang on, a revolver in each hand and a determined scowl on his face.

Ned, too, palmed an Allan's in each hand. The trail lay so narrow the horses had no choice but to stay on it; Ahead, it lay blocked by half a dozen hard men, but so was their retreat.

As Ned nudged the mustang forward, he hoped Sherman's small troop of dragoons was having better luck than he and Jourdan. Ned patted the nugget deep in a leather bag hanging from his saddle horn and wondered what the fat-whiskered bandit chief, who snapped an order to the others, then spurred his horse out of the waiting half dozen, would think when he claimed it. With it, he would become the *rey de ladrones*—the king of thieves.

As his mustang closed the gap behind Jourdan, Ned decided that this rough-looking man would never see his reign—for Ned would kill him first when the shooting started.

CHAPTER EIGHTEEN

The fat bandit chief held out his hand. "*Alto!*"

But Jourdan gave the spurs to his game little mustang and it leapt forward, slamming into the bandit's mount.

Both horses fought for position in the narrow trail, rearing and pawing with flashing hooves—and when they quieted, Jourdan had a revolver jammed into the folds of the bandit's double chin. The other revolver he had trained on the men behind, and unequal display of firepower as each bandit carried a musket and pistol in addition to a machete. Ned spurred forward until his mustang's head hung over Jourdan's mount's hindquarters. All the other bandits trained their muskets on the travelers, and grasped their machetes nervously. Any second, Ned knew, they might be shot full of holes and hacked to pieces.

Jourdan spoke quietly. "Your Spanish better. Tell him he will die where sits if others don't move."

Ned repeated the order loudly in Spanish just as the half-dozen riders behind them closed the gap and reined to a sliding halt in the narrow trail. They, too, held muskets and machetes.

"There are too many of us," the fat man spat. But his words faltered. "Surrender your valuables and your guns, and you can each keep a horse and ride on."

"You're generous! See these fine pistols, *amigo*," Ned threatened. Keeping one trained on the bandit chief and holding the other aloft so all could see the multiple barrels. "They carry enough shots to leak the fat from you and each of your men. Stand aside."

The fat man didn't speak. Jourdan jammed the Allan's deeper into his double chin, making his eyes bulge and his cheeks quiver.

"Ride on, Jourdan," Ned commanded.

"How ride on and keep gun in fatso's face?" Jourdan questioned.

Ned pondered, and turned half in the saddle to keep an eye on the men behind. "Make him get in the saddle in front of you," he said, his eyes on the ladrones.

Jourdan glanced at the size of the man, then back at Ned as if he had had too much sun. The flies buzzed around them in the silence while Jourdan searched for an alternative. Finally, he backed off the saddle to the horse's hindquarters, still keeping both pistols trained on the fat bandit and the reins gathered in a pistol-filled hand.

The man gulped a sigh of relief when Jourdan pulled back the pistol—but it left an angry, six-holed red welt on his dewlap.

"Tell him," Jourdan said with a growl.

"Hey, *gordo*, climb into the saddle in front of *mi amigo*," Ned said. The others had begun to grumble among themselves, and Ned began to worry that they might have so little regard for the bandit chief that they would merely shoot him and Jourdan out of the saddle and damn the consequences. The fat chief did not move.

"Move it, *gordo*," Ned demanded, bringing both his pistols to bear on the fat man. "If you're not in the saddle in a heartbeat, yours won't anymore. We'll both give you two pills . . . and even your fat belly couldn't handle that much lead."

Once the man decided he had no choice, he was surprisingly nimble. In a flash he had switched directions and squeezed into the saddle in front of Jourdan.

"Hands on head," Jourdan ordered, and Ned repeated the order in Spanish. Jourdan knocked the man's wide-brimmed hat off the front of *gordo's* head, and it flopped to the trail. He clasped his blunt fingers together on top of a head full of thick black hair.

"Ride away," Ned snapped to the others, "or as many coyotes will feed on *gordo's* belly tonight as hombres have lain on his mother's."

"Do what they say;" the leader spat when Jourdan shoved the six-barreled weapon roughly behind his ear. "There is no need to disgrace my sainted mother," he mumbled to Ned.

Complaining loudly, the riders in the trail ahead turned their horses and finally, after much clamoring and cursing, faced the other way. They gave the animals their heels and clattered up the rock cleft.

Ned turned to those behind. "Don't follow, amigos, or the *gordo* will surely die . . . as will many of you."

A thin-faced man leading the group behind, fingered his old Spanish musket and spat on the ground, raising a puff of dust, but nodded. Ned glared at him, and the man lowered his muzzle to the ground. Ned urged the mustang forward, feeling a small surge of triumph as his horse stomped the bandit chief's sombrero flat in the narrow trail .

Carefully picking their way up the steep trail, Jourdan's mustang straining under its load with each deliberate footfall, they passed the six riders who reined off at the crest of the rise.

Ned turned in the saddle, wanting to wipe the sweat from his brow, but kept both pistols leveled on the bandits. The trail began a rapid descent, and Jourdan's horse slipped and slid. The two spare horses were caught up by the bandits, but Ned did not argue—it was a cheap price to pay.

A quarter mile down the trail, the bandits still in sight, Jourdan yelled back over his shoulder, "Are you ready?"

"As ready as I'll ever be," Ned answered.

Jourdan brought the Allan's across the fat bandit's head with a thump like hitting a melon, and the man tumbled from the saddle. Jourdan's horse plunged forward before *gordo* plopped to the ground. Ned's horse jumped to avoid the fallen man.

They flew down the trail, clattering and sliding, lather flinging from the horses. Ned glanced back and was shocked to see the bandits less than a hundred yards behind. The trail dropped off into a steep arroyo, and Ned feared they would not reach the bottom before the pursuing riders could rein up at the top and fire at them while they were still in the range of the muskets. He carefully quieted the little mustang, then snapped off four shots while Jourdan began the descent. The riders behind scattered off the trail into the brush.

The hill was so steep Jourdan's tired mustang had to set its front feet and slide most of the way. As soon as the animal reached the sand bottom, Jourdan reined around to cover Ned as he made the plunge. The game little mountain horse took the steep side—almost a cliff—at a run. Ned, leaning far back in the saddle, his back along the mustang's rump, marveled at the horse's balance. They hit the bottom at a dead tun. Ned regained his upright seat and flashed past Jourdan, who spurred his horse after.

The arroyo widened when they moved down it. Finally it opened onto a broad, alluvial fan, and they gained the cover of a thicket of scrub oak. They reined up under the shade and studied their back trail.

"Let's leave trail awhile," Jourdan suggested.

Ned eyed the hard ground, knowing it would be difficult to track them and soon impossible in the failing light.

"Lead the way," he said, puffing almost as much as the heaving horse under him. Jourdan reined off the trail, and for the next several hours they fought the through branches of the scrub oak in the pitch-black darkness while letting the horses pick their own way. Finally they collapsed out of their saddles and rested.

"I'll take the first watch, amigo," Ned suggested. "You did well, getting us out of that last tangle."

Jourdan nodded, stretched out on the ground, and was snoring almost as soon as he was horizontal.

Even though the days were scorching hot, the nights were cool, and they slept well, when they weren't standing guard.

By the time the heat of the next day reached its peak, they could see Mexico City in the distance, and by supper time, when it began to cool, they reined up in front of the American minister's residence. Ned thought he had never seen such a welcome sight as the Marine guards at attention at the sides of Nathan Clifford's wide double doors.

Washed, combed, and brushed, Ned soon stood in the long dining room, sipping a brandy.

"It's amazing that you got through," the tall, graying Clifford said for the fourth time since he had met Ned. "We've been advising all travelers to ride with the *diligencia*."

"I've no time to wait on wagons and guards," Ned said. "The news I carry must reach Congress."

"It's amazing, what you've told me about this gold discovery." Nathan Clifford shook his head in wonder. "What providence that this should come only after we have liberated the territory." His wife, a fine-featured, silver-haired woman who reminded Ned of his mother, entered the room and was introduced to him. Ned got a flash of homesickness.

Several dragoon officers had also been invited to supper, and were due at any minute. As Mrs. Clifford left to attend to something in the kitchen, the minister turned to Ned, moved closer, and in a most personal manner asked, "I understand you were there during the siege at San Pasqual?"

"Hardly a siege. But I was there."

"Tell me, did old Kearny really make such a fool of himself as rumored?"

"I'm no judge of Army officers," Ned said, quelling his urge to condemn Kearny and refute the accusations against Fremont.

"Hell, it's no matter now, Beale," Clifford said. "Tell me the real story."

''No matter? Did Kearny retire?''

"Retire? You didn't know? Kearny died a couple of months ago. He came here directly from Washington to take over the Army of Occupation. Instead he took a fever and has gone to meet his Maker."

"I'm sorry to hear that," Ned said sincerely, for Kearny had been a brave man if a somewhat foolish one.

The sound of the butler answering the door caused the two of them to turn away from the conversation, and Ned was just as glad that they had. He would not be goaded into making any disparaging remarks about a brave man, particularly a dead one who could no longer defend his honor.

Clifford walked to the doorway of the dining room and returned with several dragoon officers in tow—including a strikingly handsome gray-eyed brigadier general named Franklin Pierce.

After Clifford made the introductions, he asked Ned, "Perhaps you would like to take a tour of the troops tomorrow?''

''No, sir,'' Ned said politely. ''I'm in the saddle again at midnight."

"Midnight? My God, man, you've just ridden in from San Blas in record time."

"And I plan to make Veracruz in record time. Midnight, but thanks for the offer. " The dragoon officers shook their heads in bewilderment at this Navy officer in Spanish dress, and Ned knew they thought him a little bit touched. He was particularly taken with Franklin Pierce, especially after learning that the general had worked his way up from private. Before they took their seats at a table laden with more food than Ned had seen since he left California, he turned to Clifford.

"Would you please make sure my . . . my guide . . .is properly fed?"

"He's in the stable. I've already made sure the waiters took him out a plate."

"Same as I'm eating?" Ned asked, and received a strange look from Clifford for his trouble.

"Same as the servants eat."

Ned did not comment, but received another strange look when he wrapped a thick slice of beef and a half chicken in his napkin and stuffed it inside his shirt during supper. He took brandy in the minister's parlor with the officers, listening to their tales of glory in the late hostilities, until the gilded French clock struck eleven-thirty; then he excused himself to the stable. They rode out on fresh horses, again each trailing a spare thanks to Clifford's generosity, into a moonless night while Jourdan gnawed away on a cold roasted half chicken.

They traveled in reverse the same route used by General Winfield Scott and his conquering army of twelve thousand Americans to enter Mexico. As dawn gave testimony, the signs of the recent war stood, or laid, everywhere. Towns and villages had been destroyed, leveled by General Scott's artillery. Burned-out buildings and burned fields of corn testified to Scott's wrath.

They came upon only one more group of *ladrones*, and this time it was Ned who saved the day on the rough trail. When the bandits reined out of the thick forest ahead, Ned jerked rein off the trail with a leap and a vaquero yell and plunged into a deep ravine. Sliding and spurring the horses, branches and thick cover slapping at their faces, he and Jourdan astonished the bandits, who reined up and looked in wonder at their fleeing prey. They were so taken aback, they did not attempt to follow the loco fleeing pair.

After sleeping a total of only eight hours in sixty, riding horses nearly dead, they reached Veracruz, 270 miles from Mexico City, in that record time. Ned hired a rowboat and rowed directly to Anton Lizardo, the American anchorage. After the wild ride, he found it would be two days until a ship, the *Gremantown*, sailed for the States. He and Jourdan slept fitfully, frustrated for most of that forty-eight hours.

Finally, they rested in earnest, in familiar swaying hammocks on the sloop of war, sailing for Mobile, Alabama.

Forty-seven days out of La Paz, on September 14, 1848, Ned Beale stepped from a coach in front of the Capitol Building in Washington. With Jourdan standing in the lobby, and with his own uniform torn and mussed, Lieutenant Edward Fitzgerald Beale strode down the aisles of Congress while a fat congressman debated the merits of adding a new device to the halls of the Capitol building, mechanical air cooling, like the system just installed in New York's Broadway Theater.

As Ned descended the long aisle, catching only slight notice from the dozing members in attendance, he decided he wasn't interrupting much. Still, a haughty sergeant at arms met him at the foot of the aisle. The man stared at the bundle Ned carried as if it might be a bomb of some kind.

"You are not a member of Congress," he said in a low voice so as not to interrupt the man at the podium. "Visitors belong in the balcony."

"I've ridden and sailed over three thousand miles to bring a message to Congress." Ned's glance brooked no interference. "I'm here at the direct orders of Commodore Catesby-Jones," Ned stretched the truth and moved forward. The Speaker of the House rose from his chair at the rear of the podium and stared at Ned. He stepped forward when Ned gained no more than a glance from the sweating congressman at the podium. The Speaker quelled the sergeant at arms with a wave of his hand.

"What's your business, young man?" the Speaker asked.

"I've an important message, all the way from California, sir.''

"This is hardly the place—"

Ned let the nugget roll out of its cloth cover onto the polished wooden floor of the House of Representatives. Both the Speaker and the sergeant at arms jumped back as if the golden lump were a viper.

"Gold!" Ned said with authority.

The Speaker stared at the lump for a moment, then walked over and whispered to the fat-jowled congressman at the podium.

The man glared at him, mopped his brow as if to solidify the point he was trying to make, but turned back to his dozing audience and offered a placation.

"Gentlemen, I've agreed to yield the podium for a few moments." He waddled back up the aisle.

"Speak your piece, young man," the Speaker said, his eyes still fixed on the massive gold nugget.

Ned bent, retrieved the nugget, then walked to the podium. The House quieted as he set the nugget up in plain view of each and every member of the group. Some of them elbowed their neighbor awake at the new development.

"This, gentlemen," Ned said in a loud, clear voice, "is proof of the rumors you've heard regarding the gold strike in California. This nugget is pure gold and weighs eight pounds."

A murmur rippled through the crowd.

"I've personally seen bags of gold, simply picked up by men who had no more expertise than any of you. . .at mining, I mean."

"Mr. Speaker!" a voice called out from the rear of the house.

"The speaker recognizes the honorable Congressman Johanson from Pennsylvania."

"Since when do we allow common military men to interrupt these proceedings? Surely there's a more proper forum for mining information—"

"This 'mining information' will change the face of this nation," Ned said deliberately, recognizing yet another slight from Norvell Johanson.

"Here, here, let him speak!" the crowd yelled, drowning Johanson out. Reporters, who had also been dozing, moved forward to get a better look at the nugget, and the members of Congress sitting near the front also rose and moved forward. Soon Ned was speaking as if he were standing in a saloon, surrounded by other beer-drinking patrons who laughed and admired his prize.

Finally, Norvell Johanson, who had not come near, deigned to move forward, and managed to shout over the throng, "I know this man, and he's untrustworthy. Take that chunk of rock to the Bureau of Mines for proof that it's more than fool's gold."

Ned pushed his way through the other congressmen until he stood face to face with Johanson.

"I bought that 'chunk of rock' with my own money, Johanson. And I'll let any man here, other than you, take it wherever they wish to test its worth. You keep your hands off it. And keep your comments to yourself, unless you want them shoved back down your throat."

Johanson reddened, and several congressmen laughed and patted Ned on the back as if he had said something they had been wanting to for a long time. The sergeant at arms moved between them. Ned, once more inundated with questions, turned his attention away. He did not notice Johanson, or several members of the press, leaving the House of Representatives.

The following morning, Ned addressed the Senate at the invitation of Senator Benton and Senator Foote of Mississippi, with whom Ned had traveled part way from Mobile.

That afternoon at Bloomingdale, with Ned and his mother at the table and with the nugget as the centerpiece, Mary Edwards commented for the tenth time, "That is simply the biggest hunk of gold that's ever been seen."

"Not as big as it was yesterday," Ned said with a wide smile, taking her hand in his.

"Why not?" his mother asked.

"Because"—he turned to Mary—"I stopped at Stanton's Jewelers on the way here and had them carve off a chunk."

Mary and his mother looked at him in surprise.

"For a ring."

Mary furrowed her brow, not comprehending.

"For an engagement ring," Ned repeated, somewhat exasperated.

Finally, Mary Edwards smiled, then blushed, but she clung tightly to Ned's hand.

During the next few days, the East Coast papers were filled with Ned Beale's exploits and news of confirmation of the gold strike rumors—including an article that would bring Ned national attention. William Carey Jones, a reporter for the Washington *Intelligencer*, was an old friend of Ned's and was John Charles Fremont's brother-in-law. After a number of inaccurate articles appeared, Ned consented to an interview with Jones—if he would keep to the facts. His article, *A Ride Across Mexico*, would confirm Ned as a national hero. Only after receiving such acclaim was Ned invited to meet with President Polk, who treated him as an advocate of his enemy, John Charles Fremont's father-in-law, Senator Benton. After a short conversation, Polk dismissed him with little comment and seemed to Ned to doubt his word about the gold. That night Polk wrote in his journal, "Nothing of consequence happened today." But he was wrong, for Ned's arrival marked the beginning—albeit a slow one at first—of the greatest migration the United States had ever seen.

Some time later, half of Ned's nugget went on display at the U.S. Patent office—after he turned down this offer, via a letter from new York:

> Dear Sir:
> Mr. Harding of the *Enquirer* has just in formed me that you have in your possession an 8 Ib. lump of California gold. As I am always anxious to procure novelties for public gratification I write this to say that I should be glad to purchase the lump at its valuation if you will dispose of it and if not that I should like to procure it for exhibition for a few weeks. A line in reply will much oblige.
> Your obedient servant, P. T. Barnum

He did have one meeting of great eventual consequence before he left Washington. His old friend and mentor Robert Stockton had retired from the Navy and been elected U.S. senator from New Jersey. Ned accepted an invitation from Stockton to attend a private dinner at Willard's Hotel. Only three men were in attendance: Stockton, Beale, and New York financier William H. Aspinwall. Ned left feeling he had made a positive impression on one of the country's most successful capitalists—and with a business proposition to look for opportunities in California for Stockton and Aspinwall.

The following week, tiring of the attention, Ned and Mary traveled to Chester and Mary's home. in addition to Mary's company, Ned was pleased to renew his friendship with Mary's brother, Harry Edwards, who pleaded with Ned to allow him to join in the adventure of traveling west. Ned was concerned with Harry's physical ability to stand the rigors, and refused him, suggesting that he have the lumps on his head read again.

Less than a week later, on October 14, Ned said good-bye to Mary, now wearing the wide engagement ring fashioned from a chunk of the nugget, and he and Jourdan headed west, this time overland. He carried dispatches for the newly installed government in Santa Fe and the commanding officer there, Colonel John M. Washington; for Colonel Mason in California; for General Joseph Lane in Oregon; and for his own boss, Commodore Catesby-Jones, who against Sherman's advice, had sailed for San Francisco.

Before Ned left the East, he read one of the few newspaper articles critical of his exploits. It was an interview of several congressmen, including Norvell Johanson:

> Beale is a self-serving exploiter, only interested in obtaining government contracts for himself and his new business contacts. This will never happen. All that glitters is not gold, and one nugget does not a gold discovery make. Even the president has dismissed Beale's dubious nugget without comment. He has, however, demonstrating his usual prudence, dispatched official messengers to California to obtain verifiable samples of any gold or other minerals for study by the United States Mint....

Again he left Washington soured on politics and politicians. Shortly after Ned and Jourdan left to return to California, the Army couriers arrived with additional proof of the value of the California discoveries. But the new rash of newspaper articles was directed to Beale, his ride across Mexico, and to the Navy more than to the Army. Johnny-come-latelys were congratulated quietly. and Ned Beale was regaled for the daring initiative he had shown. While Ned traveled west, another

Mexican War hero was recognized by the American public in the first national election where voting took place nationwide on the same day. Old Rough and Ready Zachary Taylor, was elected president, defeating Polk's ordained successor, Lewis Cass. Polk had fired Taylor as commanding general of the Mexican forces after Polk had agreed to a two month armistice. Taylor, considering orders from the politicians in Washington to be "advice," took his own path, defeated Santa Anna in a critical battle, and gained the admiration of Americans.

Ned stopped at Fort Leavenworth on the Missouri long enough to engage the services of the well-known trappers Andrew Sublette and Baptiste Perrot as guides. He also offered his services to the Army, who had seventeen raw recruits destined for Oregon billeted at the fort. Ned agreed to see them to California, reconciling the move as one that would save the Navy money—for he would use the recruits as packers and obtain the use of Army stock. He convinced the colonel in command that the recruits could cross the southern route in the winter, saving the Army the cost of having the men lay over until spring. and catch a ship north out of San Francisco. The party of twenty set out westward from the Missouri River across the flatlands of Kansas, following the Santa Fe Trail into the gradually rising plains of eastern Colorado. Passing Bent's Fort on the Arkansas River, they swung southwest to Raton Pass—and headlong into bitter cold.

CHAPTER NINETEEN

Ned headed west from Fort Leavenworth with a chest swollen with confidence. He had been the toast of the   East Coast, Mary Edwards wore his ring, and he had an offer of a business proposition from men with money to back their words. Nothing could go wrong now. His confidence chilled to a living nightmare.

As they climbed into the mountains, cold tortured them and rain and snow battered them continually. And worse, the dragoons proved to have no mettle.

Late one afternoon, after two weeks on the trail, Ned decided the frosty camp would be cheered by fresh meat and went in search of a deer. Baptiste Perrot offered to accompany him, as did Jourdan, both cautioning him about the Apache signs they had been seeing all day. Jourdan had a splinted ankle from the mule he rode taking a hard fall, so his company on a hunting trip was out of the question. Ned was tired of company, and said he could hunt better alone.

Tine   More than a mile from camp, on the gentle slope of a cedar brake, he felled a doe with a single shot from the Sharps he carried. He carefully searched the horizon before dropping from his horse to dress the doe out and load it across the mustang's rump. He was concentrating on preserving the liver and not breaking the bile glands in the failing light, with a whistling freezing wind buffeting him, and so did not hear the pounding hooves of the dozen Apaches on the soft hillside until they were almost upon him. His echoing single shot had given him away. Leaving the deer, he scrambled to catch his spooked horse. The mustang leapt to a dead run with Ned clinging to the saddle horn, until he finally swung into the saddle. The old trick of plunging into a steep, shouldered ravine at full gallop bought him a few precious seconds as musket balls kicked up puffs of dust and arrows whistled death songs over his head.

He pounded on. As he rounded a turn in the ravine, he could see the lights of his men's campfires in the distance. He hunkered low in the saddle. Chancing a glance over his shoulder, he confirmed that the Indians were not discouraged by the fires in the camp ahead or the failing light. Only a half-mile more. A lead ball ricocheted off his belt, almost knocking him from the saddle but doing no real damage. The last sliver of sun dipped below the horizon, and in the lee of the mountains, shadows became one.

Darkness would be his friend.

He plunged in and out of ravines, ducking among the low cedars, picking the roughest route, hoping against hope he could out ride the savages.

Just as he was sure he would make camp ahead of them, a blue-coated dragoon broke from the brush on his right in a panicked run. The man screamed to Ned, his voice taut with fear, "Help me! I've got six children!"

Ned sprung from the saddle, hit the sand in a stumbling stagger, and handed the reins to the running bluecoat. He had not liked the man, he had been a shirker, but he was in Ned's trust. Ned planned to mount behind him, but missed the boot-filled stirrup—not offered to him—as the trooper gave heels to the horse so hard the animal's ribs thumped like a bass drum. He raced away.

"Take him in, you som'bitch!" Ned shouted over the pounding hooves of the escaping horse. "Send back a party to bury me!" Wide-eyed, the man glanced over his shoulder, but at the Indians, not Ned. The rider hunkered down and pounded away without bothering to answer. Ned dove into the brush, cursing the dragoon private and pulling his brand-new

Walker's Colt. He palmed back the hammer on the big weapon. He could feel the pounding of the Indian ponies' hooves over his own pounding heart.

Well, this time you've done it, Ned Beale. Mary Edwards will be a widow before she's a wife.

But the Indians, screaming and yelping, galloped right on by, so close he was splattered by the gravel thrown by one pony's hooves.

Ned rose from the sage in wonder and stared after them as they rode away. Thinking back, Ned realized the Indians had dipped into a ravine and had not seen him give up the horse.

He heard gunfire from the camp as a dozen men fired, and knew the small party of Apaches would turn tail. After he was sure they were not retracing their steps, which would bring them back across his position, he put shank's mare to the test. Just before he reached camp, Jourdan, a stiff-braced leg extending out from the saddle, reined up beside him.

"I been looking for you."

"Good. Thanks," Ned said, tight-lipped, angry at the dragoon who had left him to rot with his scalp hanging off some Apache belt.

"Good to see you one piece," Jourdan said. "You want climb on behind?"

"Nope," Ned snarled. "I'll walk this out."

"Okay," Jourdan said, content to rein in behind the striding Beale.

They entered camp just as the burial party was leaving to find him.

Baptiste guffawed when he walked in. "You look about as 'appy as ze woodpecker in ze petrified forest."

"I'm happy," Ned snapped, forcing a grin. "I've got my hair, and my yellow steak doesn't wrap all the way around to my brisket." He turned to glare at the group of dragoons, who kept their own company. "There's fresh meat out there, if any of you Army boys want to fetch it.'' They flashed him a look, but said nothing and cut their eyes away.

"Salt pork, she is looking good to everyone," Baptiste said, then guffawed again.

"You want I cut that bluecoat's gut out?" Jourdan asked, sensing Ned's anger.

"He's all gurgle and no guts," Ned said. "It'd be a waste of time. Let's fry up some salt pork." Somehow, that night, the salt pork actually tasted good to Ned.

Before they reached the pass, after two more run-ins with Indians, from an Indian powwow known as Big Timber where several friendly tribes camped, Ned sent a letter back by a trapper headed to Fort Leavenworth. It was addressed to his future brother-in-law, Harry Edwards:

> I have had a most unpleasant journey so far, and the men I have with me are so utterly worthless not a day passes that I do not punish two or three. There are thousands of Indians here, mostly of friendly tribes, but I have had two affairs in which I came so very near losing my hair that I am not positive at this moment that my scalp sticks to the top of my head. The weather is most cruelly, bitterly cold and freezing. It is said the Raton Mountains, which I am about to cross, are impassable but I have crossed impassable places before.
>
> Love to those who love me.

Raton Pass lay in snowdrifts twenty feet deep. During the fourth night in the pass, the dragoon sergeant and six recruits deserted—including the man who had abandoned Ned. The cold continued to torture them, freezing mules at night and providing them with plenty of Missouri elk meat. By the time they reached Santa Fe, on Christmas Day, several of the men had to have hands or feet amputated. All of the horses and most of the mules had frozen on the trip.

Ned told the rest of the recruits they could stay in Santa Fe if they wished, and all chose to do so. On January 11, Ned, two packers, Baptiste, and Sublette left Santa Fe and headed west. They crossed the Sierra de los Mimbres in a blinding snow. The weather eased up when they reached the Gila River. At Yuma, Ned tried new country, proceeding north rather than crossing to Warner's Ranch over the Mojave Desert. Finally, after seeing thousands of antelope on a grassy high desert plain, he turned west, entered the mountains, and again turned north, hoping to hit California's great central valley, called the Tulares by the Spanish. He knew it would lead him to San Francisco.

He passed through a mountain valley thick with live oaks, and looked down on a lower valley that stretched so far to the north he could not see the end. As he descended a narrow, wild-grapevine-tangled canyon into it, he admired the country. He would have liked to have stopped to visit and study the quiet Indians whose villages spotted the foothills on the valley's edge, or lined the larger lakes in its bottom, but he had no time. They watched him with interest as he passed, but made no hostile moves. It was a place he would not forget.

After five days of hard riding north along the eastern edge of the long valley covered with lakes and ponds from the mountain runoff, then crossing it fighting tule thickets and mud bogs in a northwesterly direction, Ned decided the place, if drained, would grow anything. He noted the variety of plant and animal life—elk, grizzly, water birds of all kinds, antelope, and wild horses. Finally, they pulled up out of the valley into the oak-covered coastal range. He began to pass parties of miners on foot, on their way to the Sierra, cheerfully singing *"Oh, Suzanna"* even though burdened down like pack mules. Two days later, on April 1, 1849, after passing through San Jose, where he had once been provisional governor, Ned rode into San Francisco, a town that no longer resembled the one he had left.

Already, tents of canvas and Mr. Goodyear's rubber covered every available spot. Shanties and shacks, constructed from anything available, stood with little regard for streets— little more than dirt roads churned to mud by a thousand boots and hooves. Ships, including the *Pride of Mobile*, had been dragged up onto the mud flats and were being ravaged for their lumber and fittings, or stood shored upright with their own crossarms and booms and used, basically intact, as hotels and restaurants and general stores and gaming houses. Unlike the last time he was there, the town teemed with activity. What had been hundreds of occupants was now many thousands.

Ned and the scouts reined up at the bay's edge to study the ships anchored there. The former dozen had become a hundred, but among the forest of masts he could not make out the three-masted, full-rigged ship *Ohio*.

He yelled to a crew of men unloading a longboat, "Where's the U.S. Navy?"

"Anchored in Sausalito, across the bay."

Ned hired a small catboat, surprised when the man informed it would be fifty dollars for the afternoon. But he paid rather than argue, spurred on by the fact that three men tried to hire it away for a trip up the Sacramento while he was negotiating. Only his hand on the butt of the Walker discouraged them and encouraged the boatman. He shoved off and sailed her across the swift current of the Golden Gate.

Catesby-Jones was anchored well out into the bay beyond swimming distance for most of his crew. He welcomed Ned like a long lost son.

"By God, it's nice to see a man who's not crazed by this gold mania," the commodore said with a smile, clasping hands with Ned.

"It's good to be here, Commodore. I've been almost six and a half months on this crossing. The weather was hell."

"I'll give you a couple of days to get some rest."

"I plan to."

"The weather will be better on the return."

"Pardon me?"

"You're going back, Ned. I need dispatches carried to Washington."

"But ... I've got dispatches for Oregon, and for Governor Mason in Monterey," Ned said, not believing his ears.

"I'll assign another to take them. You're the only man for this job." Catesby-Jones slapped Ned on the back.

Ned stood, exhausted and speechless. What he wanted to say to the commodore decorum and his fatigue would not allow. He sighed deeply, and asked where he could bunk.

The next day, somewhat rested, he requested leave in San Francisco. To his surprise, while he wandered down a muddy street listening to the chatter of a man beside him trying to sell him a twenty-five-by-hundred-foot city lot for twenty-five dollars, he heard a familiar voice—a female one.

He turned to see Jessie Fremont, skirts flying, running toward him from the door of a shanty.

"My God, Mrs. Fremont!" Ned said. He could not have been more surprised had it been Mary Edwards. "When did you get here?" she asked.

"Just yesterday. It was a terrible crossing. Where is John?" Ned knew that Fremont, due to Senator Benton's influence, had received a railroad contract to study a southern rail route and had left Washington just before Ned had arrived.

"We don't know," Jessie said with a hollow voice. "He should have been here long ago. We heard his crossing of the Rockies was disastrous, and I had so hoped he would be here to meet me. My daughter, my daughter's nurse, Lilly, and I arrived a few days ago."

"John will be all right, Jessie," Ned assured her, but he wondered. He knew how tough the weather had been from his own experience. The horrible sight of frozen mules lying splayed-legged and the men's frostbitten hands and feet being hacked away filled his mind's eye. "He may have turned back to St. Louis. I'm taking a steamer out for Panama tomorrow. Why don't you let me escort you back there, where you can wait for him at your father's home in comfort and safety?"

Ned glanced around at the rough-and-tumble miners going every direction in the street—Californios, Peruvians, Australians, Chinese, Chileans, Sandwich Islanders--and an the obvious lack of females. "God knows this is no place for three ladies."

"And God also knows I promised to stand by John Charles Fremont. I'll be here when he gets here. Besides, I took the fever in Panama and the last thing I want is to go back. This is the first day I've felt good enough to be up and around."

"Still, you shouldn't try to stay in this godless town."

"John's coming, and I must wait."

"Let me try to convince you differently. How about over supper?"

That afternoon, after excusing himself from Jessie's company, Ned went from saloon to saloon, talking to miners and seeing firsthand the pouches of gold. Gaspar's Cantina's plank bar now supported three scales for gold on its fifty-foot length. Good whiskey, which had once sold for a dime a shot, now brought a dollar. On the back bar, polished to a high sheen, rested a twenty-five-pound nugget, eclipsing the one Ned had carried east.

A number of Chinese had become established in the boomtown during Ned's absence. Chinese carpenters erected prefabricated Cantonese houses, shipped over and put together like puzzles. He heard reports that one Chinese woman was becoming rich merely by allowing the female-starved miners the chance to sit with her for a few minutes, viewing her litchi-nut-colored body—without touching—if they had enough gold.

He visited Delmonico's, the most fashionable eating house in the city, with boiled eggs at seventy-five cents each, or dinner from a dollar and a half for watery soup to the astronomical sum of five dollars if beef, pork, or chicken and vegetables were favored.

Even muslin tents sported fancy names such as Irving House or Holtenstein's General Merchandise and Gambling Emporium, and housed billiard tables and grass bowling alleys. But the gambling houses, the Eldorado being the largest, were the ultimate in slapped-and-glued together glitter, with hundreds of monte, roulette, and faro tables draining the city's gullible.

Among the most profitable establishments were the smallest, some only a table with a canvas stretched overhead to quell the dampness. Moneylenders commanded fourteen percent per month for their services and employed brawny men to make sure the money and exorbitant interest were returned on time.

In one section of the city near the bay, men worked laying flooring over ashes still smoldering, erecting buildings where others had only two days before been destroyed by fire.

That night, awed by the cataclysmic change in the city, Ned rejoined Jessie, her daughter, and the nurse, Lilly, for dinner, and was surprised to learn that the skinny pullet they shared had cost ten dollars. Still unconvinced by Ned's pleas to leave, Jessie asked him to drop by on his way to the steamer the next morning. If she changed her mind, she would be packed and ready—getting a ticket out of California was no problem. When he arrived the next morning, she did not have satchel in hand. Rather, she held an open letter that had been delivered shortly after Ned had left for the evening.

"John's with Kit at his house in Taos." she said. "He plans to meet me here as soon as possible."

"Do you have enough money?"

Jessie laughed. "The way things are going, I don't' know if anyone has enough money to live here."

"I have some—"

"I've enough, but I thank you."

Ned took the liberty of hugging her good-bye, and as he rejoined Jourdan and headed for the *Oregon*, assured himself that he would never put Mary Edwards to the tests John Fremont had put Jessie to.

Two days later, Ned and Jourdan walked up the gangplank of the *Oregon*, a steam-driven ship of the Pacific Mail Steamship Line, on the coast as a direct result of Beale's meeting with William H. Aspinwall, now president of that line. And four days after that, he saw the coast of Alta California fade in the fog.

Panama City teemed with two thousand argonauts when the *Oregon* arrived. Going against the traffic was no problem, since hostlers and skinners returned to Charges with hundreds of head of riderless stock at half the cost of traveling west. Ned and Jourdan boarded an almost passengerless bark, the *Florida*, bound for New Orleans, where he caught a steamer for New York. He arrived from San Francisco in a record forty-four days and went straight to the Wall Street office of William H. Aspinwall.

After a brief meeting, Ned and Aspinwall appeared on the street and confronted a throng of merchants, brokers, newspapermen, and speculators waiting to hear Beale's tales of California. Ned related stories of overnight fortunes, and the twenty-five-pound nugget displayed on the back bar of Gaspar's Cantina.

The next day the New York Herald reported, "Every one is getting rich in California" and that "Beale's news is the most extraordinary and astounding intelligence yet received from there." Ned was quoted, "100,000 men will be in California by midsummer, working the diggings."

The following day, Ned left for Washington and reported to the Navy Department. He was surprised to be handed a bill from the Army charging him, personally, with the services of an "Army escort" from Santa Fe--more than a year's pay. His face reddened and his fists clamped at his sides.

Ned promptly sat down and penned a bill back to them for his services as a guide and for his expenses. He was forced to spend a month in Washington, arguing with a chain of bureaucrats, while Mary waited for his arrival in Chester. He fought a relentless battle with the Army, receiving continual criticism in the newspapers, admonishments he knew originated from Congress and from Norvell Johanson and his cronies. Only after he was invited to the White House for a meeting with President Zachary Taylor did the press turn in his favor. Taylor, among other things, promised to look into the matter of the Army's bill. Ned left for Chester to see Mary, but his enthusiasm was again dampened by the sting and bite of politics.

Ned's brother, Truxtun, now a civilian executive employed by the Washington Navy Yard, was left to sort out the matter. Truxtun also took a forceful stand to defend Ned. Ned had been carried on the books of the Congress as her master, and as both an acting lieutenant and passed midshipman from 1845 through 1847—and had not received a dime since he had left her. Knowing that the best defense is a good offense, Truxtun aggressively went after Ned's back pay.

Thoughts of the Navy and politics left Ned when Mary Edwards greeted him at her father's door.

"We got word you were on your way." She smiled and flew into his arms. "How long will you be here?" she whispered, her lips next to his ear.

He had received orders from the Navy Department the day before he was scheduled to leave for Chester, and what he had hoped would be at least a month with Mary had been reduced to two days.

"Not long," he managed, barely able to breathe as she clung to him and unwilling to break the news of his imminent departure and spoil the moment.

"I was afraid of that." She pushed back from him, and at first he thought she was angry. Then he realized the look was both determined and anxious.

''The invitations were hand-delivered yesterday,'' she offered tenuously. "The Navy chaplain, Mortimer Taylor, will marry us. . .I thought you would like that. Our wedding is set for tomorrow here at the house."

Ned's mouth dropped open.

"If you want to flee, Ned Beale, there's still time."

"Flee? I couldn't be happier—or more unhappy about having to leave so soon," he said with a grin.

"Good; then that settles it. Will the Navy allow me to go with you to . . . to wherever?"

"That's another matter," Ned began, then continued dissuading her all evening. He was successful at convincing her not to attempt to return to California with him.

Ned knew he was cheating her of her honeymoon, if not a great deal more.

The day after he and Mary were married, Ned left with Jourdan for California via New York, where they boarded the merchantman Falcon, Navy dispatches in hand.

He was surprised to see an old friend on board, Bayard Taylor, now a reporter for Horace Greeley's *New York Tribune*. It was Taylor's hope to write the definitive work on the California gold rush. Ned had read his book *By Ways of Europe* and had no doubt Bayard would do so. The trip was made much more pleasant with his company and conversation. Jourdan took an interest in Bayard and decided he would like to learn to read. Ned accepted the new challenge. By the time they reached the Pacific, Jourdan, the half-black, half-

Kiowa ex-slave, not only could read but also pestered them with continual questions, and every one else on board or in camp for books to borrow.

Among others Ned met on the trip was John Weller, the recently appointed boundary commissioner whose job it was to settle the disputed boundary between Mexico and the United States. Beale did not mention that among the dispatches he carried was one from the secretary of state to John Fremont, offering him Weller's job.

The trip was an uneventful and pleasant one, but still Ned dreamed of a warm-weather road across the country.

While he was east, San Francisco had gone through further metamorphosis. Now almost fifty thousand elbowed and crowded along her mud streets and fought for space in her tents and shanties. Buildings of stone and brick with panes of glass now rose in the downtown section. The El Dorado saloon was transformed from a tent to a brick building with over a hundred feet of glass panes—a small fortune's worth—fronting the street. The Irish had arrived, and ghettos of various other nationalities were being established in different parts of the city, some of them places where only the bravest or most foolish dared tread. Telegraph Hill, where signals had been sent to the occasional ship only two years before, was now vied for by the Irish on the East Side and the Sydney Ducks--Australians--on the West. Eight hundred vessels rocked at their anchor rode in the harbor, most of them awaiting the wreckers' wrenches and pry bars. Men mined the distant mountains, and others, less hardy but no less entrepreneurial or energetic, mined the miners when they returned to spend their hard-won wealth.

As Ned surveyed the rough-and-tumble, ramshackle town, he congratulated himself on his hard stand with Mary Edwards in insisting she not accompany him—even though he missed her terribly.

304

Beale delivered his dispatches—all but Fremont's--and was given a few days' leave, and he, Bayard Taylor, and Jourdan promptly changed into Spanish dress and left for San Jose, where Ned heard John and Jessie Fremont had taken up residence. As they rode out of San Francisco, they heard the peal of the *Ohio*'s guns firing across the bay in a salute to ex-President Polk, who had died.

John and Jessie Fremont greeted Ned warmly. The explorer had not let grass grow under his feet. He had arrived in California and obtained a large land grant in the Sierras called Las Mariposas. Actually, he explained, he had left Larkin with the responsibility of buying him a property, and at first was enraged when he found the businessmen had purchased a Sierra rancho rather than a coastal urban parcel. Enraged, until gold was promptly discovered in the rancho's creeks, and good-as-gold beef on the hoof. Great herds grazed contentedly in its oak and pine-covered hills. He informed Ned that he had a crew of men mining gold there.

Fremont read his call to duty, the dispatch requesting he take the job as head of the border commission, and told Ned the president and secretary of state had left him little choice in regard to the boundary matter. He penned a tentative acceptance but privately informed Ned he would only work at the border problem until his first opportunity to leave gracefully. There was too much promise in California's private life and business. His rancho was a greater call.

As Ned watched Fremont, Ned reflected more and more on his own life in the Navy and on the opportunities of California. He now had a wife and responsibilities, and hoped soon to have a family.

It's time to think about security, he decided, and money and property are security.

Finally overcome with gold fever, Ned left Fremont's, with Bayard Taylor and Jourdan riding beside him, and headed for the diggings at Mokelumne Hill.

To Ned's surprise, he was greeted warmly at a distant mining camp in the hills by Andres Pico and a group of Californio miners -- many of whom had been among the lancers at San Pasqual. They spent an evening drinking *aguardienre* and admiring each other's bravery at that fated battle. Ned, as he had done many times, left the campfire with many newly won friends.

Jourdan elected to stay in the diggings with Andres Pico and the Californios. He, too, had been infected by the gold bug. After a sorrowful good-bye, Ned left the foothills and went straight to Monterey, where Fremont, who had his eye on a senatorial seat, had informed him a constitutional convention would be meeting. They mixed with the delegates at the convention. During the meeting, slavery had been excluded from California, but Negroes and Indians—including Indian descendants—had been denied the right to vote. The Californios were angered, since many of them proudly claimed Indian ancestry. The convention settled the eastern boundary question, setting the border in a line just east of the Sierras.

Shortly after returning to San Francisco, Ned was ordered back to Washington. Among other dispatches and documents entrusted to him was the first printed copy of the California Constitution, in the process of being ratified by the electorate of California as Ned went east. He left San Francisco on November 1, and arrived in New York, on board the *Crescent City*, on December 7, carrying the first news that a new state had organized on the West Coast and now demanded admission to the Union.

More and more, when Ned made crossings via the pest- and disease-infested Panama isthmus, he wished there was a road that crossed the southern portion of the United States. Crossings of wagons over northern routes were becoming commonplace in the summer but always were risky. A real road, where weather was only an irritant, not life-threatening; where bridges, rather than block and tackles, allowed wagons across, rather than up and down, clefts; where water was a given and within a day's ride; and above all, where forts offered protection and supplies.

It would come. He knew it would come. As California continued to grow and became a state, political pressure would force it. For the first time, as he thought of what would bring a road across the Southwest, he did not cringe at the word "politics."

The fact that California was demanding admission as a state was not a surprise to Easterners, but Ned received a surprise when he went straight to Chester to see his wife.

Mary Edwards was pregnant.

CHAPTER TWENTY

Ned decided he would stay in Chester until the baby was born, and he requested and received a long furlough from the Navy. During the next months he attempted to write a journal of his trips across the country but had little success, and spent most of his time pacing. He did make a trip to New York; where he accepted a job as manager of Aspinwall and Robert Stockton's mining interests in California. He also visited his friend Bayard Taylor's boss, Horace Greeley, to inquire about Bayard.

In March, his daughter, Mary, named after her mother, was born, both mother and daughter doing well. His closeness to his wife grew, and he could not imagine being separated from her again.

He found he had helped conceive another "chi!d" when he received a letter from Bayard Taylor, who asked if he could dedicate his new book, Eldorado, to Ned, since he had been so much help. Flattered, Ned accepted. The dedication read:

> TO
> Edward F. Beale, Lieut., U.S.N.
> THIS WORK IS DEDICATED
> With the Author's Esteem and Affection

Ned considered resigning his commission from the Navy, but instead, still undecided, requested and received another long furlough. But it was soon to end.

In April 1850, Ned received orders to return to California with dispatches. He left his Marys, his wife and the baby, who was sick at the time. He wrote in his journal, "this departure almost broke my heart." This time, Harry Edwards accompanied him.

Ned traveled in two capacities: as a Navy courier, and as an employee of Stockton/Aspinwall. The ship, again the *Cresent City*, carried the first ore-crushing equipment ever shipped to California and was bound for a Stockton/Aspinwall lease just below John Fremont's Las Mariposas. The heavy equipment had to be barged, then moved on timber rollers over the spine of Panama. Over a month after they began the arduous trip, they reached Panama City. Ned had carefully protected the interests of his employers, seeing the equipment safely transported across the isthmus and loaded on the *Tennessee*—another Pacific Mail Steamship Line/Aspinwall ship. But the trip had taken a great deal out of him. Several men had been injured, and Panamanian politicians had badgered him every step of the way. He had greased palms, argued and threatened, and many times thought things would come to gunfire.

Harry Edwards was a great help. He watched and learned, and quietly helped make the trip easier.

The steamship built a head of steam, preparing to leave Panama City on a midnight high tide, when Ned heard the growing, grousing voices of many men raised in anger. He excused himself from a game of whist and, with Harry close behind, walked topside. The heavy Walker's Colt he had carried had been replaced by a lighter .36 caliber Baby Dragoon strapped to his waist. With special dispensation as a dispatch courier, he wore civilian clothes and looked much like the other passengers—or the hundreds of men he saw gathered on the quay.

Over three thousand Americans, Chileans, Peruvians, and Panamanians were already awaiting transportation to the goldfields, and Panama City, with its dysentery and a variety of fevers, and without adequate shelter or food, grated on waiting nerves. Ned and Harry propped their booted feet on the rail near the gangplank and eyed the nervous crew members preparing to sail.

Captain Layton Price moved alongside Ned and crossed his arms apprehensively. Ned had worked with him for two days, arranging the precious cargo on the *Tennessee*'s decks, and knew him to be a calm man, not easily riled. But his face was lined with worry.

"This is not a good situation, Mr. Beale," he said quietly, watching the crowd on the quay shake their fists at the ship.

"Were I in command, I would hoist that gangplank and slip my dock lines," Ned suggested. "Just let her drift out into the bay . . . out of reach of those drunks."

"Can't yet. Paid passengers still ashore. We barely have steam to maintain a headway. We sail at midnight, just as the schedule says." Price seemed determined to demonstrate to Ned, who shared the same employer, that he ran a tight ship, no matter what the threat from shore.

"Then I would place armed crewmen in plain sight along the rails," Ned offered.

"The crew have their duties, Mr. Beale. That riffraff won't try anything—" A rock ricocheted off Price's back, belying what he had said. He was not hurt, but he cast an angry look at the growing crowd, walked to the head of the gangplank, and folded his arms as if he alone could repel any attempt to board. Ned had noticed the men on the quay passing bottles back and forth and knew that more and more they were fueled by *pulque* and *aguardiente*—and that the scene would do nothing but get uglier.

Finally, as Price glared down at them, a dozen men stomped up the gangplank. He met them halfway, his first mate and another crewman at his back. Neither Price nor his men were armed.

A thick-shouldered man led the boarding party, but he stopped to face Price. Even with the tilt of the gangplank, the man stood eye to eye with Price, and the captain was not a small man.

"You've got room for another hundred men aboard this tub, two hundred if ye get rid of that junk iron all over yer decks!" the beefy man challenged in an Irish brogue.

As the two began to argue, Ned studied the situation.

Again he heard the Irishman curse the equipment lashed to the decks—hauled at great expense of money and limb to get it this far.

"Bloody junk's not as important as men—men sick with the fever, who'll die if they don't get out of this hellhole! Make room, Capt'n, or we'll make room for ye." The men behind the Irishman cheered and waved their liquor bottles along with other weapons of many kinds.

The crew of the *Tennessee*, concerned with the ship's welfare and their own, began to stop work and gather at the rail. Price put a stubby finger firmly on the Irishman's thick chest; the brawny man responded by shoving a stout pocket gun into the captain's stomach. Price stood wide-eyed and suddenly speechless.

"Stand aside," the Irishman spat.

Ned turned to Harry, whispered a quick order, then moved forward and onto the gangplank, his .36 in one hand, a heavy two-foot belaying pin in the other. Concealing the Colt and pin behind his legs, Ned slipped past the first mate, who had backed up a step or two, and took up a position directly behind Captain Price.

"I said, stand aside," the thick-shouldered Irishman repeated, and the crowd surged forward, shoving him into the captain when more of the rabble crowded onto the narrow gangplank.

Ned glanced over his shoulder as the men pushed and shoved, to make sure his orders to Harry were being carried out. Without a word, he reached over the captain's shoulder and smashed the heavy pin across the Irishman's head. To Ned's surprise, the man merely widened his eyes and snarled at the blood gushing down his face—but for a second, he shifted the aim of the pocket gun away from Price's gut.

Again, Ned slammed down the belaying pin. He heard the groan and creak of timber against timber as he desperately slammed the snarling Irishman again, wildly smashing at the pocket gun with his own Colt's as he did so.

Then the water from the *Tennessee*'s fire hoses hit the crowd with battering vengeance, sweeping some of the riff-raff off the gangplank.

"Jump!" Ned yelled to Price, who suddenly realized what was happening and lunged for the deck of the ship just as the gangplank began to drop away from her sides. Ned, too, scrambled behind, but the Irishman's pistol roared and spit flame.

Ned dove. He barely caught the gunnel of the *Tennessee* where the gangplank had rested. His Colt tumbled away and splashed into the bay, but he clung desperately. Harry and a member of the crew grappled for him, then hauled him over the scuppers to the deck. Safe, Ned glanced down and saw a dozen men in the dark water below, clinging to the floating gangplank. He gave a satisfied laugh at the sight. Then he realized his side burned terribly. He lifted a hand to the pain and brought it away covered with blood.

The bastard had shot him! Someone shoved him to the deck as the men onshore began to fire in frustration at being left behind. Lead splattered into hull and rigging and ricocheted off iron stacks and mining equipment, but the Tennessee slowly began to gain headway. The crew lay below the protection of the solid bulwarks until they were well out into the harbor. Finally, regaining their feet, they looked back in morbid fascination and some satisfaction to see several of the quayside buildings in flames. In the dancing light of the fires, mounted policia of the disease ridden, now riotous town swung at the crowd with whips and clubs, and men scattered in every direction.

Later in the wardroom, the ship's cook bandaged what proved to be only a bloody crease in Ned's side. Ned shared a brandy with--Harry until Captain Price came below and confronted them.

"You overruled my orders, Beale."

"You gave orders to stand fast before you faced that mob, Price . . . and before you had a gun barrel biting at your belly."

"I would have had the situation under control without your interference. I have a gangplank left floating in the bay, and four cut dock lines—"

Ned felt the heat crawl up his backbone. "I'll bend you a couple more lines, Price, if you don't have a sailor aboard who can do so. It's a damn sight better to lose a gangplank than thousands of dollars' worth of equipment . . your bosses' equipment, I might add."

"Still . . ." he said, suddenly sheepish, "I'll have to enter this in the ship's log."

"Please do. If you enter it properly, you'll probably get a bonus from Aspinwall."

"There was a sign on the fire hoses," Harry said, with a glint of humor in his eye. "It said, 'only in case of emergency.' Maybe I should have left them coiled?"

Price gave Harry an angry look but spun on his heel and walked out.

"That trick with the fire hose your idea?" Ned asked.

"Thought it the best way to quench their thirst to come aboard," Harry said with a laugh.

Ned studied his brother-in-law with new respect. He had ordered him to chop the dock lines and tell the engine crew to put the steam to her, but he hadn't thought of the fire hose.

For the rest of the voyage tensions remained strained between Ned and Captain Price, but Ned arrived with the equipment and made no mention of the incident in his reports to Aspinwall.

The city of San Francisco had made another transition. Buildings of cut granite blocks rose three and four stories tall, hopefully impervious to the fires that had badgered the city.

Shortly after Ned unloaded on the new Long Wharf, he received word that his old friend Jourdan and his new friend Andres Pico were in serious trouble in the diggings—if not already hanged.

Ned immediately contracted for some shallow-drafted boats to barge the equipment by water as far as the new town of Stockton, named for Ned's former boss. In the burgeoning city, tents and makeshift shacks lined the slough behind a tall stand of tules, where the San Joaquin River dumped into the swampy delta.

Ned arranged for wagons, mules, and teamsters to haul the equipment, then bought himself a fine sorrel stallion and a quiet bay for Harry. Ned rode as far as the foothills with the freighters, left Harry in charge of the slow train with instructions to take them on to Las Mariposas, then swung off the trail and headed for Mokelumne Hill .

Almost every ravine in the oak-covered foothills along the way showed telltale signs of mining: piles and piles of gravel tailings.

Ned was surprised when three armed guards met him shortly after he passed a rough sign, nailed to a cottonwood, noting his approach to French Camp.

"Hold! Do you pass on through?"

The man who stepped forward, with ice-blue eyes and a long, straight nose below slick, center-parted, coal-black hair, wore a plaid wool shirt and canvas pants stuffed into high-top laced boots. His belt held both pistol and knife. His French accent proved that the camp was properly named, and the double-barreled shotgun he carried, its muzzle trained on Ned's midsection, gave the soft voice authority. The two men behind him ignored Ned, sweeping the hillsides beyond him with their gaze.

"On my way to Mokelumne Hill. You fellas some kind of reception committee for this place?"

"French Camp has had its trouble. But if you are passing on, and alone, you are welcome to proceed."

"And if not?" Ned asked, a little affronted at the man's demanding attitude.

"This area is all claimed. No room for you, so move on to where you are welcome."

"No saloon?" Ned pressed, his dry throat reminding him he had not had a drink since the tents of Stockton.

"We have a saloon, and I personally will buy you a drink … one drink … then you will ride on."

Ned smiled tightly, dismounted, introduced himself, and extended his hand, which the Frenchman accepted. Leading the sorrel, he walked on up the trail with the man, who introduced himself as Henri Tucolette.

"What's brought on all this hospitality?" Ned asked wryly.

"Your people, that is what," Henri said without a smile. "The Americans have killed many who dared to try for a share of the wealth of California. Over ten Frenchmen have been hung, and I do not know how many Chinese have been shot or hung … dozens, I would guess."

"For what reason?" Ned asked, doubting what the man was saying.

"As I said, for wanting to share in the wealth of California. The Chinese have only followed the camps, working what the others leave behind. Even then, the Americans burn their tents and steal their tools. The Chinese are treated worse than dogs."

Ned remained silent, working what he had been told around in his mind. The ravine opened up into a wide flat dotted with tents and shanties flanking the narrow trail. Men stopped working the diggings on the hillsides or rocking cradles near the tiny creek to give Ned a hard look as he passed. Not one waved or shouted a greeting.

They entered a canvas tent with willow branches as its bows and its rear cut into the hillside, and bellied up to a rough plank bar. The man behind raised his eyes from a newspaper. Setting the Alta California aside, he rested his hands on the bar, waiting. His finely waxed mustache extended in sharp-tapered points beyond his narrow cheeks, and piercing topaz eyes studied Ned. ''Henri, que prendrez-vous?'' he asked.

"Speak English, Bernard; for our American friend M'sieur Beale," Henri instructed, and the man cast Ned an even more suspicious look. "He will have one whiskey. On me."

Bernard, unsmiling, poured a short shot, then went back to his newspaper.

''So, where are you bound for, M'sieur Beale?'' Henri asked.

"To find some friends." Ned wondered if he should tell this man more.

"Many argonauts used to pass through here, but not since the trouble started. As you saw, we meet and discourage them at the trail. Most go into the hills and around French Camp now."

"These men were probably not welcomed here ...a Californio and a zambo."

"Zambo?"

"Half Negro,'half Indian."

"We have some Californios here. They were here before the French. We have no problem with them. As long as they keep our laws."

Encouraged, Ned decided to confide in Henri Tucolette. "My friends are Andres Pico and a man named Jourdan."

"Aww, I have heard of them. You may be too late. They fought in Mokelumne with the Americans. Killed one. And the last I hear, they had fortified a place the Americans call Greaser's Gulch, where they defend their diggings. Do not go to Mokelumne Hill if these men are your friends, M'sieur Beale."

"Can you direct me to this Greaser Knob?"

"Not a wise idea. They were surrounded, and the Americans vowed to starve them out, if they have not already. I am sure your friends have surrendered their lives by now." Henri smiled, then saw the hard look on Ned's face. "That is, of course, unfortunate. You have finished your drink. I will walk you to the edge of camp and give you directions. It is only a few miles ... two beyond Mokelumne. But I suggest you give the Americans the ... how do you say? ... the wide berth`."

The situation in the goldfields was all but lawless, Ned decided, as he rode away from French Camp. He certainly would avoid no Americans, but decided he would wisely not mention Andres Pico or Jourdan. Californios had as much right, and probably more, to the wealth of California as did the Americans. Jourdan, because of his color, would be denied property, as would the Chinese, who were considered nonentities under new California law. But the Californios? At one time Ned would have been truly surprised by this turn of events, but now he had lived longer and seen more, and little surprised him. Shadows lay long by the time he reached Mokelumne Hill, and the men were already gathering at its two makeshift saloons and gambling halls. Ned nudged the sorrel between a mustang and a mule at the rail outside the first, whose sign, in gold-flecked, foot-high letters sang its praises, Emory's Gilded Well, and smaller letters under those cautioned, and games of chance. The sign and gambling tables must have been the only items Emory moved from camp to camp, for the walls and roof of his "gilded well" were of tattered canvas with lodgepole pine corner poles and rafters.

Egg and peanut shells littered the floor so thickly as to carpet it in a crunching pad over the hard-packed earth. The two dozen customers surrounded a spot at the plank bar in a three-deep semicircle. Emory stood behind, demonstrating the art of shucking an oyster.

"Y'all slide a slim ol' blade in just so, an' with a slip of the knife . . . yeow!" he barked as the knife did slip, and sliced his finger. The oyster remained happily sealed. "Damn, the pluperfect little beggar," he mumbled over the laughter and catcalls of the canvas-panted and linsey-woolsey-shirted group of whiskered men. Ned shouldered up among them and spoke to a gray-bearded man, still chuckling through it at Emory's clumsy attempt. "Is this the best food on the Hill?"

"If you favor oysters, pilgrim. Emory's out of beef and beans, an' the hard-boiled eggs come all the way from Sonora. We ain't seen a chicken 'round here since Methuselah was a whelp. He's doin' his damndest to convince this crowd that those slimy beggars are worth two dollars and fifty cents each."

"That's a little proud for my taste," Ned said with a smile. "Where would a fella get some tortillas and frijoles?"

The miner's smile faded, and a couple of the other nearby men cut their eyes at Ned.

"Greaser's Gulch is just down the road a piece," the miner said, "but there be a hundred or more men fixin' to start lobbin' lead into it the first time a greaser shows his dung-colored face. If you want to try wanderin' up there and not gettin' your hide fulla leaks, help yourself. But they haven't had a shipment of grub for more'n two weeks—we haven't let one through. I doubt if the fare's too good there."

"I don't understand," Ned said innocently.

"We're runnin' the greasers out of there. They been pullin' more'n their share of water out'n the crick."

"Hell, I'd like to shoot myself another greaser," Ned said with a laugh. They studied him skeptically. "I shot my share at San Pasqual."

"Hell, then you'll fit right in here. That general who led the greasers at Pasqual ... he's the same ol' boy whose leading' this bunch. If'n your sure you'd like to see him strung up."

The men crowded around Ned, slapped him on the back, and bought him a drink. By the time he walked out of the saloon it lay pitch dark, but he had learned the name of the man in charge of the raiders' gathering at Greaser's Gulch.

Ned mounted and gigged the sorrel, letting the big stallion find his way through the darkness along the trail for over a mile, until a voice challenged him.

"Hold up and state yer business."

"I'm a friend," Ned offered easily. "Heard a fella could make a grubstake here." As Ned dismounted, he was careful to keep his hands in plain sight.

"He's no greaser," another voice added, seemingly assured by Ned's voice. Two men stepped out of the underbrush .

"Hell, no, I'm no greaser," Ned said with a snarl. "1 was told Big Harvey McCracken headed this operation. Where is he?"

"He's at the fire. You signin' on?"

"Might, if the pay's right. Take me to him."

"Follow up," one of them said and started away into the brush. Ned followed, leading the sorrel, and the other fell in behind. Fifty yards off the trail, through heavy buckbrush, they came upon a dozen men around a campfire, some drinking coffee, some sharing a bottle being passed around. It was easy to spot the boss man. even sitting on his haunches—he stood big enough to eat hay and leave the droppings in the road if he wanted. Ned walked over and extended his hand, which was lost in the massive palm of the bear-sized man.

"Who sent you here?" McCracken asked.

"The fellas at Emory's said a man could earn a grub-stake.''

"Pay's ten dollars a head for every greaser or chink you bag . . . an' a dollar for a Indian, split tail, or handle," Harvey said with a guffaw that rocked the hillside. He scratched a flea in the curly black hair that fluffed out from his pony-keg-sized head and made it look even bigger.

"Bring us a right ear and you get paid in Mokelumne Hill dust.''

Ned wondered how you told a Chinese, Mexican, or Indian ear apart.

"An' there's a big o' bandy-legged nigger up there worth one hundred dollars in pure dust to Emory Kleinfeldt." Again he laughed. "A black ear is the brass ring here'bouts." His eyes narrowed and he spat a stream of tobacco juice into the fire. "T'was Emory's brother the nigger kilt."

Ned had never thought of Jourdan as bandy-legged, but big was close enough. He was sure it was Jourdan he was talking about. "Fair fight?"

"Don't matter. They been a boil on Mokelumne Hill's butt for most a year, and the boys want 'em outta here. . an' they got the dust to get what they want."

"They're holed up atop some hill?"

"Granite-crowned hill, cut through and through with a gulch fulla thick buckeye trees where those boys been grubbin' after some dust among the roots. Next hill over the rise," Harvey said with a gesture of his big head. "They been layin' in the cracks and crannies, fifty or more of'em, harder to pry out than a tick in a sheep's tail. But we ought to get 'em this time."

"We going at this every man for himself?" Ned asked as if he was not too sure he wanted to participate.

"Hell, no," McCracken said with a growl. "We're hittin' 'em all together at sunup. First man on a dead Mex with a

Bowie'll get hissef a ten-dollar ear. Some of the fellas have teamed up and are splittin' the take. You want a partner?"

"Have you tried this before?" Ned asked.

"Not me, or it woulda got done. Another fella tried it afore they hired me . . . but he's toes-up." McCracken scratched his head, seemingly unconcerned about the fate of the former. "They gotta be low on powder by now an' we been keepin''em back from the water—" As if to verify what he said. two shots rang out up the canyon. McCracken laughed. "Buggers are tryin' for water again."

"Count me in," Ned said. He looked from man to man around the fire. "This all of us?"

"Hell, no. Those was our boys you heard shootin'. We got another fifty or more spaced around Greaser's Gulch. Soon to be called Greaseless Gulch." He guffawed, and the others joined in.

"Where are the rest of your men?" Ned asked and got a suspicious look cast at him for his effort. He quickly added, "I don't want to be cuttin' an ear off of some dago thinkin' he's a greaser." Ned laughed. louder than necessary.

McCracken pointed a corncob-size finger. "Some of us are about two hundred paces thataway. where there's a high spot with a good view of the hill 'cross the way. Others are spread out along the creek on the other side o' the hill, keepin' the beggars off'n the water.

Ned settled down by the fire and accepted a pull of the bottle. Then, as soon as he thought he could get away with it, he yawned and stretched widely. He spoke to no one in particular.

"Been in the saddle since before sunup. Believe I'll get a little shut-eye."

He stood and, without further explanation. walked out of camp. After untying the sorrel, he wandered quietly into the brush until he figured he was halfway between the fireside bunch and the other group on the high spot on the hill. He tied the sorrel to a scrub oak. As a precaution he pulled his bedroll off the saddle and spread it out. rumpling it up as if someone was wrapped in the canvas slicker. Then he slipped quietly into the buckbrush in the direction of the spot known as Greaser's Gulch.

Judging by the distance the moon traveled in the night sky, Ned figured it had taken him two hours, moving quietly, to travel down the hill and up the next to crest Greaser's Gulch. Getting shot by the men he was determined to help was a fate he carefully avoided. Finally having to climb, he poked his head carefully up over a rocky escarpment and hoped his outline was not backlit by the clear night sky. Without a movement, he let his eyes wander over the brush-covered hilltop—but made out no sign of life.

Surely they have posted guards, he pondered, just as a match flared nearby, delineating the bean-brown gray-whiskered face of an old vaquero. It disappeared with a puff of breath; then only the glow of a cigarillo could be seen.

In a voice almost unheard over the chirping of crickets, Ned ventured in his most precise Spanish. *"Amigo, donde esta Don Andres Pico?"*

The man sprang back into the brush; sparks flew from the cigarillo as he flung it away.

It was silent for a moment before a tentative voice asked, *"Quien es?"*

"Un amigo. Donde esta?"

Finally, after a long pause, Ned heard the man begin to move away. *"Espara!"* the man called behind him. "Wait!"

In a moment, Andres Pico's voice rang out from the underbrush. "Who seeks Andres Pico?"

"Ned Beale!" Ned announced from his perch atop the rock ledge.

Ned heard the man chuckle as he rose out of the brush and moved forward. He was not surprised that Jourdan was beside Don Andres when he stepped into the clearing.

322

"You're a long ways from home, Navy!" Jourdan said, extending a calloused hand.

Ned shook. "Too damn far. You've managed to get half the gold country after your hide."

"Only half?" Jourdan chuckled.

"There's an old boy down there who calls himself Big Harvey McCracken, and big's an understatement. He said your right ear was worth a hundred dollars if the man bringing it left the rest of you for the crows."

"Hell, I'll sell him both ears for that price. . .but the crows'll have to make out somewhere else."

"Seriously," Ned said, his smile fading, "these boys are ready to charge this hill and try to pry you fellas off of it. I sneaked up here to see what I could do to help."

"They've tried before," Andres said. "The *hijos de putas* won't let us work in peace."

"Not like you to wait for someone to bring the fight to you," Ned suggested.

"What are you thinking?" Andres asked.

"They plan to hit you at dawn with a bunch of paid shooters—while the miners in Mokelumne Hill sit fat and sassy in camp. Why don't a few of us hit them where it hurts? If they see it's going to cost them more than money, maybe they'll decide it's time to negotiate."

Ned turned to Jourdan. "You got a big claim working here?"

"We haven't been able to work in more than two weeks. It's no glory hole, anyways."

"Then why don't you ride on out of here with me. I've got a job waiting for you at Las Mariposas, and with you gone, maybe Andres can negotiate with the miners from Mokelumne Hill. Seems like a little creek water and you killing this brother of Emory's are the main gripes." "I killed that bastard in self-defense," Jourdan said, grumbling.

323

"That's comforting to know," Ned said with a wry smile. "Maybe those miners will take only twelve turns on their hangman's knot instead of thirteen. That'd be a lot more lucky . . . but it'll still pop your thick neck."

"That is a comfort," Jourdan repeated. "Maybe I will ride out with you, if Andres can spare me."

Andres laid a hand on Jourdan's shoulder. "You go. We'll work your claim and send you a share. To be truthful, it would be easier to talk with them if you were gone." Andres turned to Ned. "You're right. Let's go heat up that cucaracha-infested camp; then maybe they'll decide it's too expensive to keep after us here at Canon de Oro."

"Canyon of Gold?" Ned repeated. These Californios had a more complimentary name for the spot. "Get your men and mounts, Andres. We can slip back the way I came. Then, after we hoorah the tent town, you fellas can circle around and come back here. McCracken and his bunch will hightail it for Mokelumne when they see the flames." Andres started away. "I don't want anyone killed, Andres. If they fire on us, shoot back. But instruct your men, no shooting unless absolutely necessary."

"They have been shooting at us for over two weeks," he said angrily. "We have buried two men, and two more nurse bad wounds."

"If you try to negotiate a settlement over pools of blood, it'll be impossible."

Andres studied him, then gave a wave of his hand as he walked away. "Agreed."

"They've got to get some law in these diggings," Ned said quietly to Jourdan.

"It's more than that," Jourdan said. "Chinese, Californios, Indians, and blacks have no rights. Law or no law, there's still no right to it."

Ned nodded in agreement but said nothing.

The dozen mounted Californios had to take a slightly different route down the steep escarpment. Andres explained that they only had a small spring on the hill, just enough for the fifty men and a dozen horses. Most of the horses had been turned loose to make their own way. Even then, they had had to slip down to the bigger creek below to supplement their water supply for those left.

The men managed to broach the raiders'- lines without being discovered and gathered in a patch of sage outside of Mokelumne Hill. They could see the lantern-lit saloons and hear the roaring laughter of drinking men there, but the rest of the camp was quiet and dark. Silently the Californios cut sage torches and bound them with rawhide, soaking them with a can of whale oil Andres had brought from the gulch.

Jourdan whispered to Andres and Ned that he would slip into the camp and make sure the saloons caught fire. Then he moved away.

They spread out across the canyon, awaiting Andres Pico's lead. Andres waited until he saw men begin to pour out of the saloon tents, and they flamed up from the rear. He lit up his torch, and the others followed suit. When Andres was satisfied they were all ready, he gave his stallion the spurs. They swept down through the camp, each man lighting the brush and grass as they galloped along, then flinging his torch in a likely spot against a tent. Rid of the telltale torches, they put their reatas to work. Tents bounced across the camp behind swift riders, and two vaqueros lasso the primary sluice and pulled it over. Water rushed and tumbled down the center of Mokelumne Hill, sweeping downed tents and rockers along with it.

Rubbing their eyes, many clad only in long underwear and nightshirts, men stumbled out of tents and shanties as the riders pounded past. Men from the saloons hustled to form a bucket line while the tents rose in flame. Even some of the digger pines flanking them flamed up.

The Californio riders gathered at the far end of the canyon and looked back on their work. The miners believed merely another fire had hit a gold camp; not a shot had been fired.

Within minutes, McCracken and his group galloped out of the darkness into Mokelumne Hill and joined in the fire fighting.

Ned nudged his sorrel up beside Andres. ''Looks like a good time for you fellas to work your way home. Jourdan and I'll head for Las Mariposas.''

''*Via con Dios.*'' Andres said, extending a hand.

Ned picked his words carefully. "Things will settle down in California, Don Andres. Fight for what's right ... but stay alive."

''I wish I had your faith in the future of my country,'' Andres said, and Ned could read the sadness in his eyes. "There needs to be a law for all men, but I fear that will not happen."

"It will happen. It'll take a while, but it will happen."

Andres touched the brim of his sombrero, and he and the Californios reined away into the darkness.

Ned and Jourdan headed for Las Mariposas. During the two-day ride, Ned spent a great deal of time wondering what could be done to enforce the law fairly in the new territory. Something had to be done, or it might just explode in another revolution. He wished he were in a position to help.

As soon as Ned arrived at Las Mariposas, Harry Edwards handed him a letter from John Charles Fremont. He and his father-in-law, Senator Benton, had proposed Ned as the federal marshal of California, and they expected a confirmation from the president and the Senate at any time.

Edward Fitzgerald Beale sat under a digger pine and studied the letter, not reading, but thinking. He knew California needed help. You had best not wish for something, because you just might get it, he decided. Then he arose and went to inspect the installation of the crushing mill.

Later that night, in the privacy of his tent, Ned read several letters that had arrived from Mary. The baby was doing well, he was relieved to read in one of the first Mary had written. He was distressed by the last, written in someone else's handwriting—Mary's eyesight was failing, and she had to dictate. The physician had no idea what was wrong.

He decided that as soon as the equipment was operating smoothly, he would return to Pennsylvania.

But in a few days, he received good news. Andres Pico and Mokelumne Hill had come to an understanding, splitting the water and adopting the same set of camp laws. Still, Ned knew the true test would come when it was necessary to apply the rules equally to white, brown, and yellow.

Ned prepared for his journey home. Jourdan would go with him, as his poorly drawn picture on hundred dollar reward posters was plastered all over the Mokelumne Hill country. They caught a Pacific Mail Line ship.

When they arrived in Washington, a storm was brewing over Edward Fitzgerald Beale's appointment as federal marshal. It came as no surprise to Ned that some members of Congress were politicking against him—he didn't have to ask whom. Compounding the problem was the fact that a new man was secretary of state, Daniel Webster, and worse, the president had taken ill and died, even before Ned had left California, he learned. He was saddened. Zachary Taylor had been a good president and a good friend.

Millard Fillmore, Taylor's vice president, had taken the oath of office. Ned did not know Fillmore, but knew that he and Norvell Johanson were good friends, having served in Congress together.

Ned applied for and received another year's furlough from the Navy, then left Washington with the matter of his appointment still up in the air. He was assured by the debates going on that California would be a state soon. The only question was, free or slave?

CHAPTER TWENTY-ONE

Ned was relieved to find that Mary's eyes were improving, but saddened to find that his father-in-law, Samuel Edwards, now retired from Congress but still active in the private practice of law, was very ill.

Ned had only been home a few days when Samuel died.

After an appropriate mourning time, Ned, who had received a letter from Stockton again requesting his assistance in California, proposed to Mary that she and their daughter accompany him west. Happy to get away from Chester and continual sad reminders of her father, Mary packed.

Ned's appointment as federal marshal had been effectively blocked by several members of Congress, and Ned resigned himself to the fact that Norvell Johanson had won another round of their long-lasting feud. Ned marked it up to experience. He decided that if he had to resort to Johanson's brand of politics—and a vindictiveness he would never understand—he would almost as soon not win. California was as far from Washington and federal politics as you could get on the northern continent, and he was happy to be returning there.

With poor results from the rock-crushing equipment, Stockton and Aspinwall had decided they were not gold miners, and instructed Ned to return and dispose of the equipment and send the men home by the cheapest possible route. Afterward he was to look for other opportunities for the money from the sale of their property and machinery.

While crossing Panama, Ned investigated another Aspinwall enterprise—a railroad from east to west across the isthmus. The bed for a good portion of it had already been laid. Still, he decided, even with the railroad, it would not circumvent the eventual building of a wagon road across the United States. Besides, a wagon road would open up the whole Southwest.

In Panama City, Ned and his Marys boarded an Aspinwall steamship, and arrived in San Francisco to find the city practically burned to the ground—an occurrence repeated far too often. Jessie Fremont, all but alone in a new house John had bought her, with a brand-new baby in her arms, had lain in her bed and watched the fire advance, pushed by a strong wind. It had died at the foot of the hill on which she resided, and spared her and the baby.

To the Beales' surprise and Mary's pleasure, the resilient city welcomed Ned as one of California's leading citizens, and for a few days they were the toast of the town--what was left of the town. Ned left Mary and the baby with Jessie and went to Mariposa, practically in the center of the new state, where John Fremont worked his rancho. Within days Ned had disposed of the Aspinwall/Stockton equipment, but he had no idea how to reinvest the money until he received an estimate for the cost to move some of the companies' property back to San Francisco—a dollar a pound, for packed mule freight.

Roads were still only a dream in the gold country, where almost all shipments were made by mule—and mules Ned Beale knew better than he did any other critter. The price of mule train freight had risen from thirty cents a pound in 1850 to one dollar in 1851. Ned made a long trip through the valley, buying mules along the way. He also rented livery and office space in both Sacramento and Stockton. With his excellent command of Spanish, he hired Mexican drovers and freighters, and within days Aspinwall/Stockton were in the freighting business—Ned carrying Aspinwall's promise that he would receive 13 percent of any profits. Aspinwall not only controlled the freight traffic from the East Coast to the

West Coast, but also from San Francisco to the goldfields. Freight arriving on Aspinwall steamers now transferred to Aspinwall mules.

The business carried Ned all over California. He visited almost every nook and cranny of the new state, admitted to the Union as free during the Congressional Compromise of 1850—Senator Henry Clay's supreme attempt to forestall civil war, a dark cloud he knew hung over the United States. President Taylor had opposed Clay's plan, but his successor, Fillmore, endorsed it.

California was admitted as a free state, but residents of other states created from the territory acquired from Mexico would decide for themselves to be free or slave—thus satisfying the slave states. The borders of Texas were defined, and Texas was granted ten million dollars to pay off its debt, effectively buying the Texas slave state vote for the compromise. The Territory of New Mexico was established. The Territory of Utah was established. Slave trade, though not slavery itself, was abolished in the District of Columbia. And the most controversial of the conditions, the Fugitive Slave Act, was passed, requiring the federal government to take an active part in returning run away slaves. Fugitives were denied the right to trial or to defend themselves at a judicial proceeding. This resulted in many freed blacks, who claimed the North as home, being extradited to the South based on often false claims of Southerners that they were runaways. And those aiding and abetting fugitive slaves along the newly created Underground Railroad were subject to stiff criminal and civil penalties. For a while, at least, civil war was averted, but it proved a tenuous trade, and a compromise Ned Beale personally found offensive.

Ned retreated deeper into his hatred of politics. He buried himself in his work and his re-acquaintance with old friends. Among old friendships renewed was one with Alexis Godey, who was now in the cattle business, buying cattle in southern

California and driving them to the gold fields, where thousands of hardworking men consumed all he could deliver. Ned also was treated to dinner in the tent restaurant of Baptiste Perrot. Both scouts had rapidly tired of grubbing for gold and were now busily satisfying the hunger of the miners, but in different ways.

Ned's travels also allowed him to witness firsthand the wretched condition of California's true native inhabitants—the Indians. Three Indian agents—McKee, Wozencraft, and Barbour—had been appointed for California, and one of them, George W. Barbour, had been working hard to find land where the Indians could gather and be taught to farm, a solution Ned Beale endorsed. Barbour issued drafts all over the state for land and cattle, assuring the recipients that Congress would honor them. Congress did not. He promised tribes land, cattle, food, and farming implements. Congress denied those promises, negating eighteen treaties Barbour had negotiated.

One of those drafts was issued to John Fremont for the purchase of cattle from Las Mariposas, but luckily, in need of money as always—and now politically astute—he had discounted and sold it sometime before it was dishonored.

Ned, appalled at the condition of the Indians and heartsick at his country's callousness, took note of many incidents of cruelty and mistreatment, murder and mayhem, and, even more repugnant to Ned, the conscription into slavery of the Indians. He wrote several letters to friends in Washington appealing for political help for the California tribes.

His freighting business prospered all year, and Aspinwall/Stockton mules ventured into every far-flung nook and cranny of the state. But the state was changing. Roads were being constructed everywhere in the gold country, and roads meant wagons, a better, more efficient freight hauler than mule trains. At the end of the year, Ned decided it was time to sell out. He sold the assets of the company and returned Aspinwall/Stockton's original investment, plus a profit of one hundred thousand dollars. With his commission of thirteen thousand dollars, he had earned ten times his annual Navy pay for that year.

California had roads, and roads led east from Santa Fe, but there still was not an all-weather road, and nothing but the roughest trails, connecting the two.

The Beales made the long and difficult passage back to Chester via Panama. There, Ned promptly resigned from the Navy. At twenty-nine years old, for the first time since he was fifteen, Edward Fitzgerald Beale was a private citizen.

But not for long. Again the call of California reached out and whispered to him. With the Indian situation in California becoming critical—several attacks had been made on whites, usually in reprisal for depredations--residents were demanding a solution. Governor McDougal, the state's second governor, had called for the removal of Indians from California. Friends suggested Ned Beale as the appointee for a new federal position, superintendent of Indian affairs for the State of California. Again the politicking began.

Ned endorsed the notion and promptly submitted a written plan to the recently created Department of the Interior calling for the establishment of ten reservations in California, the teaching of farming to the Indians, and ten reservation directors to do that teaching and administer those reservations. It would require, in Ned's opinion, five hundred thousand dollars. Ned was summoned from Chester to a joint committee meeting of Congress, to be interviewed in an open courtroom full of observers and reporters. Among those half dozen seated behind the long table was Pennsylvania congressman Norvell Johanson, now in his mid-thirties and beginning to show the effects of the good life—an ample belly and jowls that vibrated with his oratory.

His first question—an attack—startled Ned, for it was a complete fabrication.

"Isn't it true, Mr. Beale, that you were a partner of court-martialed John Fremont in a cattle transaction that defrauded the government of the United States of thousands of dollars? Now you expect to have almost dictatorial power over what you say will cost the better part of a million dollars.''

Dumbfounded and angry, Ned could not answer for a second.

Johanson continued, "You actually expect this Congress to receive your nomination for this trusted post, and recommend a man whose past includes the murder of Indians? How many Indians have you killed, Mr. Beale? A hundred? Why don't you walk out of here now, Beale, and forget this folly?"

By now Ned had collected himself and quelled the urge to leap over the table and throttle Johanson.

''If the honorable congressman will refrain from rambling on and ask one question at a time, I'll be happy to answer. "

"Answer any of them, Beale."

"I have never been a partner of John Fremont in any business transaction. I did happen to be present when Indian agent Barbour negotiated for and purchased several hundred head of cattle From Fremont—purchased, by the way, at twenty cents per pound, which was the going price for cattle in California at that time. These were prime animals, rounded up out of heavy chaparral at great expense. It was a completely aboveboard transaction and one, I might add, that could have resulted in the ruin of this great American hero, John Fremont, for, as you know, Congress denied payment of that draft. So, in fact, it cost the United States nothing. Luckily, Fremont had discounted the draft—"

"Your opinion of this court-martialed opportunist is not the issue here, Beale. His discounting of the note proves that the cattle were overpriced in the first instance," Johanson gloated, a triumphant look on his face.

"Proving only that Fremont needed the money for other opportunities and that he understood politics."

"Are you suggesting that Congress was wrong in disallowing those payments in California? Those agents far exceeded their authority. Are you also going to exceed authority if it's given you, Beale? Of course, it's my—"

"You're doing it again, Congressman. Oratory with you seems an affliction. One question at a time, please." The crowd behind Ned hummed in agreement and laughter. Johanson's face reddened.

Senator Thomas Benton, among those who had lobbied for Ned's appointment, had been required at another committee meeting, but entered the courtroom from the rear and strode forward through the swinging gates, walking stick tapping the polished wooden floor. He folded into a chair at Ned's side. Entwining his fingers on the tabletop, he glowered with cold eyes under bushy gray brows directly at the congressman from Pennsylvania. Johanson's brow furrowed, for he hated being outranked.

The congressman decided that rather than face the wrath of the senator by berating his son-in-law, Fremont, he would take another tack. He unfolded a parchment from his inside coat pocket and, with great ceremony, spread it in front of him.

''This letter is from the new governor of California,'' Johanson said stiffly. "Governor McDougal writes, and I quote, 'A temporizing system can no longer be pursued toward the American Indian. The policy of removal to reservations must be abandoned and the only alternative is to civilize or exterminate them.' '' He folded the letter back up. Ned again sat dumbfounded at the callousness of his fellows.

"And you propose the better part of a million dollars to create reservations?" Johanson asked with a smirk.

Ned started to answer, but Senator Benton laid a hand on his forearm and spoke in a mellifluous voice that reverberated through and quieted the room.

"In case the honorable congressman is having trouble reading or understanding Mr. Beale's clearly presented recommendations, the figure suggested by him is five hundred thousand dollars, which I believe is a penny short of being 'the better part' of a million." The crowd tittered in laughter, but Benton ignored them. The chairman rapped his gavel as the senator continued. "Are you agreeing with the governor, Congressman? I don't think it is the policy of the United States to promote genocide. if that's your stand, perhaps you should make it clear to the gentlemen of the press, whom I note are in attendance here."

"I ..." Johanson stammered.

"I want to answer the question." Ned said. "I do not agree with the governor. I have known many Indians."

"Killed many!" Johanson said, recovering.

"Known many to be hardworking and industrious. I worked many Indians and mestizos in the freight business—"

"Mestizos?" Johanson asked, interrupting just for the sake of it.

"Half Mexican, half Indian, or at least part Mexican."

"And how many Mexicans have you killed, Beale?"

Benton's voice rang over the room. "Congressman, if you would like, I will be happy to read into the record of this hearing Edward Beale's magnificent war record and his record of unfailing and valuable service to the United States of America over the past fifteen years."

"That won't be necessary, Senator," Johanson snapped, for it was the last thing he wanted to see happen. "Just answer the question, Beale."

But Benton would not let it lay. "With your own rather lackluster Navy record, Congressman, you of all people should appreciate Beale's."

The crowd roared with laughter, and the chairman rapped his gavel repeatedly. As soon as the noise abated, Johanson glared, red-faced and trembling, while Ned responded.

"I've fought the enemies of the United States, and if some died, it was in the service of my country. But as has been proven so often in our illustrious history, the enemies of today are the friends of tomorrow. Take note of our relationship with England, as an example. I now respect and value the friendship of many Mexicans, Californios, and Indians."

Johanson was an English supporter and a proponent of the Clayton-Bulwer Treaty, wherein the United States and Britain agreed to the neutrality of any canal project across the Isthmus of Panama and that neither country would occupy any part of Central America. It had been heavily rumored that Johanson was on the payroll of the British Embassy. It was a subject he wanted to avoid, since the treaty he had worked so hard for was about to be signed. He immediately clamped his jaw, and kept it so for the rest of the hearing. Ned had found his Achilles' heel.

With Benton's help and continual lobbying, Ned was appointed by President Fillmore as superintendent of Indian affairs for California on March 4, 1852. Confirmation was adamantly opposed by the Army, which was not in favor of any civilian, particularly one with a Navy record, who would be required to work closely with Army forces in California. The Army, with Johanson's covert help, kept Ned from being confirmed for over a month. When it finally happened, the newspapers quoted several senators and congressmen who complained, "Beale is given carte blanche authority, and will be vice-regal in breadth and scope." Ned silently agreed, knowing it would take a great deal of power and initiative to solve the Indian problem in California.

He waited several anxious months for Congress to approve the funding, including his salary. Watching Congress disallow Barbour's drafts precluded him from leaving and trusting that illustrious body to reimburse him. Finally, Congress did approve half what he had asked for, and the establishment of five of the ten reservations. They did not approve the expenditure for schools on the reservations, justifying, "The state of development of the savage is such as to preclude the possibility of their appreciating the benefits to be derived from such instruction."

Ned decided he would find other methods of educating them, for he believed that was the only way the reservations would survive.

Ned immediately hired his brother-in-law, Harry Edwards, who now had a great deal of experience in California, and his wife's cousin, Fred Kirlin. He knew this would be considered nepotism, but he wanted men he could trust.

By the time they were ready to leave, California had another governor, her third since becoming a state. Governor John Bigler was as adamantly opposed to the Indians as McDougal had been. Ned read a quote by the new governor in the newspaper after they boarded the steamship.

"The commissioners are giving to barbaric savages the most fertile lands. White settlers will want those lands, and the entire United States Army will be powerless to stop them. The savage must be relocated or eliminated." Bigler asked for federal troops to protect the settlers, while Ned Beale wanted federal troops to protect the Indians. He was not encouraged, and knew he was in for the battle of his life—and his primary weapon would be one that had burned his hand almost every time he had reached for it, politics .

This time they rode the train across the isthmus, a much easier trip than before, but still not as good as an all-weather road across the United States would be. Ned continued to hate the fact he had to cross a foreign country to cross his own. When they reached San Francisco, the Indian Office was quickly established at 123 Montgomery Street, a location that had almost been in the bay when Ned had first set sight on Yerba Buena. Now two blocks of recent landfill separated his office from the busiest port in the Pacific.

As soon as he got his Marys established, he set out for Vallejo and a scheduled meeting with Governor John Bigler at the new capital. Although he could have taken a side-wheeler directly to Vallejo, Ned instead purchased a tall bay stallion, crossed the bay via a ferry to the Alameda area, now becoming established as a community called Oakland, and headed north on horseback. He wanted to get the feel of the land again, and had business that would require him to go inland. He changed his clothes in a Vallejo barber's tent, donning a tailored coat and trousers and a high hat, and walked into the capital offices a few minutes before his after-noon appointment. Bigler kept him cooling his heels in the office foyer for two hours before receiving him. And when he did, he had a state militia officer in attendance.

"Mr. Beale, I've heard a lot about you. This is Major James Savage."

Ned shook hands with both men, noting that he had heard a great deal about Major Savage. His name suited him well in regard to his reputed treatment of the San Joaquin Valley In-dians.

Ned took a seat across the wide desk from Bigler next to Savage. A handsome man, Bigler eyed Ned tentatively.

"I presume you're here to discuss the location of the pro-posed reservations in California?" the governor said, his tone straightforward and decisive.

"I'm empowered to locate them anywhere on federal lands," Ned answered in a pleasant manner but one meant to establish immediately the relationship between the Depart-ment of the Interior, which Ned represented, and the State of California.

The governor smiled, placating. "Of course, you would not attempt to go against the wishes of the state?"

"If the newspaper reports are correct, the state would pre-fer no reservations. My primary concern is the welfare of the

Indian. I will, of course, listen to and weigh your recommendations."

Bigler's brow furrowed, and Savage spoke for the first time. "You've been in the East for quite a while, Beale. Are you aware of the atrocities committed by the heathens?"

"Atrocities have been committed on both sides, Savage. You should know that better than anyone."

The major leapt to his feet, his fists balled at his sides. "You're not one of those blithering, Bible-thumping Indian-lovers, are you, Beale? I heard you fought—"

"The fighting is supposed to be over, Savage," Ned said, glaring up at the major until Bigler interrupted.

"Sit down, James."

Slowly, without taking his eyes off Ned, Savage took his seat. Bigler turned his attention back to Ned, and the standard politician's smile Ned had learned to hate spread across his broad face.

"I'm sure we can learn to work together. After all, California is a big state." The governor reached for a humidor on his desk, opened it, and extended a big cigar across to Ned, who shook his head in refusal. Bigler bit off the end and spat it on the floor, then lit up, expelling a cloud of smoke. "There are great expanses of land east of the Sierras. Indians have made do in much worse country."

"I don't intend to locate valley and coastal Indians into a desert they have no familiarity with, Governor. My intent is to locate them on decent agricultural land with adequate water."

Savage groaned loudly, and Bigler took a couple of rapid drags on the cigar, then expelled the smoke in a rush. In moments he regained the same placating smile—but flat, cold eyes belied his curling lips and tone. "To the south, then, below Tulare Lake, where there are no settlers."

"Possibly. I'll have recommendations soon. First, I mean to investigate reports of Indian slavery. You do recall that

California was admitted as a free state?" Ned cut his eyes to Savage. "I expect the complete support of the militia in suppressing these barbarous acts and arresting the perpetrators."

Not satisfied with the growl he received from Savage, Ned turned back to Bigler. "And the support of the state courts in prosecuting them."

The tone of the meeting did not change as they discussed other aspects of the relationship between the Department of the Interior and the State of California. When Ned left, Savage did not bother to shake his hand.

By the time Ned left the governor's office, the town was lighting its lanterns, and he decided to take a room in Vallejo that night. But before the sun rose over the low hills to the east of the bay city, Ned headed south, to Contra Costa County and Rancho San Pablo. One of the letters he carried had been found slipped under the front door of the Indian office the day after INDIAN OFFICE had been painted on the door—and the letter was unsigned.

Back in Californio clothes, he sat easily in the saddle of the quick-gaited bay. He was comfortable as he rode the eleven miles off the main road onto the big rancho, but not at what he saw as he approached. Wind whistled through the long canyons that opened onto the bay, and even with leather *calzonevas* over woolen pants, Ned felt the cold. Yet in the fields, nearly naked Indians worked under the watchful eyes of quirt-carrying vaquero overseers. The hacienda of Don Gaspar Armenteros received Ned warmly, and his wife, the dona, assured Ned that the don would soon return from the fields. Ned agreed to wait and take supper with them, but informed the dona that he could not take advantage of their hospitality to spend the night. He asked permission to look around the hacienda's buildings, and Dona Louisa Armenteros granted it.

Ned walked to the *establo*, the stable, interested in seeing the stock—he knew all Californio dons prided themselves on their horseflesh—and secretly he hoped he would find an Indian who spoke Spanish. He found the barn full of beautiful Andalusians but was disappointed to find himself in the presence of only the don's young son, Arturo. No Indians would venture the truth about their treatment with this young man at his side.

"I have heard a great deal about you, senor," the thin young man ventured, setting aside the romal he repaired. "I am, however, surprised to see a gringo city man in *calzonevas* and *charro*."

"If you heard I was a city man, you heard wrong," Ned said as they walked from stall to stall.

"Si, Senor Beale. Now a city man. You visit us to see how our Indians are being treated."

Ned looked at Arturo in surprise. "What makes you think so?"

"You see, I wrote the letter that was delivered to your office." Ned took a minute to digest that. "My father was among the lucky ones, and our claim to Rancho San Pablo was reaffirmed by the Lands Commission. As you know, the gringos had fifty men who sat on the commission—none of whom were Mexican Californios—to determine and settle the claims to land ownership in the state. Those Commission hearings, and even the risk of losing the land, changed my father. He now believes he must act as the gringo does in order to preserve the land and our way of life."

Ned knew about the Lands Commission and the injustices that had been committed. Over thirty years ago some of the capital buildings of Mexican Alta California in Monterey had burned, destroying many of the records of old California. Most of the lethargic Mexican grant-holders had never bothered to re-file and reestablish their claims to their ranchos. Ownership, and occupancy, and their historic right, would be enough, they presumed, never guessing they would have to deal with Anglos in the future. Many former rancho owners had tried to fight for their land, which had been declared back in the public domain by the Lands Commission, but they found the state militia too much. A few had been killed defending land harboring the graves of several generations of their forebears, and many more had taken to the hills and become bandits. It was another of California's many problems.

Ned did not comment. He was fascinated with this young man, a man who would go against his own for the sake of the Indian.

"You might think it strange," Arturo continued, as if reading Ned's thoughts, "that I would do such a thing. My mother is half Maidai. Most of the Indians on this rancho are of that tribe. I am one-quarter Maidai. My father is a man possessed by the land and will do anything to keep it, including the mistreatment of his wife's own people."

"You take a great risk," Ned finally offered.

"A calculated one. I have heard of you, Senor Beale, and of your affection for the Californio and the Indian. You are said to be a fair man. Still, I expected you to ride in here in a high hat accompanied by a troop of Army soldiers."

Ned felt a twinge of guilt, happy he had the high hat folded and stuffed in one of his saddlebags. And he gained a respect for the young man's insight—and courage. He resolved to wear Californio clothes whenever he was out of the city. "Not my style, Arturo. Still, the treatment I see in your fields will have to stop. And if it takes troops to convince your father . . . "

"Good," the young man said adamantly. "I do not wish my father harmed, but he must change his ways with my mother's people." The supper gong rang. "Come," the boy said sadly. "You will now have the pleasure of meeting Don Gaspar."

Ned left Rancho San Pablo with two Armenteros promises: that the Indians working there would be given the choice of leaving of their own free will, and that Arturo Armenteros would come to work for him at the Indian Office and report the following week. Ned also arranged to send a wagon back from Oakland to bring in a dozen Indians he found too ill to work. He later placed them in homes in San Francisco, and promised to do the same for whatever healthy ones decided to apply at the Indian Office.

He learned something else from Arturo, while he was there, which caused him to contact the Contra Costa County and request a grand jury hearing. Subsequent to that trip, Harry Edwards, serving as clerk of the Indian Office, transcribed the following letter from Ned to his boss in Washington, Commissioner Luke Lea:

> I went over to San Pablo Rancho in Contra Costa County and found seventy-eight on the rancho and twelve back of Martinez, most of them sick and without clothes or food. Eighteen had died of starvation. They were the survivors of a band worked all last summer and fall, and as winter set in, when broken down by hunger and labor and without food or clothes, they were turned adrift to shift for themselves as best they could. Californians named Ramon Briones and Ramon Mesa have made a business of catching Indians and disposing of them in this way, and I have been informed that many Indians have been murdered in these expeditions. I have distributed the healthy Indians among families to clothe and protect them, and made provision for the sick to be fed and cared for. These people could easily be made to support themselves and their condition changed for the better. The

grand jury of the county found bills against the Californians mentioned and I presume their trial will come up next term.

Our laws and policy with respect to the Indians have been neglected or violated in the state. They are driven from their homes and deprived of their hunting grounds and fishing waters, and when they come back to get the merits of their sustenance they are killed, thus giving retaliation to wars. The condition of the Indians is truly deplorable. They are caught like cattle and made to work, and then turned out to starve and die when the work season is over.

To remedy this state of things and make some compensation for the country taken from them, several treaties were made, all of which were rejected. So now the Indians remain with out protection from law or treaties. Supplies of cattle were contracted for but in their deliveries, great irregularities occurred, to the great injuries of both Indians and government.

Later that month, Ned spent all his time scouring the countryside with Arturo and talking with Indians.

Ned estimated that fifteen thousand Indians had perished from starvation the previous winter. The remaining were dying with regularity from whiskey, disease, and murder. He read and agreed with a statement of Washington Irving's. ''The moral laws which govern the Indian are few, but he conforms to them all. The white man abounds in laws of religion, morals, ethics, and manners, but observes them more in the breach than practice."

Ned heard of a massacre of Indians, mostly women and children, and applied to the United States district attorney for warrants, knowing that Governor Bigler would do nothing, since he personally knew the perpetrators to be his voters. Ned was later forced to write to Bigler:

> As the gentleman who commanded the party in this unfortunate affair was a county judge, consequently I did not think it worthwhile to prosecute him in his own county. The United States District Attorney informs me that he was not aware of any law that would apply in the case as the federal court had no jurisdiction in cases where life is taken.

Frustrated, Ned wanted to take up his pistol and go after the men himself, but he was again beaten down by politics. He appealed to the commander of the United States troops in California when he heard the Army had been in the vicinity of the atrocities and had taken no action. General Hitchcock informed him that the mission of the U.S. Army, as he understood it, was only to punish Indians, should that be necessary. The murder of Indians by whites was a civil matter. The realities were that the murder of whites by Indians always elicited an Army response.

The Indians did score one. Major James Savage was killed by a band of Indians not far from Fremont's Las Mariposas.

Beale again went to Vallejo to make a pact with Governor Bigler, who was facing a coming election and had come to appreciate Beale's contacts and influence, particularly in San Francisco. Ned decided that all politicians were the same, and any he supported would probably be equally bad. To the great surprise of the Army, and more so of the politicos and his bosses in Washington, Edward Fitzgerald Beale was appointed a brigadier general in the California State Militia. He was beginning to learn to use politics as a raft to propel him where he wanted to go. rather than continually swimming upstream against the current. Now militia officers would be compelled to listen to him.

Ned knew enough about the military to realize that the glimmer of brass blinded those who had less, or none, and now he just might be able to rush in where less shine would fear to tread.

CHAPTER TWENTY-TWO

Ned promptly headed south, to a part of the state he knew would feel no pressure from settlers for a long time to come. He remembered the spot where he had first seen the San Joaquin Valley, or Tulares, as it had been called by the Spanish. At almost the extreme southern end of the great valley, he crossed a turbulent river called the Kern, after Fremont's topographer, to a sloping plain below a mountain whose hump-shaped top reminded him of a grizzly, where he established an experimental farm. He left Harry Edwards in charge of several hundred Indians.

Ned had decided to begin his experiment here for many reasons. To the north, the miners were well armed and had few cattle for the Indians to prey on. To the south, near the coast, the mission system had long ago tamed the red man. But in the lower central valley, the Indians had made their subsistence from raiding over the passes into Los Angeles and Santa Barbara, stealing cattle and more so horses, for horseflesh was the mainstay of their diet.

The Tejones, Cowilla, Cowchillas, and Freznales were considered bold and enterprising. Ned would concentrate his efforts on bringing these, the wildest of the California Indians, into the reservation system. And he could do so in a spot that held no interest, as least yet, to settlers.

President Fillmore must have been pleased with Ned's progress, for among the last of his acts before leaving office in 1853 was to appoint Ned superintendent of Indian Affairs in Nevada, the most southwesterly portion of the Territory of Utah, as well as California. And the incoming president,

Franklin Pierce, in early 1853 confirmed his appointment as well as that of Ned's old friend Kit Carson as Indian agent for New Mexico, and another old friend and scout, Tom Fitzpatrick, as agent for the tribes on the upper Platte and Arkansas rivers.

Under Harry Edwards' guidance the farm in the southern San Joaquin was proving a tremendous success. Over a thousand Indians of various California tribes resided at the foot of Paso Creek, which flowed out of mountains the Indians called Tehachapis. Ned began calling the reservation Sebastian, after William King Sebastian of Arkansas, chairman of the Senate Committee on Indian Affairs—Ned continued to demonstrate his political astuteness. The reservation was divided into rancherias, or villages, and each assigned a plot of land. Ned needed Harry elsewhere, so he hired another trusted old friend, Sam Bishop, a Virginian who had come to Los Angeles in 1849. By the end of the first year, zanjas, or irrigation ditches, crisscrossed the Sebastian, and over a thousand acres had been cultivated in wheat, barley, and corn.

As a general in the State Militia, Ned was invited to all San Francisco Army social functions, and of late to a reception for the newly arrived Fourth Infantry Regiment, there to man the Presidio. He struck up an immediate friendship with a young quartermaster, Lieutenant Ulysses S. Grant. Ned spent many of Grant's leaves gaining a real insight into the workings of the federal Army—and the two saw the bottoms of more than one bottle of fine Kentucky whiskey during that time.

Ned decided it was time to appeal to Congress for real help for the Indians, and packed to return to Washington. He took only Jourdan as traveling companion, leaving his precious Marys in San Francisco and leaving Harry Edwards to watch over matters.

Ned's report to the Department of the Interior contained many incidents of atrocities; among them:

At the Trinity River, local militia attacked an Indian village. Only a woman and child managed to escape. The attackers returned from the foray with a bag containing one hundred and thirty scalps. Similar massacres occurred at Happy Valley, Humboldt Bay, and other locations in the state. These were slaughters of helpless human beings, mostly women and children. Slave hunters prey on the natives in Northern California. Juan Berryessa and other large landowners enslave Indians from the Clear Lake region and force them to work as laborers. Indian slaves are sold at a profit to white settlers.

The report went on and on.

With President Franklin Pierce in office Ned knew he would be compelled to begin politicking all over again. He tendered a report to Commissioner Lea, holding a trump card in reserve for presentation to the president--a letter from his old enemy, now his political ally, Governor Bigler, strongly urging General Beale's retention in office and stating that the prosperity of the state depended on the success of the Indian superintendent policies.

Ned Beale, now becoming a skilled political tactician, leaked the private report to the press. Ned was also now astute enough to appeal to his old and influential associates in New York, including Samuel F. DuPont, his former commander, and to use his new status as a general to its best advantage. DuPont passed his letters and the report on to the New York Times. The day before Ned was ordered to present his findings to the new president, the Times reported:

The white trespasser upon Indian territory commit barbarities without precedence in the history of Christendom. To call such men savages and brutes would be a libel upon the animal kingdom. The article went on to praise General Beale's proposals, and lauded his courage in revealing such a shocking tale of massacre and fraud.

Franklin Pierce, a straightforward, open man, welcomed Ned and made him immediately at ease. With a Roman nose bracketed by gray eyes, and curly black hair he let fall across a high brow, Pierce was known as the most handsome president ever to hold the office. He also had been a brigadier general in the Mexican War, having distinguished himself from Veracruz to Puebla, Mexico, in that war, and had been among the officers at the reception at the minister's residence in Mexico City when Ned made his wild ride with the gold nugget. They struck it off immediately, and Ned shared a brandy and talked over old times with the president before he left his office.

The president acted without delay, approving Ned's plan for the California Indians and instructing the new secretary of the interior, Robert McClelland, to take the necessary steps to put Ned's plans into operation. McClelland ordered Beale to report without delay to California, granting him wide latitude in his instructions and telling him to adopt whatever measures in his judgment were necessary to accomplish the objective, but to make sure the funds were "legally, judiciously, and economically expended."

Ned accepted an invitation to dinner at Senator Benton's with his old employer Aspinwall, where he was greeted as a returning hero. And, as he suspected, he almost immediately received another business proposal. After they had enjoyed a delightful formal dinner of aspic and quail, venison in brandy sauce, and all the trimmings, Aspinwall sipped a brandy.

"Government service is truly satisfying, Ned," Aspinwall began. "But, of course, by the nature of the beast, profit while in its noble endeavor is always suspect."

"The politicians wait to criticize, lying like vipers in the bushes, attacking your legitimate expenditures, hoping against hope to find a chink in the armor," Ned said with a smile. "And perch on their lofty Washington branches, watching like buzzards awaiting a last breath."

"Still," Benton added, "a prudent man can carry on his private affairs at the same time. I have done so, and had my share of success."

Ned laughed. "The bush has been beat around, gentlemen. What is it you've got in mind?"

The two older men gave each other a knowing look. Then Benton, in his most eloquent manner, began to lecture Ned on the future of railroads, "Tying the great country, the fulfillment of Manifest Destiny, together like ribbons of hope," he said.

"You've got to return to California anyway. Why not lead a survey party while you do so?"

Ned sipped his brandy, then shook his head. "It's less than two months by ship, gentlemen. With luck, overland would be four. I'm instructed to return forthwith."

"But not," Aspinwall said quietly, "by ship. Forthwith could be by land. Besides, have you been in the Nevada section of your responsibility yet?" Aspinwall knew he had not, for Ned had mentioned it at dinner. "This will give you the opportunity to see what Fitzpatrick and Carson are doing in their areas, and scout reservation locations in parts of your territory you haven't yet seen." Ned sighed, beginning to weaken. "That's true."

By the end of the evening, Ned had agreed to lead a private survey party—Congress had not seen fit to appropriate funds for one—investigating the possibility of a central railroad route across the country. He had always dreamed of a wagon road across the Southwest, but this potential railroad route across the center of the country might even be a better way to reach California. The hope of seeing Carson again was the factor that sealed his determination, not to speak of the fact that he would see country he had never seen, and be able to investigate firsthand the settling of country he would have seen before other white men arrived.

The next morning, Ned received a summons to another congressional committee, mostly made up of Whigs who had supported the failed candidate Winfield Scott for president in 1852 and who wanted Ned to produce all of his Indian Office records. His California expenditures were being audited.

Norvell Johanson, now a senator, to Ned's chagrin, did not sit on the committee this time, but did appear in the audience several times and conferred with the committee members in closed caucus. Ned knew he stood at the heart of the inquiry. Although some of Ned's records had been lost, and the committee's questioning turned ugly on several occasions, General Edward Beale came out unscathed. He prepared to leave for California. The politicians had not been able to overcome his positive press, and Benton and Aspinwall kept the press rallied to his side during the week of investigation.

He did attend one more reception before he left Washington. Jefferson Davis, the new secretary of war, was being entertained at the British Embassy, and General Edward Fitzgerald Beale had the opportunity to spend several hours being questioned by the inquisitive Mississippian, both during the reception and, at Davis's invitation, at the Willard Hotel afterward. Davis, to Ned's surprise, endorsed Aspinwall and Benton's hope of finding a central railroad route. The secretary had hoped to have his own crews of Army surveyors doing the same job soon, though he did not yet have the budget, and he endorsed Ned's interest in leading the private party that was suddenly the talk of Washington. With his parting words, Davis requested that Ned keep up a correspondence with him regarding his findings, and he presented Ned with a book to entertain him on the long mountain nights ahead of him *Recollection's of a Journey Through Tarrary, Thiber and China,* by Abbe Evariste Huc.

With Aspinwall's money in hand, Ned contracted Henry Young to provide all necessary stores, weapons, and animals for the journey, but he also drew on the Department of the Interior for a portion of the funds needed, since he was going to inspect reservation locations in the Nevada portion of his area. His new boss, Commissioner Moneypenny, grew angry at the small expenditures and referred the matter to Secretary McClelland, who had campaigned with Pierce as an advocate of fair dealing and no graft, particularly in Indian affairs—and who immediately ordered Ned to stop spending the government's money until he reached California. His federal bosses were obviously angry at his decision to return overland, but Ned had given Aspinwall and Benton his word, and he continued with his plan.

They set out from Westport, Kansas, on May 9, 1853. At least this time, the crossing would start in the spring.

Ned Beale again hired family—his cousin Guinn Harris Heap, who wanted to see California. To accommodate a request of Aspinwall's, Ned employed two Washington City men looking for adventure, William and Elisha Riggs. In a more practical vein he hired Henry Young; Richard Brown, a Delaware Indian scout; Gregorio Madrid and Jesus Garcia, Mexican muleteers; George Simms, a black guide; and Jourdan.

The trip had a less than auspicious beginning. On the first night out of Westport, a thunderstorm as only the Great Plains can have them set the mules off, and they tore up the camp on their way. Wet and muddy, the men had to find them on foot the next morning. Still, they managed to average thirty-five miles a day across the Plains along a route Ned was now distressed to find lined with graves. Most of the occupants had died of cholera. More than once, their camps rested next to graveyards, where wolves had dug the bones and spread them over the prairie.

Their first destination was Fort Atkinson, where William Riggs decided he had had enough of Plains life and stayed behind to return to Washington. To Ned's surprise, his brother, Elisha, decided to travel on. Ned had to fire Gre-gorio Madrid, who could not pull his weight.

When they neared the Rockies, they cut off the Santa Fe Trail and headed into unknown country, staying with the Arkansas River and heading for Raton Pass. Then they followed the Huerfano River into the heart of the towering Sangre de Cristo Mountains, crossed to Ute Creek, and followed it to Fort Massachusetts—Colorado's first Army post—arriving there on July 13. Ned was both disappointed and pleased to find he could not purchase additional mules. Since the nearest stock available was at Taos, eighty miles south, he was forced to head for the hometown of his old friend Kit Carson.

While Ned and Jourdan headed south, the rest of the party waited. But Carson had left for California, driving sixty-five hundred head of sheep to sell. Ned and Jourdan bought the mules they needed, and returned. At the fort, Ned was introduced to a buckskinned scout, Felipe Archulete, who asked him for a scouting job. At first Ned was reluctant to hire him, even though he carried the recommendation of the officers at the fort. He had a peg leg, and was so nicknamed, and Ned could not imagine that a man so disabled could be much help. It was only after Peg Leg challenged Jourdan to a wrestling match and beat him soundly, as well as every other man in the party, that Ned took Felipe on. He let Peg Leg select some additional men as muleteers, and they got under way again.

More and more, the party came across Indian signs. The Utes had the worst reputation in the Rockies, and Ned knew that the season before they had killed several parties who had tried to cross their mostly unexplored land. But that was exactly the reason he had picked this route and became the reason he was glad he had hired Peg Leg Archulete. Ned searched for an easy, unknown crossing in the center of the country, and knew he would not find it following established trails. Peg Leg had lost his limb to a Ute ball and seemed to have a second sense about where the Indians would be and how to avoid them.

They dropped into the San Luis Valley, and Guinn Heap kept detailed maps of their progress. They reached what they knew must be the Rio Grande and turned south, then west again into a valley the Indians called Saguache. Now all streams flowed westward. They reached a spot on the trail blocked by a twenty-foot-wide elk horn fence, a sign from the Utes to stay out, but they rode around it. The high mountains were still snow-covered on the peaks, and they had crossed many patches of snow even in the lower passes, but the weather was mild.

Coochatope Pass took Ned's breath away with its beauty. Wildflowers covered its rocky slopes. The stream there, called Rio de los Cibolos, or River of Buffalo, by the Mexicans, flowed with free abandon, and animal signs were everywhere. Ned rode in pursuit of an old buffalo bull, but it avoided him. While he was gone the Delaware scout Richard Brown killed a mountain sheep, and there was fresh meat in the camp when Ned returned.

The weather turned hot after they reached the Grand River, and the snows above began to melt. They followed it until the country became an impassable area of high, black buttes.

Blocked, they searched north, skirting the roughest of the country, and reached the Grand again after it exited from the great black canyon they had avoided. But here it roared with white defiance to their crossing. Although the river heaved and pitched over a quarter mile wide with great white roiling waves, they had to cross.

Ned studied the situation and finally began giving orders. "Cut that cottonwood. We're going to make a canoe."

"She'll be heavy and hard to handle," Peg Leg advised.

"You got a better idea?"

"Nope," the scout answered, "but that won't make 'er any easier to paddle." They fell to the tree with axes. They would ferry the packs and men, and swim the mules across. It took the better part of a day to hollow and shape the clumsy craft, with all of them working in shifts.

Working rather than resting was the favored pastime, since mosquitoes and gadflies filled the air. Even during the day, they built smoky fires to find relief from the swarms, but it helped little. They discovered the chips cut from the sappy center of the cottonwood were so heavy they sank when they hit the water, and they decided it would be necessary to dry the canoe. They built fires along its edges and inside the hollow, taking another day to dry the wet wood, then hack out the burned charcoal center. Finally it was ready to launch.

Peg Leg offered to lead a string of the mules across, riding a tough little dun-colored mustang he favored, and with three mules strung out behind, he plunged into the heaving river. He managed to hang on to the saddle horn, and the mules tracked behind, but a fourth mule, still packed heavily, dove in behind them on its own and was swept down river, rolling feet up, until it disappeared into the deeper water below the spot they had chosen.

The mule had carried most of the cornmeal and several weapons in its pack. It was a devastating loss.

Ned took the bow for the first canoe crossing, and they set out with four men paddling. The craft proved clumsy and almost impossible to guide, but it wallowed forward, cutting into the heavy, heaving river and over a hundred yards below where they had entered, they reached safety. After tying pack ropes to it, they dragged the canoe far upriver for the return trip, sinking to their waists into the deep mud several times. The mud covering them proved a godsend, since it kept the gadflies and mosquitoes from eating them. From then on, they purposefully muddied themselves. Guinn Heap and Peg Leg volunteered to take the canoe back across for the next load of men and the rest of the packs. They made it, but were swept a hundred fifty yards down the river doing so. They had almost been swept into a narrows, where the river rose in ten-foot waves. Then again, with the help of the men waiting, they tugged the raft far back upriver.

George Simms, the black scout, and Jourdan took up the rear paddles and Peg Leg and Guinn Heap the forward. The center of the canoe lay piled with the majority of their remaining equipment. Ned, having remained behind, began making a camp, for the men would be exhausted when this day's work was done.

He heard the shouts of the men in the canoe as he hacked a camp clearing in the heavy riverside growth, and ran to the shore where he could see. The canoe was broaching, the packs soaking up water as the waves broke over the side.

Richard Brown dove into the river on the far side of the stream and cut through the water like an otter toward the floundering craft.

The men in the canoe kept up their mad paddling, maintaining headway until the canoe broadsided one of the few rocks in the center of the river that rose above the water level. The heavy craft seemed to want to climb the hindrance. Its downriver side rose up against it, and the upriver side lowered dangerously until it almost took in water.

The men scrambled to the high side, and Guinn Heap leapt out onto the rock. Then the downriver side suddenly dipped and the pressure of the water on the bottom flipped the canoe so quickly it flung men and packs into the river and almost knocked Guinn Heap from his perch.

The log-canoe slowly swung around the rock and headed downriver, but not soon enough to help the men, who bobbed away out of sight and into the terrible narrows.

Ned ran for a mule, and with only a lead rope, mounted and gave the animal his heels, galloping downriver, where he hoped to intercept the men and some of the equipment, though he knew the heavy packs were lost.

He crashed through a thick stand of river willows, the mule's sides heaving from exhaustion in the deep ooze, and saw Peg Leg and George Simms, covered with mud and dripping wet, struggle out of the willows.

"Where's Jourdan?" Ned yelled, and both men shook their heads in confusion. Ned dismounted and tied a Spanish hackamore from the lead rope so he would have reins to guide the mule, then remounted and searched on. For hours, as the other men via Richard's strong swimming got a rope to Guinn Heap, who sat stranded on the rock, Ned searched the river's edge for his old friend. Finally, well after dark, with half the party, including Guinn Heap, still on the far side of the river, he plodded back into camp. He prayed he had somehow missed Jourdan, and that the big zambo would be warming his hands at the campfire—but he was not.

The next morning, exhausted and dejected, Ned instructed the seven men on the far side of the river to return to Santa Fe and issue government drafts for more mules and supplies—in direct contradiction to his orders from Secretary McClelland. It was a major challenge for Guinn Heap, and Ned hoped he was ready for it. Ned and the remaining party would wait here and continue the search for Jourdan, hoping that by the time the men returned, the river would be much tamer.

Two days of searching proved fruitless. On the third, they found what they did not want to find—Indians, in full war paint. Over two hundred Ute braves tracked and flanked them as they returned to their makeshift camp. Ned had long ago learned that Indians respected brazen action. While the Utes watched from a hillside, Ned and Peg Leg had one of the scouts throw buckeye balls, plucked from the trees, far out into the heaving stream, and blew them apart with a few shots of their remaining ammunition while they bobbed along. Finally, after the demonstration of their marksmanship, Ned set the rifle aside, brushed his hands off, and, alone, began climbing the hillside to where the long line of braves sat their ponies, watching. The men in camp took up positions where they could cover him, but it was a fruitless endeavor. They had less than ten shots apiece, not even one per brave.

As Ned climbed the hill, he felt less than confident. His party was anything but awesome. Every man of them was covered with mud, and the uniform he would have preferred to have worn for such a meeting had been swept downriver along with several hundred pounds of trade goods he brought as gifts for just such a confrontation.

A tall brave astride a piebald horse nudged his animal forward to meet Ned's approach. His hair hung in two long black braids down his chest, and polished bones and beads formed parts of the braids' design. A few feathers lay gathered atop his head. A bone, tooth, and claw choker proved his feats as a bear hunter. A beaded loincloth hung from his waist. A cartridge box, for paper cartridges, dangled from the loincloth's band. He was painted over his body with alternating yellow and black stripes. A yellow and blue cavalry hat and low moccasins were the total of his remaining dress. His horse stood unpainted and without saddle. Not even a blanket separated horse and rider, but the bridle was a Cavalry Curb, of good bright steel with brass buckles and leather reins, adorned now by a few bright feathers. The Indian carried a large-caliber Sharps of the most recent design—probably a .52-caliber Beecher's Bible, so named because as they had been shipped to Kansas by a man named Beecher in crates marked "Bibles" and traded to the Indians—and a Bowie knife with some unfortunate's initials still carved into its bone grip—old W.C.H. had probably lost his hair by his own knife. It was obvious the warrior had been successful in battles other than just those with bears.

He hooked a painted leg over the horse's neck and, dropping the reins, slipped casually off the animal's back to await Ned's approach.

The man wasted no time in getting to the point. "Do you have presents?" he signed, his brown fingers moving deftly.

"No, they were lost in the river," Ned signed back, his look remaining hard and confident, belying the empty feeling in his gut. "But many more men, well armed, are coming behind, and they will have many presents."

Ned heard the grumbling of the braves at this news, and glanced to see that many more of them had white man's gear, and one even sat on a saddle blanket with the insignia of an officer of the Engineers' Corps on the frayed corner, its makeshift elk hide belly strap tied to the slits where the officer's saddle cinch had passed through. Another brave carried over his shoulder a haversack filled with God only knew what, the "U.S." plainly visible on the leather flap.

The brave signed, "You and your men will come to our camp, and we will wait together there for the presents."

It was better than the possible alternative, Ned decided quickly, and turned to retrace his steps and order the men to pack up. Peg Leg, who had read the signing from afar, furrowed his brow at Ned's approach. "Damn fool thing to do, General."

"You got any better ideas, Peg?" Ned snapped, and the scout admitted he did not.

They rode a few miles then into a beautiful mountain valley, where hundreds of wigwams of buffalo and elk hides rose at the foot of aspen groves and pines and lined a meandering stream. Ned noted a herd of over three hundred goats being tended by several Utes. An even larger herd of horses grazed at the far end of the lush valley. Peg Leg spoke the language, and seemed to be known and respected—and maybe a bit feared—by the Indians. The travelers were given four of the large tents to share, and they bedded down on buffalo robes for the night after sharing a stew they prepared from an elk loin the Utes had provided them.

"It will begin tomorrow," Peg Leg said as he rolled in a buffalo robe.

"What?" Ned asked, not liking the scout's ominous tone.

"You'll see, General," he said, and yawned.

"Damn it, Peg Leg. What the hell are you talking about."

"Games. The Utes are great on games."

Well, games can't be so bad, Ned thought, but he tossed and turned all night. He put it off to the loss of his old and very good friend Jourdan.

But Jourdan's ghost was not through haunting him.

CHAPTER TWENTY-THREE

The next morning, squaws brought them an early meal of boiled corn and roast venison, and Ned, who had been suffering from a touch of dysentery, found it as fine a meal if not better than his last dinner at Senator Benton's.

But the meal was nowhere near the surprise that followed.

Jourdan, dressed in Ute buckskins and carrying a bow and quiver of arrows, arrived to welcome them to camp. He explained he had been found by the Indians far downstream from where he had been swept away, and they had brought him nearly unconscious to the village. Ned did not know whether to punch him or hug him when he asked Jourdan why he did not find his way back to camp, and he answered with a wry smile, "Many women here, and no mosquitoes. I was coming soon."

On finishing the meal, they were taken to a central campfire, where the first of many Indians challenged Peg Leg to a wrestling match. The travelers were expected to bet on each match, and, of course, they won much more than they lost, only betting what little tobacco they had left.

The Utes seemed fascinated with the skill of this one legged man at wrestling. One brave followed another, until finally, out of shear exhaustion, Peg Leg was thrown and bested by a large brave. The Indian was beaten in turn by Jourdan, who redeemed himself for losing to Peg Leg back at the fort.

Then all of them and their animals were tested as the horse racing began. A course of three hundred yards was set out, and every man was expected to race against the finest of the Indian ponies. By the end of the day, more than fifty races

363

had been run, and the Indians had won back all they had lost and more. Ned would have bet on the mule he rode in any endurance contest against the Indian ponies, but in a straight-out race he was not surprised to come up far in the rear. Tests of hatchet throwing and spears flung at rolling hoops went on well into the night.

The Indians were fascinated with the revolvers carried by the men, apparently never having seen the smaller modern weapons. Ned demonstrated the use of his own Baby Dragoon and allowed a number of the chiefs to fire it. He was amazed when they fired groups almost as tight as his own.

That night they rolled in their robes feeling it had been a good day, and their relationship with the Indians had been maintained, but Ned lay awake and worried about how long it could last. He hoped his cousin Guinn Heap got back within the twelve days Ned estimated it would take him.

The days wore on, seemingly interminable to Ned. Both sides quickly tired of the games, but the Indians continued to feed them handsomely, and Ned and the men gave them what they could in return, which was very little. Ned dispatched Peg Leg to return to the Grand to await Heap and the others. And it was a good thing.

Guinn Heap and the men rode into camp in record time, having averaged forty-five miles a day. They carried adequate shot and powder and had replaced the lost weapons so each man had at least a rifle, and most had Baby Dragoon revolvers. They also carried a number of bull-skins of thick and well-tanned leather that would serve as skin for willow ribs—boats to cross the Grand and other waterways they might encounter.

Unfortunately, the bare necessities were all he had gotten from Santa Fe. There were no presents for the Indians. As they prepared to leave the Indian camp, a group of the older chiefs approached in a friendly manner, and one man spoke to Peg Leg for all of them. The scout turned to Ned.

"He wonders about the presents," he asked in an I-told-you-so manner.

"I was afraid of that," Ned grumbled, searching his mind for a solution. Surrounded by hundreds of Utes, he knew he was in dire need of one. "You got any ideas, Peg?"

"I was the one who didn't wanna come around these coons in the first place."

"That's not an idea, Peg Leg. Give me a way out of here."

"*Cojones* is the only way out, General. *Cojones grande*."

"Tell him I'll bring presents the next time I'm passing through."

"He'll be happy as a mule draggin' his dong through prickly pear," Peg Leg muttered, but walked away to the group of chiefs while Ned and the men continued to pack and load their animals—the pace noticeably increased. Ned could hear the grumbling begin, and glanced back to see a number of the younger men gathering behind the chiefs. Peg Leg wandered nonchalantly over to his horse and sucked up the latigo, as if he knew he was in for a wild ride. He spoke without looking at Ned.

"I suggest we sashay on out of here, General. The old chief suggests we leave our sidearms, since he's been showing us hospitality and giving us graze for our animals."

"Fat chance of that," Ned said, and swung into the saddle.

"Don't get in a rush!" Peg Leg shouted to the rest of the party. Ned reined over to the chiefs and bent from the saddle to shake hands with them and gave them all the sign for thank you. The other men reined away and began to string out through the camp, meandering along as if they were not very close to losing their hair. Ned and Peg Leg, took up the rear.

"This is no hill for a stepper," Ned said confidently as he and Peg Leg neared the edge of the wigwams. He was starting to believe they could make their exit without a confrontation.

"Don't count your coon dogs till they get back to camp," Peg advised, glancing back at a hundred or more mounted Utes who were forming up behind them. "It may just be that these fellas don't want to mess their own nest. They'll wait till we're well out of camp before they try anything."

Ned pulled his Baby Dragoon and checked the loads.

"Let me handle 'em," Peg cautioned. "This moccasin requires a fine stitch."

"Here they come," Ned warned. He shouted to the men ahead, "Hold fast, men! Just ride on!"

A half dozen of the younger braves, including' the one Ned had originally approached on the hillside over the Grand, came galloping down on them from out of the main group of riders. They got very close before they jerked rein, their horses almost sliding into Ned and Peg Leg. Then they reined away as quickly as they had come, shouting.

"What did they say?" Ned questioned.

"You don't wanna know," Peg said quietly. "Jus' keep a'ridin'' on."

"Another bunch coming," Ned said, and again a group of a half-dozen braves charged forward. Ned's horse danced nervously and sidestepped as they rode within arm's reach. One of the braves actually tapped Ned with his lance before they wheeled away.

"This could get nasty as maggot pie," Peg Leg said as the original group of six charged forward again. This time the brave painted in yellow and black stripes slammed his horse into Peg Leg's at a gallop, knocking both horses aside. When they recovered, the warrior and Peg Leg both had a firm grip on Peg Leg's rifle. The horses stood facing in opposite directions, both nervously dancing in place. Peg Leg and the glowering brave sat astride them, each glaring at the other, each with a death grip on Peg's rifle. The other riders in Ned's group reined around, and each man sat where he was. The other Indians rode in two groups, flanking the column of men, mules, and horses. "Hold, men, let Peg handle this!" Ned cautioned.

The muzzle of Peg's rifle aimed at the Indian's stripped belly, but still he foolishly jerked at it. Peg jerked back with equal determination. They stopped the struggle, but held tight and stared unblinking at each other.

In the silence of the forest morning, the ratcheting of Ned's hammer rang up and down the trail. The other men in the column followed suit, cocking their rifles and palming the revolvers so feared and respected by the Utes. The sound was as loud as a buffalo stampede among the quietly brooding men.

Still no man moved, nor blinked, nor even breathed.

The last rifle cocked was Peg Leg's, its muzzle now marked with paint from the brave's belly.

Ned could see the man's eyes noticeably flare, though he struggled to retain his fierce disposition. Peg muttered something in the man's tongue, but quietly under his breath so the other Indians could not hear.

Stripes flung the muzzle aside angrily and in a single motion reined his horse around and galloped away. The other Indians slowly followed suit, shouting insults as they retreated back down the trail to the village.

Peg Leg shook his head and rebooted his rifle. "Close as a tick."

"You handled that remarkably well," Ned complimented, and got a shrug from Peg for his trouble.

"They wanted to shout and take coup and show off for their squaws. . .still and all, it coulda got outta hand."

"I admire your ability to keep calm," Ned said, still a little astounded at how controlled the scout had remained .

"I never got a hurt tongue from talkin' quiet."

Ned chuckled for the first time that morning and vowed to remember the advice. "What did you say that made him give it up?"

"I told him he was a brave man, but that his squaw would lie with his friends and they would howl his praises while copulating, while he was alone and roaming the after world."

This time Ned guffawed loudly.

They followed the Grand to the Red, known to some as the Colorado, and crossed in the bull hide boats.

On July 24 they reached the Green River, and used the bull skins for the third time. The country had changed from forest to high desert, and though game abounded, graze became more and more scarce. Several times they crossed paths with Indians, but other than the braves trying to run their mules off in the night, and wounding one with a volley of arrows, they had no serious encounters.

At Paragoona, where thirty Mormon houses of adobe sat in a quadrangle with fences between them to form a sort of fort, they rested. The Mormons worked smelting iron ore from nearby mines they claimed were inexhaustible. Almost as soon as Ned and his party arrived, the Mormons began moving their whole community to a place they called Patawan, in compliance with an order from their governor, Brigham Young. War had broken out with the great Ute chief Walkah, and Young thought Paragoona unsafe. Ned and his party helped dismantle the town, and accompanied them on their move. The graze remained good at the new town site, with underground streams watering the pastures in a natural fashion, and the mules rested and gained strength and weight. They would need it for the desert ahead.

The Mormons had published a reward for the Ute chief Walkah, offering the huge sum of fifteen thousand dollars for his carcass. Ned was worried that some of his party might foolishly go man-hunting—an endeavor he was sure would end with their hides strung on Walkah's tanning frames.

But they did not, and the party moved through the rough country unmolested. Ned continued to visualize how a road and a rail bed could be constructed through this rugged country. Streams cut deep canyons, even where the desert floor was flat and inviting; then suddenly the country would become a series of almost vertical rises and falls, and the party would ride miles to avoid impassable areas. He hoped there might be a better route than this.

They were well out of the Ute country, and now the Indians were Paiutes. Much less refined than the mountain tribes, these were nearly if not totally naked.

The party moved down the Santa Clara River, then the Rio de la Virgin. The country became cactus and greasewood. The mules and men were holding up well, as water was adequate, if scarce, and feed was tolerable. They paused and rested again at the Vega Quintana, with its two streams and abundant mesquite and willows, where they feasted on wild grapes.

August 15 found them at the Armagosa, or Bitter Creek, sweltering in true desert heat. Now even the rifles were too hot to touch. Water, when found, was usually brackish. The Mojave River offered them relief, but the rugged, dry mountains in front of them were only desert ranges, as uninviting as the sands behind.   The Sierras were still far from sight.

But soon after they reached the intermittent sinks of the Mojave, Richard the Delaware killed an antelope, and Ned knew they were nearing verdant California.

They reached the narrows of the Mojave, and soon after passed through mountains, oak and pine-covered, into the San Bernardino Valley. On August 22 they sat sipping wine at Rancho de Cucamonga, where they obtained fresh horses for the ride into Los Angeles.

They had accomplished the trip from Westport on the Missouri in exactly one hundred days with the loss of only three mules.

Ned received a letter from Senator Benton shortly after his arrival in San Francisco, offering to have Ned's journals "published in the *National Intelligencer*, whence it will go all over the U.S."

Three other government expeditions had been organized to explore the central route, and to Senator Benton's chagrin, none had been assigned to his son-in-law, Fremont. Still, Benton was quick to praise Ned, repeating many times that Ned's expenses totaled only eighty-six dollars, thirty cents for the entire journey, and noting that a column appeared openly quoting the commissioner as saying Ned owed the government money he would not pay, was misappropriating funds, and would soon be recalled to Washington. Ned could not believe that his own boss, a Democrat like himself, would spread lies about his own party members.

Ned did not wait for a recall. Within three days from receiving a copy of the article in the mail, sent by Senator Benton, who explained that he and a number of Ned's friends had made a personal visit to the *Morning Star's* office and demanded a retraction but had not gotten one, Ned packed and boarded a steamer headed for Panama.

In Washington, he went straight to Moneypenny's office, but found the commissioner out to lunch. Ned, dressed in his best high hat and frock coat—already angry at having to leave his work and his Marys—tried his best to remain calm. He fought to remember his wife, Mary's, parting words: "Remember, Ned, this is politics. Win with words and wile and influence."

He would convince Moneypenny with the valise of journals and receipts he carried that the man was wrong and that Ned's work with the Indians must go on. Ned went to Senator Benton's office but found he was also out.

Finally, frustrated, Ned grabbed a hack and headed for the Willard, where he would kill some time over lunch and wait for the politicians to get back to their offices. The old hotel, still among Washington's finest, attracted the elite of Washington's political and social circles.

Deciding a drink would calm him before he met with Moneypenny, he walked into the Willard's dark walnut bar and ordered a bourbon. Standing alone at the bar, he downed the drink in a gulp. He searched the room for someone he knew, but spotted no one among the crowd of well-dressed men. Letting his gaze drift to the cut glass windows separating the bar from the dining room, where a few women and a crowd of men busily polished off oysters and other well-prepared delicacies, he spotted Senator Norvell Johanson.

Johanson, always a big man, had begun to go to fat. Puffy-cheeked, he laughed loudly, obviously enjoying the company of three other men. Ned walked to the swinging doors separating the two rooms, feeling the heat rising in his back at even seeing Johanson. Then it pierced to his neck like a hot poker. One of the men with Johanson was George Moneypenny, and he and Johanson were toasting. Ned balled his fists at his sides, but remembering Mary's last words, turned to walk back to the bar. He decided to leave, and had almost made the door when again the loud, hollow laugh of Senator Norvell Johanson rang across the room.

Ned spun on his heel, pushed through the batwing doors, and made his way across the dining room. He stopped at the table, between Johanson's and Moneypenny's chairs.

At Ned's intrusion, George Moneypenny appeared as surprised as Norvell Johanson appeared angered.

Ned fingered the newspaper article, now worn from repeated readings, out of his pocket, unfolded it, and dropped it print up in George Moneypenny's lobster bisque.

"Did this reporter quote you accurately?" Ned asked, his quiet tone belying his anger. "If so, you're as big a crawfish as the one you're eating."

Moneypenny fished it out with his spoon and set the dripping article on the white linen tablecloth. He seemed to be at a loss for words—but beads of sweat broke out on his liver-spotted pate among the few wisps of remaining hairs.

371

"You're out of line, Beale!" Johanson roared, his fat jowls shaking. But it was Moneypenny who rose, his face red, his hands trembling.

"You're dismissed, Beale, fired, through. Don't even come around to the Department of the Interior," Moneypenny said, and he made the mistake of following Ned's firing with a smile. "In fact, with great pleasure, we'll send your final check by mail; . . if there's any left after we deduct what you've taken.

"You're a joke, Commissioner, and a traitor to your party as well as a liar," Ned said, cutting his gaze to Johanson. "And you've always been ugly and a blowhard, Norvell, and now you've gotten fat." He looked back to Moneypenny. "The government trough feeds one hog as well as another."

"Get out, Beale!" Moneypenny bellowed, almost choking with his anger, his watery eyes bulging.

"No, Moneypenny, it's you who's going out," Ned smiled. His left fist, backed by powerful shoulders, cracked into Moneypenny's nose. His arms reeling, the commissioner stumbled back into a waiter, who pushed him forward again. Ned sidestepped and shoved Moneypenny over the table, burying his face in the bisque.

Norvell leapt to his feet, swinging, but Ned ducked and jerked his dripping ex-boss to his feet. Two more solid punches sent Moneypenny back, wings wind-milling like a wounded goose. Without the waiter to stop him, he crashed through the window, over the sill, and disappeared headfirst down onto the boardwalk.

Ned spun back just in time to partially block an overhand right from the puffing Johanson. Driving a fist deep into his fat midsection, Ned doubled him, then slowly and very deliberately straightened him up. Bystanders scrambled to get out of the way, knocking chairs and tables over and spilling food as they did so.

Washington's finest formed a semicircle around them, and Ned did not disappoint them. He drove a solid right into Norvell's face, and the other two astounded men who had been lunching with them finally gained courage and leapt at him. Ned managed one more blow, snapping the senator's head back and splattering his blotched nose, before the other two were on him, pinning his arms to his sides. But Ned had no quarrel with these two, and stood quietly, disappointed and disgusted that his old nemesis had been such an easy conquest. Norvell Johanson managed to crawl back to all fours. Partially eaten quail, roast beef, gravy, and broken crocks and crystal mingled with the blood that flowed freely from his broken nose and the yawning cut in his brow.

Outside, a physician from the crowd attended to Moneypenny, who had not moved and lay bleeding from not only Ned's blows but also from the broken glass.

Eyeing the two men holding him, Ned calmly commanded, "Let me go, gentlemen, unless you want to join this pile of pig shit here."

The men cautiously released him and backed out of range. Ned picked up a linen napkin to wipe his hands. The room began to buzz with comment, and the waiter ran over to check on the senator. The man trembled, wringing his hands, and his voice sounded at least two octaves above normal.

"What have you done, what have you done?" he said, moaning.

"Settled a very old grudge," Ned said with a grin, then walked to the shattered window and looked out to see that a physician, a Willard diner, had Moneypenny on his feet, apparently not seriously injured. Ned walked back to the waiter. "And a recent one," he said as he dug into his wallet for some bills and handed a wad to the man.

"This is for the damage. Send the change to Bloomingdale. I'll need it. Seems I'm among the unemployed."

Ned carefully fitted his high hat, which had been sent reeling across the floor, onto his head at a jaunty angle, and left the Willard, unmolested except by a reporter who hurried along beside him, firing questions.

The next day the following story appeared in the Evening Star:

> After the article charging Mr. Beale with being a defaulter appeared, and his accounts were admitted to be correct, a number of his personal friends called upon the editor of the *Star* and were frankly informed the information was furnished by the commissioner (Moneypenny), who had himself written the article charging Beale with the defalcation.... Mr. Beale embraced an opportunity to meet his accuser. He encountered Moneypenny at Willard Hotel, upon whom he inflicted a severe castigation with his fists.
>
> If an assault can be justified in any case, then was this castigation right and proper? An attempt had been made to ruin the reputation of an honest man in his absence; and now the vindication of the charges, extorted from the accuser, and his public punishment go together.

The press was once again on Ned's side. He heard nothing more from either Moneypenny or Johanson, but knew somehow that the matter was not over. He returned to California.

Shortly thereafter, Thomas Jefferson Henley was appointed superintendent of Indian affairs for California. Ned Beale had been fired. But he had gone down swinging, and he knew he had been fooling himself—he should have expected no less from politics and politicians.

During his trip across the country in what came to be known as the Beale/Heap expedition, Ned had managed to keep at hand the book Jefferson Davis had given him, and after he had completed it, realized what the secretary of war had meant when he advised Ned to read it carefully and see if some of the author's experiences might be useful in the equally arid Southwest. Huc raved about the camels he had encountered, going on and on about the animals' usefulness. He went on to suggest that they could be put to good use in the American Southwest.

Ned had begun to wonder if camels would work as well in the American deserts as they worked elsewhere in the world. Then he learned that Guinn Heap and a contingent of Navy officers were even then in the Near East, acquiring a seed herd of the strange beasts.

Ned and Mary Beale, with little Mary in tow, decided that they had had enough of California, and returned to Chester, Pennsylvania. Ned had no idea what he wanted to do with his life, only that he wanted to rest and enjoy his family—a pleasure long overdue.

But as he relaxed on the porch swing, he wondered about Guinn Heap's adventures in the Near East, and although he did not say as much to Mary, he envied him.

CHAPTER TWENTY-FOUR

During his tenure as Indian superintendent, Ned had made a recommendation to the Army for the location of a fort in the canyon above the Sabastian Reservation. The Army took his advice, and built Fort Tejon in a wide oak flat, with abundant water, up a long, narrow canyon leading out of the San Joaquin toward Los Angeles.

Major General John Ellis Wool, Army commander of the Department of the Pacific, issued the order to establish Fort Tejon on June 24, 1854. It lay on a route often used by the Indians in their former raids on Los Angeles, and a fort there would help prevent further atrocities. Now that the Sabastian Reservation was in the valley below, there was even more reason for the route's existence.

Later, it was discovered that both the fort and the reservation were on private property. They rested on old Mexican land grants, but the more recent Mexican grants had come under the jaundiced eye of the Lands Commission far more so than the older Spanish grants, and title was suspect. Four grants—Rancho los Alamos y Aqua Caliente, Rancho la Liebre, Rancho Castaic, and Rancho el Tejon—lay contiguous on the slope of the Tehachapi Mountains and extended over into Antelope Valley. A quiet title action had been implemented, and now the title of all the properties was assured, due to the government's action in bringing the quiet title suit.

In midsummer of 1855, the lure of California again beckoned the Beales. On August 8, they purchased, in the name of Ned's wife, Mary, the 48,825-acre Rancho la Liebre for twenty thousand dollars.

Under the new Indian superintendent, Henley, the reservations failed rapidly. He had seen no reason why the Indians should raise their own cattle—it precluded him from his important and potentially profitable duty of negotiating for their purchase—and one of his first acts had been to sell off all the Indian livestock. That and his other policies drove the Indians off the reservations, and by the time the Beales returned to make the rancho their home and become patrons to the Indians remaining there, only one hundred fifty of the onetime population of twenty-five hundred remained.

Ned left his Marys in San Francisco, with Mary pregnant with their second child, went to his new property, and began building an adobe. Beale's old friend Alexis Godey had a contract with the Army to provide Fort Tejon with cattle; and Samuel Bishop, whom Ned had given a job at the reservation, had purchased an adjacent property, Rancho Castaic. He operated Castaic in partnership with Alfred Packard, the city attorney of Santa Barbara.

Ned immediately negotiated a partnership with Bishop, whose skills with stock he admired, then hired Godey, and found himself in the ranching business. A number of Californios were employed, as were many of the Indians. The rest were welcomed to continue living on the rancho in the manner they had been, if that was what they wished.

Well before the baby was due, Ned left Godey in charge of the rancho and headed for San Francisco. On March 6, 1856, Mary gave birth to their first son, and they named him Truxtun after Ned's grandfather, Commodore Thomas Truxtun. Ned busied himself in San Francisco while Mary and the baby gained strength. He hoped to take them soon to the completed adobe on the rancho.

Then the news rocked California that the Indians of the San Joaquin were on the rampage.

The worst of Ned's old fears had become a reality. Indians in the Four Creeks Tule River areas had finally decided to

377

take up their weapons as ranchers and miners moved south into their territory. Indians destroyed a sawmill, burned homes and crops, and stole cattle and horses. Governor John Neely Johnson called on Edward Fitzgerald Beale to help quell the uprising, and when he accepted, commissioned him a brigadier general in the California State Militia.

Ned's appointment as general was a paper one at best. The governor allowed him only five hundred dollars to perform his task of talking the Indians back onto the reservations—a feat Ned knew would be all but impossible under Henley's reign. The governor also had no troops to assign him. Ned was a general in name only, all but without funds and without an army. And his appointment put him in direct conflict with Superintendent Henley, whose policies were diametrically opposite to those Ned advocated.

But Henley was in the East, attempting to placate his own detractors, who were up to their old games of criticizing government employees—and Ned knew something of the Army. Brass was brass. Ned took a steamer to Los Angeles, bought a horse, saddled up, and rode out. He headed for Fort Tejon, and when he arrived in spotless uniform and polished brass, wearing the saber given him by his fellow officers for his action at San Pasqual, gleaming and clanging at his hip, he charged directly into the office of the fort commander, Captain Billy Ray Shenneshay, who had taken command of the fort during Ned's absence in San Francisco.

"Captain," Ned commanded with the ring of authority in his voice, "you are to prepare a detachment of soldiers, a full platoon if you can spare them, but not less than forty men and a field piece, and have them ready to ride out of here at daybreak. Field rations for two weeks."

The captain was taken by surprise by this well-dressed officer who had ridden into his camp unescorted. He jumped to his feet and saluted. "Sir!"

"Daybreak, full battle gear. Rations for two weeks in the field. And the field piece."

"Yes, sir," Shenneshay replied, willing to accommodate this senior officer but obviously confused. "For what duty, sir?"

Ned shot him an annoyed glance, then spoke very slowly, as if speaking to a child. "Are you aware, Captain, that we have an Indian uprising on our hands?"

"Not here, sir. I made a tour of the rancherias only yesterday, and they are busily working in the fields." "Are you a federal soldier, soldier?"

"Of course, General, you know—"

"Then your jurisdiction is wherever and whenever your country calls. True?"

"True, sir."

"Then snap to, Captain. Duty calls to the north. I'll require quarters for the night."

"Yes, sir. Sergeant!" the captain yelled to the wide-eyed man who sat in the anteroom outside his office. The man front-and-centered in the doorway and snapped a salute that left a mark on his forehead. "Sir?"

"The general will enjoy the guest room in the officers' billet for the night."

"Thank you, Captain," Ned said, and started to follow the sergeant out.

"Sir?" the captain called behind him, his voice rather tenuous.

Ned spun back.

"You'll pardon me, sir, but who are you?"

"I'm Brigadier General Edward Fitzgerald Beale, Captain. California State Militia, operating under the direct orders of the governor and legislature of the State of California, with the cooperation of your commander, General Wool."

"Yes, sir."

Ned again turned to leave, and again the captain stopped him. "Sir?"

With a hint of irritation, Ned turned to face him.

"Sir, supper is at eighteen hundred sharp. Should I have cook prepare something special for the general?"   "I'll   eat with the troops, thank you, Captain."

As Ned strode out to his quarters, Captain Shenneshay could not help but admire the officer. That's my kind of general, he thought, and wished he could go on the planned expedition with the decisive officer.

Ned pulled his boots off, put his feet up on the bed, and relaxed after the long ride from Los Angeles. He grinned with self-satisfaction as he thought, *cojones*, as old Peg Leg would say, *cojones grande*.

The next morning, he rode out for the Tulares country with fifty men and a six-pound field piece at his rear. He stopped at the Rancho la Liebre adobe, picked up his own guide and Indian expert, Alexis Godey, and with Godey at his side, continued north. Without roads, the cannon and caisson were not easily trailed, and they had to build a raft at the Kern to get it across—but Ned planned to put it to good use.

As they neared the country where the Indian atrocities had taken place, Ned made arrangements with Godey for a meeting on the banks of the Kaweah River, and sent him on ahead with instructions to contact the Indian chiefs and get them to the rendezvous.

At Camp Easton in Tulare County, a small federal Army installation, Ned ordered Henley's field man, Indian agent M. B. Lewis, to accompany him. The field agent had not been in touch with his boss, Henley, for months. Lewis, thinking that Beale, brightly uniformed and backed by a large number of federal troops, was acting under Henley's direct orders—a perception Ned did not discourage—hired a wagon and team and followed the troops.

With Godey's help, Ned arranged meetings with twelve chiefs from the tribes who had left the reservations. He established an impressive camp on a sand-spit under the spreading limbs of huge live oaks and immediately put the troops to work building breastworks. When the chiefs arrived, Ned welcomed them and offered them food. Offhandedly he instructed Lewis to issue drafts to cover the expenditures. Lewis did so without question.

The general kept his troop drilling, and firing the cannon, in plain sight of the negotiations. By the end of the week, with the impressive field force of Fort Tejon soldiers backing him up, Ned successfully convinced the Indians to return to the reservations.

Bearing presents Ned had charged to the Superintendent of Indian Affairs Office over Lewis's signature, the Indians rode out having promised to bring their people back to the reservations, where Lewis had agreed to provide them with cattle, seed, and farm implements—and Ned rode away with signed treaties. He purposefully did not leave a copy of those treaties with Indian agent Lewis, although the man had signed them under General Beale's signature, obligating his department to their terms.

The task had been accomplished in a few days before General Wool was aware that his troops had been used-he had earlier specifically informed the governor that he had no men to spare—and before Agent Henley had been able to contact his men in the field and give them the order that awaited Lewis when he returned to his outpost at Camp Easton. With quaking knees, Lewis read the dispatch from Henley, who had just returned from the East and found out about the governor's appointment of Beale. It read:

> Under no circumstances is this department or are any of its employees to assist Edward Beale in his effort to bring

those Indians, who are the responsibility
of this department, back to the reservation. I repeat, the responsibility of this department. Give him no assistance. We will
solve our own problems. Await further
orders.

Ned filed his report, submitted a voucher for nine hundred
dollars to the state, and received only the five hundred the
governor had promised. He just smiled. He had gotten five
hundred dollars' worth of satisfaction. Letters flew from Henley's Indian Office in San Francisco, including a complaint
the superintendent of Indian affairs filed with Governor Johnson—but the fact of the matter was, the Indians were back on
the reservations. Henley sent demands to Ned using very un-
complimentary language, insisting that he submit the fraudu-
lent treaties forthwith.

Governor Johnson backed Ned up and publicly stated
what a fine job he had done. In a newspaper article, he questioned if the Indian Office would "foul things up again, after
General Beale and the state government had solved the problem."

Ned responded to none of Henley's demands, then got a
chuckle when Henley finally had to concede his success. He
wrote Ned the following letter—in a most conciliatory tone.
Ned decided that Henley's sentences were as confusing and
difficult to understand as his Indian policy:

Although your authority did not ema-
nate from this department, yet as the Superintendent is expected to make provisions for carrying into effect the treaties
in question, you will perceive it to be indispensable before definite action can be
taken, that this office should be furnished

with copies of the treaties, a statement of
the pledges given, and promises made to
the Indians, so as to determine the questions that may arise in connection with
this subject.

Ned had charged the bulk of the cost of the expedition to
the federal government, via drafts on the Indian Office,
signed by their own agent, and by using federal troops. Hostilities had been quelled in the San Joaquin Valley. Beale had
most certainly cooperated with the authorities, "both civil and
military," as Johnson had ordered him to do, even though
their superiors were not aware of it. Ned had taken two turns
around the capstan with old Henley's neck and enjoyed it
immensely. He decided he liked politics—at least if played
his way.

Ned again received notoriety in the press, only this time it
achieved an end he did not really desire.

San Francisco was in turmoil again; mobs and gangs ran
rampant. The Barbary Coast had a killing or more a night,
and the streets were unsafe. The city was in the hands of vigilantes. Due to the failure of San Francisco sheriff David
Scannell to post a bond for his office, he was dismissed, and
the Board of Supervisors was authorized to fill the vacancy
by appointment. The board wanted a man of courage and
conviction to accept this dangerous position—and Ned Beale
had just returned from restoring law and order to the San
Joaquin Valley. Ned Beale's name was raised, and he was
elected by the Board of Supervisors on the first ballot.

Governor Johnson happily confirmed Ned's election. All
of it happened before Ned really had a chance to say much
about it. Ned was appointed on August 11 but did not run in
the general election of November 1856. He did work hard at
cleaning up the town in the meantime and at avoiding getting
shot in the process. His eyes were on higher political office—

not for himself, but for his friends. He left a better San Francisco to his successor.

Almost immediately after turning in his badge, Ned accepted chairmanship of the State Democratic Committee in Sacramento, meeting to elect delegates to the national convention for the presidential election of 1856.

All three candidates for president were close friends of Ned's, making his choice to support one or the other a difficult one.

John C. Fremont was sought as a candidate by factions of all three political parties. A coalition of Whigs, Free Spoilers, and other antislavery groups had united to form the Republican Party, and Fremont agreed to be their candidate.

Former president Millard Fillmore had lost the nomination for reelection in 1852, and this time accepted a bid by the American Party, a group of unhappy northern Democrats and Whigs. Ned felt obligated to the man who appointed him superintendent of Indian affairs in 1852.

And last, James Buchanan, who had just returned from a position as minister to the Court of Saint James's, had been a father figure for Ned and had recommended him for his appointment as midshipman in 1836. Ned had always admired Buchanan, particularly his tenacity. He had tried for the presidency in 1&14, 1848, and 1852. Ned liked his *cojones*, and he was a Democrat. Ned threw his support behind James Buchanan.

Buchanan won the nomination on the seventeenth ballot at the Cincinnati convention. He carried nineteen of the thirty-one states in the general election. Fremont carried eleven and Fillmore one.

Ned and Mary Beale, their daughter, Mary, and their son, Truxtun, finally were able to settle down to life on the rancho—at least so Ned thought, but the camels that he had read about were already treading on American soil. Jefferson Davis remembered the young man he had given a copy of Huc's book to, and who had written him enthusiastically endorsing his idea of utilizing them in the American Southwest—a young man who was more than capable of testing the beasts in the American deserts.

The Beales traveled east for Buchanan's inauguration. John B. Floyd had replaced Jefferson Davis as secretary of war, but he, too, maintained an interest in Davis's camel idea, and a southern wagon route was under consideration—Ned's longtime dream. Over seventy of the beasts had been collected from the Mediterranean, and this exploration and mapping of the Southwestern deserts would be the ideal mission to test their effectiveness.

Without mentioning it to Mary, Ned began to write letters and worked to be appointed to lead the expedition. He wondered about his sanity as he did it, since it would mean politicking again. But a southern wagon route, a dream of his for years—he could not sit idly by. no matter how comfortable his life, no matter how he would hate the politics involved, and let someone else have this job, a mission it seemed he had been preparing for all of his life.

On April 22, 1857, Secretary of War Floyd contacted Ned and offered him an appointment as superintendent of the wagon road from Fort Defiance to Fort Tejon. Ned informed Mary only after it was an accomplished fact.

Ned would report to New Mexico and organize his men. He would utilize ten wagons, an adequate number of mules, and "as many camels as you may deem necessary, not to exceed twenty-five, to test their usefulness. endurance, and economy." At Fort Defiance, in New Mexico, he would pick up an escort of soldiers to see him safely through Indian territory.

Ned prepared a detailed estimate of his expenses, which were in excess of the fifty thousand dollars approved by Secretary Floyd. This time what he needed he procured with little regard for what the politicians might have approved, or in their naiveté, thought unnecessary.

He promptly hired Guinn Heap as his segundo, or second-in-command. His cousin had not only proven himself on the recent crossing of the continent but also had an intimate knowledge of the beasts to be tested. Ned also hired Lieutenant Charles E. Thorburn of the Navy, who had led the camel-collecting expedition in the Near East. Geologist Lewis W. Williams would verify roadbed quality and advise them about the security and location of bridge sites. As wagon master, Alex H. Smith seemed well qualified.

Ned was not happy about leaving his Marys and baby Truxtun again. But this was a challenge. and a hope for the future of the Southwest, from which he could not turn away.

Ned, in a moment of weakness, had also hired three local boys, May Humphreys Stacy, J. Hampton Proter, and Joseph Bell, all eager for adventure, all under twenty years old. The party—Ned, Heap, Thorbunr, Jourdan, and the boys—left Chester on May 12, 1857, and headed by train for Pittsburgh, then by packet boat to Cincinnati. The stern-wheeler, *Queen of the West*, carried the party down the Ohio and the Mississippi to New Orleans. There Ned spent a week buying supplies, including the horses and mules he would need. They boarded the *U.S.S. Fashion* and landed in Indianola, Texas, in early June. Among those hired in Indianola was a guide, John Chisholm, who would lead them to San Antonio.

Ned had a gnawing doubt in his gut about the expedition. He was already under a great deal of attack in the newspapers, who questioned his qualifications to survey a wagon route. Although Ned had no formal training as an engineer or road builder, his experience in the Navy as a navigator and in leading numerous expeditions across the country certainly qualified him. But he had learned long ago that newspapers needed to fill space, and like hens pecking at their sisters' bloodspots until they killed them, would exploit any weakness to their own ends. Still, it galled him. Even his old friend and relative Guinn Heap had been giving him trouble and seemed argumentative and distracted. A few miles out of Indianola, a teamster, whom Ned suspected was sneaking a few pulls from a bottle, confirmed it by falling off his own wagon and being run over.

Ned was forced to dispatch a wagon, team, and driver to return the injured man, who had a broken leg, to Indianola. Ned was furious. An inauspicious start.

On the third day out, a number of the mules escaped the night's camp, and Ned led a party to recover them. He instructed Heap, his segundo, to stay with the wagon train, not lead it, as he seemed to be inclined to do, until all the wagons and stock had crossed the stream where they had camped.

Guinn, eager to see the country ahead and sure that the wagons would have no trouble crossing the stream, led out. When Ned returned, the last two wagons wallowed, mired in the mud, unable to cross. Guinn Heap and the others were long gone. Ned and the teamsters worked into the hot summer late afternoon to free the wagons, and when they finally caught up with Heap and the others, it was long after dark.

Ned rode directly up to where Guinn Heap reclined by the campfire and started cursing even before he dismounted: "By damn, I'll stand for no insubordination. If you can't obey, then by God, I'll find a second-in-command who can!"

Guinn Heap rose from his reclining position, looked his cousin in the eye, and said quietly, "Then do so."

Guinn packed his personal things on the back of a horse and rode out at midnight. Ned went to his bedroll, disgusted at himself for dressing Guinn down in front of the men, and more so at the way the expedition was beginning. The next morning he decided to put the bad start behind him, and he rode on with renewed vigor.

They reached Major Howard's ranch, where the Army now maintained and bred the camels that had been collected, and where two of their keepers, Hadji Ali, a Greek who had been nicknamed Hi Jolly, and a Greek called Greek George, greeted Ned and the survey party—and seemed happy to see Lieutenant Thorburn, with whom they had sailed to the United States. Ned circled his wagons in a clearing near the main ranch buildings, far from the corrals containing the camels, and he and the men walked to inspect the beasts.

Ned surveyed the cumbersome-looking creatures, met their slovenly keepers, and wondered if he was not on a fool's mission. If the writer Huc had stretched the truth, they would be in for a hell of a time. Ned rode on to Camp Verde that same afternoon and presented Captain J. N. Palmer, quartermaster, with a requisition for eight dromedaries and seventeen Bactrians.

From many hours of conversation with Thorburn and Heap, Ned understood the difference between the beasts: The Arabian dromedary, with one hump, was considered the swifter of the two; the larger and stronger Bactrian, with two humps, was the pack animal. The animals seemed quiet and docile, but Ned wondered if it was the quiet before the storm. Ned returned to Major Howard's, and for the first time mounted a white camel, Seid, suggested by Hi Jolly. In record time, while Thorburn. Hi Jolly, and Greek George prepared the others to leave, Ned and two of the other muleteers, mounted on riding camels, headed to Camp Verde, and rode up to its corrals.

He spotted a sergeant running from the barns, waving his arms as Ned approached, and reined the animal in that direction. The others followed. A six-mule team hitched to a heavily laden supply wagon waited in front of the barn, and other mules and horses were tied to corral posts and rails. A squad of cavalry rode just ahead of Ned. Pleased with his new animal's speed, Ned passed them, grinning like a schoolboy.

The cavalry exploded in a tangle of hooves and legs and pitched men as horses flattened ears back, arched backs, and landed stiff-legged trying to shed themselves of their riders—and distance themselves from the approaching animals ridden by Ned and his men. Ned's smile faded as the mules hitched to the wagon brayed and broke away from the sergeant who fought to contain them. The man hung onto the traces, stumbled along beside the lurching team, then abandoned the task as useless. The wagon careened off, rounded the barn behind the panicked team, and rolled, spilling goods in every direction. The mules charged on, dragging the wagon on its side. Finally they broke their traces and galloped away in different directions.

The cavalry fought to calm their animals, some of those less fortunate chasing theirs on foot after eating the dust of the parade ground.

The animals who had been tied to the railing of the corral sat back, jerking the top rail off. It became a battering ram, tossed this way and that as they kicked and bucked, trying to shed themselves of it and get away.

Finally Ned turned his lead camel and rode it to the far edge of the field, leading his men away. He tapped it behind the foreleg with his quirt, as he had been instructed to do. It knelt calmly, and he dismounted. He stared in awe at the destruction he had wrought, turned and hobbled the camel, then strode across the parade ground to the sutler's store. He paused long enough to glance back at the great white beast. Seid calmly stood surveying the scene, chewing his cud in total oblivion.

Ned entered and. without comment, bought a case of whiskey. Before leaving, he pried the lid, then returned to the barn with the case under one arm to make peace with the cavalry and hostlers.

It required all twelve quarts to do so.

That night, after almost as much trouble, he hobbled his own mules and the camels within fifty paces and began the arduous task of getting them used to each other.

He hoped that tomorrow would be better, since they were about to set out for Fort Defiance, across all of Texas.

But, as he was beginning to expect, with the dawn came more bad news: The Comanche nation was on the warpath. And he had to pass through six hundred miles of their country.

What more could go wrong?

CHAPTER TWENTY-FIVE

On sweltering June 25, 1857, they set out across Texas, along the Old Comanche Trail. And a stranger caravan was never seen on the western plains. Sixty miles; as many horses; a small herd of cattle—steaks on the hoof; dogs; wagons, including an ambulance painted bright red; Texans and Louisianians as muleteers, teamsters. and hostlers; Turks and Greeks, and, of course their charges--twenty-five camels of one- and two-hump variety. Wagons and traces clattered and clanked, dromedaries and Bactrians bawled and roared, dogs barked, horses and mules brayed and neighed, and men cursed and swore in several languages. The muleteers generally ignored the camels, thinking them large and clumsy and totally without usefulness. The animals displayed large teeth, emitted a roar rivaling that of a Bengal tiger—embarrassing the muleteers, who fled in fright; spat streams of regurgitated hay in great green, slimy streams when angry; and appeared lazy. Greeks and Turks swore at the Texans and Louisianians in their native languages, then, when challenged, denied having cast aspersions on the ancestry of the muleteers—but laughed after their denials.

It was true that as the journey began, the camels, soft from a long period of idleness at Major Howard's, did not fare well. It had been reported that the animals could be packed with six hundred pounds each, but Ned insisted that they receive only four hundred at the outset, and still they did not do well.

In addition to Hi Jolly and Greek George; Mimico Tedora, nicknamed Mico; Hagiatis Yannaco, nicknamed Long Tom;

391

Anastasio Corali, nicknamed Short Tom; and Yanni Illiatio were on the journey, having already accompanied the camels all the way from the Mediterranean. As they had not been paid in several months, the Turks and Greeks almost revolted at the beginning of the trek; some of their party had already quit and left the country. Ned calmed them with a token payment that left him almost out of money before the journey even began. The local Texans had had many bad experiences with government drafts and laughed when offered them.

Ned had forbidden whiskey to be carried on the trek except for medicinal purposes. That order sat well with none of the men, and Ned knew it would be disobeyed, but at least it gave the men caution about the free use of courage-in-a-bottle. His order carried even less weight when, after being drenched in a driving rain on July Fourth and melancholy about being away from the holiday festivities in Chester and Mary and the children, Ned drank a bottle of medicinal brandy. Enough snakebite medicine to offset the results of falling into the worst snake pit. His self-applied medicinal treatment became apparent to the men when they called him out to quell an argument between a muleteer, John Hoyne—who had been the source of problems several times—and Long Tom; Ned's obvious condition did not help the already dubious discipline of the group, and at the next fort, several of the men, deciding they had been given leave to do so by the general's own actions, got drunk and brawled with the soldiers.

The next day, Ned decided they all needed the easy solution to bickering and complaining, and the schedule became: up at three A.M., On the road by four, stop at dusk. The men were too tired to argue, and Ned was too exhausted to spend much time remorsefully thinking about his Marys and little Truxtun.

Ned had hired the three boys from Chester almost as a lark, but they did prove to lighten the hard journey and keep him entertained with their naiveté. Immediately upon leaving

Camp Verde, Ned had warned them, tongue in cheek yet in the sternest tone, about Indians. Thereafter, every rock and bush was well inspected as they progressed. Ned could not have had three better lookouts had they been situated high in the crow's nest of a brig, sailing across the hill country of Texas.

One of the boys, May Stacy, was given the job of clerk assisting Alex Smith, the wagon master, and acting in the capacity of Ned's old job—ship's master. Stacy's accurately maintained journal almost immediately became useful to Ned, who had been ordered to file quarterly reports with Washington—a job he despised. When the first report came due, he used Stacy's journal to complete it with much more ease than he would have had otherwise.

After a few days without accident or incident, Ned felt reassured that the camels would prove their usefulness. The animals browsed as they traveled, eating whatever the country offered, from grass to mesquite, and never seemed to require water. Ned was amazed at the jaw strength and toughness of the camel's mouths as they tore great bunches of thorny. screwbean mesquite away without pausing in their rolling, trail-eating gait.

After Fort Clarke, the country became dry and uninviting, and Ned's admonitions about Indians became serious. He, too, checked every patch of cactus and pile of rock.

By this time, Ned's admiration of the camels was immense. He noted in his journal:

> The camels are now keeping up easily with the train, and came into camp with the wagons. My fears as to their feet giving out, as I had been lead to believe from those who seemed to know, have so far proved entirely unfounded, though the character of the road is exceedingly trying

393

to brutes of any kind. My dogs cannot travel at all upon it, and after going a short distance run to   the wagons and beg to be taken in. The camels, on the contrary, have not evinced the slightest distress or soreness; and this Is the more remarkable as mules or horses, in a very short time, get so sore-footed that shoes are indispensable. The camel has no shuffle in his gait, but lifts his feet. This enables them to travel continuously in a country where no other barefooted beast would last a week. I have never seen one stumble.

The caravan reached Fort Davis, near El Paso, on July 16, where they remained several days to rest. So far the trip remained without serious incident. But to the north lay Fort Defiance, where the real trip was about to begin.

At each village along the way, the locals treated the caravan as if it were an arriving circus. Riding into one small group of adobe hovels along the Rio Grande, Ned, at the front of the train, was met by a mounted group. The man in the lead reined up beside him, his eyes wide with wonder at the sight of the camels following. He appeared undecided about getting closer. After doffing his sombrero but still staring back over his shoulder at the animals, he questioned Ned in his broken border English.

"Dis show wagon, no?"

Ned chuckled. The man had mistaken the red ambulance for a showman's wagon.

"Yes."

"Ah, ha! You be de showmans, no?"

"Yes, sir!"

"What you gottee more den *camelos*? Gottee any

dogs?"

"Yes," Ned agreed with a guffaw, getting into the swing of the conversation. "Yes, trained dancing dogs, and monkeys, too, and more!"

"Whatee cando horse?"

"Stand on his head and drink a glass of wine."

"*Valgame Dios!* What a people these are, to have a horse stand on head and drink a glass of wine.

Ned got the best laugh of the trip as the man reined his horse around and, followed by his friends, rode back and alongside the camels—still maintaining a respectful distance. Ned had to forgo showing the villagers, to their great disappointment, his trained dancing dogs and head-standing wine-imbibing horse, since they were compelled to forge on to Fort Defiance.

At Albuquerque, Ned could not pass up the opportunity to ride north to visit his old friend Kit Carson. This time Kit was in residence, and Ned not only spent a pleasant repast with the scout but also purchased a hundred head of sheep from him. Kit agreed to loan him a couple of Mexican shepherds and personally to help him drive the mutton back to his camp.

When Ned returned to his camp outside of Albuquerque, he was not particularly surprised to find half his men, and all the camel drivers missing. It had been a long trip from Indianola, and the temptation of a nearby town, and its promise of women, had just been too much. Ned strapped a Colt's on his hip, wisely asked Kit to accompany him, and went to town in search of his men.

The village of Albuquerque huddled on a wide flat east of the shallow, brown Rio Grande and was backed by tall, pine-covered mountains rising in the east, and low, sparse brown bluffs on the west. The mission and its few dozen adobe cantinas, *establos*, and haciendas fronted dirt lanes populated by the villagers, horses, donkeys, pigs, chickens, and an occasional snake or lizard.

Ned picked the hitching rail with the most horses and mules tied outside. He grunted in satisfaction when he read the sign. His search was over. Carlita's Cantina y Casa de Banos—Catlita's Saloon and House of Baths. Steam rolled into the dry New Mexico air from the rear of the low building.

"If they're here, they won't be easy to pry loose," Kit said with a chuckle, looking forward to the fun. Ned shoved the black-and-white cowhide door covering aside, then backpedaled out of the way, running into Kit and knocking him aside, as two men lunged out of the inside darkness. One had i pistol in hand.

Ned pawed for the Colt's at his side before he realized the two were fighting each other and not attacking him, as they tumbled by him and rolled between the legs of a mule. The animal sprang up on all fours, clearing the ground, but his lead rope, securely tied, jerked him back onto the fighting pair.

Ned regained his composure. Kit came up from the crouch he was in, Bowie in hand. Ned realized the battlers were Joe McFeeley and John Hoyne, two of his teamsters. McFeeley struggled to keep Hoyne's revolver shoved aside.

"They're mine!" Ned yelled to Kit, so the scout would not open one of them up too quickly if the fight came his way.

Ned pulled his own Colt's to use as a bludgeon, but before he could step into the fray, Hoyne's old Colt's roared, and blood splattered over Ned's chest and face. He felt no pain and so decided he was not hit. He stepped in and cracked Hoyne soundly across his hard skull, just as the frightened mule cracked McFeeley in the ribs, knocking the wind out of him and sending him reeling away.

Hoyne dropped like a rock.

Kit stepped in just far enough to hook Hoyne's Colt's with a moccasined foot and kick it out into the road, well out of reach of thc man. Ned bent and snatched Hoyne up by the collar, pulling him away from the wrath of the mule, then dropped the teamster on his face near the door.

McFeeley regained his feet and staggered forward, holding his chest where blood flowed freely down the front of his shirt. Ned feared that the man had been fatally shot, then realized McFeeley was holding the spot where the mule had kicked him—and doing so with a ragged hand shot through the palm.

McFeeley tried to kick the fallen Hoyne in the chest, but Ned shoved McFeeley back against the adobe wall. The man glared at him in anger but made no move to retaliate— besides, he had Kit Carson's Bowie shoved into his face.

"The som'bitch tried to shoot me," Hoyne said with a snarl.

"Tried? You are shot, man," Kit said, and Hoyne's eyes widened as he patted himself on the chest and down across his stomach.

"You're shot through the hand, Hoyne," Ned said. Hoyne held both his hands in front of his face and turned white as he saw the gaping hole.

"Damn the flies," he managed to mumble, sitting unsteadily back on his butt in the dirt. He stared at his hand as if he could not believe it.

Mexicans and muleteers and scantily clad whores crowded out of the cantina behind Ned. Hi Jolly walked out wearing a foolish grin.

"Crazy teamsters fight," he offered in broken English, "when whiskey to be drunk and ladies to be loved."

"And work to be done," Ned snapped. He turned back to Hoyne and McFeeley, who had begun to come to their senses. "You two are fired." He dug in his pocket, fished out a few gold coins, and dropped them on the ground. "Don't bother to come back for your gear, I'll leave it at camp. I don't want to see either of you again."

They stumbled to their feet and unsteadily walked away together, cursing under their breath.

"Do any of the rest of you want to stay in this garden spot?" Ned asked. Most of the teamsters and camel drivers looked sheepish and drunkenly remorseful and did not answer. ''Then get your rumps back to camp. We pull out before dawn."

"I stay," Hi Jolly said, and Greek George stood behind him, nodding his head in agreement. Of all the men Ned could not afford to lose, these two topped the list. They were the only ones who could truly handle the camels.

"You're staying?" Ned asked, his voice low and ominous. Kit sensed his old friend's intent and moved around behind Greek George.

"I stay," Hi Jolly said adamantly.

"Then I guess I'll buy you a drink," Ned said with a false smile only the drunken Hi Jolly and Greek George would believe.

Hi Jolly smiled, too, and turned to the cantina door. He had not taken a step before Ned poleaxed him with the butt of the Colt's and Kit brought the heavy bone hilt of the Bowie across Greek George's curly locks. Both men hit the ground and lay unmoving.

"Load 'em up," Ned commanded, and several of the others hoisted them across their mules.

Ned started to walk away to fetch his own, when a voice called to him in Spanish.

"Alto, hombre!''

He turned to face a barrel-shaped Mexican who shook a blood-stained meat cleaver in Ned's direction.

"Are you the *jefe* of these flea-infested men of the desert?" the Mexican asked with a scowl that showed yellowed teeth and the spot where a front one was missing. "Who wants to know?"

"I am the owner of this cantina. These *hombres* owe me thirteen dollars and eighty-five cents."

"You're Carlita?" Ned asked with a smirk, eliciting a chuckle from Kit Carson. The man did not pay the slight any mind. He extended his hand, palm up, for his money. Ned dug into his pocket and handed the man fourteen dollars, then turned to the others.

"Can you find your way to camp?" They silently turned and went to their own horses and mules and reined away, leading the unconscious Hi Jolly and Greek George tied across their mules like sacks of flour.

Ned headed for the doorway, calling to Kit over his shoulder. "This may be the last chance I have to share an *aguardiente* with you for a while. Besides, ol' *gordo* Carlita owes me fifteen cents."

He and Kit drank up a two-dollar gold piece before they said their good-byes again.

When they crossed the Rio Grande and headed west, the menagerie increased by a hundred head of mutton on the hoof. Ned, with a well-earned headache, did not yell at the men, who were happy he did not, since they had their own throbbing heads.

That night Ned entered in his journal:

> ...getting the men out of Albuquerque was no easy chore, as the fandangos and other pleasures had rendered them rather troublesome. I was obliged to administer a copious supply of oil of the boot to several, especially my Turk, who had not found the positive prohibition of the Prophet a sufficient reason for temperance but was as drunk as any Christian in the train. To move a stubborn, half-drunken

Turk, give me a good tough piece of wagon spoke, aimed tolerably high!

Brigadier General John Garland, commander of the Department of New Mexico at Santa Fe, where Ned had stopped
on his way back from Taos, had issued an order to his commander at Fort Defiance assigning a sergeant, three corporals,
and thirty-five hand-picked men to Ned's caravan. They came
well provisioned for sixty days and hauled two mountain
howitzers. Ned had expressed his pleasure to the general that
he had passed through Comanche country without incident,
only to discover the Apache and Navajo were on the warpath.
Still, Ned turned down the howitzers. He sold five of his
wagons to General Garland, who needed them to carry supplies for the escort Ned was to pick up at Fort Defiance. This
relieved Ned of the expense of thirty mules and five teamsters, laying their cost on the Army and replenishing Ned's
depleted reserves.

In retrospect, Ned concluded that no self-respecting Comanche would attack a caravan as strange and wondrous and
slightly frightening, in a bizarre way, as his, and hoped the
Apache and Navajo would feel the same.

The last ten days of the trip to Fort Defiance covered the
parched mesa country, a true test of the camels. They outdistanced the mules easily and disdained water holes the smaller
pack animals crowded around. A few miles outside the fort,
Captain Josiah H. Carlisle met the train. He had received a
report of their coming and, having taken that trip many times,
knew the best possible respite for Ned and his weary men. He
threw a blanket off a tub resting in the bottom of his wagon
and exposed a large block of ice. Within moments, the two
commanders and their men were enjoying a red-eye on the
rocks, courtesy of the U.S. Army.

On August 27, Ned and the train, accompanied by an additional twenty soldiers and a large work group of Mexican la-

borers, making them now seventy men strong, headed out of Fort Defiance to begin the real work of the mission. Ned took careful sightings at each landmark, watched his map makers, corrected, and made suggestions. He thought as a teamster would think as he judged the capability of the country to carry a road. Finally, after years of contemplating the possibility, he was surveying a road—an all-weather wagon road—through to California. Ned noted in his journal:

> No one who has not commanded an expedition of this kind where everything is dim, uncertain, and unknown, except the dangers, could possibly imagine the anxiety with which I start this journey. Not only responsible for the lives of my men, but my reputation and the highest wrought expectations of my enemies, all dependent on the next sixty days of good or evil fortune. Let us see what I shall say in this journal, if I live to say anything, on the day of my return here.

The fun was over; now the work began. The country from Fort Defiance on was unsurveyed and mostly unexplored.

Ned followed the stars along the thirty-fifth parallel and carefully mapped his progress. Making careful note of ravine and watershed crossings, he estimated the bridge requirements as he plodded forward. He named landmarks after his friends and his men. He had little trouble with the Indians for the first days, but had a great deal of trouble with the country—but it was trouble he had expected and none he believed would preclude a road. He left the land of the Zuni and entered the vast fairyland of the Painted Desert. Then to his great surprise, he entered a land of pine-covered mountains. No maps showed anything other than dry desert in this country. He was fascinated with the game-filled mountains, but pressed on. Still, he saw no reason a road could not follow the path he carefully surveyed and noted.

Ned had hired a guide in Albuquerque and was shocked to find the man continually lost. He put him to work as a swamper, and worked him harder than the others for his treachery in claiming he knew the country they were scheduled to travel over.

After they left the mountains and probed deeper into the desert, the true value of the camels shined though. They carried oats and hay and water that the mules would have perished without, never taking a bite or a drink themselves. They lived off the land, and the scarce water holes at great distances were more than enough for them.

Ned screamed in anger when he caught the Turks and Greeks cutting into the humps of the live camels and carving out the fat to roast. Ht forbade them ever to touch the animals with their knives again. They shrugged as if the camels were indestructible, but agreed to anything that would not incur his wrath.

On October 1, Lieutenant Thorburn failed to return from a water-scouting expedition. Ned immediately ordered a search party, sending Jourdan and two others, but had to order a search for water at the same time. They were desperately low.

Jourdan was more than glad for any excuse to get away from the camels. In Texas, almost before they had left camp, a camel had kicked him. Jourdan had kicked back, and the camel roared and covered him with a coating of green slime. Since that time, Jourdan had not gotten within twenty feet of the animals—spitting range.

But the faithful Thorburn wandered back into camp after three days, reporting he had discovered water thirty-five miles ahead. When they arrived, Ned realized that they had also discovered another Indian tribe. Signs were scarce, but Ned had become a passable tracker. Finally they came on several villages, abandoned when they reached them but always showing signs of recent occupancy, sometimes with fires still burning. The Indians, probably fearing the camels, were fleeing ahead of them.

They reached the Colorado and its several thousand Mojave Indians. It was obvious they were not the first white men to come upon this particular band, for a brave ran out to meet them and proudly exclaimed, "God damn my soul eyes! How-de-do, how-de-do!"

They were refreshed to discover the Indians well fed, and traded for pumpkins, watermelons, cantaloupes, beans, and corn.

Two hard days were spent floating the wagons across the Colorado. They experienced their first losses there, as several mules were swept away and drowned in the swift flowing stream.

Ned had been told the camels could not swim, a "fact" confirmed by both Hi Jolly and Greek George. The camel Ned still preferred to ride, the great white beast called Seid, was an animal Ned considered beyond all others. He could not believe that Seid could not swim, but the other men were convinced they must build rafts for the camels.

"They are cowards when in the water over their hocks," Greek George said with great authority, folding his arms across his chest.

"And how many times have you tried to get a camel to swim?" Ned questioned.

"I have had many camels at the sides of many oceans, and never have I seen one enter the water."

"And what reason did these camels have to go in the ocean?" Ned pressed, beginning to get irritated at the pigheadedness of Hi Jolly and Greek George.

Both men shook their heads and said in unison, "Camels do not swim."

Ned walked to Seid and motioned him down. The beast knelt, and Ned mounted him. All the men in the caravan walked forward, expecting to see the first loss of a camel—not necessarily a loss in the eyes of the more stubborn muleteers.

Ned quirted the animal toward the river, and Seid entered up to his knees before he balked. Ned allowed him to exit the water, then turned him back. Seid arched his great neck and looked back at Ned, who wondered if he was about to be spat on or roared at, but Ned confidently urged him forward.

To the shock of those watching, and possibly even more so to Ned, the animal not only entered the water but also did so with a great leap and stroked across with ease, crashing out the other side from deep water up into a stand of willow so thick a mule would have been unable to get out and would have drowned.

The men, even the muleteers, cheered. They lashed the camels in groups of five, and Ned swam back and led them into the Colorado. They crossed with ease, and another absurdity about the camel had been dispelled.

Within days they reached the narrows of the Mojave River, and Ned, who had been instructed to terminate his route at Fort Tejon, sent two riders with camels on into the San Bernardino Valley and to Los Angeles, where word of his safe arrival could more readily be sent back to Washington. He and the rest of the party branched off across Antelope Valley and arrived at Fort Tejon on November 26.

Ned stayed at the fort until he was satisfied that the camels had proper corrals and that the soldiers there were familiar with their requirements, then went on to Los Angeles himself—but not before he took the opportunity to visit his rancho and Alex Godey. Ned found his herds thriving—he now was the patron of more sheep and cattle than he could count.

When he arrived in Los Angeles, expecting somewhat of a hero's welcome, he was surprised to read the following article that had been saved for him, printed in the *Alta California* shortly after the arrival of the two camels he had sent on to that city:

> They caused a great curiosity and scared all the horses, mules and children. When the docility of the animals was proved, they were all anxious to take a ride on the humps of those awkward locomotives. They remained but two days and then went to join the remainder of the train which had followed up the east side of the mountains to Tejon. The road has been duly surveyed to the Colorado, but it is understood that Mr. Beale intends to terminate it at Tejon, without coming to Los Angeles, and much dissatisfaction is expressed.

Ned was enjoying the article until he reached the last paragraph:

> Lieutenant Beale has used the national dromedaries to build a road up to his rancho at the Tejon and he alone will benefit by it.

He flung it down in anger. The press, he knew, had to sell newspapers, and nothing did that as well as controversy. The fact that his orders had stated that he was to conclude the road at Fort Tejon, California's largest and most improved military installation, was of no consequence or interest to the reporter, whom Ned would be happy to place face first into a bowl of lobster bisque if he had the chance.

Angrily, he reached for a bottle of whiskey, which shared the chest of drawers with a bone-white pitcher and bowl, and poured himself a taste to wash the trail dust from his throat. Then he laughed aloud, the sound echoing through the silent room as he thought back over all of the newspaper articles criticizing him over the years. Had he bothered to shove all of their faces in the soup, he would have had time for little else. He had learned to keep his own counsel, listen and evaluate all, but take to heart only self-criticism.

His room on the second floor of the Angeles Hotel opened onto a common verandah, the sun was dipping into the west, and a warm breeze beckoned him out.

He was out of government money, which was no new problem for him. He would use his own or issue government drafts for what he needed, and fight it out later with watery-eyed, limp-handed politicians.

Tomorrow, he and Jourdan, Peg Leg, and two packers would saddle and pack mules and start back, making a detailed investigation of the necessary bridge locations along the route. But more important than even the bridges was water. Dependable water holes would have to be located no more than a day's wagon trip apart through the burning Southwest. Jourdan had proved himself several times as having a nose for the simple but critical substance, claiming he had conversations with mourning doves who showed him the way. Jourdan would find water, and it would be the determining factor as to the final location of the road. When those two chores had been done, Ned could return from Fort Defiance to Washington and begin politicking for funds to begin building the road in earnest—that thought caused him to down the last of the whiskey—but he would not give himself that unpleasant task until he had spent some time with his Marys and Truxtun.

Ned splashed another dollop of whiskey into a snifter, then wandered out onto the verandah. Scattered clouds in the west gleamed gold over the setting sun, and the mountains to the north and east were highlighted on their peaks, shining up out of deep purple shadows, shimmering in anticipation of darkness and well-earned rest. Ned sipped his whiskey and surveyed the street below, where clerks closed the iron shutters of the few eastern-style buildings beginning to rise among the pueblo's adobes. Only two women stood chatting on Alverado Street below the verandah, and both of them were dark-haired Californios—but Ned knew that would change. Children with towheads would soon play among the dark-haired ones, and they and their families would have arrived in safety, thanks to the southwesterly route.

Even in October, the weather was mild. Ned relaxed in shirtsleeves, placing a booted foot up on the verandah's railing.

An all-weather wagon road would soon offer California's beauty and opportunity to the rest of the country.

Ned sighed deeply and wondered why he had not succumbed to the disease and other perils of so many crossings from the East Coast to the West Coast through Panama, or from the freezing snows of high mountain crossings through the center of the country. Even with his road, the Indians would have to be tamed, the water problem resolved, and a thousand ravines and canyons graded and bridged, but those were surmountable. The snows in the Rockies and northern Sierras, he knew, could never be tamed by man. His road had gone around them, just as he had gone around the worst of the obstacles, politicians, so many times.

A reality, because he, and men like him, had embraced a rush to destiny, damning the doubters, hungering for adventure, thirsting for challenge. Ned raised his glass and toasted the nearby Pacific, satisfied that Manifest Destiny had finally become a reality.

AFTERWORD

On his return to Washington, Ned came across an old friend fallen on hard times, Ulysses S. Grant, cutting and hauling wood for a living, wearing a tattered Army jacket. Ned and Grant renewed their friendship over a bottle of bourbon.

Ned Beale had followed the thirty-fifth parallel on his survey to California, and on his return to Washington convinced the politicians that his route was the best one across the country. For the next two years, Ned Beale labored to improve the old route all the way from Fort Smith, Arkansas, to Albuquerque, New Mexico, then along his new route to California.

Finally Ned became fed up with the slave issue and became a Republican to support Abraham Lincoln. Lincoln appointed Ned surveyor general of the State of California. When the Civil War began, Ned repeatedly wrote the president and asked to be relieved of his duties and given a command in the Union Army. Lincoln, concerned with the volatile situation in California—its population made up mostly of Southerners—needed Ned there. California was the only state in the Union not to be saddled with conscription during the war; Ned Beale insisted it would be the final straw that caused the populace to revolt and join the South: California remained in the Union, though thousands defected to the South.

During this time, against the wishes of most Washington politicians and the law of the land, Ned ran guns to assist his old enemies the Mexicans, who were trying to drive Maxmilian out of their country. They succeeded.

Ned went on to acquire all four of the old Mexican land grants, and Rancho El Tejon became a holding of over two hundred seventy thousand acres of prime ranch and farmland. It remains, to this day, almost intact, dotted with oil wells among its cattle herds and surrounded with communities.

After the Civil War, the wood hauler, Grant, became president. He appointed Ned as minister to Austria/Hungary. The boy had gone from a Navy uniform--with its old-fashioned buttons, to buckskins, and then on to the pomp of Europe's finest palaces.

Edward Fitzgerald Beale always went where others feared to go, and wanted a road so others could follow. Now an eight-lane freeway bisects his rancho. But under its pavement lay the bones of elk and grizzly, of Indians and Californios, and it passes Fort Tejon, still standing and the site of Civil War reenactments.

Beale died in Decatur House, his Washington residence, on April 21, 1892, survived by his Marys and his son, Truxtun.

HISTORICAL NOTES
AND ACKNOWLEDGMENTS

The author makes no claim to being a biographer, but has attempted to utilize history accurately in his writing, incorporating actual dispatches, letters, and newspaper accounts. Hopefully, this novelistic style offers accurate history, dates, and events in an entertaining form.

The author would like to express his admiration and appreciation to the following, whose wonderful nonfiction books were of immeasurable help:

Stephen Bonsal, *Edward Fitzgerald Beale: A Pioneer in the Path of Empire.*

Carl Briggs and Clyde Francis Trudell, *Quarterdeck and Saddlehorn: The Story of Edward F. Beale.*

Gerald Thompson, *Edward F. Beale & the American West.*

William A. DeGregorio, *The Complete Book of U.S. Presidents.*

And others too numerous to mention.

Almost all of *Rush to Destiny* is founded in fact, either gleaned from the biographies noted above, from the Beale Papers in the Beale Branch of the Kern County Library (named after Edward Fitzgerald Beale and located on Truxtun Avenue, which was named after his son), or from other related biographies or journals. The Beale Memorial Library has microfilm copies of those documents on file in the National Archives, where they require nine feet of shelf space. The actual flow of events in the novel is very close to accurate, as are all dates. Ned Beale, as you have noted, was a busy man. The author has used creative license to re-create actual but unknown conversations, to invent conversations to inform the reader, or to fill in action. Where Beale's journal might note, "Indian attack, killed a mule," the author has expanded that into a whole scene. Even using this creative license, the author is sure, after intensive research that Ned Beale's life was even more exciting than portrayed here—and it was certainly of more import than was possible to portray within the limits of novel length.

Of interest, since they played such an important role in Beale's life, are some of the following, referred to lovingly as "her":

The *Independence*: Ned sailed on the third *Independence*, built in 1814, and razed from an eighty-four-gun frigate to a fifty-four-gun frigate in 1836. She was sold by the Navy in 1914.

The *Congress*: Ned sailed on the fourth *Congress*, a frigate of forty-four guns. She was launched in 1841 and sunk by the Confederate ram Virginia on March 8, 1862. The wreck was later raised and sold.

The *Levant*: Luckily, Ned was not aboard the second class sloop when she was later lost in a storm with all hands in the Pacific in 1860.

The *Savannah*: A frigate of forty-four guns, Ned was aboard the second, built in 1820. She was sold by the Navy at the Norfolk Navy Yard in 1883.

The *Cyane*: Also a second-class sloop, of eighteen guns, she was built in 1837 and sold in California in 1887.

The *Constitution*: A forty-four-gun frigate, she was built in Boston in 1797. She is still afloat.

The following notes or explanations are offered in chronological order, beginning with the Prologue:

Beale family memoirs relate young Ned's scrap in the Washington streets, its motivation, and the fact that Andrew

Jackson broke it up. Later, Emily Beale took advantage of Jackson's reputed offer, and relied on his referral to get Ned his Navy appointment. Jackson was called Andy-by-God as a result of his propensity to use the phrase.

When Ned entered the Navy, as a result of his father's death and family financial problems, he wore a coat on which his mother had sewn his grandfather's large, out-of-style buttons. Those buttons became the cause of a fistfight, as a result of which, it was said, Ned gained the additional respect of his peers. Still, Ned prudently acquired a more conventional coat shortly thereafter.

Norvell Johanson is a fictional character, a combination of several enemies, both in the Navy and in politics, whom Beale acquired during his lifetime.

It is not known exactly how much time Ned spent in England, nor exactly what he did there as he would never, during his long life, talk about his exact mission.

George Bancroft, the secretary of the Navy whom Ned reported to on his return from England, is the same Bancroft who wrote several definitive histories of the United States, which were referred to by the author. He is no relation (at least the author could not establish one) to Hubert Howe Bancroft who wrote the definitive several volume history of California, another several-volume history of Mexico, and a ten-volume history of the United States—all of which were referred to many times in the past by this author for this work, and which will be referred to many times in the future for other historical works. Among other accomplishments, George Bancroft founded the U.S. Naval Academy at Annapolis, served as U.S. minister to Great Britain, and was minister to Prussia and Germany.

Ned's exploits while with the Brazilian Squadron were one of the wild times in the young man's maturation. He made many notes in his journals, giving rise to the fictionalization portrayed herein.

The slave Jourdan was actually purchased and promptly set free by Ned in New Orleans just before the camel trip, but in many instances prior to that, Ned had Mexican, Indian, or black traveling companions. Jourdan, for the sake of this novel, has become many of them combined. The real Jourdan remained a free man, staying with Ned Beale as a trusted friend and working as his body servant until Beale's death.

The dispatch Ned carried from Bancroft to Commodore Stockton, when Ned rejoined the Congress at Callao, Peru, is verbatim. A great deal of controversy among historians over the years contemplates other possible unwritten orders. The author has taken liberties in assuming what those were.

The passage made by the Congress from Callao to the Sandwich Islands (Hawaii), under Ned's command as ship's master, set a new crossing record for sailing vessels.

Sam Brannan's ship, the chartered Brooklyn, was in harbor with the Congress, and Stockton did sell him and his Mormons one hundred muskets and one hundred fifty Allan's six-barrel revolvers—the finest weapon of its time. Though inaccurate, it would faithfully fire six shots without reloading. Unfortunately, sometimes it would also jump-fire, and more than one cylinder would fire at a time. Later, Ned would come across Brannan many times in San Francisco, where the Mormon leader became active in the Vigilantes. The dispatches read by Sloat's fictional secretary, O'Connel, are practically verbatim, but annotated, as is the proclamation that was posted wherever the flag was raised. Daingerfield Fauntleroy was the name of the purser of the *Savannah* and was the officer Sloat ordered to establish communications among the northern Alta California communities. This is an instance where I'm sure the reader believed the author took great literary license-but the name is factual.

The *Collingwood* did, in fact, enter the harbor at Monterey while the American fleet was anchored there, and the actions outlined in the novel are those of both groups. A good portion of the verbal exchange between the English admiral Seymour and Commodore Robert Stockton is taken from a secondhand account of that conversation and should be close to the actual strained, but still relatively cordial, conversation.

The interactions among Commodore Sloat, Commodore Stockton, and John Charles Fremont during the first days of the California revolt have caused a great deal of speculation and argument among historians. Later, when General Kearny entered the territory, the friction intensified, culminating in Fremont's eventual court-martial. Fremont was basically condemned and court-martialed for obeying orders—the problem was that he, as an Army officer, obeyed naval orders. Kearny, far outnumbered in California by naval forces, remained on the sideline—a position Fremont never relegated himself to. Even so, Fremont's role in the revolution was invaluable from a political standpoint, though he did little from a military one. Had it not been for the Mexicans'—Alta California's own divisiveness, it is possible we would even now be applying for a visa to visit California's beaches. Possible, but not likely, as the country truly believed the Pacific was part of our Manifest Destiny.

Stockton did issue a crowing dispatch to the secretary of the Navy after he first marched on Los Angeles and the Mexicans handed it to him without conflict—and the text, as dictated to Ned, is almost verbatim. It would come back to haunt him when the Mexicans decided his occupancy could not be tolerated, due to Gillespie's strict and intolerant interpretation of his orders, and again at Fremont's court-martial .

John Brown's ride from Los Angeles to Monterey was heroic and well documented.

William Manchester was killed by attacking lancers on one of Ned's trips to bring stock back to Stockton's force at San Diego.

The dispatch sent from Kearny to Stockton, carried by Edward Stokes, is almost verbatim, and it, too, is the subject of great controversy. Had Kearny been more explicit about his severe problems with near-dead stock and lack of rations, Stockton undoubtedly would have set out immediately with the largest force he could muster. As it was, he waited, sending only Ned, Archibald Gillespie, and a few men.

Kearny's actions at San Pasqual speak for themselves. He sorely underestimated the Mexicans, which may, in part, be blamed on Kit Carson. Carson never held his enemies in high regard. This also may be the reason Kearny later denied Carson's heroics or even knowing the scout.

At various times during the revolution and the early occupancy of California, Kearny, Stockton, and Fremont signed documents as governor of California. One gets the impression that each of them was unsure as to his actual status but did not lack ambition.

The Battle of San Pasqual is as faithfully reproduced as the author is able, with the wounds and deaths as reported.

The message sent back by Stockton in response to Kearny's letter carried by Stokes, and entrusted to Godey, was found by a vaquero years later, in a knothole in an oak tree where Godey had hidden it when fearing his capture.

When Ned and Kit Carson left Mule Hill to sneak through the Mexican lines and go for help, another man accompanied them. He has been variously reported as being an Indian and/or a servant of Ned's. The author put Jourdan in this position, as explained earlier in these notes.

Ned took over a year to recover fully from wounds received at San Pasqual, and from the arduous rescue trip to San Diego—even though he continued to do his job during that time. The commendation Ned received from his fellow officers is verbatim.

The orders Ned delivered to Secretary of the Navy Mason are verbatim and reflect the hopes Stockton had for Ned's career. The orders were a commendation and a notice to others of Stockton's regard for his passed midshipman who carried an acting-lieutenant designation.

General Kearny did claim he had never met Kit Carson and gave no credit to Carson for leading him back to California, or for his action in going for help with Ned.

Ned did go through a bad spell after the Fremont trial. There was an incident, in Mexico, where he was punished for a display of horsemanship while only partially clothed—details were unavailable to the author.

This extraordinary man Ned Beale seemed to lead such an amazing existence that his story may lack credibility to the reader—no one could have known so many prominent figures. But with respect to the limitations of space, the author did not include nearly all the persons of then current and later fame Ned actually encountered in his career, but did elect to include William Tecumseh Sherman and Ulysses S. Grant. Sherman was nicknamed Cump. Grant and Ned did become good friends—a great many letters between the two still exist—and shared a liking for John Barleycorn. Ned assisted the ex-president when he had financial problems late in his life.

Ned's ride across Mexico was a harrowing adventure, and made in record time. He carried proof of the California gold strike—proof he had purchased with his own money. It is not known the exact quantity, nor nugget size, of the gold he carried, but in a later letter P. T. Barnum did inquire about Ned's "eight-pound nugget." That letter is verbatim in the novel.

Polk did enter into his diary that "nothing of consequence" happened the day Ned met with him and reported the details of the California gold strike—a report that began the greatest migration in the history of the country was not "of consequence" to the president. At least he did not recognize it as such.

During Ned's next westward crossing, he was chased by Apaches and almost caught after killing a deer for camp meat, and one of the dragoon recruits did scream for help. Ned gave up his horse when the man pleaded that he had several children. The Indians overran his position, but did not see him in their mad pursuit to catch the mounted man. Six of the dragoons deserted on that trip, including the sergeant. They were never heard from again.

The excerpt from the letter sent from Ned to his future brother-in-law, Harry Edwards, from Big Timber regarding the worthless dragoons is verbatim.

The trip across the Rockies was horrible, and was probably one of the reasons Ned steeled his resolve to see a warm-weather wagon road reach California. When Ned finally did reach San Francisco, Catesby-Jones turned him right around and sent him back—this time one would imagine Ned was glad for the Panama crossing.

The twenty-five-pound nugget mentioned was not the largest, by far, taken out of the California goldfields. A nugget in excess of seventy pounds was found later.

Ned actually ran across Jessie Fremont in Panama City, not San Francisco. He did try to convince her to return to St. Louis, as he thought booming, bawdy San Francisco no city for a woman without her husband, but the letter from John caught up with her there.

Bayard Taylor's book *Eldorado, or Adventures in the Path of Empire* is dedicated to Ned Beale. Ned shepherded Taylor all over California. It is an enjoyable read, currently available in trade paperback from the University of Nebraska Press, and a must-read for those interested in the California gold rush.

On Ned's return trip to New York, another record crossing of forty-four days was made. When he arrived, the *New York Herald* made the statements quoted. The Army did try to charge him, personally, for the services of an Army escort—men who had deserted and acted as he reported to Harry in his letter, verbatim excerpt given, from Big Timber.

Zachary Taylor, an ex-military man himself, did much to further Ned's career.

When John Fremont accepted the draft for the cattle from Indian agent Barbour, he discounted it and was subsequently sued by the buyer. Ned Beale loaned him twenty thousand dollars to pay the judgment. Ned later had to sue Fremont to recover his money. It was the only blemish in their long friendship, and they later patched it up and remained friends for the rest of their lives.

There seemed to be some legitimate question about Ned's involvement in Fremont's cattle transaction, and historians differ on the subject. If he had been so involved, Fremont lied on Ned's behalf when Ned was being considered for superintendent of Indian affairs. Later, when Ned sued him to recover the twenty thousand dollars he loaned him, Fremont claimed that Beale had been a partner in the loss, but lost as a result of his testimony at the superintendency hearings—where he denied Beale's involvement.

California governor McDougal did write the letter to President Fillmore stating that the only solution to his Indian problem was to civilize or exterminate them. It was a popular solution within the state.

Congress did appoint Ned and give him a reduced budget, and their belief that the Indians could not benefit from school is illustrative of the thinking at the time—and of Ned Beale's farsightedness.

Captain James Savage was later killed during an Indian action in central California.

Ned's letter to his boss Luke Lea is actually a combination of two communications but accurately states his findings regarding the Indians.

The letter Ned wrote to Governor Bigler wherein he groused about the federal government being unable to prosecute murderers illustrated a problem that again rise in the 1960's during the civil rights activities.

Ned's report to the Department of the Interior is annotated but almost verbatim.

The private survey Ned undertook on his return trip to California became known as the Beale/Heap expedition. Scout Felipe Peg Leg Archulete was a wonder to Ned, who reported that he could do far more with one leg than most men with two.

The river Ned encountered and knew as the Grand was renamed the Gunnison, after Captain John Gunnison, whose party was murdered by Utes at the Grand shortly after Ned had crossed there. Gunnison had been sent to map the area for a central railroad crossing by Secretary of War Jefferson Davis, who finally appropriated the money to do so.

The fight in the Willard happened, though Norvell Johanson, a fictional character, was obviously not part of it. The newspaper report of the fight, taken from the *Evening Star,* is verbatim.

Ned was appointed ·a brigadier general in the State Militia a second time to quell the Indian uprisings, and the basic facts of his relationship with Henley are correct. The letter of concession written to Ned by Henley is annotated but verbatim.

Ned's arrival in Indianola for the start of the camel expedition was actually the first instance of his buying and freeing a slave. In his personal papers is a bill of sale recording his purchase of Jourdan, for a boy "supposed to be from twenty-five to thirty years of age, is healthy, sensible and a slave." A handwritten note on the back of the bill of sale reads, "I bought the slave referred to within and gave him his Freedom. E.F.B." Later family pictures show Jourdan with Beale in Chester and Washington, D.C., and he is referred to as "body servant."

The guide he hired in Indianola to see them to San Antonio, John Chisholm, was the same man the great cattle trail was later named after.

The camel expedition is a topic for a book in itself, and several have been written on the subject. Greek George later went on to receive nefarious fame in the Southwest.

Beale's camel route is very close to that of Interstate 40 and the Atchison, Topeka, & Santa Fe Railroad. For many years, well into the twentieth century, it carried the name Beale's Road.

Ned's entry in the journal regarding the camel's feet is taken almost verbatim from the actual text. His conversation with the villager wherein he claimed to have a head-standing, wine-drinking horse is also from his journal.

May Stacy's journal not only helped Ned file his quarterly reports but also provides us with an accurate portrayal of the affair.

The excerpt from Ned's journal regarding the camels is verbatim and demonstrates his high regard for the animals.

Ned did ride north over a hundred miles to visit Kit Carson and did buy a hundred head of sheep from him. There was no record of Kit returning with' him, or of Ned being present at the fight between McFeeley and Hoyne, but the fight was mentioned in Ned's journal, and the quote following is nearly accurate to the word regarding his problems with getting his men out of Albuquerque.

Ned's seriousness with the job at hand is reflected in the entry quoted verbatim. This was one of the few times he made an entry expressing his personal feelings and his own vulnerability.

Ned did swim a camel across the Colorado after his Near East experts advised him they could not. He was never good at accepting a "can't."

Jefferson Davis, the secretary of war who showed such initiative importing camels for use in the Southwest, ended his career paroled from a Union prison after becoming president of the Confederacy. Had it not been for the Civil War, camels might have become a common sight in American deserts.

The rest of Ned's life was as fascinating as the first half, no less a rush to destiny. But that's another story for another time.

Works by L. J. Martin in print and eBook:

Shadow of the Mast
Tenkiller
Mojave Showdown
El Lazo
Against the 7th Flag
The Devil's Bounty
The Benicia Belle
Shadow of the Grizzly
Rush to Destiny
Windfall
Condor Canyon
Blood Mountain
Stranahan
McKeag's Mountain
McCreed's Law
O'Rourke's Revenge
Wolf Mountain
Nemesis
Venomous (Fourplay)
Sounding Drum (Last Stand)
Bloodlines
From The Pea Patch
Write Compelling Fiction
Killing Cancer

Internet Rich (with Mike Bray)
Against the Grain
Tin Angel (with Kat Martin)
Crimson Hit (with Bob Burton)
Bullet Blues (with Bob Burton)
Quiet Ops (with Bob Burton)
Myrtle Mae (cartoons)
Cooking Wild & Wonderful
Write Compelling Fiction
Cornucopia: How to Build a Greenhouse
Mr. Pettigrew
The Repairman
The Bakken
Gee Whiz G5
Who's On Top
Target Shy & Sexy
Judge, Jury, Desert Fury

Made in the USA
Lexington, KY
18 December 2019